EMIL AND KATHLEEN SICK SERIES IN WESTERN HISTORY AND BIOGRAPHY

With support from the Center for the Study of the Pacific Northwest at the University of Washington, the Sick Series in Western History and Biography features scholarly books on the peoples and issues that have defined and shaped the American West. Through intellectually challenging and engaging books of general interest, the series seeks to deepen and expand our understanding of the American West as a region and its role in the making of the United States and the modern world.

D1604024

GOLD RUSH
MANLINESS

• —————————— •

RACE AND GENDER
ON THE PACIFIC SLOPE

CHRISTOPHER HERBERT

CENTER FOR THE STUDY
OF THE PACIFIC NORTHWEST

in association with

UNIVERSITY OF WASHINGTON PRESS
Seattle

22   21   20   19   18   5   4   3   2   1

CENTER FOR THE STUDY OF   UNIVERSITY OF WASHINGTON
THE PACIFIC NORTHWEST   PRESS
http://cspn.uw.edu   www.washington.edu/uwpress

LIBRARY OF CONGRESS CATALOGING-IN-PUBLICATION DATA ON FILE

ISBN 978-0-295-74413-1 (hardcover), ISBN 978-0-295-74412-4 (paperback),
ISBN 978-0-295-74414-8 (ebook)

Cover photograph: California miners ca. 1850s, courtesy California Historical Society, CHS2010.238.tif

For Cambria . . . this is as much yours as it is mine.

CONTENTS

Acknowledgments ix

Maps xi

INTRODUCTION Mining Gold, Remaking White Manhood 3

CHAPTER 1. Getting to Gold
Migration and the Formation of White Manliness 17

CHAPTER 2. A White Man's Republic
Republican Ideology and Popular Government in Colonial California. . . . 46

CHAPTER 3. English Principles Encounter American Republicanism
Colonial British Columbia 78

CHAPTER 4. Pursuing Dame Fortune
Risk and Reward during the Gold Rushes 109

CHAPTER 5. Dirty Clothes, Clean Bodies
The Body and Costume of White Manliness. 136

EPILOGUE Endings and Beginnings 163

Notes 171

Bibliography 241

Index 263

ACKNOWLEDGMENTS

Looking back, it is hard to imagine how I would have completed this project without the support I received. I was fortunate to find at the University of Washington a community of scholars who encouraged my work and challenged me to do better. First and foremost among these was John Findlay, who showed great dedication in reading more drafts than I care to admit, always doing so with the close attention to detail for which he is renowned. Alexandra Harmon challenged me to think about how power and identity are created and construed and to never lose sight of the people about whom I write and how I write about them. Moon-Ho Jung posed challenging questions, forcing me to grapple with theoretical and methodological issues, while encouraging me to remember that the stories we choose to tell have power and implications for today. Stephanie Camp, Quintard Taylor, Adam Warren, Richard Johnson, Linda Nash, Sandra Joshel, and Tracy McKenzie all provided valuable insights or pushed me to approach questions from a different direction. Nathan Roberts, Katharine Chapman, Laura Erickson, Holly George, Juned Shaikh, and Jason Shattuck all read and offered feedback on different aspects of the manuscript while also being some of the best friends one could ask for.

I am also particularly indebted to the editors and anonymous reviewers at the *Pacific Historical Review,* which published sections of a prior version of this book. Peter Boag, Albert Hurtado, and Elizabeth Jameson also offered keen and insightful criticism at various points.

I have been fortunate to find a home at Columbia Basin College in Pasco, Washington, where the manuscript has benefited from a warm and collegial atmosphere and, most importantly, from the invaluable feedback and criticism of my friend and colleague, Dave Arnold. Dave's close reading sparked some significant changes.

This project entailed extensive research trips to various archives, and in each case I was fortunate to encounter knowledgeable and professional staff. Bill Quackenbush, curator of the Barkerville Historic Site and Archive, and his staff provided great support and company as I spent several cold weeks sleeping in a tent while visiting their archive. The staff at the British Columbia Archives went to great lengths to help me track down leads. Despite being in the middle of a move, the staff at the Bancroft Library did their best to locate gold rush correspondence for me, as did the staff at the California Room of the California State Library.

This research would not have been possible without generous financial support from the Department of History at the University of Washington and from the University of Washington. Special thanks must go to Ellen Barth, who not only endowed the Gunther Barth Award that allowed me to spend several weeks at the Bancroft but also opened her home to me.

Only other authors can really understand when I say that this book would have been far inferior but for the careful guidance and feedback of the editors and staff at the University of Washington Press. The support and insights they offered helped me refine my argument and prose. Any remaining flaws in the book are, of course, entirely my own.

And above all else, I owe an immense debt to my family. To Uncle Terry, Aunt Louise, and my cousins, who not only have been interested and supportive but also let me live with them while I was doing research, thank you. To the Nelson family, who also unrolled a mattress for me and who were, over the course of my graduate career, to become my in-laws, thank you. To my parents, for their unwavering support, thank you. And finally, to my wife, Cambria, and to our children, Taylla, Avery, and Carina, for believing in me and this work and for reminding me that there is more to life than books, thank you.

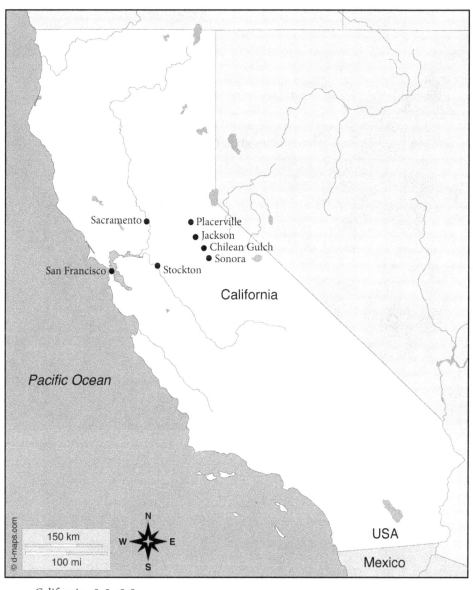

Sacramento

Placerville

Jackson

Chilean Gulch

Sonora

San Francisco

Stockton

California

Pacific Ocean

USA

Mexico

150 km

100 mi

N

W E

S

© d-maps.com

California, 1848–1858

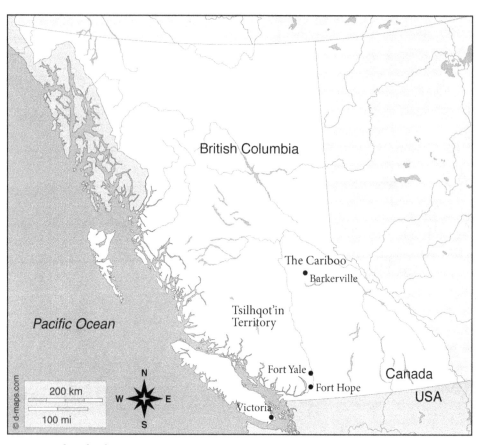

British Columbia, 1858–1871

GOLD RUSH MANLINESS

Introduction

Mining Gold, Remaking White Manhood

THE GOLD RUSHES OF THE MID-NINETEENTH CENTURY bring to mind bawdy, raucous mining camps and hastily constructed cities filled with gambling, prostitution, and disorder verging on anarchy. And yet many of the men who went to the goldfields were products of the Victorian era: the same people who exist in popular memory as straitlaced, repressed, and order-loving. It is clear that the men who went to the goldfields acted, spoke, and worked differently than they had in their eastern homes. For some gold rushers, the looser, rougher society of the goldfields presented a chance to prove that they were the embodiment of a revitalized white manhood, the sort of men who could do "the hardest kind of work," which took "a real man to do."[1] Others worried that gold rush society might imperil their status as respectable white men and longed to return to "civilization."[2] These aspirations and apprehensions were part of a larger debate over the meaning and form of white manhood during the gold rushes. This debate, which profoundly shaped colonial regimes in California and British Columbia, forces a reconsideration of traditional understandings of the gold rushes of the Pacific slope.

The California rush began on a cool morning in January 1848 as James Marshall stood looking down at a few small gold nuggets in his hand. Standing on land that the United States had seized during the recent war with Mexico, and whose inhabitants were overwhelmingly of indigenous and Mexican descent, Marshall had no inkling of the sweeping transformations those pebbles would unleash.[3] Marshall's discovery sparked one of the largest voluntary migrations in world history and accelerated the incorporation of California into the United States. In turn, the California gold rush catalyzed a series of rushes throughout the western United States, Canada, the South Pacific, and eventually, Alaska.[4] In each case, the discovery of precious metal was a watershed moment in local histories of colonialism. The sudden and massive influx of outsiders, and their intense focus on extracting wealth from the landscape, forced sweeping changes on preexisting colonial societies, with especially disastrous results for aboriginal populations.

Newly arrived colonizers faced their own challenges. Gold rush society forced a group of predominately male English-speakers of European descent who shared a set of values to contend with a complex and unfamiliar environment and to challenge, experiment with, and ultimately, reconfigure ideas of race and gender. Exploring how these men used ever-changing ideas of race and gender to define acceptable identities for both themselves and a range of racialized and gendered Others provides an interesting case study that suggests our understanding of white manliness has been fixated on the eastern United States and Britain, whereas much of the national attention and imagination at the time was focused on the West, where new ideas of white manliness prefigured later formulations undertaken elsewhere.

The process of movement was crucial to the development of these new understandings of white manhood. While English-speaking men brought cultural beliefs with them to the goldfields, they soon found themselves both creating new ideas and adapting old ones. This process began en route to California, but as other gold discoveries were made throughout the Pacific Rim, these ideas were transmitted to each new rush. Ideas of what it meant to be a white man, and the place of white men within a colonial gold rush society, underwent constant evolution. We can trace the development and transmission of these ideas by comparing the gold rush societies of California (1848–58) and British Columbia (1858–71) and weighing the relative impact of local, regional, national, and global forces influencing ideas about white manliness and about the place of white men in a colonial society.

The discovery of gold in California in 1848 occurred in the midst of a particularly dramatic transformation in the United States and Britain. Although the United States remained profoundly attached to agrarian and rural virtues, an ever-increasing percentage of its population lived in towns or cities. From 1830 to 1860, towns with populations of twenty-five hundred or more grew by at least 60 percent each decade; and from 1840 to 1850 that growth rate reached 92 percent.[5] More and more, urban men dreamed of making enough money to start their own businesses, but in reality most made their livings as permanent wage laborers, including in the developing area of white-collar work.[6] Across the Atlantic, the same economic and demographic transformations had been under way for some time, albeit in a modified form. In England and Wales, 41 percent of the population lived in urban centers of twenty-five hundred or more by 1850. A decade later it was 46 percent and rising, prompting widespread social dislocation and discontent.[7] As in the United States, young urban working men, ranging from laborers to clerks, dreamed of accumulating enough capital to open their own business and perhaps employ others, but found a lifetime of wage work instead.[8] These demographic and economic changes, simultaneously affecting the two major empires of the English-speaking world, led to a trans-Atlantic conversation about the changing nature of society and its repercussions for young men and women.[9]

These changes, and the social disorder they created, encouraged the formation of a distinctive form of middle-class white manhood. Like any ideology, middle-class white manhood was not a static or stable construct but was instead constantly being re-created and interpreted from a variety of perspectives. As a result, there were significant regional and class variants, one of which emerged in the gold rushes in the North American West, encouraged by the similarity of the backgrounds of many Anglo-American gold rushers. Gold rushers from the eastern United States and Great Britain tended to be from middle-class societies where public discourse emphasized prudence, hard work, thrift, self-restraint, and sexual repression.[10] In other words, the particular strain of middle-class white manhood dominant in much of the urbanizing and industrializing eastern United States and Britain taught men to embrace the values of a restrained manhood. This form of gender identity centered on the cult of "true womanhood" and the glorification of the household as the moral center of the world. Its proponents valued, as the name suggests, self-control framed by an explicitly Christian worldview.[11] The appeal of restrained manhood was that the values it promoted, having arisen partly as a response to the social dislocation of an industrializing and urbanizing landscape, appeared to offer stability and order in the midst of change.[12] Given the long-standing and deep ties between the

United States and Britain, it is unsurprising that these values took hold on both sides of the Atlantic, albeit with significant variations.[13] But while this particular strain of white manliness was dominant among middle-class society, especially in the towns and cities of the eastern United States and Britain, it was not uncontested.

Some middle-class white men rejected restraint as a path to manhood and argued that white men should be martial. Where restrained manhood celebrated expertise, martial manhood valued dominance over subordinates, which had particular appeal for those heading west.[14] Unsurprisingly, western stereotypes of the frontiersman, the pioneer, and the like were strongly associated with ideas of martial manliness and widely distributed in the popular culture of the eastern United States and Great Britain.[15] While martial manhood remained a minority position in more settled regions, linked to the working class, soldiers, and sailors, or associated (in slightly different forms) with the South or the "frontier," many men appear to have been eager to at least temporarily throw off the constraints of restrained manhood and embrace a martial identity.[16] These men would define social and political order in the gold rushes of California and British Columbia.

Ideas of martial and restrained manliness relied on an array of racial and gender Others to give them meaning. Only when values such as bravery, self-restraint, self-denial, and hard work were coded in racial and gender terms, tied to white male bodies, and juxtaposed against supposedly impulsive, hedonistic, and lazy people of color, women, the poor, criminals, or children did they take on real meaning.[17] In the nationally diverse and racially plural context of gold rush societies, ideas of race and gender would be crucial to formulating alternative versions of white manhood.

The men who went to the goldfields of California and British Columbia debated and sought to enact visions of white manliness that both differed from and overlapped with existing versions of white manliness. Overwhelmingly, this discourse was carried on between people of European descent. Of course, at different times and in different ways women and people of color either challenged, subverted, or co-opted this discourse, but these challenges remained largely peripheral to the central debate among English-speaking people of European descent. With firm control over the military, police, government, courts, press, and the economy, men of European descent had a vastly disproportionate effect on how people would be talked about and treated in the gold rush societies.

Race, gender, and class existed in an intricate balance in the gold rush societies of California and British Columbia. White people generally believed that only men of European descent could attempt to live up to the high ideals of white manliness. Americans and Britons of all stripes believed that manliness required certain key characteristics, such as bravery, emotional control, and self-reliance, while darker bodies, and especially black bodies, were incapable of these virtues. Being a white man was a prerequisite for, though not a guarantor of, respectability and status.

A similar influence is evident in contemporary concepts of race. In the mid-nineteenth century, people's behavior and way of living shaped perceptions of their race. For instance, behavioral differences led some middle- and upper-class Britons to see the lower class of England as dark skinned, even black; and in other contexts Britons saw the Irish and Spanish as "off-white" or "not quite white."[18] In the United States, too, the more "noble" Native Americans were generally described as resembling Europeans, while the "ignoble" ones were described as being darker.[19] The emphasis on behavior, which could change or be interpreted differently by different observers, meant that concepts of race and gender were open to debate in gold rush society and that men of European descent had ample opportunity to degrade themselves if they failed to act respectably.

This emphasis on behavior and action brought with it profound insecurities for middle-class white men in the mid-nineteenth century. Not only did the ever-expanding influence of the market threaten both the urban and the rural dweller's financial and social status, but also white men could not even rely on innate characteristics such as sex and European descent to guarantee their self-worth. Contemporary society interpreted financial failure, mental breakdown, criminal or socially disreputable activities, and even social missteps as evidence of a weakness of character. This was especially troubling because character set respectable white men apart from criminals, women, children, and nonwhites.

One value shared among white men of all kinds caused particular consternation: independence. For many men, concerns about being independent compounded the fundamental uncertainty of their position in a rapidly changing world. In both the United States and Britain, the idea of independence was exalted and made into a key trait of manliness and whiteness. Being independent—or more to the point, not being dependent upon others—distinguished a man from a woman, a child, the aged, or the infirm.

At the same time, being independent set one apart from an array of racialized others, most notably peoples of African descent.[20] This trait, more than any other, seemed imperiled by the very processes that helped bring these ideas of white manliness into being.

The changing economic structure of the rapidly industrializing societies of Britain and the United States compelled more and more men to confront the possibility that they faced a lifetime of wage labor.[21] Frequent economic depressions, called panics, made it painfully obvious that independence was not only hard to obtain but also increasingly precarious. It was in this context that news of gold was first received, and that middle-class whites gave meaning to gold rush society.[22]

While men went to the goldfields because wealth would allow them to be independent and manly, the actual conditions of gold rush societies challenged ideas of restrained manhood. Some migrants tried to uphold manly values in the goldfields, but it was not easy. The diverse, mobile, and relatively anonymous gold rush societies of California and British Columbia lacked many of the social institutions that provided the framework for order in the metropoles of the eastern United States or Britain. Families were fairly rare, and with them, so were the supposed moderating influences of white women, parents, and other authority figures. Churches were only weakly established and haphazardly supported by the mass of miners. Many of the miners, motivated as they were by a desire to challenge or reject some of the social mores of the metropole, and believing themselves to be only sojourning in the goldfields, had little desire to entirely reproduce the values of the East.[23] But while the journey westward eroded the different strains of white manliness, the gold rushers still remained firmly vested in their rudiments. These men could not help but view the society around them through the lens of their experiences in the East, and while some might have celebrated transgressive aspects of gold rush society, most sought to impose a colonial order based on middle-class racial and gender values that had been adapted to the local conditions.

THE GOLDFIELD SYSTEM: TRANSNATIONAL FLOWS OF MEANING

Two decades ago Ann Laura Stoler and Frederick Cooper observed that "colonial historiography has been so nationally bound that it has blinded us to those circuits of knowledge and communication that took other routes than those shaped by the metropole-colony axis alone."[24] Histories of gold rushes are particularly vulnerable to this criticism. When the gold rushes of the mid-nineteenth century are treated as anything other than localized, episodic events, they are viewed through the lens of national development. In many of these narratives, the gold rush stands as a turning point in which the nucleus of a new state or social order arises from the massive demographic, economic, and cultural transformations that occur after the discovery of gold. The underlying narrative of many accounts is that of the extension of state control and the transformation of a previously "rowdy" goldfield society into one with more "respectable" behaviors and pursuits.[25] The vast majority of gold rush histories pay scant attention to more than one rush, and especially not to rushes that occurred outside current national borders.[26]

And yet there are good reasons to compare different gold rushes. First, gold rushers during the mid-nineteenth century generally shared the same concerns about their place in a changing society and especially about their ability to become economically self-sufficient heads of families. Second, gold rushes tended to take place on the periphery of imperial expansion. The discovery of gold marked a watershed moment that created a new, or dramatically reshaped an old, colonial order, often with adverse effects for the indigenous inhabitants. This is particularly important because the nature of colonial gold rush society encouraged gold rushers to justify domination through the language of race and gender. Third, settler colonialism took place in both California and British Columbia. Settler colonialism is characterized by conquest and migration, in which the colonizing immigrants dislocate and replace indigenous populations. As a result, the rushes share fundamental structural similarities as a basis for comparison.[27] Fourth, and most importantly, an interconnected web of ideas, capital, technology, and people extended between the rushes, creating, transmitting, and maintaining a set of ideas and practices about life in the goldfields that was related to, but distinct from, the values and behaviors promoted in the eastern United States and Britain. This web constituted a goldfield system: a set of shared practices, technologies, and languages that meant that gold rushers working in diverse goldfields often had more in common with each other than with family and friends in their respective metropolitan centers. This particularly influenced how these men came to articulate and perceive white manliness in the gold mines.

This is not to say that the goldfield system lent itself to creating a static, unchanging concept of what it meant to be a white man. Existing roughly from 1848 to the 1870s, the system spanned a period in which rapid changes were occurring in economics, society, culture, technology, and politics.[28] Large-scale economic and cultural changes in the eastern United States and Europe influenced the goldfield system, most particularly urbanization, the rise of large corporations, and the growing acceptance of wage labor. Indeed, the goldfield system eventually evolved from the social-cultural system it had once been, into an economic network of mines that persisted long after the "rush" had passed. Gold rushes end, not when the gold runs out, but when the gold becomes less accessible and major companies employing wage labor dominate what remains. Ultimately, gold rushes are the result of shared fantasies of triumphing over the ever-present fear of failure so central to nineteenth-century Americans' sense of themselves.[29] Inevitably, however, the rise of corporations in mining exploded this fantasy. This transition helped fuel the gold rush system, because the end of one rush, as in California, encouraged gold seekers to create new rushes, as in Nevada, Idaho, Colorado, Montana, and British Columbia. Nor was the goldfield system ever homogenous. While the connections encouraged homogeneity, local conditions such as the environment and demographics, and local histories of colonialism, all affected how gold rushers understood and talked about white manliness and the nature of goldfield society.

Though the goldfield system encouraged homogeneity, it was also the primary avenue for the propagation of change. The system inspired participants in a particular rush to look to earlier and concurrent rushes for innovations. These, most obviously technical innovations but also social, economic, and cultural innovations, moved through the goldfield system, where they were adopted or modified to local conditions.

What made the gold rush system of the mid-nineteenth century so unusual was the way that it bound together various American and British colonial possessions all around the Pacific Ocean and North American West. Comparison of different sites in this system provides a means for examining the impact of the goldfield system itself and for throwing into stark relief the common trends and specific differences of colonialism in California and British Columbia. The proximity of the two rushes intensifies and makes obvious the connections within the goldfield system while simultaneously allowing for a more effective contrast of two neighboring forms of settler colonialism.

The gold rushes were profound moments of settler colonialism. Both California and British Columbia were territories claimed by aggressively expanding empires in which the newly arriving settlers dramatically altered older forms of government and society. These changes disproportionately benefited the settlers and their countrymen while systematically denying rights and privileges to those deemed nonwhite or otherwise unsuitable for colonial society and government. While people of Chinese, African, and Hispanic descent all pressed for a greater degree of equality and inclusiveness, their voices remained a minority, and most European migrants never seriously questioned the idea of a racially stratified society dominated by white men. And though gold rushes lasted anywhere from months to years, the changes they wrought had lasting repercussions.

Nor were these impacts limited to California and British Columbia. As part of the expanding colonial holdings of the United States and Britain, California and British Columbia were fundamentally bound up with the societies from which they had emerged. Capital, goods, population, and ideas flowed from the metropole to the colonial periphery and back again, and the logics of racial and gender domination that formed in colonial societies like California and British Columbia affected the social order and cultural beliefs of the metropole.[30] As gold rushers wrote and returned home, they brought with them ideas and practices that would shape the evolution of ideas of race and gender in the East.

The settlers of European descent who went to California and British Columbia thought about, talked about, and performed identities as white men. How they conceived and categorized both themselves and others cannot be divorced from the relationships of power that existed in the goldfields. The question of how to define whiteness, and who qualified as white, stimulated considerable debate among settlers in California and British Columbia. At the crux of these discussions were the ways in which the gold rush societies of California and British Columbia challenged existing ideas of white manliness. Indeed, an oft-remarked, but little analyzed, observation is that the category of whiteness was more inclusive in the West than in the East, particularly with regard to the Irish.[31] Arguments that race was largely irrelevant in California, or that racial categories easily expanded to encompass a wider range of people in the West, miss the mark, however. [32] Instead, what happened was that national origin and religious affiliation lost some importance in determining whiteness at the same time that other signifiers (largely based on behavior and appearance) accrued greater meaning. The shifting boundaries of whiteness both affected and were influenced by the relationships of power in the colonial societies of California and British Columbia. This study tells that story.

Whiteness cannot be understood in a vacuum, however. Instead, an individual's or group's self-identification (or labeling) as white, nonwhite, or off-white intersected with a variety of other identities, including gender. In the colonial project, as Anne McClintock has argued, "gender power was not . . . an ephemeral gloss over the more decisive mechanics of class or race. Rather, gender dynamics were, from the outset, fundamental to the securing and maintenance of the imperial enterprise."[33] The relative dearth of families or "respectable" women, combined with the fact that so many gold rushers were responding to perceived economic and social challenges to their status as men in the East, made gender exceptionally important for understanding how these men thought of themselves and of others. Indeed, considerations of gender and race were so bound up together in the gold rushes that one category is illegible without the other. Gold rushers in California and British Columbia never aspired to simply be men, nor did they want to be only white. They wanted to see themselves, and have others see them, as white men.

FIRST GLIMMERS

The discovery of gold at Sutter's Mill in California in late January 1848 was only one of several major events that reshaped much of the Western world that year; and initially, it was of minor concern when compared to events elsewhere. In the United States, far more attention was given to the end of the Mexican-American War, the expansion of the United States, and the reopening of old debates over the extension of slavery.[34] Americans also looked east, across the Atlantic, where an ongoing famine forced more and more Irish to emigrate to the United States, where they congregated in major port cities, exacerbating racial and religious tensions.[35] In Europe, a series of revolutions challenged governments from France to Austria-Hungary. The social turmoil caused by these revolutions, and the counterrevolutionary reactions they provoked, added to transatlantic migrations in the following years.[36] With Europe aflame, domestic problems in the East, and a war successfully concluded in the West, it is understandable that eastern audiences initially paid little attention when newspaper reports began to circulate claiming gold had been discovered in California.

Other considerations, too, dampened early enthusiasm about the gold discovery. The most important factor was a well-placed skepticism about any news from California. Those Americans familiar with California knew it mostly through accounts like Richard Henry Dana's *Two Years before the Mast* and John C. Fremont's report on Oregon and California. Both accounts depicted California as an isolated location with potential agricultural or ranching wealth.[37] Readers in the East were cautious of being made fools and were well aware of the long tradition of questionable reports and tall tales that emanated from the West.[38] Consequently, most readers seemed to have adopted a wait-and-see attitude, believing that even if gold had actually been discovered, it was uncertain in what quantities.

All this changed on December 5, 1848, when President Polk informed Congress that "the accounts of the abundance of gold in that territory [California] are of such an extraordinary character as would scarcely command belief were they not corroborated by the authentic reports of officers in the public service.... The explorations already made warrant the belief that the supply is very large, and that gold is found at various places in an extensive district of country."[39] There was now no question that gold existed in significant quantities in California. The rush was on.

The desire for wealth was the primary unifying feature of all gold rushers. News of the gold discovery in California opened up a world of possibilities for a wide range of individuals. That so many decided to go to California gives some indication of both the opportunity they believed awaited them there and, to an extent, the increasing perception of life in the East as economically and socially constraining. Gold rushers anticipated that wealthy capitalists would not control mining, and that the difficulty and danger would mean that individuals with flawed characters would fail. In other words, California gold was alluring because it represented a chance for economic advancement that seemed to rest almost entirely on an individual's worth as a white man.[40] In a period of economic and social change, the gold rush not only appeared to affirm one of the central morality tales of white manhood (that hard work was the key to success) but also linked this tale to imperial expansion and ideas of manifest destiny and promised unmatched wealth. With such a potent combination of economic incentive, manliness, and for Americans, nationalism, it is little surprise that so many men decided to rush to California. They would soon discover that their ideas of white manliness would have to be adapted to new circumstances.

The modification of ideas about white manliness began on the journey to the goldfields. As chapter 1 demonstrates, faced with conditions that differed dramatically from what they were used to, gold rushers experimented with new ideas of what it meant to be a white man on the way west. This chapter analyzes the two major migration streams to California—the Overlanders, those who traveled across the continent, and the Argonauts, those who took sea routes—and their experiences to reveal shared assumptions and telling differences, before comparing the California-bound migration to the later migration to British Columbia. In both cases, the migration westward served as a training ground where settlers developed their ideas of race, gender, and colonialism. Before they ever set foot in California or British Columbia, these men had already begun to redefine white manliness to cope with what they believed the conditions would be like in the goldfields.

Arriving in California, Americans and Britons, along with thousands of migrants from around the world, rapidly overwhelmed the preexisting forms of colonial authority. Chapter 2 explores how self-described white men set about reestablishing colonial authority in California on the basis of "republican virtues"—that is, according to the ideal of a government controlled by citizens who were independent of any outside influence and who put the greater good ahead of individual gain. In the process of reestablishing this authority, white settlers were forced to confront the problem of how to determine who qualified as a proper and respectable citizen and why. In the United States during the nineteenth century, citizenship was strongly linked to whiteness. Echoing the consensus in the eastern states, the vast majority of white men on the West Coast never doubted for a moment that they were the one people truly capable of functioning in a republic. But in California, who exactly was a white man, and how that status was marked, was debated in the legislature, the mining towns of the Sierra Nevada, and the urban hub of San Francisco.

Ten years later, the gold rushers in British Columbia encountered a very different preexisting colonial authority. As chapter 3 makes clear, the British

Columbian colonial elite, which had developed during the era of the fur trade, maintained and expanded its authority during the gold rush. To this colonial elite, the greatest threat was white Americans whose perceived republicanism and aggressive expansionism suggested the possibility of insurrection, filibustering, or social disorder. In response, the colonial elite articulated a policy of "colorblindness," claiming that British colonial authority did not recognize race, virtually ensuring that race would remain central to questions of power, authority, and identity in the colony as the gold rush continued.

Chapter 4 shifts gears and explores changing understandings of white manliness as articulated by attitudes toward risk and gambling. Gold rushers hailed from a society in which hard work and dogged determination were believed to be the sole criteria for success. Financial success or failure (and how one handled each) therefore served as a metric of an individual's character. But in the gold rush societies of California and British Columbia, risk and chance seemed to characterize both the act of mining and the leisure pursuits of the miners. Mining itself was a "gamble" that seemed to reward men of dubious character as often as, if not more often than, men of moral worth. Yet the risks involved in such labor differed from those in games of chance. Whereas the former could be portrayed as at once daring and respectable, the latter could not. Gold rushers used the risk of mining to identify as white men, but understood the risks involved in gambling as having the potential to collapse boundaries between themselves and "others." In order to cope with the role of luck in mining and gambling, these men ascribed racial and gender meanings to both activities that became a critical way for settlers to define white manliness and to justify a colonial order that placed white men at the top of society.

In California and British Columbia, gold rushers were confronted with a vast array of people from around the world at the same moment that they were deprived of the circles of family, friends, church members, business partners, and the like who had conveyed their reputations in the East. Lacking specific background knowledge of others, settlers in the gold rushes came to rely heavily on appearance to judge a person's worth. Chapter 5 traces how gold rushers in California and British Columbia depended on evaluations of dress and bodies to determine if an individual or group measured up to idealized standards of white manliness and, therefore, to determine the place of that individual or group in their colonial society. The problem was, of course, that those ideals kept shifting over the course of the gold rushes. Standards of dress proved particularly problematic for gold rushers; and over time, these men increasingly emphasized what they believed was the unalterable truth of the body. Focusing on the body, and in particular on its perceived racial and gender characteristics, had the effect of consolidating understandings of race and gender, which had, in turn, serious implications for the colonial order, especially in British Columbia, where this trend was the most pronounced.

In the gold rush societies of California and British Columbia, ideas about white manliness were thrown into question. Likewise, as ideas of white manliness were challenged and redefined, ideas of white womanhood had to adapt to the tumultuous conditions of the gold rush. The ideas about race and gender that emerged out of these two colonial societies eventually came to foreshadow the development of ideas of masculinity in the latter part of the nineteenth century. But first, for all that to happen, these men had to go to the goldfields.

• • •

Note to readers: This book reproduces the racist language of the time, not to celebrate it, but to draw attention to the underlying ideologies and structures of power that gave this language meaning. While racist terms are, thankfully, considered offensive in today's world, they were in common circulation at the time, and obscuring them and their meanings would misrepresent the racial animus of so many while letting us underappreciate the bravery of those who stood for a more just and equitable world.

CHAPTER 1

Getting to Gold

Migration and the Formation of White Manliness

"TO BREAK OFF THESE TIES OF ASSOCIATION WITH A Father, Brother & Sisters," wrote twenty-seven-year-old Peter Decker in April 1849 as he set out for California, "is too much for cool regret. I have lost control of my feelings."[1] For gold rushers like Decker, the journey to the goldfields was the first step into an uncertain future away from family and familiar social networks. It was the first time they experienced a world in which they were not clearly socially, economically, and politically dominant. In the absence of these networks, the migrants struggled to come to grips with what being a white man meant, and these efforts reveal both the diverse and shifting ways that gold rushers understood the idea of white manliness and how they related that idea to social and political order.

Gold rushers can be sorted into two categories: the Overlanders, who crossed the continent by land, and the Argonauts, who traveled by water. Despite their very different methods and routes of transportation, the Overlanders' and Argonauts' migrations had marked similarities. Both groups of migrants were overwhelmingly male, both imported cultural baggage from the East while improvising new responses to conditions they encountered as they moved west, both expected to encounter nonwhites, and both usually feared the worst. Whether they traveled by sea or by land, colonialism fundamentally shaped how Argonauts and Overlanders experienced the people they met and the places they visited while en route to the goldfields. At its core, colonialism was characterized by the assumption that white people had the right, ability, and sometimes, duty, to rule over non-whites. The people whom the migrants met and the places they saw encouraged the migrants to begin the process of adapting older beliefs about white manliness to account for a more racially diverse, socially fluid, and homosocial goldfield society.

The route migrants took to the goldfields exposed them to slightly different understandings of the relationship between themselves and the peoples they encountered. Overlanders encountered indigenous peoples who were firmly in the path of the expanding United States, while Argonauts encountered Latin Americans who, occupying tropical locations of dubious healthfulness, were more peripheral to the concerns of most nineteenth-century Americans. A comparison reveals that while white Americans understood white "civilization" to be *replacing* indigenous "savagery," they believed that a small number of white men could *rejuvenate* the decayed society of Latin America. As a result, gold rushers had a far harder time imagining a place for indigenous persons in the colonial societies of California and British Columbia than they had for other nonwhite groups.

Attitudes toward, and experiences of, migration to the goldfields changed over time. Changing demographics, combined with advances in technology and infrastructure, distinguished the rush to British Columbia in 1858 from the rush to California ten years earlier. In the decade after the discovery of gold in California, the population of the state had grown to almost 400,000, from around 135,000, a rate of growth even more astounding when the massive demographic decline of the indigenous population— from around 120,000 to between 20,000 and 40,000 during the same period—is taken into account.[2] With this demographic transformation came the shift to wage labor, statehood, and the emergence of San Francisco as a regional center of capital and political power and a key site in the gold rush system of the mid-nineteenth century. Building on its early dominance of the California gold rush, San Francisco provided capital and expertise to miners working the Australian goldfields and then to miners who took part in the numerous rushes that occurred in mountains and streams throughout the western portion of the North American continent.[3] With San Francisco acting as the hub, men, material, capital, and ideas moved through the goldfield system from one rush to another, both disseminating new ways of doing things and bringing knowledge and experience of older methods.

The gold discovery on the Fraser River meant that British Columbia was quickly incorporated as another site within this gold rush system, with California being the dominant source of gold rush migrants to British Columbia in 1858, the first year of the rush. For example, in a two-week period in June, an estimated six thousand people arrived in Victoria, the vast majority of whom were from California.[4] With travel to British Columbia being relatively cheap and easy, the gold discoveries themselves seemed to herald a return to "days of '49" for many Californians.[5] The Fraser River offered a place where the abundance of gold would allow miners to work in small companies, with little or no capital, and stand a reasonable chance of success. This was particularly meaningful in California, where wage work dominated mining by 1858, undercutting the dreams of many men to gain financial independence.[6] In much the same way that the California gold rush had been fueled in part by a reaction against the growth of industrialization and wage labor in the East, many who rushed to the Fraser were reacting to similar developments in California mining. Ultimately, by land or sea, to California or British Columbia, migration to the goldfields provided the first opportunity for gold rushers to articulate what being a white man would mean in the gold rush societies of the Pacific coast.

STARTING OFF

Important regional divisions existed in the motivations and demographics of the two main streams of migrants from the United States to California. Although the Overlanders did draw some of their population from urban centers, rural folk from the western states dominated the migration. For most Overlanders, the trek to California was a continuation of a process that had repeatedly seen whole families migrate westward in the previous decades.[7] In contrast, the Argonauts came mainly from ports on the Atlantic. Even those Argonauts who did not live in urban centers themselves had observed and felt the changing economic and social conditions that resulted from the growth of manufacturing and urbanization.[8] Families made up approximately one-quarter of the California-bound overland migration, far more than went by sea.[9] Those differences aside, both Overlanders and Argonauts shared similar cultural values and concerns that encouraged similar conversations among migrants regardless of whether they traveled by land or sea.

Overlanders and Argonauts envisioned the West and westward move-ment as an integral component of the "American character."[10] Both eastern and western Americans shared an intellectual heritage that stressed west-ward expansion and celebrated the pioneers who "opened" the West.[11] The California gold rush occurred when the expansionist ideology of Manifest Destiny still enjoyed wide support in the United States. Furthermore, Ameri-cans shared basic assumptions about the place of white men in the westering expansion of the country. At midcentury two streams of manliness, restrained manhood and martial manhood, competed for dominance among middle-class white Americans. While restrained manhood celebrated self-control and social responsibility, martial manhood emphasized conflict and aggres-sion as a path to manhood.[12] Strongly associated with martial manhood, westward expansionism had broad appeal to many segments of American society in both the East and the West. Americans could see individuals who moved west as exemplars of independent and self-reliant manliness.[13] Memo-ries of the opening of the Mississippi and Ohio River valleys, along with the more recent celebration of the Oregon settlers as "America's finest citizens," served as symbolic touchstones for this rhetoric that linked martial white manliness with national expansion and colonialism.[14]

Like the Overlanders, the Argonauts thought of themselves, and were perceived by their supporters, in much the same manner. This is particu-larly evident in the attention many Argonauts gave to Juan Fernandez Island, the island off the coast of Chile where Alexander Selkirk, the inspi-ration for Robinson Crusoe, was shipwrecked. Frequently visited in 1849, before the Panama and Nicaragua routes became dominant, the island linked the archetypical solitary, self-reliant, and martial white man to the Argo-nauts.[15] As George Payson put it, "The idea of a life in the mines was rather agreeable. It had about it a smack of Robinson Crusoe."[16] Even the name Argonauts reflected an idealized link between these men and the ancient Greek hero Jason. Among the gold rushers and their spectators, significant support existed for the idea that the Argonauts were embodiments of a range of manly, martial virtues.

Both streams of migrants shared other traits, the most significant of which was a nearly complete lack of direct experience with non-Europeans other than people of African descent; even then, black populations were concentrated in certain areas, most obviously the slave-holding South, where many migrants had never lived. Importantly for gold rushers, the migration to the goldfields marked the first time most of them encountered Native Americans or Hispanics. By the mid-nineteenth century, with the eradication or removal of the vast majority of Native Americans from east of the Mississippi River, most Americans knew about indigenous peoples only through popular culture.[17] These imaginary Indians buttressed, critiqued, and celebrated middle-class white American society, culture, and imperial expansion.[18]

As Overlanders approached the starting points for the transcontinental trek, they heard more and more stories of attacks and treachery by Native Americans.[19] Drawing on the ideals of martial manhood, potential Overlanders responded to these stories in an amazingly uniform manner, buying prodigious quantities of firearms, ammunition, and knives.[20] Whatever their prior concept of indigenous peoples, the vast majority evidently decided to err on the side of caution, a decision that, not coincidentally, allowed them to act the part of the brave frontiersman. Nor were the Overlanders alone in embracing the costume and accoutrements of martial manhood. As future California state senator Elisha Crosby noted in 1849, even among Argonauts "it was pretty well known that every passenger had stowed away his small arms and enough powder for a California campaign[,] and any one of these trunks contained enough powder to blow the steamer to attoms."[21] Besides allowing migrants to symbolically link themselves to representations of martial manhood from soldiers to pioneers, the emphasis on weaponry also revealed the widespread sense among migrants that whatever social order existed out West would have to be maintained in the face of possibly violent resistance.

Argonauts shared with Overlanders a distinct lack of experience but a surfeit of beliefs about the people and places they would encounter on their voyage. Most knowledge of Latin America came from tales about Spanish colonization, travel narratives, and, most immediately, accounts of the Mexican-American War. Additionally, Protestants on both sides of the Atlantic were only too willing to believe that the Catholic nations to the south were despotic, corrupt, and backward, the antithesis of the democratic, progressive, and energetic white Protestant North.[22] When Samuel Morse asked, "Is it not clear that the cause of Popery is the cause of despotism?" most of Protestant America agreed that it was clear indeed.[23]

Perceptions of environmental and biological difference, too, predisposed gold rushers to see Latin America as different and backward. In the nineteenth century, middle-class whites on both sides of the Atlantic divided humanity into Orient and Occident, as well as along a North-South spectrum. At the bottom lay Africa, with its black inhabitants who were "oversexed and not fully human; less far southward resided the Spaniards[,] . . . worthier than Africans but vitiated by their propensity for unmanly conduct."[24] The warm climate and abundance of Central and South America suggested that Latin America and its inhabitants would be degraded.[25] To middle-class whites, residents of tropical areas had their wants too easily supplied, resulting in laziness and degradation, while residents of northern climes had to struggle for basic necessities, encouraging an energetic and competitive character.

Before the Mexican-American War very few Americans traveled to Latin America, so a small group of travel writers disproportionately shaped public perception. Books like John Lloyd Stephens's *Incidents of Travel in Central America, Chiapas and Yucatan* and Richard Henry Dana's *Two Years before the Mast* were incredibly influential.[26] Indeed, Dana's account was so widely read by gold rushers that when he visited California again in 1859, he discovered that "almost . . . every American in California had read it"—though, as he admitted, this was largely due to the fact that in 1848 "there was no book upon California but mine."[27] Travel writers like Stephens and Dana described Latin Americans as lazy, poor, insolent, overprideful, and racially suspect.[28]

Accounts of the Mexican-American War demonstrated the link between imperial expansion and the nation's white, Protestant republicanism.[29] As more people read stories about the war in the burgeoning penny press, these confirmed and consolidated preexisting stereotypes and images of the region and its peoples. American newspapers identified Catholicism as one of the key factors undercutting Mexican morale and rendering the Mexicans meek, cowardly, and apathetic. A series of lopsided U.S. victories demonstrated to Americans that because of their greater virtue, American citizen-soldiers could easily defeat the racially degraded armies of Mexico.[30] The war demonstrated that Americans were strongly inclined to imagine imperial expansion through the rubric of the expansion of the white republic.[31]

The gold rushers who traveled to British Columbia would inherit this "knowledge" about indigenous peoples and Latin Americans. By 1858, ideas about the California gold rush and the minor gold rushes that followed it had entered popular culture on both sides of the Atlantic.[32] American emigrants went to British Columbia with expectations not only about the sort of society they would find when they arrived but also about the sort of people they would encounter along the way. As a result, the migration to British Columbia had many similarities to the earlier rush to California; but owing to changing technology and the dynamics of British encounters with Americans, this later migration would have different ramifications.

SETTLING INTO THE TRIP

Starting in 1849 and continuing throughout much of the early 1850s, both Overlanders and Argonauts often organized themselves along the lines of joint-stock companies to travel to the goldfields. For the Overlanders, this made sense. Previous overland migrations had been organized around families, but the overwhelmingly male character of the gold rush migrations made this impractical.[33] Still, with few exceptions, migrants believed that a safe transit across the country required large numbers for mutual aid and defense.[34] The result was that most started off the migration as members of some form of joint association with resources pooled to purchase supplies. These associations often appointed a leader, but one with little coercive authority. Much of the decision making was actually far more consensus-driven than the paper organization of these companies suggested.[35] Once on the trail, dissatisfied members could split into smaller trains or join other trains if they disagreed with the leadership of their group.[36]

In the early years, before regular fare passage was inaugurated, the Argonauts demonstrated a similar tendency to organize associations or joint-stock companies. With their combined funds, these companies either bought or chartered a vessel and purchased supplies for the trip to California and for mining after they arrived.[37] Not only did mining companies organize the resources necessary for departure, but they also usually included in their charters regulations for behavior on the journey to the goldfields and provisions for trading and mining as a company once in California.[38] The prevalence of this type of organization among the Argonauts is even more striking given that, while at sea, these democratic companies had to contend with the autocratic authority of the captain. The outcome was predictable: account after account details conflicts between the passengers and the captain. While many of these were fairly mild disagreements, some exploded into near mutiny or resulted in criminal trials or lynch mobs targeting captains when the vessel arrived in California.[39]

Because mid-nineteenth-century Americans saw democracy as a key signifier of white manliness, membership in these organizations helped mark an individual as a white man. This trend linked the settlement of California to a particular colonial order, one vested in the idea that free, independent white men should be politically dominant. This idea encouraged gold rushers to differentiate between themselves and the peoples they encountered en route on the basis of race.[40] Their experiences with recalcitrant compatriots and, in the case of the Argonauts, ship captains, suggested other threats to such a society, either from authoritarian outsiders or from corrupt or foolish members. Settlers would have to act aggressively to preserve their prerogatives as white men against these threats, eventually finding the solution not only in colonial government but also in the language and practices surrounding ideas of risk and appearance.

The practice of forming associations does not appear to have lasted until the rush for British Columbia. By 1858, regular steamship service and a rail connection across Panama made the ocean route the far more popular choice for migrants. Regular service, shorter trips, and lower fares all combined to encourage gold rushers going to British Columbia to travel as individual passengers, not as members of a company.[41] As a result, the migrants who had not been involved in earlier rushes—like to California—lacked direct experience with democratic organization en route to the mines. This may have, in turn, contributed to their willingness to accede to preestablished colonial authority upon their arrival in British Columbia.

But while the absence of joint-stock companies may have reduced the appeal of democratic organizations, Cecil Buckley's journal provides some of the strongest evidence that some miners remained deeply concerned about ideas of independence and equality. Buckley left Southampton in April 1862 for British Columbia on a second-class ticket because he "wished to be well acquainted with the style of people who were leaving England for the same purpose and who I fancied would be chiefly met with in the 2nd class."[42] Buckley, of middle-class background, fancied himself a miner and sought to surround himself with other laboring men to bolster his claims to that identity. Another gold rusher, Byron Johnson, who was, like Buckley, of "a good deal better class," also traveled in steerage to British Columbia.

Johnson remembered that the "hard sun-burnt fellows in rough miner's dress . . . were our heroes," and that the "new chums" would gather around each one to collect "fragments of his advice."[43] Traveling in second class, Buckley witnessed the third-class passengers threatening his second-class companions that "we shall be all alike at the diggings, and 'them as tries to make theirselves exclusive now, had better look out'" in British Columbia.[44] A belief in the perceived leveling effects of the gold rush was part of the attraction of the gold rush for some members of British society. It need hardly be said that the equality espoused by the third-class passengers was almost certainly predicated on a common racial, gender, and possibly, national identity. In other words, it was equality for (British) white men atop a hierarchical colonial society.

Both the Overlanders and the Argonauts first experienced the repercussions of a homosocial world during their migration to the goldfields. For the Overlanders, one of the biggest changes to which they had to adjust was the necessity of doing what would have been called women's work at home, particularly washing, mending, and cooking. While some migrants celebrated their newfound ability to cook (one wonders if their messmates did as well) and perform other domestic chores, more were like Peter Decker, who, after his "first washing (except socks) last evening," concluded that "the washerwoman earns all & more than she gets."[45] Indeed, for many men, the practical realities of homosocial life stimulated a profound nostalgia for women or, at least, women's labor. D. A. Millington probably spoke for many of his fellow travelers when he opined, "My camp fare with the cold ground and a little straw for a bed and food served up by our rude cookery does not well compare with a downy bed softened by the delicate hands of woman and the neat and wholesome fare sweetened by her smiles, neither does the boisterous company of a crowd of men replace the gentle influence of female society. But I must get accustomed to these changes whether I like them or not I suppose[,] and so I shall pretend to like it well enough as long as I can stand it."[46] While men at least claimed to celebrate their manly independence, the reality of making do without the labor of women, combined with the other hardships of the trek, encouraged them to think more fondly of what they had left behind.

Although women were more common on the Overland trails than on the sea routes in the first years of the rush, the Argonauts' accounts do not tend to have the same note of longing for absent women. To be sure, many men while in the throes of sea sickness or an Atlantic storm were "all for giving up and count[ing] their share of stock worth but a verry little and would sell out for almost nothing." They wished, as did Nelson Kingsley, that they were back among the "many blessings . . . enjoy[ed] at home," but these sentiments usually lasted only until the storm or sickness subsided.[47] One of the key reasons for this difference appears to be that for the Argonauts the daily task of cooking usually fell to the ship's cook, who was very often black.[48] With a black cook to fill in the role of subservient and effeminate domestic labor, it is unsurprising that the Argonauts did not express the same sort of longing for women's labor as did the Overlanders. Indeed, about the only domestic chore the Argonauts engaged in was laundering, which they did with far less frequency than the Overlanders; and, on the rare occasion when they did wash, they did not find themselves "particularly handy at the business."[49] Even this limited amount of domesticity worried Richard Hunt, who feared "the girls would think . . . we look more like a laundry than a California droger."[50] While Overlanders lamented the loss of women's labor, Argonauts like Hunt worried more about their own performance as men.

This is not to say that Overlanders were unconcerned about performing identities as white men; indeed, the performance of white manliness was as central to the Overlanders as it was to the Argonauts. Both Argonauts and Overlanders sought to assert an identity as white men by claiming expertise related to their mode of travel. Expertise served as a way for the migrants to divide themselves into two groups: seasoned, experienced men and "greenhorns" who were unskilled and unprepared for the realities they would encounter in the goldfields.[51] For the Argonauts, expertise was manifested in the use of nautical terminology, recording latitude and longitude in their diaries, and engaging in some of the basic tasks of the crew.[52] Although some Argonauts thought the "effort to play the part of the old salts" was "amusing," even they conceded that "a lot of the verdant passengers" did so.[53]

For Overlanders, the context was slightly different. The skills that Overlanders expected to master were necessary to their trip. As a result, most Overlanders acquired those skills early. Unlike the Argonauts, Overlanders had to learn how to make camp, pasture their animals, stand watch, and, most importantly, deal with Native Americans.[54] So it was that John Carr, the "kid" of his company, spent his days getting ready in Weston, Missouri, by practicing with a "'Pepper-box,' or Allen's revolver[,] . . . as the

Comanches were liable to make a raid on us while passing through their hunting-grounds."[55] Argonauts, miles out to sea, practiced with their weapons for amusement and to ensure they would be prepared for what they expected to encounter in California, be it a lawless society or marauding Native Americans; but few expected to have to use their weapons on the journey to the goldfields.[56] Nevertheless, both groups believed that at least appearing to be able to dominate a range of nonwhites, criminals, or other threatening people was a necessary part of their conception of themselves as white men. That they felt this way speaks to their expectations about the nature of a colonial society that would require individuals, rather than the state, to enforce a racial hierarchy at the point of a gun, if need be.

These attitudes were reflected in the spirit of play that infused both the overland and overseas migrations. With copious free time, Argonauts had more opportunities to engage in a wider array of play than their overland counterparts, but the men on the overland trail also seized virtually any opportunity to engage in play that hearkened back to schoolboy games or fantasies. Play, of course, is a fairly subjective and fluid concept, encompassing recreational activities but also describing a mind-set about those activities. In the mid-nineteenth century, play, at least for school-age boys, embraced a vision of manliness tied to martial manhood.[57] Adults, on the other hand, were expected to fill their leisure time with reading, metaphysical and political debates, lectures, and prayer, all recreational activities strongly tied to the ideology of restrained manhood and which explicitly rejected the loss of self-control evident in childish behavior.[58] This division of recreational activity speaks to the multifaceted gender implications of engaging in play. Migrants' play was a reaction to eastern standards of restrained manliness and an assertion of martial manhood, hence the frequent use of the term *boys* to denote fellow gold rushers. In the East, the term *boy* was a diminutive, with connotations of paternalistic superiority.[59] On the migrations west, however, gold rushers seized on the term *boy* as a self-descriptor at the same time that many embraced play as an expression of identity. Playing with the "boys" was, therefore, a way for migrants to clearly differentiate their identity from the expectations about middle-class manhood on the East Coast, dominated as it was by ideas of restrained manhood.

Even this is too simple, however. Many men on the western migrations were like Alfred Doten, who would race, dance, play cards, and pretend to hunt whales one day, then practice singing, read, and listen to debates the next.[60] Like Doten, many men participated in leisure activities linked to both martial manhood and restrained manhood. For some, this meant an embrace of alcohol and gambling; for others, those activities remained beyond the pale, even as they engaged in practical jokes and gunplay. Whatever the specific activities engaged in, the result was the same, a blending of martial boyish play and restrained adult leisure activities that helped set the stage for the articulation of new understandings of white manliness in the goldfields.

The link between play, boyishness, and westward migration was evident in a wide range of migrants' activities. Many migrants evidently felt liberated, as Overlander A. J. McCall did, on having been "relieved from the conventionalities of social life." For McCall, being under "the broad sky, upon the free earth" caused "the wild shout, the boisterous laugh" to well up "from the pent up bosom like a bursting torrent. Grave men become boys again." Further underscoring the link between westward migration, boyhood, and martial manhood, the experience caused McCall to recollect an incident from his "youthful days" in which some boys had run around howling like "wild, untamed savages" and disturbed a pious old neighbor.[61] Aboard ship, play was evident in the appropriation of sailors' rough culture, in particular the equator-crossing ceremony that often involving drenching or being shaved with a "very dull" razor with "tar and slush" used for lather.[62] For Richard Hale, the trip west was a chance to link the westering experience with "boyhood's fancy"—an opportunity to visit what he called "the most fascinating spot, to me, on the face of the globe! Robinson Crusoe's island!"[63] For Hale and his fellow passengers, visiting the island was a "great adventure," and the trip quickly came to resemble boyhood play, complete with jungle explorations, daring each other to climb a mountain peak, "some rough sport—storming each other with cabbage balls made from the spongy pulp of the tree"—and racing downhill.[64] For these men, playing indicated not immaturity but some of the earliest attempts to reconcile the demands and appeals of martial manhood and restrained manhood.[65] It is little wonder then, that migrants to British Columbia engaged in boyish play and jokes with as much enthusiasm as the migrants to California.[66]

Hunting, target practice, and gunplay were other ways that both Overlanders and Argonauts asserted an identity as martial white men. Argonauts

THE AUTHOR À LA ROBINSON CRUSOE.
E AR

Browne dressing up as Robinson Crusoe on the Juan Fernandez Islands en route to California. This sort of boyish play was common on the way to the goldfields. Source: Browne, *Crusoe's Island*, 150.

and Overlanders alike had outfitted themselves with "pistols and Bowie-knives, dirks, and other offensive weapons" before departing from the East.[67] John Faragher has argued that the Overlanders' frequent hunting was a way to "measur[e] themselves against the already romanticized images of their heroic pioneer fathers and grandfathers traversing the Wilderness Road and the Cumberland Gap."[68] It was that, but in measuring themselves against the pioneer archetype, these men were also embracing a standard of manliness that emphasized toughness and martial ability. Washington Peck described his first buffalo hunt in terms deliberately evocative of a military engagement. Men on horseback accompanied by "five or six foot men started to atact the buffaloes" but while "the herd sho[w]ed fight, . . . they did not come in close contact enough to have a regular battle."[69]

Unsurprisingly, given attitudes like this, it turned out to be a short distance for some Overlanders to go from hunting game to hunting indigenous peoples. The determination of hunting enthusiast Alonzo Rathbun to get a "scalp or to" was realized just over a week after a buffalo hunt, when seventeen of his party ambushed three Native Americans and "shot down" one of them, with "7 or 8 balls through him."[70] Despite the perception at the time that Overlanders faced constant danger of attacks by Native Americans, violent incidents were rare; and when they did occur, they were often, as with the murder recorded by Rathbun, instigated by the Overlanders.[71] Though armed conflict between Argonauts and the peoples they encountered en route to California was rarer, Argonauts demonstrated a desire to shoot at targets, birds, and even fish.[72] In one conflict in Panama, arising out of a dispute between American and Panamanian boatmen over control of the river trade, not only did the Argonauts take part in the fighting, but also one of them, Stephen Davis, made special mention of the martial prowess of a "Rocky Mountain hunter who . . . with his long, heavy rifle picked off the black rascals who were working the cannon at the fort and doing so much damage to the town."[73] On both routes, the linking of hunting, pioneering, and the violent suppression of nonwhite peoples powerfully buttressed emerging ideas about the ideal colonial order for the goldfields.

The practical jokes played by migrants are particularly revealing, because in order for a joke to work, migrants needed shared values. While many of the jokes were only "the exploits of . . . unimaginative jokesters," others had significant cultural meaning.[74] In case after case, on land and at sea, jokes were designed to ridicule the victim's claims to martial manhood. A favorite joke on the overland trail involved simulating an attack by indigenous peoples with the intent to reveal the victim as cowardly or panicky.[75] Likewise, the passengers and crew of the *James W. Paige* went to great lengths to simulate a pirate attack, causing the victim to rush up on deck armed only with a pump handle to defend the ship. On the *Edward Everett*, the captain and crew convinced a group of men they could avoid the discomfort of rounding the Horn by hiking from Patagonia to Valparaiso. To be prepared to deal with "cannibals and ferocious wild beasts," they were drilled by "a sailor, dressed in an old uniform with a sword at his side." After about an hour they caught on to the joke.[76] One man on the *Falcon* turned the tables on his tormentors after they paid the black cook to dress up like him and imitate his "Napoleon-like" demeanor. Turning to the laughing passengers, the man remarked to them, "You have sent me a very fit representative of yourselves." The laughter quickly stopped.[77]

All of these jokes functioned on the basis of racial and gender punch lines that mocked the victims' claims to being martial white men by encouraging them to overreact or panic. That the threat they reacted to was, in many cases, a racialized Other, only underscored the point that these men were not the stuff of which imperial adventurers were made. This is why the *Falcon* passenger's response was so effective. He quickly and efficiently reversed the racial and gender coding of the joke. No longer was his Napoleon-like demeanor ridiculous because a black man was imitating him. Instead, the black man now represented the jokers, throwing their own claims to white manliness into question.

Migrants' play and jokes remained remarkably consistent over a twenty-year period because of the way these activities underscored key aspects of the experience of the gold rush for some, if not most, of the migrants. Boyish play and jokes encouraged men to embrace a martial form of manhood and, often, to do so in a way that encouraged them to think of themselves as dominant over a range of racial and gendered others. In so doing, these men identified restrained manhood as the dominant male gender norm. Men who revealed themselves as gullible, cowardly, or averse to rough play ran the risk of being the ultimate punch line to their fellow migrants: the over-civilized and effeminate easterner, woefully unprepared either to withstand the rigors of mining or to exercise authority in the goldfields.[78]

MEETING THE LOCALS

One of the most important events on the migration to the goldfields was an encounter with indigenous peoples or Latin Americans. For many migrants, this was the first time they encountered significant populations of people who were not white, not Protestant, and not enslaved. These encounters proved to be crucial early experiences that foreshadowed and helped condition the response of migrants to the diverse populations and unsettled conditions of the goldfields. Migration allowed only the most transient of relationships, lasting, on average, from a few hours to a few days. As a result, migrants showed little awareness of Native American or Latin American motivations, perspectives, or situations beyond the most cursory level. Migrants expected to see certain behaviors and practices, and Native

Americans and Latin Americans had little opportunity to break these stereotypes. Migration also shaped the types of interactions gold rushers would have with indigenous peoples and Latin Americans. The main concern of the Overlanders and Argonauts was movement, and most relationships on the overseas and overland routes revolved around permitting, denying, or aiding passage.

The first thing that struck migrants was the environment of the places through which they traveled. Gold rushers placed great meaning on the environment, believing that it had a determining impact on the characteristics of people who lived there. The relationship between the character of Latin Americans and the environment, particularly in Central America, was straightforward: a lush environment was allegedly a direct cause of Latin Americans' perceived decadence. The linking of tropical environments to moral, social, and physical decay had a long lineage in European thought.[79] In 1849, while crossing the isthmus, William M'Collum summed up this prevailing thought when he observed that "idleness and sloth meet you at every turn; you feel that you are in the midst of an inferior race of men, enervated by the climate, whom bountiful nature has made stolid and indolent, by exempting them from the necessity of enterprise and industry."[80] The association between tropical environments and perceived character flaws would remain consistent throughout the two gold rushes.[81] Despite the greater attention paid to notions of biological difference, British Columbia–bound migrants still put considerable emphasis on environmental and cultural factors in determining the nature of Panamanians. As Samuel Bowles noted in summary, "The climate and their rude wants invite a lazy, sensual life, and such is theirs."[82]

Latin American laziness was explicitly contrasted with the energy of Anglo-Americans.[83] In spite of accounts that "the streets were filled with women selling fruit, cake and bread, cigars, wine and all sorts of stuff," Panamanian economic activity was dismissed as "pestering" or as being of less importance than the industries dominated by foreign white men.[84] Argonauts believed that a small cadre of enterprising white men could seize control and remake Latin America.[85] Anecdotal evidence seemed to confirm this. Argonauts recorded having met with a variety of Americans and Europeans who had arrived previously in Latin America and risen to positions of economic and social dominance, such as "Capt Cithcart," an American living in Rio de Janeiro who had "amassed considerable of a Fortune" and owned "a large plantation and Several negro Slaves."[86] While degraded, Latin Americans simultaneously seemed potentially valuable as colonial subjects.

The comparatively bleak and harsh landscapes of the Great Plains and the Western Cordillera also shaped how Overlanders thought about indigenous peoples. The Plains peoples encountered by the Overlanders, for instance, had adopted a nomadic or seminomadic lifestyle heavily dependent upon the horse and buffalo. Linking this lifestyle to essential characteristics, Overlanders particularly admired the hunting prowess of Plains peoples, seeing in the buffalo a suitably challenging and impressive prey.[87] Nomadism therefore represented both the antithesis of civilization and the potential for military ability. In stark contrast, gold rushers saw the mainly pedestrian Native Americans of California and the Great Basin, whom they pejoratively labeled "Diggers," as cowardly and poor hunters who ate, among other things, insects.[88] The contrast gold rushers perceived between the Plains peoples and "Diggers" helped justify, they believed, relegating the indigenous population of California to the bottom tier of the colonial hierarchy.

Perhaps most importantly for the colonial projects in California and British Columbia was migrants' belief that indigenous peoples and Latin Americans represented a martial threat but not a manly martial threat. Overlanders worried that "the great warriors, arabs, and terror of the plains," would attack them while en route to California.[89] Though some migrants entertained visions of massive battles with "lots, gaubs, fields, and swarms of [Native Americans]," for most migrants the actual threat Native Americans represented was through theft or attacks on "some solitary hunter or isolated band, with an occasional effort at stampeding stock."[90] Indigenous peoples, in the eyes of most migrants, were not interested in fighting fairly and instead resorted to surprise, darkness, and overwhelming numbers.

To Overlanders, Native Americans were bullies, all threat and intimidation but very little courage. Standing up to them confirmed the manly status of the overland migrants. The men in Sarah Royce's 1849 overland train evidently reached this conclusion when they encountered "Indians, by the hundreds," who demanded "the payment of a certain sum per head for every emigrant passing through this part of the country." Instead of paying the toll, as they almost certainly would have if it had been whites they were encountering, the Overlanders "armed themselves with every weapon to be found in their wagons" and marched on, threatening to "open fire with all their rifles and revolvers" if the warriors attempted to stop them. Royce's perception of indigenous peoples as inherently cowardly was confirmed when she believed she saw "in their faces the expression of sullen disappointment, mingled with a half-defiant scowl, that suggested the thought of future night attacks when darkness and thickets should give them greater advantage."[91] Conversely, Royce's status as a white woman made her an important arbiter in asserting that the strength of white men was not only in their weaponry but also in their character. To the Overlanders, while Native American warriors might have weapons, they lacked the character necessary to be a manly threat.

This supposed lack of manliness had other repercussions for indigenous peoples. As Glenda Riley has argued, "The more dangerous and shifty Indians could be portrayed, the more their defeat assured white males of their own prowess. Any tricks the white man could get away with or damage he could inflict on Indians upped his image in other men's eyes."[92] This is why Alonzo Rathbun celebrated when seventeen members of his overland party ambushed and killed a Native American who visited the previous night's camp, presumably to scavenge anything left behind.[93] Surprising, ambushing, or tricking Native Americans did not imperil migrants' claims to white manliness any more than would beating up a bully. Facing down a group of warriors and ambushing an unarmed Native American were two aspects of the same logic. Both actions demonstrated that indigenous peoples, as nonwhite Others, lacked the essential virtues of white men and did not need to be treated with respect. Actions ranging from insults to brutalizing violence therefore confirmed for migrants their white manliness instead of imperiling it.

Though similar colonialist assumptions underlay how migrants perceived Latin Americans, the latter did not occupy the same place in the American psyche as Native Americans. Since at least the conflict between the Powhatan and Jamestown colony, indigenous military power was a concern for Americans. In contrast, not only had the Latin American world long been peripheral to American awareness, but also, when it jumped to center stage during the Mexican-American War, the events of that conflict underscored the perception that Latin American martial abilities were markedly inferior. Latin American military fortifications held particular fascination for Argonauts, who saw them as a "true index to the state of the country" and their "present condition a lamentable commentary on the ruthless spirit that has pervaded the countries of South America."[94] Argonauts described Latin American fortifications as "castles" and stressed the decay of the "old" fortifications in the face of an untamed nature.[95] The weakness of "Old Spain" was reflected in "these walls and towers that once helped to mark its greatness even in this far off Colony [that now] is too feeble for foreign conquest."[96] Argonauts found even less to admire in the inhabitants of the fortifications, describing them as in "their habits & appearance . . . similar to our Indians,"[97] "coal black negroes,"[98] or "as if they were the descendants of Falstaff's company."[99]

The Argonauts, therefore, feared little more than petty theft or isolated muggings when they encountered Latin Americans.[100] When violence broke out in 1851 in Panama, according to one participant, "the cruel wretches" were easily defeated by the outnumbered Argonauts, whose weaponry, discipline, and martial prowess won the day.[101]

The "Incidente de la Tajada de Sandia," or the "Watermelon Incident" of April 15, 1856, began when an American Argonaut, Jack Oliver, drunkenly refused to pay Jose Manual Luna, a Panamanian merchant, for a slice of watermelon. Luna warned Oliver, "Careful, we are not in the United States here," at which point Oliver pulled a pistol, Luna a knife, and the situation rapidly escalated into an armed skirmish. White Americans again depicted Panamanians as a blood-thirsty horde, but this time, riding allegations of attacks on white women and nineteen American deaths during the episode, the United States justified the first in a long series of military interventions in Panama, linking the contest of manhood between Oliver and Luna directly to American imperialism.[102] These incidents were aberrations, however, and the vast majority of Argonauts never engaged, or really expected to engage, in armed conflict with Latin Americans.

This disdain for Latin American martial ability shifted only slightly between the Californian and British Columbian gold rushes. Completed in 1855, the Panama Railroad transformed the trip across the isthmus so that by 1858, British Columbia–bound gold rushers could take a comfortable three-hour ride instead of what had been a strenuous and dangerous multiday journey.[103] Like their California-bound predecessors, gold rushers en route to British Columbia viewed the local population as immodest, dirty, and lazy.[104] At the same time, in the aftermath of armed American intervention following the Watermelon Incident of 1856, the sovereignty of the Panamanian state was clearly compromised. The corresponding growth in the power of the region's white inhabitants, most obviously manifested by the Panama Railroad Company, further underscored the growing irrelevance of the Panamanian state and, therefore, removed the need for migrants to comment on the weakness of the Panamanians.[105]

The lessons that migrants took away from these encounters would have significant impact in California and British Columbia. Argonauts passing through Latin America learned that Latin Americans were degraded, shiftless, and lazy but also a potentially useful colonial population. In contrast, the Overlanders tended to see Native Americans as dangerous, duplicitous, and threatening. These attitudes may help explain why Overlanders would become so strongly identified with the near-genocide of the indigenous people of California.[106] It is suggestive that the British Columbia rush, which largely avoided massacres of indigenous people, lacked a significant Overland migration. Of course, even though British Columbia lacked a significant Latin American presence, Argonauts bound for there still learned generalized lessons about subordinated nonwhite populations as they passed through Latin America.

The isthmus crossing was significant as an early and sustained encounter between British migrants and their American "cousins." The British were of two minds about the Americans they encountered in Latin America. On the one hand, Americans, especially the Yankees, seemed to embody everything the Panamanians were not, particularly in the realm of economic activity. Bowles, an American himself, noted that not only was trade carried on under "English and American superintendence" but also the "well-built stations with handsome yards" were the product of "American occupants." Bowles explicitly contrasted these residences with the "crowded negro hamlets and villages."[107] Reginald Pidcock, a British subject, agreed, claiming that "nearly all the Hotels and Restaurents are kept by Americans and are generally very clean and comfortable."[108] When comparing the Latin American population to Americans, some British subjects perceived the latter positively.

On the other hand, other British subjects found these early encounters with Americans profoundly disturbing, often focusing on American behavior and attitudes. Cecil Buckley quickly concluded that "the Americans certainly are an ugly race of people, and no mistake," an opinion that he "d[id] not think they would attempt to deny, . . . it is too evident." In Panama, Buckley found the Americans he encountered rude, brutal, and often drunk.[109] On board ship, John Emmerson recorded that "the Canadians looked upon us Englishmen as their own people, and treated us with the greatest kindness and consideration; while the Americans looked down upon us with supreme contempt, and sought for an opportunity to insult us, both nationally and individually." Especially galling for Emmerson was that "the Americans generally manifest a bullying, domineering, overbearing manner, arising from the idea they entertain of their superiority over all the world."[110] Much of what men like Emmerson and Buckley were actually upset about was the more democratic nature of American society, manifested through such activities as drinking rituals that enforced egalitarianism at the bar.[111] Of course, this egalitarianism was racially coded, as Byron Johnson discovered when he witnessed an American bartender denying a black man a drink.[112]

ARRIVING IN CALIFORNIA

When the migrants arrived in California, they soon discovered that the ideas they had formed before departure and along their journey were inadequate to the task of dealing with the society that confronted them. Indeed, the reality of gold rush society seems to have been overwhelming for most new arrivals. Migrants sought to make sense of gold rush society by contrasting their perceptions of California with the homes they had left and the people and places they had encountered when traveling.

The Argonauts, passing through the Golden Gate to San Francisco, arrived in what Gunther Barth has evocatively described as an "instant city [that] came into existence Athena-like, full-blown and self-reliant."[113] In San Francisco "everything bore evidence of newness, and the greater part of the city presented a make shift and temporary appearance."[114] For commentator after commentator, the speed at which San Francisco was being built or, in their language, "progressing," set it apart from any other city they had encountered.[115] For many, like John Letts, the city indicated the character of its inhabitants. As Letts said of San Francisco, "The scene around me was animated. Everything appeared to be propelled by the most indomitable perseverance. The frame of a house would be taken from the ship in the morning, and at night it was fully tenanted. The clatter of the innumerable hammers, each answered by a thousand echoes, seemed the music by which the city was being marshaled into existence."[116] For many migrants, the "exuberant life, energy and enterprise of the place" marked San Francisco as different, not only from their homes in the East, but also from the societies they had encountered while traveling to California.[117] As one account put it, "In no city in the world, perhaps, has more been accomplished in the same space of time, by the enterprising spirit of its inhabitants, than in the city of San Francisco."[118] Descriptions of San Francisco stand in stark contrast to descriptions of Latin American settlements with their crumbling fortifications, decaying churches, and "very narrow, very filthy, and very gloomy" streets occupied by "an inert race."[119]

To the newly arrived Argonauts, the population of San Francisco seemed to be the key to the difference between California, which had a long history of Spanish colonization, and Latin America. In California, and especially San Francisco, Argonauts saw the proof of their assertion that a small population of energetic white men could rejuvenate and reshape a degraded Latin American society.

The deciding factor in this process was the Yankee population from the Northeast, who dominated California demographically and symbolically. In San Francisco, the stereotypical Yankee was "easily detected by his bustling habits, nasal intonation, and eccentric speculations." It seemed to some observers (many of whom were from New England themselves) that the Yankees' "indomitable assiduity" would eventually lead them to "manufacture the means of a livelihood, and lay even the foundation of a fortune." As a result of this energy and enterprise, Yankees were "in most cases the instigators of every thing permanent and good" in the city.[120] But San Francisco was not simply New York on the Pacific. Instead, the "California Yankee" was the "New England Yankee" but "with all his peculiar power centupled. All his sharpness is sharpened; all his 'cuteness is more 'cute."[121] Richard Hale attributed the difference to the fact that "in the east the Yankee was walled about by forms, creeds and conventions. . . . But here there were no questions asked about pedigree. 'Can he fill the position? If he can, well and good, if not—let us have one who can fill it.'"[122] Gold rushers in California believed that the lack of social supports that buttressed ideas of restrained manhood allowed them to reach their full potential, to become wealthy, to succeed or fail on their own merits. In other words, gold rush society seemed to offer the opportunity for gold rushers to lay claim to an identity as martial white men in a way they could not in the supposedly more restrictive East.

At the same time that some accounts celebrated the rapidity with which San Francisco was being built, the nature of the built environment raised concerns for other observers. From a practical standpoint, the built environment of San Francisco was scarcely preferable to Panama City and other Latin American settlements. Especially in the early years of the rush, newly arrived Argonauts found that, instead of "substantial brick buildings,"[123] San Francisco was "a mass of wooden hovels and cloth tents."[124] The streets were crowded, dirty, prone to flooding, and, in the case of the wooden streets built on pilings over the bay, filled with dangerous holes.[125] Despite the buildings "exhibit[ing] evidence that they were put up in a hurry," commentators did not attach the same negative traits to San Francisco's inhabitants as they had to Latin Americans.[126] Instead, this disorder could be tolerated, even celebrated, because gold rushers saw it as transitory stage. The very haste that made the built environment of San Francisco so problematic also ensured that it could not be mistaken for the built environment of Latin America. Where Latin American buildings were supposedly dilapidated owing to lack of energy and care, San Francisco's shoddy buildings and streets were the product of energy and ambition. While they might lament the current condition of the city, white residents of San Francisco were confident that the city would eventually become a counterpart of the major cities along the Atlantic.

British subjects bound for British Columbia remained divided in their opinions of Americans after reaching San Francisco. Matthew Macfie, a British Congregationalist minister with American sympathies, found the city's buildings "magnificent," "tasteful," and "monster" in size and noted that "an air of activity, comfort, and grandeur pervades the well-dressed multitudes that incessantly cross one's path."[127] George Styles also linked the built environment with its "wide and noble" streets and "handsome" buildings to the population, made up of "the strongest built and tallest men I ever saw."[128] And it was in San Francisco that Byron Johnson came to the conclusion that it was not "impertinent curiosity" but friendliness he experienced among the American population.[129] Arthur Birch, a senior colonial official en route to British Columbia, found in San Francisco "a charming cosmopolitan feeling and an intelligent and delightful social society," which compared especially well to Civil War–era New York.[130] These positive accounts tended to identify San Francisco as an emerging metropolis on a par with New York, Paris, and London, and Americans as energetic, productive, and polite. In other words, to some British Argonauts, San Francisco and its inhabitants were the embodiment of mid-nineteenth-century ideals of middle-class white manhood.

But other migrants saw a decidedly different San Francisco. Negative depictions of San Francisco tended to link its built space to the perceived corruption and vice of the city's inhabitants. In his description of San Francisco's waterfront, W. Champness noted that "there are frequent deaths, from unwary persons falling, or being thrust, at night, into the water, through some of the large openings occurring at intervals in the super-marine streets."[131] Where Champness found a link between shoddy construction and immoral behavior, Francis Poole drew the opposite conclusion, linking the American Theater in particular, and by extension all such grand buildings, with the "coarse and undisguised immorality" of the activities that went on inside. Furthermore, given the manipulation of "passions" inside these buildings, it was "no wonder" to Poole that "they should often take the direction of murder, that the most hideous crimes should be easily condoned, and that the general tone of morality should have descended to the very depths, as I was given to understand is the sad case at San Francisco."[132]

Negative depictions also focused on the "go-ahead" attitude of the city. Commentators like James Nelles proclaimed "San Francisco . . . about the worst place I ever was in" because the Sabbath was so flagrantly disregarded in favor of leisure and work activities.[133] Faced with the same built environment and population, these observers saw disorder and corruption. Poole articulated the logical conclusion of these observers' comments when he noted that San Francisco's society, and particularly its standards of justice, demonstrated that it could only "pretend to civilization."[134] British society and British governance were the clearly preferable alternative. For these men, national differences were everywhere evident in San Francisco, and Americans fell short of idealized standards of middle-class white manliness, foreshadowing the impact that the intersection of ideas of race and national identity would have in shaping the colonial order in British Columbia.

On one topic, however, British Columbia–bound Argonauts shared a remarkable concurrence of opinion. Visitors frequently commented upon the Chinese population of San Francisco. Indeed, whereas newly arrived Argonauts in 1849 and the early 1850s had stressed California's diversity with laundry lists of national and racial groups, most accounts produced by Argonauts heading to British Columbia focused almost exclusively on the Chinese, stressing their numbers and their distinct Chinatown.[135]

By 1858, the Chinese population had emerged as the racial touchstone for San Francisco. Observers almost always described the Chinese as an impediment. One of the more positive accounts noted that "the only benefit derived from them . . . is from a tax of four dollars per month each."[136] John Emmerson, though surprised at Chinese "thrift and activity," noted that Chinatown was "wallowing in almost [an] iniquitous state of filth," and that Chinese faces "betrayed an ingrained demoralization shocking to behold."[137] These attitudes closely paralleled an increasingly entrenched fear of the social, economic, and political threat of the Chinese among the American residents of California.[138] Some Chinese Americans, such as Pun Chi and Norman Asing, contested these interpretations and, aided by prominent American allies like Presbyterian minister William Speer, tried to portray themselves as ideal American citizens. But these challenges seemed to have escaped notice by the British Columbia–bound migrants, much as they were largely dismissed by the majority of the white population of California.[139] Instead, regardless of their opinion of United States society, Argonauts bound for British Columbia learned in San Francisco that the Chinese were different from other nonwhite immigrants. These attitudes would inform their reactions to the Chinese population in British Columbia, particularly in the Cariboo Mountain gold mines, and speak to the existence of widely shared racial conceptions that bridged national divisions.

For the Overlanders, arrival in California was a reentry into "civilization." The Overlanders saw the mining communities they encountered in the foothills of the Sierra Nevada as frontier settlements "on the borders of civilization."[140] When Bernard Reid found "the 'town'" of Weberville to be little more than "tents and rough log huts," he was neither surprised nor disappointed. If anything, he was simply happy at being able to eat "very heartily . . . under an awning supported by trees and poles" before sleeping on a "parcel of pine chips beside some hewed timber."[141] Likewise, upon arriving at nearby Placerville after crossing the Sierra Nevada, John Carr found it "to be two rows of houses with a street between them." The simple buildings and the large population of gamblers and rough-looking miners located Placerville firmly within the trope of the frontier town.[142] For the Overlanders, then, their arrival in California was both an entry into a new sort of society and a reentry into the world of frontier settlements they had left months before. By linking the mining camps of the Sierra Nevada to stereotypes of frontier towns, Overlanders affirmed California as a place where "civilization" was just beginning to assert itself over "savagery." This understanding, combined with their experiences of the previous several months, encouraged them to see their own identity as white settlers engaged in the securing of land and resources at the direct expense of indigenous peoples and, by extension, other nonwhites. In a telling example, at least one Overlander claimed that the "watch word" among the emigrants shortly before arriving in California was "to shoot every Indian they see."[143]

ARRIVING IN BRITISH COLUMBIA

In 1858, nine years after the first wave of gold rushers began to arrive in California, another wave arrived in British Columbia. Initially, the vast majority of the migrants came from California; but starting in 1859, migrants increasingly came from Britain. As Adele Perry has demonstrated, elites in both British Columbia and England attempted to encourage immigration to the colony, particularly of white women from England, but with middling success.[144] However, even without these official efforts, the letters of Donald Frazer and other enthusiastic reports in the British press fueled interest in Fraser River gold in Britain during a period when British emigration to North America was already strong.[145] The news of gold in British Columbia followed hard on the heels of the Panic of 1857 in the United States, which, though it depressed overall British migration to the nation, may have encouraged more potential migrants to look for destinations and occupations that were relatively unaffected by the recession.[146] The British Columbia gold rush also drew heavily on British residents of the United States, much as the California gold rush had done a decade earlier.[147]

The status of British Columbia as an imperial colony seems to have added to its appeal among some migrants, placing it within the larger context of imperial expansion and migration. In much the same way that men who went to India and elsewhere in the empire asserted their status as white men through their movement to the imperial periphery, so too did British men find that migration to British Columbia represented a chance for them to participate in the imperial project. Concurrently, other factors worked to dissuade Americans from the eastern states from going to British

Columbia. The tense period leading up to the start of the Civil War, and the conflict that followed, dramatically curtailed American migration to British Columbia. In 1859, coinciding with conflicting reports about the gold deposits in British Columbia, the discovery of silver in Colorado provided an accessible alternative destination for those inclined to mining. By the end of the Civil War, the peak years of gold production in British Columbia had passed, and the colony had experienced a considerable outflow of Americans back to the United States.[148] For all of these reasons, British subjects would make up a greater portion of the population in British Columbia than they had in California, despite the short distance between the two locations.

Because Governor James Douglas of British Columbia had closed navigation of the Fraser River to any but approved vessels, the vast majority of the gold rushers entered the goldfields by way of Victoria on Vancouver Island.[149] The first to arrive were those from California. Perhaps because they were old hands at gold mining and saw British Columbia as just the latest in a series of gold rushes, these Americans left few accounts of their impressions of Victoria. Even letters to California newspapers usually had few details about the city. Those that described it contained little direct mention of the built or natural environment. One of the few detailed accounts of the built environment of Victoria noted that it was "very 'forty-nineish' in its character," by which the correspondent seemed to mean that it was still largely undeveloped but growing rapidly.[150] William Nixon, freshly arrived from San Francisco and apparently easily impressed, found it "the greatest city I ever saw, composed of about 70 or 80 wooden buildings, one brick house, and about 550 tents."[151] Nixon's enthusiasm was unusual, however. Many of the American commentators, who stopped at Whatcom or other American ports before proceeding to Victoria, tended to contrast Victoria unfavorably with those places.[152]

For these California veterans, Victoria's boomtown appearance was unremarkable, and so they focused on describing the population and the Hudson's Bay Company (HBC). The company, for instance, was derided for maintaining an unfair trade monopoly on the mainland but praised for keeping prices low on Vancouver Island.[153] Writers usually condemned Governor Douglas and, by extension the colonial authority, particularly for the obstacles Douglas placed in the way of competition with the HBC and direct immigration to the mines.[154]

Both Americans and Britons asserted that the treatment of Native Americans was an important marker of national difference, even as both groups of migrants tended to share similar assumptions about the racially defined character of indigenous peoples.[155] Americans like Henry Fitch commented on the "docile" indigenous population, which signaled that British Columbia had a different history of colonialism, but one that was compatible with the interests of American migrants.[156] At times, however, this alternate form of colonialism seemed to go too far in its tolerance of the indigenous population. One joke making the rounds in Victoria targeted the HBC for "their old fogy way of doing business," part of which was giving preference to "the negro or Indian."[157] Pacifying the indigenous population through fair treatment was one thing; appearing to prefer them to white men was another matter entirely. For the newly arrived American population, British colonialism could be admirable or dangerous, depending on the context.

As British subjects began to arrive in the months following the first influx of Americans to the colony, they expressed different sentiments. Francis Poole looked forward to soon being "again under the good Union Jack of Old England," while Sophia Cracroft finally felt "*at home . . .* once more among our own people only, after many months residence with Americans."[158] For at least some of the British migrants, their experience with American society and governance en route to British Columbia had reinforced their sense of national difference and superiority to their "cousins."

But while the migration to British Columbia underscored a sense of national difference, the spatial organization of Victoria and the mainland gold rush towns suggested common, or at least related, conceptions of race between the two groups. During the gold rush period, a Songhee village across the harbor from Victoria located Native Americans as intertwined with, yet distinct from, the white settlement.[159] Adjacent to the Songhee village, across a bridge, was Victoria's Chinatown.[160] The working classes also tended to occupy "small wooden shanties" in the "suburbs" around the town. These "suburbs" were a racially mixed space where "Indians and Chinamen" lived alongside people of European descent.[161] These spaces were juxtaposed with the more "respectable" white-controlled space of central Victoria. Over the course of the rush, white settlers attached more and more meanings to these outlying spaces, thereby necessarily encoding the towns more and more explicitly as whites' spaces. The presence of Britons and Americans intermixed throughout the towns from the earliest days of the rush, combined with the existence of racially and class-segregated settlements, facilitated the coming together of British and America settlers under the banner of white supremacy later in the gold rush. Nevertheless, while there were some shared attitudes, particularly regarding the formation of a racialized hierarchy, there were also profound national divisions. Both British and American immigrants arrived with serious reservations about each other, signaling an attention to national difference that would characterize much of the British Columbia gold rush.

CONCLUSION

The impact of the migratory experience has been an overlooked factor in the creation of colonial societies in the California and British Columbia gold rushes. Migratory experiences gave meaning to the world that gold rushers found at their destinations and the world they attempted to create. Between 1848 and 1871, on both the overland and the oceanic routes, gold rushers began to articulate an understanding of white manliness that emphasized martial manliness while still retaining aspects of restrained manliness.

Gold rushers' encounters with indigenous peoples and Latin Americans while en route to the goldfields deeply shaped this emergent form of white manliness and revealed that the migrants were already coming to ascribe key traits to these two groups and, in the process, to themselves as well. In so doing, these migrants defined white manliness against a range of racial and gender others within an explicitly colonial context. As a result, whether they were arriving in California after 1849 or British Columbia after 1858, these migrants were already prepared to understand gold rush society as a colonial society organized along a racial and gender hierarchy with themselves, as white men, at the top. The exact nature of these societies would be shaped by the particular contexts of California and British Columbia.

CHAPTER 2

A White Man's Republic

Republican Ideology and Popular Government
in Colonial California

ON TUESDAY, JUNE 20, 1848, WALTER COLTON, ALCALDE of Monterey, watched as a man just returned from the mines drew lumps of gold from his pockets and passed them around a crowd of eager onlookers.[1] "The excitement produced was intense" recalled Colton. Soon "all were off for the mines, some on horses, some on carts, and some on crutches, one went in a litter." Within a month, Colton was alcalde of a virtual ghost town. By August, the "gold mines [had] upset all social and domestic arrangements[:] . . . the master has become his own servant, and the servant his own lord."[2] As Bayard Taylor observed, "The results of the gold discovery produced a complete revolution in society, upturning all branches of trade, industry or office, and for a time completely annulling the Government."[3] The political and social order that would emerge to take the place of the rapidly disappearing old order would be a specific form of settler colonialism vested in ideas of white manhood and republicanism.

Scholars have been reluctant to acknowledge that gold rush California, as much as the Philippines, Hawaii, or Cuba, was a colony.[4] More specifically, California was a settler colony, in which migrants sought to seize control of the land and either replace or subjugate the indigenous population. Owing to the cost of transportation, which raised a formidable barrier to poorer migrants, middle-class white men quickly came to dominate the region.[5] Middle-class white settlers used the ideal of the republican citizen to define and rank participation in California's colonial society. Drawing on preexisting racial and gender attitudes, these men claimed a place for themselves at the top of a colonial hierarchy and then attempted to define the place of a range of Others, both in the gold mines and in the towns. However, three factors complicated this project. First, though gold rushers would try to impose a social order brought from the East, California was not on the Atlantic, and the migrants had been changed by their journeys. Second, the disordered nature of California encouraged local governance. Third, California's diverse population included groups whose position as white, off-white, or nonwhite was unclear, and who actively sought to reshape the emerging colonial hierarchy in their favor.[6]

Before the gold rush, California had been ruled first by a weak Spanish regime, then by a Mexican colonial regime, and then, for a brief period, by a "thinly staffed, badly financed [American] military government."[7] The discovery of gold dislocated the newly conquered territory's residents and brought about a massive influx of population from around the world that overwhelmed both the military government and the Mexican colonial system onto which it was grafted. The new immigrants sought to create a social, political, and cultural order where they saw none and to replace, modify, or co-opt the existing order where they recognized it. This process was necessarily a process of re-creating and redefining racial and gender roles. The particular context of California, its heterogeneous population, the nature of gold mining, and the weak presence of a federal government meant that attitudes toward race, gender, and the state that had been developed in the East could not be transported to, and implemented in, California intact. Instead, these attitudes were adapted to the particular context of gold rush California through a series of conflicts and negotiations that took place in three main venues: in the state government, in the mines, and in San Francisco.

The disruption of the formal state apparatus (such as it was) and the attendant social disorder of the goldfields elicited contradictory responses from many gold rushers. The gold rush coincided with the end of years of Mexican rule and seemed to herald not only a new beginning for California but also a new beginning for the thousands of Americans who arrived there.[8] Middle-class whites believed they were freeing California from the oppressive rule of Catholic priests and Mexicans while simultaneously freeing themselves from the social and economic constraints that had come to dominate life in the East.[9] In particular, gold rushers saw in the West a chance to embrace a more martial form of manhood than the restrained manhood that pervaded middle-class life in the East.

At the same time, the lack of state control raised deep concerns among many commentators. For men like Joseph Benton, working on the Sabbath and swearing spoke both to the lack of the influence of churches and to the rough character of "the *natives & foreigners*," as well as the Yankees.[10] The belief that the republic needed the support of a strong and active state apparatus to survive was reflected in the multitude of conspiracy theories about secret criminal organizations flourishing in California.[11] These fears were compounded by the unprecedented diversity of the population of California. In the United States, only in California could sizable populations of Europeans, Anglo-Americans, blacks, Native Americans, Latin Americans, Asians, and Pacific Islanders be found in proximity to each other.[12] The weakening of social controls was, therefore, as Walter Colton warned, "an ill wind that blows nobody any good: the nabobs [elites] have had their time, and now comes that of the 'niggers.'"[13] This was the crux of middle-class white concerns about social order in California—not that there would be anarchy, but that an alternative way of ordering society, perhaps that of the "niggers" or of "*natives & foreigners*," might come to dominate.

American gold rushers talked about these fears, as well as their hopes for an ideal society, through the language of republicanism. Republicanism, as a political ideology, had deep roots in American psyches by the time of the gold rush and was connected to ideas of work, race, and citizenship.[14] But Californian republicanism was not classical republicanism. Indeed, California's "liberal individualist ethos," with its celebration of self-interest and nonagricultural economic activity, conflicted with some of the basic assumptions of classical republicanism.[15] However, much of the language used to discuss and think about the characteristics of white men and the colonial state drew heavily on classical republican tropes. Americans in California asserted that racial, gender, national, and religious attributes affected an individual's ability to be politically independent and, as a result, determined their place in the colonial hierarchy that middle-class white Americans were attempting to create. Middle-class whites in California quickly developed a shorthand for describing whether an individual or group conformed to their expectations of republican behavior by labeling them either "good citizens" or "bad men."

New Yorker Elisha Capron bluntly highlighted the confluence of race, gender, and republicanism in California when he argued that, relative to "the Chinese, South and Central American, and Mexican, . . . all classes of Europeans are superior . . . in those qualities which are essential to the security of a republican form of government."[16] In so doing, Capron claimed that while Europeans of various nationalities might be considered inferior to white Americans, they were fundamentally superior to nonwhites.[17] This made it extremely unlikely that the Chinese, South and Central Americans, and Mexicans (among others) would gain admission to California's colonial society as full citizens during the gold rush. Though the broad contours of Californian colonial society were set (the state's status as an American territory guaranteed that self-professed white Americans would dominate the society), the specific meanings attached to different groups were dynamic and flexible, responding to the actions and arguments of a wide range of actors and events. Over the course of the gold rush, white settlers gradually consolidated racial and gender identities as they developed and elaborated California's colonial settler system.

STATE POLITICS: CONSTITUTION AND LEGISLATION

In September 1849, forty-eight delegates met in Monterey to draft the legal framework for what they hoped would soon be the thirty-first state to join the union.[18] Working at a time when questions of race and citizenship were at the fore of public debate, each delegate sought a constitution that would both reflect his own view of the ideal form of Californian society and facilitate speedy admission into the union. It was this latter concern that prompted the majority of delegates to make California a free state. Prohibition of slavery did not mean, of course, the delegates endorsed equality between blacks and whites. Indeed, a lengthy debate over whether free blacks should be prevented from entering the state was eventually resolved against exclusion only because of pragmatic concerns over a speedy ratification.[19]

Although ultimately unsuccessful, the arguments of the pro-exclusion delegates reveal widely shared assumptions among white settlers about the danger that nonwhites generally, and African Americans specifically, posed to the social, political, and economic order of California. Although African Americans had already been excluded from voting and testifying in

California, the pro-exclusion delegates argued that their degraded nature, whether enslaved or free, made them a social and economic threat.[20] According to pro-exclusion delegates, African Americans were undesirable because they were degraded: they were, in the eyes of many whites, lazy, brutish, and prone to irrational vicissitudes of emotion.[21] Even worse, these traits supposedly made African Americans susceptible to the will of others. When delegate James McHall Jones voiced his concerns that African American labor could be used by slaveholders to "degrade the white labor of the miners," his warning resonated with widely shared ideas of republican virtue that warned that dependent and servile people were the tools of tyrants and despots.[22] Even the opponents of exclusion tended to agree with these basic principles, arguing only that exclusion would impede the ratification of its constitution.[23] Although influenced by concerns about federal ratification, the delegates to the state constitutional convention clearly shared a vision of society in which people of African descent occupied a place near the bottom of a racialized colonial hierarchy.

But California was not the East, and the delegates were forced to confront the presence of two groups who complicated their attempts to reproduce a racial hierarchy modeled on that of the eastern states. The first of these was the state's large indigenous population. Delegates feared that Native Americans, like blacks, were an "objectionable race" because their supposed natural servility left them open to manipulation by white men. Yet the delegates ultimately decided to insert a provision allowing the legislature to provide for the future suffrage of Native Americans. On the one hand, this reflected sensitivity to the mixed-race status of some of the delegates to the constitutional convention, while on the other hand it also reflected a significant trend in American thought, which held that the ultimate assimilation of indigenous peoples was possible.[24]

Yet, while the constitutional convention opened the door to future citizenship for Native Americans, the first legislature, meeting in 1850, passed An Act for the Government and Protection of the Indians. More than any other piece of legislation, this act defined indigenous peoples as colonized subjects. Among its many provisions, it allowed for the indenture of Native American children and those indebted to the court, prohibited indigenous testimony against whites, extended state laws over Native Americans, and ruled that "any Indian able to work . . . , who shall be found loitering or strolling about, or frequenting public places where liquors are sold, begging, or leading an immoral or profligate course of life," should be "hire[d] out . . . to the best bidder."[25] In short, the first legislature moved to seal off the possibility of indigenous assimilation and instead defined Native Americans as a permanent, quasi-enslaved, colonized underclass.

The second problematic nonwhite population provided the constitutional convention with more of a dilemma. The terms of the Treaty of Guadalupe Hidalgo, which ended the Mexican-American War, complicated attempts to address the presence of a large population of Mexicans in California. This treaty provided that "those [Mexican citizens] who shall prefer to remain in the [ceded] territories may . . . acquire those [rights] of citizens of the United States."[26] The issue was that Mexico did not have the same racial classification scheme for defining citizenship that the United States had, opening the door for the franchise to be extended to people of African and indigenous descent who had held Mexican citizenship.[27] In its broadest interpretation, the Treaty of Guadalupe Hidalgo would, in the eyes of most delegates, fatally undermine the integrity of the republican system of government in California.

Faced with this possibility, the delegates began to debate whether and how to restrict the franchise. It was here that Pablo Noriego de la Guerra, a Californio delegate, asserted that while "many citizens of California have received from nature a very dark skin," some of those men had ably filled very high office, and it "would be very unjust to deprive them of the privilege of citizens merely because nature had not made them white. But," de la Guerra continued, "if, by the word 'white,' it was intended to exclude the African race, then it was correct and satisfactory."[28] In emphasizing class solidarity between elite whites and Californios, de la Guerra instead sought to focus white American animus on African Americans while portraying elite Californios as acceptable members of the republic. In so doing, de la Guerra opened the door to the potential of citizenship for all Californians of indigenous descent.

The other delegates listened to de la Guerra and then made a wholly predictable decision. In order to maintain the racial basis of citizenship but still appear to abide by the terms of the treaty, the convention limited the vote to "every white male citizen of the United States, and every white male citizen of Mexico."[29] As they left the convention hall, congratulating themselves on a job well done, all but forgotten was Edward Gilbert's comment that "the meaning of the word 'white' . . . was not generally understood in this country, though well understood in the United States."[30] As Gilbert hinted, while African Americans were decidedly nonwhite the delegates were less sure what to do with the indigenous, Mexican, European, and mixed-race residents of California.[31] It was left to the mass of miners to define white manliness and enforce it through the popular tribunals in the mines, towns, and cities that characterized the first decade of the gold rush.

THE MINES

The various forms of local governance, vested in the ideals of republicanism, that miners created were key to the establishment of this colonial hierarchy. However, while San Francisco and some of the other early settlements had pre–gold rush civic governments in place, the new communities in the mining areas that sprang up did not. Some opted to elect alcaldes, justices, or mayors; but in most, effective control was held by, or shared with, mining councils.[32] Later in the gold rush, as mining regions became more settled and the economy began to diversify, mining councils gave way to elected city councils and other forms of government.[33]

Mining councils were overwhelmingly controlled by, and acted in the interests of, native-born white Americans.[34] Europeans could support the decisions of the council, or even take part in making decisions, but it was clear that their involvement was conditional upon their acquiescence to the will of Americans.[35] Non-Europeans, such as Native Americans and Chinese, were rarely, if ever, recorded as taking part in the mining councils. As in San Francisco, participation in local government mirrored the national debate over citizenship: Europeans were divided and ranked by nationality and categorized as off-white, but still evaluated separately from the rest of the world.[36] These American-dominated mining councils, and similar organizations of "the people," were responsible for most of the approximately 150 lynchings that occurred in California between 1849 and 1852, the majority of which victimized Latin Americans.[37] The targeting of Latin Americans demonstrates that on the ground, many, if not most, Americans saw these people as "bad men" instead of potential good citizens.

Controlling access to the rich goldfields quickly became one of the primary concerns of mining councils throughout the mines. The influence of republican ideology was evident in how mining councils regulated mining districts to favor small groups of independent white miners.[38] Excluding nonwhite labor, and especially slave labor, was essential for middle-class white men to be independent and successful, the necessary prerequisites for a republican society. This is why the mining code for the Upper Yuba district was hardly alone in stating "that none but native and naturalized citizens of the United States shall be allowed to hold claims," and "that the word 'native' shall not include the Indians of this country."[39]

Such attitudes were not uniform, as an incident involving a Yankee, Charles Thompson, demonstrates. Thompson, a product of the rapidly industrializing northeastern states, believed "that men never make a fortune out of their own individual manual labor, but that it is head work & talent that must in the end succeed." Thompson, therefore, hired twenty-four Mexicans to work in his and his partners' mines. However, Thompson's mining claims were adjacent to "Western Hoosiers, Oregonians & Missourians" who refused to have a "damned greaser on the bar" and, indeed, threatened to drive off "N. Yorkers Bostonians &c" if they persisted in hiring Mexican labor. In conflict were two ways of being white men, both predicated on the assumption of white supremacy but reflecting different understandings of the nature of the colonial society in California. Thompson was thinking like a classic colonist: nonwhite labor was an exploitable resource for white men. His neighbors were thinking more like most settler colonists in California: to them, nonwhite labor degraded white labor and therefore threatened the republic. Ironically, despite Thompson's ability to face down the other Americans, his supposedly submissive laborers decided they were not going to work under the threat of violence, and left.[40]

On April 13, 1850, the state legislature attempted to reach into the mining districts with An Act for the Better Regulation of the Mines and the Government of Foreign Miners. Claiming to alleviate "the strife and bloodshed which have taken place between the citizen and foreigner" in the mines by imposing a tax on foreign miners, the bill specifically mentioned "the worst population of the Mexican and South American States, New South Wales and the southern islands" as the target of the legislation before adding, almost as an afterthought, "to say nothing of the vast numbers from Europe."[41] In a time and place where citizenship could largely be conflated with the attributes of white manliness, the language of the Foreign Miner's Tax reveals that the relationship between white manliness, citizenship, and particular bodies was neither simple nor straightforward. Most notably, the deliberate targeting of Australians as dangerous foreigners signaled the importance of factors other than skin color in determining identity.

The framers of the bill made it clear that the tax was primarily intended as a means of social control. The intended target of the tax was "the foreign proprietor [employer] of Chilian, Peon, Chinean, Canacker or convict gold digger" or "gold diggers from any other nations" who would now have to pay "some little tribute." Even more importantly for Americans in the mines, "this bill will afford our own citizen gold diggers means of controlling this foreign labor upon equal terms with the foreign proprietor."[42] American employers, it was envisioned, would buy licenses for their foreign employees, limiting their ability to break their contract, strike for higher wages, or otherwise interfere with the interests of their American employers. Of course, while the tax would tie foreign labor to a specific employer, native-born white workers would have no such constraints. The law would, therefore, help assert the superiority of white men by demonstrating their manly economic independence in contrast to supposedly subordinated and controlled foreign labor.[43]

Ultimately, local miners selectively enforced the Foreign Miner's Tax according to their vision of the ideal colonial order. This can be seen in the reaction of native-born white Americans to the largest and most organized resistance to the Foreign Miner's Tax, the so-called French Revolution that occurred in May 1850 in Sonora.[44] Though the area around Sonora had seen some expulsions of foreign miners, they were evidently not common enough for Americans in the area to think that the relationship between the American minority and the Mexican, Chilean, and French majority was strained.[45] However, the imminent arrival of the tax collector galvanized much of the non-American population to protest. The local American population was not particularly sympathetic to the Foreign Miner's Tax and appears to have been relatively unconcerned even when the French and Mexicans began arming themselves.[46] Instead, the flashpoint for this conflict was when a camp composed of foreigners "mounted Mexican, Chilean, and French flags." In response, the Americans "started out . . . to avenge the insult, and chastise the temerity of the greasers and outsiders."[47] By one account, they then shot the flags full of holes before hoisting the Stars and Stripes.[48] As one witness noted, "Our own citizens, who although generally sympathizing with the discontent occasioned by the unjust tax, are incensed that the foreigners should presume to take the law into their own hands."[49] At least one Chilean miner similarly understood the conflict to be about "who is the master and who is the slave."[50] Tellingly, the previously apathetic Americans mobilized quickly and violently to suppress this nascent opposition to their position atop the colonial hierarchy.[51]

Throughout the mines, white Americans usually permitted or encouraged tax collectors to target Mexicans and Chileans, resulting in an exodus of these groups to nearby towns.[52] On the ground, American miners had little patience for the legal stipulations of the Treaty of Guadalupe Hidalgo and the state constitution. Instead, language, along with dress, skin color, religion, and customs served as key markers of foreignness. The Foreign Miner's Tax tied the legitimacy of gold mining to ideas of race, citizenship, and gender as defined by the miners, and it shored up white American domination of the gold districts.

If nonwhite labor was problematic in the mines, then ownership of mining claims by nonwhites was even more controversial and many mining districts expelled or prohibited nonwhites. Some, like the Columbia mining district, incorporated in 1854, explicitly barred "Asiatics [and] South Sea Islanders" from mining, "either for themselves or others." The districts rules restricted mining to "Americans, or Europeans who intend to become citizens," and punished anyone who sold a claim to an "Asiatic or South-Sea Islander [by not allowing them] to hold another claim in this district for the space of six months."[53] Other mining districts expelled or prohibited Mexicans, Chinese, Hawaiians, French, Chileans, or African Americans.[54]

White Americans often justified the exclusion of nonwhites by asserting that foreign labor was unfree and a threat to the independence of white men.[55] In the mid-nineteenth century, white Americans were extremely concerned with being made into slaves by the extension of slavery or industrialization. Both forms of labor seemed to challenge the ability of the laboring white man to maintain the manly independence required by republican virtues.[56] In the early years of the California gold rush, most mining was carried on by small groups of men who often lived together and required little capital. Nonwhites, either working in American claims or in their own mines, raised the specter of the "enslavement" of white men through the degradation of white labor. This was the objection that J. M. E., a miner near the San Joaquin River, raised when he claimed that "the country is overrun by Mexicans and Chileans, so that Americans and kindred races have no chance with them. They have the advantage of cheap and combined labor in their menials who are little better than slaves." Tellingly, J. M. E. called for the exclusion of all non-Americans from the mines.[57]

At other times, white miners justified the move to exclusion on the grounds of racialized social threats. In May 1852, Alfred Jackson recorded that "the miners on Deer Creek . . . turned out last week and drove all of the Chinamen off that stream" for being "impudent and aggressive." Economic motivations remained just below the surface, however. The Chinese were perceived as impudent because they were "taking up claims the same as white men and appropriating water without asking leave." Like foreigners elsewhere in the mines, the Chinese on Deer Creek actively contested attempts to subordinate them. The conflict escalated until the Chinese destroyed a dam owned by American miners, at which point "fifty miners gathered together, ran the Chinamen out of the district, broke up their pumps and boxes, tore out their dams, destroyed their ditches, burned up their cabins and warned them not to come back under penalty of being shot if they made a reappearance. . . . [T]here is a disposition to bar the Chinks out of the district."[58] In March 1855, Ben Bowen recorded an attempt to drive African Americans from his mining camp by miners who claimed that the "niggers had got to be too saucy and therefore must leave the place." Though Bowen and other white miners called a miners' meeting that determined that the African Americans could stay if they would "behave themselves," at least one left anyway. Bowen later learned that "the intention was to drive them all off and divide the plunder."[59] For many American miners, economic and social concerns justified creating and defending a particular vision of colonial society.

When nonwhites resisted American attempts to exclude them from a mining district, events could rapidly escalate, as occurred during the winter of 1849–50 in and around Chilean Gulch in Calaveras County. Sometime late in 1849, rumors that the Chileans had expelled American miners, reports that many of the Chileans were "*peons* or slaves," and a desire to limit economic competition from foreigners fueled the move to expel the Chileans.[60] Up to this point, the events in Chilean Gulch were interchangeable with any number of other expulsions in the goldfields. However, instead of quietly acquiescing, the Chileans vigorously defended their right to mine.

Like the foreign miners in Sonora, the Chilean miners of Chilean Gulch rejected the American characterizations of them as degraded, effeminate labor. Instead, the Chileans asserted an identity as manly miners with an equal right to the gold claims. In a move that at least one Chilean claimed met with the "admiration of the Americans," the Chileans not only refused to leave but also expelled five Americans working on their ground.[61] Faced with escalating harassment from the American miners, the Chileans then appealed to Judge Reynolds in nearby Stockton, who issued a writ for the arrest of the American miners. When two judges in Chilean Gulch refused to enforce the order because "American citizens can never be arrested by foreigners," the Chileans took matters into their own hands and attacked the American camp.[62] The conflict left men dead on both sides and the Americans the prisoners of the Chileans.[63] The Chileans then attempted to march their captives to Judge Reynolds in Stockton but soon realized the Americans were mobilizing in force to stop them.[64] Eventually, the prisoners either freed themselves or were rescued, and the Chileans were captured and marched back to Calaveras under guard.[65]

By this time, the American population was incensed. Americans criticized Judge Reynolds for issuing the writ, especially because he issued it to "the lowest order of Chileans—none of whom could speak English."[66] Unsurprisingly, most of the blame was placed squarely on the Chileans, who, it was believed, falsely swore in order to obtain the writ in the first place.[67] With Stockton "red-hot" with rumors of Chilean atrocities and of a possible Chilean–Native American alliance against whites, harassment of Chileans increased, partly fueled by the alcohol of the holiday season.[68] Back in Chilean Gulch, white Americans organized a "court," hanged three Chileans, and either whipped, shaved the heads of, or cropped the ears of others.[69]

The Chilean miners of Chilean Gulch attempted in two ways to challenge white American's understandings of them as servile and effeminate foreigners with no claim to the land. First, by expelling American miners and vigorously asserting their right to mine, the Chileans believed they were acting, and expected to be seen as acting, manly.[70] Second, by appealing to the court system, Chilean miners asserted equality before the law. Unfortunately for the Chileans, the logic of republican ideology meant that, whatever the legal situation, the white miners, as the embodiment of "the people," saw themselves as the final arbiters of belonging in the mines. With their reaction, white American miners served notice that challenges to their authority would be met by escalating resistance, culminating, if need be, in state-sanctioned violence.

The regulation of foreigners underwent a significant shift in 1851 and 1852. On March 14, 1851, the Foreign Miner's Tax was repealed, largely at the behest of white merchants who saw foreigners as another market for their goods. As miner William Ryan put it, the merchants "regard[ed] it as a matter of indifference whether they dealt with Yankees or Californians, provided they could sell their goods."[71] The opposition of white merchants to the Foreign Miner's Tax reflected a vision of colonialism that emphasized the utilization of nonwhites as laborers and customers. However, the original drive behind the Foreign Miner's Tax to drive out nonwhites would outlive the legislation itself. In May 1852, the state introduced a system of mining licenses targeted, like the Foreign Miners' Tax, at noncitizens.[72] The implementation of mining licenses, though officially aimed at all foreigners, coincided with the first great influx of Chinese into California and came to be applied almost exclusively to them.[73] To understand the impact of the new mining licenses, it is necessary to examine the changing attitudes of white Americans toward the Chinese within colonial society.

While negative stereotypes had preceded the actual arrival of the Chinese in California, attitudes toward them remained remarkably fluid until 1852, when a massive influx of immigrants catalyzed widespread concern among whites.[74] At the start of the rush, popular opinion was divided, though slightly favorable to the Chinese. Described as "happy and clannish" and "very useful, quiet, good citizens and . . . deserving the respect of all," the Chinese, as viewed by many white settlers, seemed more curious than threatening.[75] Chinese immigration generally received strong support from white leaders who saw them as "peaceable [and] industrious," and from merchants in particular, who saw in them a domestic market as well as recognized the potential for overseas trade.[76] In the mines, the number of Chinese remained small and concentrated in quieter mining districts.[77] In the eyes of some settlers, the Chinese compared well to other migrants, like the Chileans or Australians.[78] At the same time, however, Americans widely believed the Chinese to be mostly "coolies"—that is, uneducated Chinese laborers under the control of the "better class" of Chinese.[79] The supposedly coercive aspects of Chinese labor, combined with Chinese "clannishness" or insularity and perceived racial differences, made the Chinese appear problematic as potential republicans. These mixed feelings meant that the place of the Chinese in a republican society remained an open question.

The massive influx of Chinese in 1852 changed this. Coinciding with an accelerated shift to large mining companies and wage work that threatened the ability of American men to stake a claim to an independent white manliness and dampened their dreams of striking it rich, the years after 1852 saw a mounting concern over Chinese labor, now identified with greater frequency as "coolie" labor.[80] Concurrently, white settlers became intensely concerned about the place of the Chinese within the republic. They worried that the Chinese posed not only an economic threat but also a threat to republican government and the right of middle-class white men to regulate and control society.[81] Commentators became increasingly anxious that the Chinese were enforcing their own laws. To the settlers, when middle-class white men asserted their right to self-government, it was admirable; but when a supposedly degraded race presumed to do the same, it was an intolerable threat.[82]

Politicians and other concerned citizens began to call for a halt to Chinese immigration, citing the danger they posed to American labor as well as the threat of "an *amalgamation* of the different RACES of men, and the consequent destruction of the great distinctive features of the Anglo-Saxon race."[83] By 1856, it was evident that legislator Wilson Flint spoke for the majority of white settlers when he argued that the "God endowed white man" could "never share with [the Chinese] the duties and burdens of self-government, the responsibility and glory of a free citizen!"[84] By the late 1850s, following increased Chinese migration and fundamental changes to the systems of mining, most white Americans in California had moved from nuanced, even positive perceptions of the Chinese to identifying them as among the greatest threats to republicanism and to the ability of settlers to claim an identity as white men through labor.[85] Mining licenses were one way for white Americans to try to control this supposed threat while simultaneously marking the Chinese population as different and threatening.

Though white settlers talked about the Chinese as the greatest economic and social threat, it was the indigenous population that felt the full weight of the colonial regime. Indigenous peoples had occupied an ambivalent position in the Spanish, and then Mexican, colonial states. Sometimes enemies, they were also a source of labor and a subject of missionization. Like native peoples in other Spanish colonies, Native Americans had the potential to occupy a subordinate position within colonial society as converts, laborers, and servants.[86] With the arrival of large numbers of white

Americans, some parts of this colonial relationship were preserved, most notably with the passage of An Act for the Government and Protection of the Indians in 1850.[87]

As disastrous as this policy was for Native Americans, it at least created space for indigenous peoples in the colonial hierarchy, even if as a permanent underclass. The other major line of thought, and the one favored by many white settlers, was that Native Americans and civilization were antithetical, and that the indigenous population should be killed or driven out by any and all means. What little legal protection Native Americans had was often dispensed with when white settlers interacted with Native Americans. And when these encounters turned violent—and they did with astonishing frequency in the early years of the rush—settlers, egged on by newspapers and government officials, showed a marked proclivity toward attempting to exterminate the indigenous population.[88]

While a wide variety of settlers took part in attacks on Native Americans, there is suggestive anecdotal evidence that Overlanders bore a disproportionate burden of responsibility for these attacks. Theodore Johnson summed up this perception when he claimed that "the late emigrants across the mountains, and especially from Oregon, had commenced a war of extermination upon [the Native Americans], shooting them down like wolves, men, women and children, wherever they could find them."[89] While Argonauts took part in the violence, and other factors influenced white settler reactions, the prevalence of Overlanders in accounts of attacks on Native Americans suggests the role that the overland migration played in conditioning certain groups of settlers to see Native Americans as expendable barriers to progress.[90]

The relationship of indigenous peoples to the colonial state served as a way to articulate two competing visions of white manhood in California. Reflecting a national debate over federal Indian policy, one side, dubbed the "protection" faction, favored slavery or the isolation of Native Americans on reservations followed by eventual assimilation. On the other side were those who favored extermination: in their view, the Native Americans were going to die out and, frankly, the sooner the better.[91] Each faction ascribed different actions and attitudes to proper white men. While the extermination faction saw Indian-fighters as heroic embodiments of martial manliness, proponents of a protectionist Native American policy, operating from the perspective of restrained manhood, saw these same men as degraded whites, little better than savages themselves.[92] While neither side completely dominated the public discourse about the nature of Native Americans and the white men who killed them, the outcome of this violence, combined with dispossession, slavery, and other actions, is clear. The indigenous population of California plummeted from approximately 120,000 in 1846 to between 20,000 and 40,000 by the 1860s.[93] Both factions were complicit in causing this massive demographic collapse.

The subordination of Native Americans was just one part of a larger project by middle-class white settlers to create and enforce a colonial hierarchy with themselves at the top. Key to this project was white American control of local government in the mines. Though off-white Europeans such as the French, Irish, and Germans could be targeted for challenging the dominance of white Americans in the mines, the energy of white settlers was, for the most part, directed toward regulating people of Asian, African, and Hispanic descent. The racial and gender values inherent in California republicanism meant that these latter groups appeared more threatening. Shared republican values such as these not only tied disparate mining camps together, but they also linked the mining region to the towns and cities. However, in the urban centers the same language and logic of republicanism, with its attendant racial and gender components, took an even more dramatic form.

SAN FRANCISCO

San Francisco, as the dominant city of the gold rush, had no serious challenger. Following the massive population explosion that transformed it from a sleepy hamlet to a burgeoning metropolis, San Francisco rose to become the center of banking, merchandising, media, and industry and the largest and most politically important city on the Pacific Coast.[94] While civil control had rested with the alcalde when California was Mexican territory, many Americans saw this concentration of legal and civic powers as despotism; and to be subject to it, even with an American filling the office, was an affront to their republican sensibilities.[95] Nevertheless, in San Francisco, backed by support from the military governors, the office of the alcalde uneasily coexisted with a series of elected town councils until it was replaced by the office of the mayor and a separate judiciary in April 1850.[96] Thereafter, until the passage of the Consolidation Act in 1856, formal authority in San Francisco was vested in the mayor and city council, and federal authority remained nearby in the form of the army and navy.[97] However, in the turbulent world that was gold-rush San Francisco, assertions of extralegal authority clothed in the logic and rhetoric of natural law that underlay republicanism in California challenged these official structures.

The colonial order that emerged in San Francisco was related to what emerged in the mines. In San Francisco, emphasis was placed on the divide between "good citizens" and "bad men." The key criterion for admission to the ranks of the good citizenry was respectability. Americans in California perceived respectability through the prism of gender, class, and racial biases, such that good citizenship was strongly correlated to white manliness. For middle-class whites, the danger of non- and off-whites was that they either explicitly challenged the authority of "proper" white men to dictate public behavior, or asserted alternative sources of authority, arguing that while American laws and codes were applicable to white men, these did not apply to them. The challenge for "good citizens" was to make other groups "appreciat[e] . . . the principle of submission to the majority." To carry out this "almost impossible task," one of the first things white Americans did upon their arrival in California was attempt to establish their dominance over other groups, often through real or threatened violence and the assertion of moral, cultural, technological, and religious superiority.[98]

In San Francisco, white settlers came to perceive crime as one of the most significant threats to social order; and in suppressing it, they sought to position themselves as the embodiments of republican order.[99] Middle-class whites believed that criminals were predisposed to form gangs or operate under the control of a criminal mastermind, making them a particular threat to the manly independence needed for a functioning republic.[100] Not only were criminal organizations filled with "bad men," but they also represented an alternative social order to the nascent colonial state. To meet this supposed threat, middle-class white men in San Francisco increasingly used the language and logic of republicanism to justify creating extralegal forms of government.

The Hounds crisis of 1849 was the earliest major example of the evolving debate over the status of various groups as "good citizens" or "bad men" in San Francisco. A group of decommissioned New York Volunteers, the Hounds banded together in San Francisco to form a mutual benevolent society.[101] The working-class men who made up the Hounds soon sought to position themselves as the muscle of the local Democratic Party, naming their headquarters "Tammany Hall" and becoming involved in several political disputes.[102] However, lacking discipline and the ability to dispense political patronage, the Hounds soon took to harassing and extorting foreigners to secure power and for amusement.[103]

The Hounds came to focus on the Chilean population in particular, arguing they were defending American citizens from "acts of violence committed by Chilenos and foreigners."[104] At the same time, the Hounds changed their name to the Regulators, a reference to a prerevolution movement in the Carolinas celebrated as an example of white men rising up against oppression, in the best tradition of republicanism.[105] Those settlers who noticed the Hounds found them to be a source of amusement, known for "displaying a want of sense, in parading the public streets in fantastic or ridiculous dresses, and by the commission of pranks of a character calculated to amuse the community at the expense of themselves."[106] Other commentators, not so generous, noted the Hounds could "be seen, attired in the most gaudy clothing, with rich-colored *serapas* thrown over their shoulders, their hats ornamented with feathers and artificial flowers."[107] In both cases the Hounds behaved not as "good citizens" but as lower-class rowdies and dressed in flamboyant or foreign clothes; even more damning, they were often seen with "the most abandoned Spanish women or Indian squaws."[108]

Emboldened by the perceived popular acquiescence to their previous attacks and fueled by alcohol, the Hounds planned, as Joseph T. Downey testified later, "to run the Chilenos out" on the night of July 15, 1849.[109] In keeping with their asserted identity as defenders of American citizens in San Francisco, the Hounds gathered near Tammany Hall, assembled in "military order," and, led by men in quasi-military uniforms playing "fife and drum" and singing the "Star-Spangled Banner," proceeded to Telegraph Hill, where the Chilean population was concentrated.[110] Once there, they apparently broke into several groups, destroying and seizing property, killing four Chileans and wounding another thirteen.[111] Throughout it all, the Hounds explicitly targeted non-Anglo-Americans. They spared two Englishmen because of their nationality, underscoring the assumption that the British were white men, even when they were living in an immigrant part of town.[112] Though the Hounds were out for a rowdy good time, their republican values clearly determined who constituted a legitimate target.

The Hounds.

The Hounds' attack on July 15, 1849, was a vicious assault on a predominately nonwhite area of San Francisco. Source: Soulé, *The Annals of San Francisco*, 553.

The Hounds had dramatically misjudged how the majority of settlers would respond to their actions. Instead of being praised, the Hounds were confronted by a citizens' meeting the day after the attack, organized by the alcalde, Thaddeus Leavenworth. Under Leavenworth's direction, but assisted by Samuel Brannan, a local figure who would go on to play a crucial role in the 1851 Vigilance Committee, those assembled at the meeting appointed two special judges, a district attorney, and 230 "good citizens" to arrest and try the Hounds. Most of the Hounds fled San Francisco before the citizenry could mobilize, but 17 were arrested and tried on charges ranging from conspiracy, rioting, and robbery to assault with intent to kill and sentenced to a variety of punishments, ranging from imprisonment and banishment to fines of various amounts.[113]

While later accounts claimed that the Hounds' behavior had gradually grown more obnoxious to the population of San Francisco, court testimony and other contemporaneous sources show that the Hounds were virtually ignored before the attack.[114] Public opinion shifted against the Hounds after the attack for several reasons. Despite their emulation of New York's Tammany Hall political organization, the Hounds did not have much more than a weak affiliation with political power structures of any kind at the time of the attack.[115] Also, while nativism had strong and deep roots in California (indeed, at their trial the Hounds used General Persifor Smith's defunct prohibition of foreign labor in the mines as a defense), the merchants, wishing to preserve and expand their market, remained a vocal and influential voice for the rights of foreigners.[116] Additionally, the Hounds' behavior and dress marked them as "brawlers, gamblers, and drunkards"—in other words, as off-white.[117] Politically, then, the Hounds were operating in an exposed position exacerbated by their own conduct.

As off-whites, the Hounds found that their actions, instead of buttressing a colonial order that served the interests of white men, seemed to threaten it. Immediately following the attacks, a consistent narrative of the Chileans as helpless, effeminate, and in need of the protection of white men emerged. The *Alta*'s description that opened the paper's coverage of the attack, set the mood: "The scene, as heard by those residing in the vicinity, is described as heart-rending. In every direction were heard the cries and shrieks of women and children, mingled with the oaths and demonic laughter of reckless and impious men, whilst the report of fire-arms, and the sound of blows falling thick and fast upon the defenseless, gave to the act its finishing touch of cowardly outrage and attempted assassination." The gendered language coding the attack as degraded-male on defenseless-female was continued in the charge that the Hounds conspired to "riot, rape and murder."[118] Within a few years this narrative had been strengthened, and as a result the response was remembered as being a reaction to "the most brutal outrages [committed] upon [a Chilean] mother and daughter."[119] The Chilean population, despite being overwhelmingly male, stood in for innocent feminine victims, which in turn cast the Hounds as unmanly aggressors and the middle-class white population as manly protectors. Conveniently for middle-class whites, this logic reduced the Hounds and Chileans, rendering them as unfit for full participation in the republic, since neither embodied the proper attributes of respectable white manliness.[120]

After the dispersal of the Hounds in August 1849, attention focused on the supposed criminal propensities of the Australian immigrants, or

"Sydney Ducks."[121] The history of Australia as a penal colony led most Americans to conflate Australian origins and criminality.[122] The liminal status of the Australians, as European-descended English-speakers who were nonetheless tainted by criminality *as a people*, attracted middle-class settlers' attention. Even the Irish, whom white settlers understood to have a criminal element among them, were not characterized as an inherently criminal people to the same extent as the Australians.[123] Given that many of the migrants from Australia were originally from Ireland, the linking of criminality with Australia may have had the effect of encouraging white settlers to think of "bad" Irish as Australian and to identify "good" Irish with Ireland. This may help explain why the "Irish" (or at least a portion of them) received a warmer welcome in California than in the East.

In the eyes of San Franciscans, the cowardliness of Australians underscored their status as off-white. After a group of Australians attempted to bully William Downie and his friends in 1849, he reported that all that had been required to scare them off was to announce that "nothing could scare us, we had just landed after a long voyage and nothing would please us better than a good live fight."[124] American settlers also singled out Australians for using the slung-shot, a "coward's weapon" associated with muggings.[125] As cowardly criminals, Australians violated the codes of behavior embedded in understandings of white manliness and republicanism, underscoring their threat to the nascent political and social order in San Francisco.

Settler reactions to Australian immigration ranged from antagonism to near-hysteria. To some commentators, the Australians were the epitome of

> the creatures that are making our State, as far as in their power, a perfect Pandemonium. They have come here by the thousands. They are like the locusts and vermin of Egypt; they are everywhere. Not alone in the mines, engaged in robbery and murder; they are in our midst. They are upon us; our motions are watched, our steps followed; the privacy of home, of the business office, of the study, and the dormitory, is nothing. They see all, know all, and if vigilance is slackened for a moment, the theft, the robbery or the murder is almost certain to follow.[126]

The "crying evil" of Australian criminality was "sapping the foundations of civil and social life." By late 1850, the *Alta* suggested immigration restrictions and deportation, but a weak federal government, a state government controlled by Democratic politicians sympathetic to immigrants, and rapidly escalating tensions between settlers and Australians meant that events would come to a head first.[127]

As concern over the Australians intensified, San Francisco's memories of the Hounds crisis began to morph, and the citizen's committee organized by Alcalde Leavenworth came to be remembered as oppositional and superior to the alcalde. Many settlers now saw Leavenworth as "a very weak, undecided and inefficient officer, who looked with fear and trembling upon the Hounds and dared not act," in contrast to the quick and decisive actions of Samuel Brannan and the citizens' committee that suppressed "the spirit of ruffianism and disorder" that had "jeapordize[d] the peace of the community." When it forgot the role of the legal authorities and idealized the actions of Brannan and other "good citizens," the *Alta* was part of a shift in California that undercut the legitimacy of official structures of authority and instead glorified the ability of "good citizens"—that is, strong, independent white men—to exercise authority when needed.[128] This shift would help enable the formation of the first Vigilance Committee, in 1851.

On February 22, 1851, two Australians, Stuart and Wildred, were arrested on suspicion of "being the robbers and attempted murderers of Mr. Jansen," a San Francisco store owner.[129] The perception of crisis galvanized much of the San Franciscan community to question the ability of the government to deal with crime. As the *Alta* put it, "Every honest man feels indignant against the vile miscreants who have fired our houses, robbed our citizens, and murdered them," a state of affairs that was "the inevitable result of a shameful laxity in the administration of our lower courts."[130] These claims that public opinion supported subjecting the men to popular justice were, as the *Alta* itself would admit months later, "farcical."[131] Multiple attempts by mobs to seize the prisoners were foiled by the militia and police.[132] A committee elected by an angry crowd, and headed by Samuel Brannan, arranged with Mayor John Geary to serve as the jury in a special trial of Stuart and Wildred, yet the jury emerged deadlocked, unable to render a verdict. By February 24, the "feverish feelings" had dissipated and the men were remanded to jail to await regular trial at the district court.[133]

The Stuart and Wildred affair demonstrates that while there was some dissatisfaction with the legal system, widespread support for lynch law had yet to emerge. Indeed, the *Alta*, which would later become the most important public advocate of vigilantism in California, voiced significant reservations about lynch law as a concept while simultaneously praising the crowd that had tried to seize the prisoners as "our best citizens."[134] The inability to present a clear and consistent narrative justifying the supersession of the government by an organization of "the people" was further compounded by the very competent reactions of what would later be termed the "law-and-order" faction. In particular, Judge David Shattuck ably defended the accused at the public trial and undercut public support for the proceedings at the same time. Shattuck directly likened the trial to lynchings in Mississippi, arguing that innocent men had been killed because of the "hot haste" of those proceedings. Shattuck repudiated the committee's claim to be acting as a cool, rational manifestation of the will of the people and, instead, suggested the trial was the result of the actions of an inflamed, irrational mob, hardly the embodiment of white manly republican virtues.[135]

Indeed, had the Great Fire of May 4, 1851, not occurred, it is likely that the vigilance movement in San Francisco would have remained a historical footnote. However, in the fire's aftermath, many middle-class white settlers came to believe that it was the work of organized Australian "incendiaries."[136] The perceived weak response of legal authorities evidently galvanized the members of the February citizens' committee to form the "Committee of Vigilance" sometime in early June.[137] This time, however, Brannan and the other members of the committee moved proactively to ensure they would have an organization in place that could replace the legal system should the opportunity arise. Working in secret, the committee secured the participation of large numbers of merchants and others who would act in accordance with prearranged signals.[138] In the absence of any new acts of arson, a theft on June 10, 1851, provided an opportunity for the committee to make its public debut.[139]

That evening, a local merchant discovered that his safe containing fifteen hundred dollars had been stolen. Boatmen at the docks noticed an Australian, John Jenkins, placing a heavy parcel into a rowboat and setting off across the bay. Giving chase, the boatmen caught Jenkins just after he dropped the safe overboard. Instead of taking Jenkins to the station house, the boatmen conveyed their prisoner to Brannan's house, where he was put under guard. About the same time, bells were rung around the city summoning members of the committee.[140] Resisting attempts by police officers

Hanging of Jenkins on the Plaza.

Urged on by Samuel Brannan, the hanging of Jenkins was a mass act. Source: Soulé, *The Annals of San Francisco*, 343.

to take the prisoner, the committee tried Jenkins in secret, and Brannan then "informed [the gathered crowd] that the man had been fairly tried by a committee of citizens, and that no doubt of his guilt existed."[141] In the early morning hours of June 11, the committee marched Jenkins to the plaza, hanged him, and left his body suspended from a beam as a warning to other criminals.

The execution of Jenkins emerged as the central performance of the committee's legitimacy. The committee's key tactic had been to create the impression that it acted as the embodiment of the will of the "good citizens" of San Francisco. When Brannan had addressed the crowd, he asked them, the citizenry, if they supported the actions of the committee.[142] Unsurprisingly, many in the crowd answered, "Aye!" and "Hang him!"[143] The committee had made the pulling of the hanging rope a mass act, with Brannan reportedly exclaiming, "A long pull, and a strong pull altogether—let every honest citizen be a hangman for once!" and later claiming that he could not identify who actually pulled the rope.[144] When the coroner named certain committee members as directly responsible for the death of Jenkins, the committee countered that all two hundred members shared equally in the act.[145] In so doing, Brannan and the committee sought to tie participation in the trial and execution to republican virtues.

The success of the Committee of Vigilance hinged on the narrative of the committee as acting in the best traditions of republicanism. First, the committee asserted that the arrival of "large numbers of the most daring, depraved and reckless men," who had come "from every part of the habitable globe, but more particularly from the British penal colonies," had left the city at "the mercy of organized gangs of the worst felons."[146] The courts and police had failed, "through want of energy or collusion," to protect the "good citizens" of San Francisco.[147] In response, the "good citizens"—"men of standing, character and influence,"[148] "industrious, orderly and patriotic men"[149]—that is, white men who embodied republican virtues, were "compelled" to organize into a body to restore order to society.[150] Following this reasoning, the committee members, many of whom were merchants, claimed that they organized not to protect their own financial interests but to protect society out of "stern necessity."[151] Furthermore, being "quiet" and "orderly" transformed the public gathering from an excited mob into a political body of independent men exercising their rights as citizens that reflected the inherent propriety of the committee's actions.[152] Finally, while rejecting the authority of a "corrupt" government, the vigilantes went to great lengths to stress that they acted in keeping with the values of republicanism.[153] In this way, the 1851 Committee of Vigilance used the language of republicanism to justify directly vesting themselves—as representatives of the good citizenry of San Francisco—with sovereignty in order to suppress the threat represented by "bad men" from Sydney. Claiming to have restored "order," the committee disbanded, allowing local government to take over once again. None of the participants were held accountable for their actions, and some would go on to play prominent roles in 1856, when local merchant elites again used the pretext of a supposed crime wave to justify their actions.[154]

Though motivated by a desire to achieve political dominance and economic control of the port, the Vigilance Committee in 1856 also drew on the language and popular understandings of republicanism to legitimize its actions. This time, however, the duration and extent of the vigilantes' actions far exceeded the 1851 precedent. The committee began acting again in late November 1855, when the *Alta* and other supporters of lynch law began agitating against what they perceived as the sure-to-be biased trial of Charles Cora, a gambler reputed to have "friends, rich, powerful, influential, talented, fertile in expedients, active and determined to rob justice of its own."[155] Anger about Cora's trial and subsequent hung jury failed to mobilize the population, however. Instead, it was the shooting of James King of William, an anti-Democratic newspaper editor, at the hands of a rival newspaperman, James Casey, on May 14, 1856, that proved to be the flashpoint. King had been an active supporter of the 1851 Vigilance Committee, and his newspaper, the *San Francisco Daily Evening Bulletin*, had been a leading voice in the antigambling hysteria of 1855 and 1856, focusing in particular upon the case of Charles Cora.[156] It took little incentive for many in the population to seize upon this coincidence as proof of a conspiracy between gamblers, arsonists, and corrupt politicians and officials.[157]

The second Vigilance Committee grew quickly from the skeleton of the first committee.[158] By May 18, when the Vigilance Committee seized Cora and Casey from jail, it claimed almost three thousand men under arms, many of whom had defected from militia units stationed in the city.[159] With the death of James King on May 20, the Vigilance Committee quickly tried James Casey and Charles Cora. Both men were found guilty and hanged on May 22 from the windows of committee headquarters.[160] Between then and the day they disbanded, on August 18, the Vigilance Committee executed two more men, caused the suicide of another, and banished, deported, or drove into hiding at least twenty-seven more.[161] Through it all, city, state, and federal officials were largely helpless without support from the U.S. military.[162]

What was initially justified as a reaction to a perceived crime wave quickly became a purge of the Democratic Party in San Francisco and an attempt by members of the executive committee of the Vigilance Committee to seize valuable waterfront property.[163] More than any other factor, it was the committee's use of the language of republicanism that enabled the shift of an organization originally publically focused on protecting citizens from the "thief, burglar, incendiary, assassin, ballot-box stuffer, or other disturbers of the peace," to an almost exclusive focus on the "ballot-box stuffer."[164] Nor did it take much to convince much of the population of San Francisco that this shift was justified.

By 1856, many middle-class white settlers in San Francisco believed they were in the midst of a crime wave, and that the legal authorities were either hamstrung by the technicalities of the law or complicit in shielding criminals from justice. Corrupt officials, though hardly rare in the nineteenth century (indeed, more notable in their absence), were anathema to republican philosophy. At the core of American republicanism was the ideal of the independent citizen, free from encumbrances, exercising his political voice.[165] Of course, this ideal was strongly gendered, as only men could vote, and also heavily raced, as nonwhites were explicitly denied the right to vote in California.[166] Ballot-box stuffing and other forms of electoral fraud were therefore more than a danger to the legitimacy of civil government: these actions threatened the racialized and gendered privileges upon which white men constructed their superiority. Without free elections, white men were no better than the women and nonwhites to whom they denied a place in government. Even more striking is rhetoric suggesting that the loss of the vote through fraud reduced white men to the slaves of corrupt politicians and their criminal allies.[167]

In place of "slavery" at the hands of corrupt politicians and criminals, the Vigilance Committee offered "good citizens" the means by which "the people" could vest sovereignty directly in themselves, purify the political system, and impose a new order on San Francisco. Practically speaking, this meant the political allies of the Vigilance Committee would run San Francisco; but this language rhetorically linked the racial and gender requirements of citizenship and the attributes of republicanism to the idealized morality of middle-class white men.

Under the Vigilance Committee, the key determinant of participation and place within the system was whether an individual qualified as a "good citizen" or a "bad man." The qualities of good citizens read like the attributes of the ideal middle-class white man. A good citizen was a calm, cool, and hardworking man who did not want violence, but who did not shy away from it when necessary.[168] Members of the Vigilance Committee, as paragons among citizens in the eyes of their supporters, were described as "men of honor, intelligence, high social worth, worthwhile integrity, and patriotic hearts; men whose hands no bribe has ever stained; men whose hearts are ever-throbbing with the pulses of a high and pure patriotism."[169] Further emphasizing their manly and rational maturity, the *Alta* described committee members as "playing no school boy game, they have well weighed the consequences of all their acts."[170] According to the committee's constitution, only "good citizens" could be admitted to the Vigilance Committee; if any "unworthy persons gain[ed] admission," they would be expelled.[171]

At drills, mass meetings, and parades, respectable women were present as silent spectators, "len[ding] their smiles to the important occasion" and occasionally showering the men with flowers.[172] These women allowed men to act out male fantasies of control and order in which they, as good citizens and family men, acted to defend their homes, their families, and their women. It is telling that virtually the only time a female voice supporting the committee emerges in the historical record, the woman, Miss Louise Dam, speaks as the representative of "every true woman" and directly links the actions of the committee to those of "patriots of earlier days."[173] That the most prominent woman associated with the opponents of the vigilantes was the Catholic prostitute and lover of Charles Cora, Belle Ryan, only underscored the status of the vigilantes.[174] This sort of recognition was crucial to the vigilantes' claim to be respectable white men and the true heirs to the legacy of republicanism in the United States.

The vigilantes relied heavily on comparisons between their actions and those of the Founding Fathers. The committee argued that the "supreme power in the State is the People," and that the "shoulder-strikers, loafers, and rowdies, who [had] pretended to govern" were not a legitimate government.[175] It was no coincidence that the *Alta* described the "Address of the Vigilance Committee" (a justification and statement of principles) as "equal almost to the Declaration of American Independence."[176] By embodying the will of "the people" against a corrupt and abusive government that denied them their rights as free men, the members of the Vigilance Committee positioned themselves as paragons of republican virtue.

Opposed to the good citizens of the Vigilance Committee was the law-and-order faction, or "Law and Murder Party" as the vigilantes sometimes styled them. These "reckless men" had "mercenary and corrupt motives" and sought to shape society for their own "private interests" rather than for the public good.[177] Moreover, unlike good citizens who operated as autonomous individuals, "bad men" operated in "organized gangs" as subservient followers of a corrupt master.[178] In the eyes of the vigilantes, these men supported Governor John Neely Johnson (who saw the vigilantes as an illegal organization and declared San Francisco to be in a state of insurrection), not out of any sense of civic duty or higher ideals, but out of a sense of self-preservation.[179]

The position of foreigners vis-à-vis the Vigilance Committee was surprisingly complicated given the linking of crime and immigration. The acceptance of men of "Anglo-Saxon" descent, as long as they supported the committee, was assumed and so went unremarked upon.[180] More surprising was the acceptance of French and Germans into the committee. Normally, the French were seen as politically radical and lazy, and the Germans, while "industrious, orderly and contented," were too easily satisfied with "slow, but constant returns," unlike the supposedly more aggressive and hardworking Anglo-Saxon settlers.[181] And yet, because both groups actively supported the committee, the pro-vigilance *Alta* praised them as restrained and orderly.[182] As long as the French and Germans, by being subordinate and loyal, mirrored the colonial hierarchy the committee sought to create, they were accepted.[183]

In contrast, the vigilantes singled out the Irish as "bad men." Though not as intensely as in the East, stereotypes of the Irish as degraded, drunk street thugs had considerable traction in California.[184] Moreover, the Irish came from the northeastern United States, where many of them had developed ties to the Democratic Party, or from Australia, further reinforcing negative stereotypes.[185] These factors led to the labeling of the Irish as "ballot-box stuffers, election bullies, thieves, murderers, and other bad characters."[186] Even so, the committee was careful to distinguish between those Irish who had "*honestly* differed" from the committee and the group it referred to as the "low Irish."[187] Here, class divisions operated to separate working-class Irish from Irish merchants, lawyers, and politicians who met the standards of public behavior expected of respectable white men. There was hope that, like the French and the Germans, these Irish gentlemen could find a (subordinate) place in the social order of the vigilantes.

The conundrum the vigilantes found themselves in was that while they wished to be associated with the Founding Fathers, they had little desire to be branded revolutionaries. Unfortunately for the vigilantes, the law-and-order faction, as well as some in the East, saw the committee as a treasonous, revolutionary group *opposed* to republican values.[188] Indeed, on June 3, Governor Johnson issued a proclamation declaring the city of San Francisco to be in a state of insurrection. Although the vigilantes attempted to belittle the decree, calling it "absurd" and "ridiculous," the possibility of military intervention was a real concern.[189] Though Governor Johnson was never able to actually enforce martial law in San Francisco, both he and General Volney Howard, commander of the state militia, continued to argue that the vigilantes were "bad men" opposed to the values of republicanism, an argument that found considerable traction outside California.[190]

The vigilantes tried to calm these fears by creating two categories—"lynch law" and "mob rule"—and identifying the Vigilance Committee's actions as in keeping with the former. Lynch law, by the vigilantes' definition, was "an American institution" that "had a more orderly and civilizing aspect . . . [and should] never be identified with 'mobs' and 'riots' and personal affrays with pistols and knives."[191] Instead, attention to the forms of the law, trials, and most importantly, cool and calm deliberation by the "people" characterized lynch law.[192] In his sermon "Vigilance and Reform," Joseph Benton argued, "If the evils suffered are absolutely intolerable, and can not be borne till the close of their [corrupt public officials] terms, then the people *must* resume their original power. For them to do so is legitimate, if not legal. Rising in their majesty, coolly and firmly, they may either depose their nominal rulers, or act as though there were none. This is the right of self-defence, and self-protection; a right belonging to communities no less than individuals. It is not mob-law, though it easily degenerates into it;—it is the law of necessity; the law of nature."[193] Mob rule, on the other hand, was the work of the "ungovernable passions"[194] of an "infuriated band of men . . . combined to effect an evil, or selfish object, in an unlawful way."[195] Indeed, mob rule was the result of the antithesis of the good citizen: the bad man.

All these concerns came to head when the committee arrested and charged Judge David Terry of the State Supreme Court with stabbing Sterling A. Hopkins, a vigilante "police officer," on June 21, 1856. Though accounts varied, a general consensus held that Terry had been present in the office of the United States naval agent when Hopkins and some other vigilantes attempted to arrest Rabe Maloney, a Democratic operative. Terry forced the vigilantes to leave and was escorting Maloney to a law-and-order armory when he and Hopkins again encountered each other. A fight led to Terry drawing his knife and stabbing Hopkins in the back of the neck, badly wounding him. Terry, Maloney, and a few others then fled to a nearby armory, where the committee quickly surrounded them. Heavily outnumbered by the vigilantes, Terry surrendered.[196] By the end of the day, the committee found itself stronger than it had ever been but also poised on the brink of a disastrous confrontation with the federal government.

While the arrest of Terry and the capture of the law-and-order armory seemed to herald the total victory of the committee, neither Terry nor the law-and-order militias had previously been much of a threat to the committee. Now, if Hopkins died, the committee would have to try a senior representative of the state government for murder, a trial that would almost certainly have to result in a guilty verdict or risk exposing the committee to charges of hypocrisy. The execution of such a high-ranking Democrat and state official risked bringing about a direct confrontation between the committee and the federal government that would almost certainly destroy the reputation of the committee members in the East. Even if Hopkins lived, the committee would have to find a way to save face by making Terry suffer some consequences without catalyzing the intervention of the federal government. On balance, the law-and-order faction was actually quite happy with the situation, recognizing that the whole affair undermined support for the committee.[197]

While both sides waited with somewhat morbid curiosity to see whether Hopkins would succumb to his wound, support for the Vigilance Committee dwindled.[198] Despite the best efforts of the vigilante press, internal divisions over Judge Terry and rumors of the disbanding of the committee persisted.[199] Only on August 7, when Hopkins was finally pronounced recovered, could the committee finish its trial of Terry. They ultimately found him guilty on two counts of assault and one for resisting arrest. Terry's "sentence" was a demand that he resign his office, which Terry proceeded to ignore.[200] A little under a month later, the Vigilance Committee declared victory and quickly disbanded.[201]

Ultimately, the 1856 Vigilance Committee was far more successful in reshaping the political order of San Francisco than the previous vigilante movements in the city had been, yet this very success engendered the committee's greatest opposition. While the republican rhetoric of the Vigilance Committee served the concrete political objective of crippling the Democratic Party, a wounded but resilient Democratic Party and the numerous non- and off-white residents actively contested this rhetoric and continued to lay claim to a place in the city on the basis of an alternative, more expansive form of republicanism.

CONCLUSION

Ultimately, for middle-class white men, the debate in California over the order of colonial society was not over who would serve and who would rule. Settlers across a wide spectrum of professions, locations, and times agreed that the economic, political, and social system should benefit white men first and foremost. But Edward Gilbert's words from the Constitutional Convention, that "the meaning of the word 'white' . . . was not generally understood in this country, though well understood in the United States," reflected a persistent problem in California society: though American settlers agreed that white men should be in charge, how white manliness should be ascertained and who qualified as a white man underwent change and consolidation throughout the gold rush period.[202]

In seeking to address this ambiguity, American settlers in California came to rely on the language of republicanism. Republicanism in California was narrowly focused on defining the type of traits and behaviors that defined a good citizen. As result, it served as a crucial nexus between ideas of race and gender and political participation. The racial and gender ideas embedded in Californian republicanism posed significant obstacles to political participation by women and non-Europeans, while the emphasis on behavior as the defining characteristic of good citizenship could move men of European descent out of the category of white and into the category of off-white. This colonial regime was still in flux when gold was discovered on the Fraser River in British Columbia in 1858. There, the presence of the British government and a different history of colonization would lead to the development of a related, but distinct, colonial regime vested in ideas of white manly supremacy.

CHAPTER 3

English Principles Encounter American Republicanism

Colonial British Columbia

A DAY AFTER ARRIVING IN BRITISH COLUMBIA WITH THE
first group of gold rushers, W. D. Moses, a leader in the African American
community of California, met with Governor Douglas. Douglas encouraged further immigration by "the colored people of California" and promised that "they shall have all the rights and privileges and protections of the
laws of this country."[1] In the coming months, many more people of African
descent would take Douglas up on his offer, joining the thirty-five black
settlers already in the colony.[2] The recruitment of settlers of African descent
was part of a larger project by the colonial elite to establish a hierarchy in
explicit contrast to California. Instead of a system of racial domination
masquerading as republicanism, Douglas and the other colonial leaders
would order British Columbia according to "English principles."[3] Foremost
among these principles was the assertion that, regardless of race, as long as
a man was a subject of the crown, he was guaranteed all the rights and
privileges of freeborn Englishmen.[4] Of course, nineteenth-century settler
colonialism in British Columbia, as elsewhere, cannot be divorced from the
language of race, gender, and class that explained and justified it.[5] Although
those who espoused English principles claimed they embraced equality

between British subjects, the reality was more complex and less egalitarian. For many British subjects, the ideal social order was one based on a series of interlocking hierarchies.

In the British vision of society, equality and hierarchy existed in harmony. In theory, all British subjects enjoyed legal and political equality, at the same time that class lines ensured social hierarchy. Of course, in reality, social stratification meant that some individuals, particularly those in the upper and emergent middle classes, enjoyed far greater access to political patronage and the levers of power than the lower classes. Gender divided society between the masculine public sphere and the feminine domestic sphere, which served to curtail female involvement in activities ranging from voting to public drinking. Race and gender distinguished whites from nonwhites—namely, Native Americans, who were depicted as childlike, irrational, and culturally inferior.[6] Therefore, while British society in the colony laid claim to a heritage of colorblindness and equality, that ethic extended only to those who met white, British conditions of respectability.[7] "Savage" Native Americans (along with the "heathen" Chinese) were, more often than not, too alien to the British—who had specific ideas about respectability—to benefit even from the rhetoric of equality. But blacks, who spoke English, were usually Protestant, dressed and behaved similarly to Anglo-Saxons, had symbolic value deriving from the history of abolitionism in England, and were useful as a way to distinguish British from American values, really stood a chance of taking advantage of the promise British society offered.

As in California, but in a significantly different manner, ideas of race and gender were used to systematically expropriate resources, claim political control, and organize society.[8] Though the basis of the colonial project before the rush was the control and domination of indigenous peoples and their resources, during the gold rush much of the energy of the colonial project was aimed at regulating and controlling nonnative society.[9] In British Columbia, especially during the early part of the gold rush, Americans formed the most problematic aspect of society. Fear of these destabilizing and possibly revolutionary white Americans encouraged the British colonial elite to emphasize national differences in the early years of the gold rush. After 1859, as the American population fell and their actions demonstrated their willingness to accept British rule, ideas of white manliness that emphasized commonalities between white American and British men began to emerge. By the late 1860s, shared understandings of white manliness underlay a system of colonial domination that paid little more than lip service to the colorblind values of a decade before.

Colonial government in British Columbia stretched back to 1805 and the establishment of a Hudson's Bay Company (HBC) fur-trading fort at McLeod Lake, but it was not until the 1820s that the HBC began to have a significant presence in the region.[10] In 1821, the Act for Regulating the Fur Trade gave the HBC political control of British Columbia; and in 1843, the HBC, fearing the outcome of the Oregon boundary dispute, established Fort Victoria on the southern tip of Vancouver Island.[11] Now British Columbia, not Oregon, was the center of HBC activity in the Pacific Northwest. From 1843 to 1849, the HBC ran British Columbia as its own private game preserve, discouraging settlement or economic activity that would impede the fur trade.[12] The British government soon began to fear the rapidly growing American population south of the border and, in 1849, created the colony of Vancouver Island to attract British settlers. It also dispatched a governor, Richard Blanshard, who was unconnected with the HBC.[13] Upon arrival, Blanshard discovered that real power lay with the HBC, which owned virtually all the land, controlled the major industry, and directly employed a majority of the colonists. Blanshard lasted just nine months; and when he quit, the Colonial Office made James Douglas the chief factor of Victoria, and the senior HBC official in the region, governor. The appointment of Douglas reflected and secured the power of a group of senior HBC officials, labeled the "Family-Company-Compact" by their opponents, in the colony.[14] Key to the influence of the Family-Company-Compact were the policies of the British government for both promoting and controlling immigration to the region.

At the time, the theories of Edward Wakefield heavily influenced British colonization. Wakefield argued that the problem of colonization was an economic one. Too often, he claimed, colonies were cursed with a shortage of labor that resulted in economic stagnation and social decay. England, on the other hand, suffered from the problems of a "surplus population" that needed to be removed overseas, where it could then enrich the mother country through productive trade. Wakefield's solution was to "make the cheapest land [in the colonies] somewhat dear" by setting the price of "waste land" high enough to ensure that laborers would be unable to afford land, which would, in turn, prevent a shortage of labor. The result would be that "Gentry" and "Capitalists" would have an exploitable labor force that would allow for the economic development of the colony. In other words, Wakefield and his contemporaries argued that the preservation of British class relations was essential to the economic development of the colonies and to the future well-being of the empire and of England.[15]

This system had obvious appeal to the colonial government in Victoria and the Colonial Office in London. Not only would class relations be preserved, but also colonization would be self-supporting, with the sales of land going to an emigration fund that would bring "young married couples, or . . . young people of the marriageable age in an equal proportion of the sexes."[16] In practice, a male British subject had to own twenty acres of land to vote, and three hundred acres, at a cost of one pound sterling per acre, to run for office, conditions that helped ensure the continued political dominance of the Family-Company-Compact.[17] Between 1849 and 1857 this policy successfully ensured that the social hierarchy of the colony remained mostly intact.[18] Faced with a choice between a large, white, and multinational immigration, and a smaller British immigration, the Colonial Office consistently chose the latter.[19]

The example of settlement run amok that Wakefield held out was the United States. There, he believed, cheap land encouraged a dangerous democratic sentiment, an equality "not before the law only, but equality against nature and truth; an equality which, to keep the balance always even, rewards the mean rather than the great, and gives more honour to the vile than the noble."[20]

Though biased, Wakefield accurately identified the link between land policy and national mythology. In the United States, squatting was common, while the Preemption Act of 1841 and the Homestead Act of 1862 both provided relatively cheap paths to land ownership. More importantly, these acts traced their ideological lineage back to Jeffersonian republican ideals, which held that cheap, easily accessible land would be a safety valve for the nation, helping preserve its republican virtues by allowing men to become economically self-sufficient.

By April 1858, Governor Douglas and the other ruling elites of Vancouver Island and British Columbia had well-formed opinions about their neighbors to the south and about the likely result of a major gold discovery in British territory. Having experienced a small rush in the Queen Charlotte Islands in 1851 and watched the California and Australia gold rushes from afar, Governor Douglas, along with the Colonial Office in London, realized that a significant discovery of gold in British Columbia would spark an immediate wave of immigration from California.[21] This prospect unsettled both the local colonial elite and their superiors in London.

When the colonial elite of British Columbia and the Colonial Office thought of social disorder, they thought of California. To the British elite, America, and especially California, represented the dangers of overdemocratic and unorganized society. For these elites, a lack of social graces, a disturbing crassness, and a tendency toward violence characterized American society. Nor did the aggressively expansionist nature of the United States soothe their nerves. The prospect of American emigration to British Columbia brought with it memories of the Oregon Question of the 1840s, the Texas Revolution, the Mexican-American War, and numerous filibustering expeditions throughout Central and South America. A worried Governor Douglas wrote to the Colonial Office in 1858, "The interests of the empire may suffer, from the introduction of a foreign population, whose sympathies may be decidedly anti-British, and if the majority be Americans, strongly attached to their own country and peculiar institutions. . . . There will always be hankering in their minds after annexation to the United States, and with the aid of their countrymen in Oregon and California, at hand, they will never cordially submit to British rule, nor possess the loyal feelings of British subjects."[22]

Additionally, the racial attitudes of Americans, their "prejudices as to colour and race," as Supreme Court judge Matthew Begbie, termed it, threatened the ability of a supposedly color-blind British government to function, as did the American attachment to republican and democratic forms of government.[23] Though some British immigrants looked upon the Americans with a more forgiving eye, many saw them as needlessly reckless and expressed revulsion at their habit of wearing weapons and other customs.[24] In response to the threat of democratic, disorderly, and potentially disloyal American emigrants, the colonial government would protect British Columbia through the legal institutions of the state and by encouraging the immigration of "suitable" subjects, including peoples of African descent.

With the start of the gold rush in 1858, the colonial elite in British Columbia saw the influx of Americans as potentially destabilizing. To the elites, the claims of Americans to be white men mattered far less than their perceived proclivity to violence and disorder. To counter the threat of white Americans, Governor Douglas appointed black men as Victoria's first police force shortly after their arrival. The significance of this act, especially for the black population, is hard to overstate. Though no government record of this decision survives, it seems likely that African Canadians were chosen not only for their loyalty and status as British subjects (many were Jamaican) but also to convey a message to newly arrived white Americans that they were now on British soil.[25] As Judge Begbie pointed out, "Their [the 'negro' or 'mixed negro population'] presence [is] . . . *the* test and pledge of British, as contrasted with U.S., domination."[26]

Predictably, white American resistance was high. American John Gibson remembered that "the Americans swore thay would kill every one of them [the 'Negro Police'] and that thay would do as thay had a mind to if thay did not put other men on the Police."[27] Not only were the black police "heartily despised by the Americans," but also, in at least one incident, an American crowd supported a thief who admitted his guilt but refused to be arrested by a black man.[28] In another instance, a white judge had to intervene to stop an angry crowd of whites from throwing a black officer into the harbor.[29] Forced by white Americans to choose between maintaining order with a white police force or facing a disorderly and surly American population, the colonial government soon replaced the black police officers with white British subjects.[30] Thus, almost from the beginning of the rush, the British elite began to compromise on the ideas about race they believed set them apart from their American cousins in order to establish a more orderly society. The Americans, for their part, had signaled that they were willing to abide by the laws and authority of the British, but only so far as they perceived that doing so did not threaten their status as white men.

But while the use of men of African descent as police in Victoria proved a small flashpoint between the British elite and the predominantly American population in 1858, the colonial elites' real concern was for the lower Fraser River, where the colonial state was weak and relations with the local indigenous populations precarious. Within weeks after news of gold reached San Francisco, an overwhelmingly American population had moved in unprecedented numbers into territory held by various First Nations and taken over prime areas along the Fraser River. Many of these miners believed that Native Americans were not only inferior but also dangerous. Given these circumstances, it is perhaps surprising that there were only two major incidents between miners and Native Americans, and that neither devolved into the genocidal conflict characteristic of California and Oregon.

By the time of the discovery of gold along the Fraser River in 1858, the HBC had over thirty years of direct experience with the First Nations of British Columbia, while some indigenous groups had upward of seventy years' experience dealing with European fur traders coming by land and sea.[31] Long experience had led the HBC and Native Americans to develop a system that, while framed in the language of paternalism, was more generally characterized by mutual obligation and respect. As a result, by the time gold was discovered along the Fraser River, the HBC and much of the indigenous population had developed a way of dealing with disputes that, while far from perfect, combined European and indigenous practices and recognized and respected the place of Native Americans in British Columbia.[32]

Governor Douglas, fearful of a wider conflagration, acted quickly and decisively to defuse an early conflict at Hill's Bar in late May and early June 1858. The underlying cause was a contest between members of either the Sto:lo or Nlaka'pamux First Nation and newly arrived Anglo-Americans, both of whom asserted their right to mine the bar.[33] These tensions were exacerbated when a man named Taylor began selling liquor to Native Americans, which the Americans believed would inflame their passions and precipitate an attack.[34] According to the miners, this action precipitated a series of escalating threats and posturing by both sides. The American miners responded much as they would have in California, by organizing themselves into a vigilante organization and preparing to unilaterally expel the indigenous population from their own land.

Aware only that the situation on the river was tense, Governor Douglas arrived on May 31 with the "sloop-of-war *Satellite* . . . and a dozen blue jackets on board."[35] He found the Native Americans "mustered under arms . . . threaten[ing] to make a clean sweep of the whole body of miners assembled there." Douglas defused the situation with time-honored tactics developed in years of service with the HBC. He spoke first with the indigenous population and then with the miners, informing the miners that they had no "rights of occupation to the soil[,] . . . that Her Majesty's Government ignored their very existence in that part of the country, which was not open for the purpose of settlement, and they were permitted to remain there merely on sufferance; that no abuses would be tolerated, and that the Laws would protect the rights of the Indian, no less than those of the white man."[36] Douglas accompanied this assertion of authority with the appointment of a British subject, George Perrier, as justice of the peace, as well as of several "Indian Magistrates," indigenous men who would "bring forward when required any man of their several Tribes, who may be charged with offences against the Laws of the country," to enforce British law on both the indigenous and white populations.[37]

By resolving the conflict at Hill's Bar in this manner, Douglas asserted the power and sovereignty of the British state over both white and nonwhite inhabitants. By asserting that the rights of Native Americans and whites were equal, he articulated a key reason that British Columbia differed from California: in British Columbia, the state was colorblind. While ensuring that the white miners could continue to mine, Douglas positioned the colonial order of British Columbia, and the white men who ran it, as a superior alternative to the government of California, one that did not endorse independent warfare against Native Americans.

The next major incident, often referred to as the Fraser River War, bore many of the hallmarks of California Indian fighting, leading at least one scholar to suggest that the Fraser River was an extension of the California mining and Indian warfare frontier.[38] In some ways, the Fraser River War was a quintessentially Californian conflict. In response to perceived "outrages"—a code for everything ranging from rumors of violent resistance, to theft, to Native Americans asserting ownership over their own territory—white miners gathered in mass meetings, appointed leaders, and organized militia units to "chastise" the indigenous peoples of the Fraser Canyon without waiting for, or seeking, approval from Victoria. Here, however, the similarities between the Fraser River and California end. The Fraser River War did not degenerate into a genocidal bloodbath but instead ended with a series of treaties between the First Nations of the Fraser Canyon and the white miners. How and why this occurred draws attention to the evolution of how white settlers in British Columbia thought of themselves and of natives, in comparison to their counterparts in California.

Tensions had been mounting with the First Nations of the Fraser Canyon since the arrival, earlier in the summer of 1858, of predominately American miners. As more and more miners began to move up the Fraser River, they pushed into territory controlled and used by various First Nations, who responded by asserting their continued right to the land. In August, near the confluence of the Thompson and Fraser Rivers, a French miner fired on some Nlaka'pamux, and the resulting firefight killed two men on each side. Matters might have ended there, but a large prospecting party of about sixty miners that rushed to the scene "immediately commenced firing on the Indians and killed nine of them." This started a wholesale panic among the miners in the upper Fraser Canyon, and hundreds fled downriver to Fort Yale or Fort Hope, British Columbia, or left altogether.[39] The Nlaka'pamux, for their part, abandoned their lower villages and moved farther up the canyon and deeper into the surrounding mountains. As they retreated down the canyon, the miners burnt several unoccupied villages, destroying homes and supplies needed for the coming winter.[40]

The miners on the Fraser acted as if they had been expecting an Indian war because, to a large extent, they had. Many of the miners came from California, with its history of genocidal Indian wars, and those who came from elsewhere had read or heard enough about indigenous peoples to "know" that they were dangerous, warlike, and treacherous. More immediately, isolated attacks by Native Americans on whites and vice versa had raised the possibility of conflict, a possibility that rumors and circumstantial evidence seemed to support. For weeks, vague rumors of mutilated bodies washing down the river had circulated among the miners.[41] Fear of Native Americans gave these stories credibility and fueled the growing hysteria.

As in California and elsewhere in North America, white miners claimed that outside provocateurs incited and encouraged Native American hostility. In the Fraser Canyon, two groups quickly came to share the blame for the state of affairs: degraded whites who sold liquor to Native Americans, and Chinese miners who supplied them with arms and ammunition.[42] The hastily formed militia units, composed of white miners, that departed Fort Yale on August 18 sought to reopen the Fraser to mining by dealing with the indigenous population and these other threats. The Fraser River War was a conflict about respectable white men reestablishing order over a range of socially marginal groups, not just Native Americans.

Mirroring California, two factions put forward different strategies for dealing with the Nlaka'pamux. The smaller faction, led by two Americans, Graham and Galloway, "avow[ed] their intention to make it a 'war to the knife,' on men, women and children." The larger faction, led by the American Harry Snyder and supported by the French Canadian John Centras, "endeavor[ed] to effect a peace with the Indians by peaceable means if possible, and only as a last resort to use force." Supported by the majority of the miners, Snyder, by threatening to withdraw and leave Graham's much smaller company exposed, convinced Graham to follow behind and come up the river only if needed.[43] The miners supported Snyder for pragmatic and ideological reasons. Snyder argued that a peace policy would yield results sooner, allowing the men to return to mining on the river. While the danger of Indian fighting had a certain appeal to gold rushers seeking to assert an identity as tough, manly, white men, it was also a distraction from economic opportunities and risks of mining.

The rough terrain of the canyon and the strategy of the Nlaka'pamux also discouraged miners from seeking to exterminate the indigenous population. By withdrawing into the rugged country around the canyon, the Nlaka'pamux virtually ensured any war would be long, bloody, and, just as important to the white miners, expensive. Indeed, the militia units that departed Fort Yale took only five days' worth of supplies with them, demonstrating their unwillingness and inability to engage in a protracted conflict.[44] These factors allowed the proponents of treaty-making to control the situation, even in the face of what many believed was the start of an all-out war in the colony.

The remainder of the Fraser River War can be quickly described. Acting on his own authority, Snyder made a series of "treaties" with the Nlaka'pamux that included the return of property allegedly stolen by the indigenous peoples of the canyon in exchange for an end to hostilities. Shortly after the first negotiations were concluded, Graham's party was attacked by warriors who had not been informed of the treaty. Graham and his lieutenant, James Shaw, were the only casualties of the attack. The death of Graham and the panic among his company took whatever wind remained out of the sails of the "war to the knife" faction. Most commentators blamed Graham for his own death, because he trampled a white flag sent by Snyder and failed to post sentries. Within days, Snyder and his men returned to Yale, accompanied by five chiefs from the upper canyon, to whom Snyder wished to demonstrate the numbers and strength of the white population.[45] Chinese miners and those suspected of selling liquor to Native Americans were harassed and encouraged to leave until the situation had settled.[46] By the time Governor Douglas arrived with a force of thirty-five men, the miners had been back at work for a week, and many had returned to the upper canyon.[47] At Fort Hope, Douglas met with the Nlaka'pamux chiefs who had accompanied Snyder downriver. Douglas reassured the chiefs they were under the protection of Her Majesty's Government, gave them gifts, and offered "much useful advice for their guidance in the altered state of the country." Seeking to address some of the perceived underlying causes of the conflict, Douglas banned the sale or gift of liquor to Native Americans and reserved some sections of the river for their exclusive use.[48]

As Douglas acted to calm relations in the aftermath of the Fraser River War, he was already embarking upon a process that pushed the American and British miners together by dividing them from Native Americans. In the immediate aftermath of the Fraser River War, Douglas approached Snyder and offered him a position in the colonial bureaucracy, an offer Snyder politely declined.[49] Though Douglas was probably trying to shore up the colonial government by incorporating an influential local leader, he was not the type to appoint someone he regarded as incapable of acting in accordance with the wishes of the British empire. By pursuing a peace policy with the local First Nations, and by controlling the excesses of the more hard-line miners, an American, Snyder, had acted much as Douglas might have in his place.

A close examination of miners' meetings during the conflict also raises questions about any assumption that the mostly American miners believed their interests were incompatible with those of the colonial government. Although a letter drafted by the residents of Fort Hope laid some of the blame for the situation at the feet of colonial officials, their solution was to call for more active government.[50] Various other correspondents also complained about the lack of colonial authority in the Fraser Canyon, particularly in view of the mining licenses most of the men had paid for.[51] Here, too, Douglas addressed the miners' concerns, appointing a justice of the peace and a chief constable in Hope when he arrived in September.[52] That American miners wanted greater British authority is important because of the strong correlation between self-identification and what constituted an acceptable form of government. Given the strong link between ideas of race, citizenship, and good government in the United States, this suggests that some Americans saw British colonial officials as fundamentally similar to white men.

Though too late to avoid the Fraser River War, a well-functioning bureaucracy is what Douglas sought to create in the Fraser Canyon. From the conflict, Douglas learned that the American miners wanted competent officials, and that the ideological distance between at least some Americans and the British colonial elite was not as great as he had first feared. It is ironic, then, that the relative dearth of capable colonial officials in British Columbia would be a recurring source of friction between Douglas and the American miners. By the end of the year, the incompetence of the colonial officials around Fort Yale sparked an armed conflict between two groups of Americans, which drew in the colonial government. This conflict came to be known as "Ned McGowan's War."

The "war" itself started just after Christmas 1858, when a dispute over jurisdiction between Justices Peter Whannell of Yale and George Perrier of Hill's Bar resulted in Whannell arresting Perrier's constable. In response, Perrier swore in Edward McGowan and twelve to fourteen other Hill's Bar men as special constables and issued a warrant for the arrest of Whannell, the freeing of the constable, and the transfer of a witness to Hill's Bar.

Edward (or Ned "Ubiquitous") McGowan was a former judge and high-ranking member of the Democratic Party of San Francisco. He had spent months in hiding while being hunted as an accessory to murder during the second Vigilance Committee's reign in 1856. Though he eventually cleared his name, McGowan realized that he was a marked man as long as he remained in California and, along with many other law-and-order faction members, followed reports of gold north in 1858. McGowan arrived in British Columbia with many friends but also with an unenviable reputation. Proceeding to Hill's Bar, he quickly emerged as a leading figure in the American community there.[53]

Arriving at Yale, McGowan's posse seized Whannell at gunpoint from his bench and hauled him to Hill's Bar, where Perrier fined him twenty-five dollars for contempt of court.[54] Whannell was then released, whereupon he immediately returned to Yale and penned a frantic dispatch to Governor Douglas charging that "a lawless band of ruffians" led by McGowan had usurped his authority and, by extension, the authority of the Crown. This report led Douglas to dispatch a small military force under Colonel Richard

Moody, a police force under Chief Gold Commissioner Chartres Brew, and the newly appointed Supreme Court judge of British Columbia, Matthew Begbie, to the scene.[55]

Historians have interpreted Ned McGowan's War as a challenge to the authority of the colonial government by a dangerous and unruly American mob, led by a known criminal, Ned McGowan. In this narrative, if not for the strong and decisive action of colonial authority, "McGowan might have turned his comic revolt into a genuine takeover and become the *de facto* ruler of the gold fields," possibly resulting in American annexation.[56] In reality, however, Ned McGowan's War resulted from two distinct, but inter-related, conflicts: one between the various colonial officials in and around Yale, and the other between remnants of the Vigilance Committee and the law-and-order faction of San Francisco. The war did not represent a challenge to British ideas of order or the authority of the British colonial state. Instead, the Americans mainly concerned themselves with their own conflict; and when they acted, they acted in support of one colonial official against the other.

At the time of Ned McGowan's War, the American population near Yale had divided into two camps: south of Yale at Hill's Bar, McGowan and other former Democratic Party operatives from San Francisco were the dominant force and, according to at least one account, harassed and threatened former vigilantes passing by on their way up the river.[57] The former vigilantes clustered in Yale, where their most prominent member was Dr. Max Fifer. Both factions remained antagonistic and looked to settle old scores.[58]

Such a tense situation would have required the united efforts of skilled colonial officials to manage. Unfortunately, the officials around Yale were particularly ill suited to their jobs. Richard Hicks, Yale's revenue officer, was denounced by the miners there as "an unscrupulous man, as well as a corrupt public officer."[59] Whannell shared these concerns about Hicks and would, over the next few months, consistently charge Hicks with bribery, corruption, "disgraceful intoxication," and dereliction of duty.[60] Judge Begbie, upon arriving in Yale in February 1859, found that "Mr. Hicks is totally unworthy of serving Her Majesty in any capacity whatever: and that it wod be . . . proper that criminal proceeding shod be instituted against him."[61]

Whannell, for his part, was a fraud. Though he represented himself as an officer of the Royal Victoria Yeomanry Corps, he had actually served only as a private before deserting to California, where he owned a saloon.[62]

According to some reports, Whannell was given to bombastic and erratic behavior, especially when drunk, which was a not-uncommon occurrence.[63] The justice for Hill's Bar, George Perrier, seems to have shared some of the weaknesses of character, if not the same checkered past, as Whannell. In Begbie's analysis, the greatest factor contributing to Ned McGowan's War was that both Perrier and Whannell were "carried away with the most unbounded ideas of the dignity of their offices and themselves."[64] More than just being unfamiliar with the law, Perrier and Whannell did not have the strength of character that British elites felt should characterize colonial officials.

In fastening the blame for the disturbances on Whannell and Perrier, Begbie emphasized a particularly British vision of society. British ideas of authority and order were "derived from the person of the official, who had to be visibly invested with the dignity of office," in contrast to beliefs in California, where order was "inseparable from the morality of the population in general" and from the forms of authority there.[65] This is why in California, vigilantes could assert legitimacy by claiming to act in the interests of the population and by assuming the roles of judges, lawyers, and juries and holding unsanctioned trials. In British Columbia, the key to preserving order was to admit only the proper type of men to the upper levels of colonial service. This had two major repercussions. First, it confirmed that most Americans, with their dangerously democratic notions, should be disqualified from public office, and it raised concerns about their participation in politics at all. Second, it meant that colonial officials were expected to act in accordance with the values of restrained manhood, in explicit contrast to the mass of settlers who embraced more martial virtues. Through their conduct during Ned McGowan's War, Whannell and Perrier demonstrated that they lacked the strength of character necessary for their positions.

The colonial officials dispatched upriver generally expressed pleasant surprise at the miners' conduct. Instead of encountering a rebel army, Colonel Richard Moody reported a peaceful march to Hill's Bar, where he received a gun salute and "three long loud cheers," after which Moody "thanked them in the Queen's name for their loyal reception."[66] Soon after, the miners held a public meeting, which commenced with "3 cheers for the Governor" followed by an address "with a good many epithets, pitching heavily into Whannell." Moody stopped the address and asked the Americans to redo it without the epithets, and they complied.[67] By so doing,

Moody and the Americans agreed to a form of public discourse more in keeping with British notions of propriety. Of course, the fact that Moody was listening to a public meeting underscored that this was actually a compromise. While the language and behavior of the meeting reflected British notions of class and status, the forum was American.

The fizzling-out of Ned McGowan's War demonstrated that the Americans around Yale, far from challenging the authority of the colonial state, actively supported it as long as it was basically competent and fair. When McGowan and his "lieutenant," identified only as Kelly, appeared before Begbie and Brew, they claimed "that they were acting under virtue of a warrant from a justice of the peace [which] they were in fact precluded from even questioning." Begbie and Brew agreed with this line of reasoning and dismissed both men.[68] The day after the trial, Colonel Moody, Lieutenant Richard Mayne, and Judge Begbie toured Hill's Bar, where McGowan toasted the queen with champagne, much to the delight of his guests.[69] Moody even speculated that with "*watching*," it might be possible to convert McGowan "into a valuable subject of the Crown eventually."[70] Moody, at least, seems to have reached the conclusion that McGowan and his countrymen could be assimilated to English principles, given time and competent governance.

McGowan's War suggests that colonial officials were finding a way to be open to a degree of "Americanness" in British Columbia, pragmatically using stereotypical American public forms like mass meetings and resolutions in a manner that supported British authority and conceptions of order. The colonial elite maintained the peace in the colony, even as they hoped to enlighten the American population to British values. By 1859, many Americans had pronounced the lower Fraser a "humbug" and returned to California; and in the coming years, an increasing percentage of immigration consisted of British subjects.[71] As the demographics began to change and the colonial elite grew more accustomed to those Americans who remained, the process of compromise and conciliation between the white American and British population accelerated.

Conversely, McGowan's War demonstrates that the American population was growing more and more obviously comfortable with British colonial authority. By embracing British colonial governance, Americans of European descent signaled that they saw Anglo-Saxon British subjects as fellow white men. To white Americans, only white men could create and administer a government that would be a tolerable alternative to a republic.

Just what this emerging American emphasis on race would mean, and whether the British population would reject or adopt it, would fuel ongoing controversies in the colony.

"SHALL WHITE MEN OR NIGGERS RULE IN THIS COLONY?"

On Vancouver Island, as the fear of American disorder on the lower Fraser began to ebb, the black population continued to be at the center of a debate over whether British Columbia should be a racially organized society akin to that of California, or one in which class, status, and nationality determined an individual's place. The British colonial elite claimed that the treatment of the black population was "*the* test and pledge of British, as contrasted with U.S., domination," but as the quick backtracking on the black police force indicates, the commitment of the elite to equitable treatment was questionable at best.[72] Indeed, equality probably would have remained a largely rhetorical gesture if not for the actions of the African Canadian community. It was the decision of this community to actively assert claims to equality, not the halfhearted commitment of the colonial elite, that propelled the issue of the place of people of African descent in British Columbia to the fore of debates over colonial hierarchy. At the same time, however, the support of the colonial government was crucial to the efforts of the black community to assert an equal status; and that support waxed and waned in response to how the colonial elite perceived the threat of white Americans and the utility of the black population in countering that threat.

When the initial group of thirty to forty black immigrants arrived in Victoria, they found an early supporter in Reverend Edward Cridge of the Anglican Church.[73] Cridge visited with community leaders shortly after their arrival and expressed support for their desire to worship in an integrated setting.[74] For several months, Anglican services were integrated without incident, but on August 24,1858, someone using the pseudonym "Sharpstone" wrote a letter to the *Gazette* complaining of the "*aromatic luxury*" of the African Canadian members and linked integrated church services to interracial unions. In arguing for segregated church services, Sharpstone conflated class and racial divisions, asserting that "the English nation are divided into classes. The negro has his place, there, and ever will have so long as his skin is black."[75] The next day, Mifflin Gibbs, merchant and future U.S. consul to Madagascar, lashed back at the man he labeled

"Dullstone," pointing out that the population of African descent had come to British Columbia on the promise that "they should have the same legal protection, and enjoy the same immunities—other things being equal—as could the most favored subject; and that the color of their skin should never debar them from their rights."[76] Cridge, for his part, informed the congregation that there was no difference between whites and blacks, before God or on Earth. However, he also reached out to the Americans in his congregation, stressed his "high respect" for Americans and insisted that the seating arrangement had not been a "studied insult" but, rather, "an honest endeavor to do the best which circumstances allowed." Cridge ended by hinting that a more "commodious" church would solve the problem.[77] Evidently, the lecture and Gibb's letter had the intended effect, as there were no more complaints until the arrival of Reverend William Clarke later that month and Reverend Matthew Macfie in September, both Congregationalists.

Despite both being sent by the British Congregational Missionary Society, Clarke and Macfie held widely divergent views on race and on the place of people of African descent within the church. Though the Anglican and Methodist churches were already integrated, Clarke, an ardent abolitionist, made it a point to appeal to the black community. Evidence does not survive, but it seems likely, given his strong views on race and his calling as a minister, that he espoused ideas of social equality and other abolitionist viewpoints. This would seem to be the only explanation for why his congregation, out of all the integrated congregations, drew such attention.[78] Clarke's stance led to a decline in the number of white parishioners, a trend that was exacerbated when Macfie criticized him for promoting miscegenation and opened a church that segregated people of African descent. The battle between Clarke and Macfie quickly escalated as Clarke found himself preaching to an ever-smaller and ever-blacker congregation.[79] Opposition to Clarke was about more than just the integration of religious services. As one speech in support of Macfie put it, the question was really, "Shall white men or niggers rule in this Colony?"[80] White Americans, in particular, perceived Clarke as a disturbing symbol of racial equality. By labeling him a "nigger preacher," deserting his church, and actively discouraging new arrivals from attending, Macfie's mostly American supporters made Clarke's position in the colony financially precarious. The deathblow to Clarke's church came, ironically, from the black population. Not wanting to be associated with a "blacks-only" church, and recognizing that Clarke was, in many ways, doing more harm than good, the majority of church-going blacks in Victoria chose to attend Reverend Cridge's Anglican Church. By the spring of 1860, Reverend Clarke had left, though the British Congregational Missionary Society eventually upheld his actions and ordered Macfie to integrate his church. Macfie attempted to comply, but, unsurprisingly, no people of color attended, and the church remained lily-white until Macfie left the colony in 1864.[81]

The church dispute demonstrated the support each vision of colonial society had. While members of the colonial elite were willing to take a stand in support of the black population, this support could go only so far before an American-led pushback made it too troublesome. The dispute signaled that the society emerging in the early years of the rush would be more racially tolerant than that of California, but only up to a point. The widespread criticism of Clarke, and the eventual collapse of his ministry, reflected the outer limits of racial toleration in the colony. As the dispute demonstrates, the notion that ideal white manliness in the colony endorsed colorblindness (and consequently emphasized national differences) was contested from the early months of the gold rush.

The reactions of the general population and the three British ministers to these disputes reveal conflicting attitudes toward race and class in the colony in the early years of the rush. Clarke represented a particularly British way of organizing society along class lines, while Macfie tended strongly toward a more American way of organizing society through racial divisions. Macfie's racial divisions repulsed many liberal whites, in addition to the African Canadian population, while Clarke's approach offended not only many Americans but also a large segment of the Canadian population that was increasingly uncomfortable with ideas of racial mixing.[82] As a result, Clarke and Macfie represent the clash of two different logics for organizing society in British Columbia. Cridge, however, represents the beginnings of a compromise between these two logics. By opposing segregation, Cridge maintained British standards in respect to race; but by reaching out to the American population and alluding to the possibility of a future compromise, he provided some legitimacy for distinctions made on the basis of race and, therefore, for the American manner of organizing society.

The debate over segregation did not disappear with the end of the church controversy. In 1860, African Canadians contributed financial support to the new Victoria volunteer fire company, only to find that while the white

Americans who ran the company welcomed their money, they balked at black participation. This rebuff led directly to African Canadians' organization of Victoria's first rifle company, to which they denied any white men admittance.[83] Critical to the initial success and eventual failure of the rifle company was the amount of support tendered by the colonial government. Under Douglas, the Vancouver Island Volunteer Rifle Corps enjoyed limited financial support and the use of outmoded rifles with which to drill. However, with the arrival of Governor Arthur Kennedy in 1864 and the organization of a white rifle company, this moral and financial support was withdrawn and the company collapsed soon after.[84]

The most serious contest, however, was in November 1860 over the segregation of the Colonial Theatre in Victoria. The Colonial Theatre had originally been integrated, but following protests by white patrons, the management restricted patrons of color to "six or eight seats in the back part of the parquette." In late October 1860, when a black man sat in the main part of the theater, white patrons pelted him with eggs. The next day, members of the local African Canadian community, led by George Washington and Thomas Anderson, had a friend buy tickets for them to the "white" section of the theater. On the night of November 3, a crowd of between thirty and two hundred black men arrived and demanded entrance. When they were refused, they forced their way in and a melee ensued. By the time the police arrived fifteen minutes later, several men on both sides had been severely beaten with chairs, slung-shots, and fists, and the protestors had set the theater on fire in two places. At the trial of three of the black men for inciting a riot, Lambert Beatty, one of the owners, testified that, in an attempt to disperse the crowd, he had told the protestors, "Gentlemen you are doing wrong," to which Adolph Richards had replied, "You white son of a bitch[,] are we [doing wrong?]" The black population saw the segregation of the theater as part of a disturbing trend within the colony to re-create the racial stratification of the United States. At the same time, they felt confident enough to protest in a manner that could have easily resulted in a lynch mob in the United States.[85] Support from the colonial government remained tepid, however, and the dispute continued to erupt periodically for the next four years.[86]

Faced with continued hostility to racial equality from many white inhabitants, the colonial government remained unwilling to do much beyond affirm the principles of racial equality. This was because, ultimately, the colonial elite had two interlocking goals: to maintain an orderly and peaceful society and to preserve its control of the colonial government. While these goals encouraged the colonial elite to emphasize the differences between British and American society, they also meant the elite had a fairly pragmatic view of the large and vocal white American population in the colony. An idealistic stance on the grounds of racial equality could threaten colonial order by aggravating the white Americans. Although official and public discourse still tended to portray British white men as better than American white men, on-the-ground experiences and official wavering were undercutting a sense of a real difference. As the first years of the gold rush drew to a close, a noticeable decrease in state and white Britons' support for the African Canadian population's claims to equality signified a greater emphasis on racial divisions and a concurrent de-emphasis on national divisions.

POLITICAL MANEUVERINGS

When it suited the interests of the Family-Company-Compact, the principles of racial equality could be enforced in sometimes startling ways. In late 1859, Governor Douglas prorogued the Vancouver Island Assembly, the token elected body that advised the governor, and new elections were held.[87] For the first time, the "government party" faced real competition, most notably from a Nova Scotian émigré (by way of California) named Amor De Cosmos. De Cosmos had changed his name from William Smith in California either to ensure his mail would be delivered or because, as he put it, "It is an unusual name and its meaning tells what I love most, viz.: Love of order, beauty, the world, the universe." From his position as editor of the *Daily British Colonist*, De Cosmos had become the leading voice of the "reform" faction in Victoria politics.[88] De Cosmos attacked Douglas as a corrupt, despotic, and incompetent official who did not know "the feelings of free born Englishmen" and who instead sought to preserve power and privilege for himself and his HBC cronies.[89] De Cosmos argued that the assembly needed to wrest power away from Douglas as the first step toward a fully representative government. Already a considerable thorn in Douglas's side, De Cosmos and his potential election to the assembly in 1860 only promised to make Douglas's problems worse.

Douglas found the solution in the black population of Victoria. Because the colony had no naturalization law, the franchise was effectively restricted to British-born males.[90] Shortly before the election, however, Judge David Cameron (Douglas's brother-in-law) and Attorney General George Cary approached Mifflin Gibbs and told him "that colored people who had no political *status* in any other country had a perfect right to vote here on taking the oath of allegiance."[91] In other words, because the *Dred Scott* (1857) decision had denied African Americans the status of citizens, they had no citizenship to be "erased" with a naturalization law. The African Americans took advantage of this opportunity to secure the franchise—which was not available to white Americans—and eighteen voted as a bloc on January 7 for Cary and Selim Franklin, giving them the two available spots in the assembly and denying De Cosmos a seat.[92] De Cosmos and the reform faction were livid. The subsequent debate highlighted the contentious place of national and racial identity on Vancouver Island.

Both the reform and the government faction claimed to act on behalf of British and "foreign" (namely, American) settlers at the same time that both disavowed American republicanism and racial attitudes in favor of British-style representative government and social order. Partly this was the result of political pragmatism. As long as the franchise was restricted to British nationals, it would be political suicide not to focus on appealing to British subjects.[93] More than this, both factions believed that British-style governance was superior to its American counterpart. Where they differed was over the ideal balance of power between the governor and the elected assembly and who should constitute that assembly.

The presumed republican and racial attitudes of white Americans were the unspoken issue of the 1860 election. When black Americans seized the opportunity to vote offered by the government faction, "Shears," a particularly vitriolic reform faction partisan, denounced them for flattering themselves in believing they had triumphed "over American prejudices, or add[ed] some imaginary privilege to the catalogue of rights guaranteed to them in common with all British subjects." Shears fumed that they "sold themselves to the worst enemy of their country" for "fair *promises* of an indefinite amount of that myth called social equality," when "neither Attorney-Generals nor Governors can increase or diminish the constitutional rights of a British subject, black or white." By making the election about race, Shears argued, the black voters had betrayed their country and their countrymen. Shears concluded by arguing that the election had demonstrated why "the world is so ready to believe that the colored race is unfit for freedom," and that a backlash by white Englishmen and liberal white Americans, combined with continued indifference on the part of the government, would make the black population "curse the day they sold themselves to a petty monopoly."[94] For Shears, at least, race had no place as a political issue in English politics, but racial categories did have explanatory value for an individual's fitness to vote. Shears was, in essence, elucidating the basis of the racial order that was emerging in British Columbia, one that used the rhetoric of colorblindness and national difference to disguise a social order increasingly predicated on the assumption of white male superiority.

The reply from the government faction's *Gazette* the next day sought to tie the reformers to American racism, noting their use of the term *nigger* and their attempts to show the African Canadian population as unfit for suffrage. The *Gazette* argued that the "manly and straight-forward" African Canadians voted for "those two candidates, whom they thought the most English in idea—the most likely to support English institutions—and the working of which they know—and thereby benefit the country." In contrast, the reformers would threaten the ideals of British political equality by "wrest[ing] from [the African Canadian population] the privileges they possess." In other words, it was the reformers who were motivated by un-British considerations of race, while the population of African descent acted in the best traditions of freeborn Englishmen.[95]

And yet, the *Gazette* also had to acknowledge that racial categories had meaning in Victoria. Underlying the defense of African Canadian suffrage was the assumption that, without an active defense, racial categories could quickly undermine the ideal of colorblind English values and political participation. It was Gibbs who most explicitly tied the reform faction to American racial attitudes, describing the election as "a victory of the philanthropic and magnanimous English principles over the rowdyism and prejudice of that portion of the population which held American sympathies."[96] Gibbs's implication was that most white Americans were fundamentally unsuited to political participation in an English colony. Ultimately, the colonial government was more than willing to push the limits of racial equality for African Canadians as long as the political value outweighed the cost. This was pragmatism gilded with idealism, the shallowness of which became apparent in the 1861 assembly election when the government sided with Joseph Trutch, a white man with close connections to Governor Douglas but whose candidacy was illegal, rather than back Jacob Francis, an African Canadian.[97]

The tenuous nature of government support for racial equality is also evident in the judicial system. In September 1860, two African Canadian men called to serve on a jury in the town of Douglas were confronted with a white-led meeting of indignant citizens opposed to sitting on the same jury as black men.[98] As a result of this protest, the government did not call a person of African descent to serve on a jury again until 1872.[99] White Americans occasionally served on juries, a trend that only accelerated after the passage of An Act to Provide for the Naturalization of Aliens in November 1861, which allowed immigrants to become British subjects.[100] Even before the law was passed, it was often difficult for Begbie and others to determine whether an individual was an American citizen or British subject.[101] In contrast, the assumed place of African Canadians, Chinese, and Native Americans in court was as litigants or witnesses, not as jurors.[102] In both the courts and at the polls, American-born whites gained power at the same time that people of color saw their influence diminish. That these trends seemed to have occurred with the tacit approval of many of the British settlers in the colony, including the colonial elite, speaks to a growing convergence in worldviews between the white American and British populations, a convergence predicated on assumed commonalities based on race.

THE CHANGING TIDE

By the middle years of the 1860s, increasing numbers of both white American and British colonists assumed common bonds of whiteness even as they acknowledged that national origins gave each group a particular flavor. This was particularly evident in the final major conflict of the gold rush period, the Tsilhqot'in crisis of 1864.[103] Alfred Waddington's attempt to build a road from Bute Inlet to the Cariboo Mountains precipitated the crisis. The proposed road went directly through territory of the Tsilhqot'in, a nation that had experienced relatively little direct contact with the colonial state until this time. By 1864, Waddington's road crews had been at work in Tsilhqot'in territory for almost two years. Then, on the morning of April 30, approximately a dozen Tsilhqot'in warriors under the leadership of a man called Klatsassin surprised seventeen workers in their tents and killed fourteen.[104] After killing a ferryman and another isolated party working on the western portion of the road, the warriors moved east and attacked the crew approaching from that direction.[105] This time, however, forewarned by the indigenous wife of one of the work crew, a running battle ensued; while three more workers died, the rest of the party escaped.[106] Word of the attacks spread throughout the colony, and most of the settler population left the affected area.

The colonial government responded to the attacks by forming an expedition composed of marines, militia units, and special constables, who would operate in two columns under Gold Commissioners Chartres Brew and George Cox.[107] Though the largest demonstration of force in British Columbian history to that time, the expedition faced the nearly insurmountable challenge of locating a small group of Tsilhqot'in in a large and virtually unknown territory. While Brew and his men endured considerable hardship hiking through Tsilhqot'in territory, Cox simply built a fort and waited.[108] Much to the surprise of the newspapers and colonial elite, Klatsassin and seven of his supporters seemingly presented themselves at Cox's camp on August 15 and were arrested.[109] Unbeknownst to the wider public, Cox had lured the Tsilhqot'in to the camp under the pretense of negotiations. After a brief trial, Klatsassin, Telloot, Pielle, Tahpit, and Chessus were found guilty of murder in September and executed on October 26 at Quesnellemouth.[110]

The attacks and their aftermath ignited an intense debate over the proper response of the colonial authorities, a debate that highlighted changing attitudes toward race, gender, and nationality in the colony. Though different factions within colonial society sought to explain the attack in different ways, by the end of May public opinion in British Columbia was in general agreement that "fear is the only power that can keep such savages in entire subjection," and that the colonial government had not impressed that fear upon the indigenous population.[111] It is clear that the mainland and island populations, both consisting of American and British white settlers, shared stereotypical views of Native Americans as greedy, irrational, and childlike—in a word, savage. To these populations, the superiority of the white man over the Native Americans justified colonialism, and the supposed racial inferiority of Native Americans meant that domination had to be "demonstrated."

This unanimity was undercut, however, by the question of whether Klatsassin and his supporters had committed an act of war or of murder, a question that had very real implications for how settlers in British Columbia thought of race and gender, particularly as manifested through political and legal systems. The dominant position, and the one supported by the colonial government, was that the indigenous people should be treated as criminals and dealt with by the judicial system in the hope of precluding a general Indian war. On June 2, however, an emergency meeting was held in Victoria following reports (later proved false) of another massacre by the Tsilhqot'in. At the emergency meeting, the speakers (who included notable community leaders such as Amor De Cosmos, Alfred Waddington, and the mayor) argued that Native Americans "knew no law but blood for blood," and that the Tsilhqot'in should be hanged without trial. Interestingly, British subjects organized this meeting, with its echoes of California's Indian conflicts, and probably made up a significant portion of the audience, suggesting the degree to which American ideals of civic participation and perceptions of the proper response to Native American "aggression" had taken root in the psyche of the British population on Vancouver Island by 1864.[112] The opposition criticized this meeting, and the sentiments it espoused, for replicating "the American doctrine of 'manifest destiny' in its most fatal form."[113] Even as American and British attitudes grew more alike in practice, the idea of unacceptable American racial attitudes remained rhetorically powerful.

Proponents of treating the attack as a criminal matter drew heavily on the idea of national difference to explain and justify their position. They argued that American Indian policy, with its perceived emphasis on warfare and extermination, was antithetical to the British goal of educating and civilizing colonized peoples.[114] In contrast, British Indian policy, as practiced in British Columbia, "assumed a paternal oversight of the Indians, treating them as minors," a policy that would lead to Native Americans being "peaceable, orderly and well disposed towards the Government."[115] For this group, the proper role of the white man in colonial society was not as a slayer of indigenous peoples but as a father figure to racialized children.

This explains why the Tsilhqot'in crisis also prompted criticism of Governor Douglas's strategy of securing the allegiance of indigenous peoples through gift giving.[116] Instead of being based in what Governor Arthur Kennedy, Douglas's newly arrived successor, called "strict justice, good faith, and the greatest firmness,"[117] Governor Douglas's Indian policy could, in the eyes of at least one critic, "be summed up in two words—*cunning* and *deceit*."[118] Another critic argued that "a policy which may have proved tolerably successful in bartering brass buttons and glass beads for skins [was] hardly the thing to regulate the intercourse of the British Government with these 'ancient lords of the soil,'" because it degraded both whites and Native

Americans. It was, therefore, crucial that a new Indian policy be implemented in the colonies, one that would reflect the changing vision of how white men should act. The result was Brew's and George Cox's Tsilhqot'in expeditions, which sought to marry a demonstration of strength with the restraint of the law. No longer, argued critics, would British Columbian Indian policy be based on deception and bribery and reflect poorly on the character of the officials who carried it out. Instead, strength tempered with restraint would subdue the naturally effeminate indigenous population and confirm the white manhood of the colonial government and population.[119] The members of the British expeditions, and particularly the two leaders, Gold Commissioners Chartres Brew and George Cox would, therefore come to be seen as symbolic of an emerging idea of white manliness that blended ideas of restrained manhood and martial manhood in British Columbia.

The capture of Klatsassin raised questions about the character of George Cox and threatened to undermine the legitimacy of the entire project. Within two weeks, reports began to circulate that suggested the capture did not demonstrate that manly strength could cow the indigenous population. According to the later reports, Cox had given the Tsilhqot'in gifts, insinuated that he wanted to make peace and "friends," and invited the Tsilhqot'in into camp to negotiate. When they arrived, the Tsilhqot'in "found to their surprise that they were surrounded by armed men, who informed them that they were prisoners, and ordered them to lay down their arms."[120] Cox's personal and professional behavior added weight to this allegation of wrongdoing. There were suggestions that Cox had taken up with a "Hideous Klootchman [indigenous woman] with one eye," thereby degrading himself as a "squaw man."[121] Even more concerning was that Cox built a fort and waited, while Brew's party endured considerable hardship hiking through Tsilhqot'in territory.[122] That Brew was considered the better officer and the more likely to succeed was evident even in the letter from Arthur Birch, the colonial secretary, appointing Cox to command the expedition. "The Governor trusts," wrote Birch, "that under the experienced management of Mr. Brew, the well disposed Indians will be induced to capture and hand over the Murderers."[123] It is clear that both the government and the public were concerned that Cox lacked the character necessary to command one of the expeditions.

The newly appointed governor, Frederick Seymour, worried that, if true, these rumors might affect future dealings with other First Nations, and therefore he ordered "the strictest investigation."[124] Judge Begbie concluded that Klatsassin "was completely in the dark as to the consequences of his entering Mr. Cox's camp," but attributed this to a lack of knowledge on the part of Cox and the deliberate manipulation of the situation by the interpreter, Alexis, a Tsilhqot'in chief who evidently wanted to maintain peaceful relations. Ultimately, Begbie concluded that because Cox had not deliberately misled Klatsassin and the others, and because the Tsilhqot'in were, in his opinion, "on the very verge" of "being fairly hunted down," the surrender was inevitable and the honor of the British state had been preserved.[125] The governor and council ultimately agreed "that no promise of any sort was made to any of these Indians by Mr. Cox on their surrender[,] and that there was no reason why the justly deserved sentence of death imposed on five of them by the Law should not forthwith be carried out."[126] In the end, Cox's reputation as a respectable white man was upheld, and through him, the justness of British Columbian Indian policy was confirmed.

The Tsilhqot'in crisis revealed how a unifying category of whiteness could exist in a colonial setting in which national identities still had significant traction. With the fears of American domination fast receding, British subjects in the colony continued to stress differences between the British and American forms of government while simultaneously welcoming greater white American participation in colonial society. Under a proper, British, style of government, white Americans could be perfectly acceptable members of colonial society. The Tsilhqot'in crisis revealed that the differentiation between white-Americans-as-cousins and republican-government-as-dangerous had, by 1864, largely laid to rest the old fears about the American population of the colony. Instead of fearing an American uprising, the concern now was that a unitary body of white men, acting through the colonial state, had to establish a secure and stable social order in the face of nonwhite challenges.

RACISM AND THE RHETORIC OF COLORBLINDNESS
IN THE CARIBOO

By the mid- to late-1860s, a trajectory toward a racially organized society that still made rhetorical nods to national differences was well established. But for the population of African descent, even these nods had very real implications. The idea that people of African descent, even without representation on juries, were the most respectable of the nonwhite groups meant they could still find their interests represented by the community as a whole. By the mid-1860s, the African Canadian community in the Cariboo Mountains was small but significant, moderately successful, and fairly well integrated. People of African descent tended to consume and invest like their middle-class white counterparts and, indeed, often owned shares in mixed-race companies.[127] African Canadians also mined as employees in mixed-race or all-black companies.[128] But in 1865, the prominent all-black Harvey-Dixon Company became involved in a legal dispute that demonstrated the fading potential of the rhetorical commitment to colorblindness for even the most accepted of nonwhite populations.[129]

The dispute originated when the all-white Aurora Company allowed their claim to lapse on William's Creek. The Harvey-Dixon Company claimed ownership of the ground and then amalgamated with the white-owned Davis Company. Shortly after, the newly amalgamated company (calling itself the Davis Company) made a large strike on the claim.[130] The Aurora Company immediately began litigation, arguing the land had been "jumped" by the Davis Company.[131]

After the initial case was thrown out by County Court judge William Cox, the Aurora Company appealed to Judge Begbie of the Supreme Court, who agreed to hear the case.[132] On June 18, the jury returned a verdict that rejected the charge of claim jumping but recognized the labor the Aurora Company had put into the land and recommended that the disputed area be evenly divided between the two companies.[133] At this point, Begbie stated that he "quite agree[d] with the findings of the Jury with the exception of one small point," but he was concerned that the ruling would "not end the litigation, and the expense of actions in one or two other branches of this Court would be heavy on both parties."[134] Supposedly to prevent future litigation, Begbie suggested binding arbitration, to which both parties consented, believing that he would suggest only minor changes to the decision of the jury.[135]

In arbitration, however, Begbie announced to a shocked court that the Harvey-Dixon Company had, contrary to the testimony provided during the trial, "jumped" the claim. Begbie went on to draw a distinction between the shares in the Davis Company owned by the African Canadians of the Harvey-Dixon Company and the shares owned by the white members of the Davis Company. Begbie ruled that the disputed land be divided up into nineteen and three-quarter sections, corresponding to the total shares in the Aurora Company and the total white shares in the Davis Company. The African Canadians, whom Begbie held accountable for claim "jumping" and who controlled two and a quarter shares of the Davis Company, got nothing.[136]

In response to this ruling, a mass meeting of approximately six hundred men, mostly miners, met in front of the courthouse in Richfield.[137] That Begbie singled out the African-descended miners as guilty, despite overwhelming evidence to the contrary, suggests that race was a factor in his decision, though one that both Begbie and the mining community did not want to acknowledge. Begbie's decision was problematic because the assertion that British law was colorblind meant that even an obviously racist decision had to be interpreted as a threatening precedent for the mining claims of white miners.[138]

As a result of the logic of colorblindness, white miners extended solidarity to the African Canadians miners, despite their status as black men. Mr. Laumeister, a white co-owner of the Davis Company, made this clear when he labeled his partners "colored" and "darkies." Yet, in spite of their race, Laumeister reaffirmed that they would earn their "pro-rata share."[139] Given little choice by Begbie's decision and the discourse of colorblind British law, Laumeister framed the Davis miners as entitled to the same equitable distribution of gold as their white partners by insisting that only their identity as miners mattered.

Indeed, the only individuals who seemed willing to raise the issue of race directly were of African descent. On the same day as the mass meeting, Colored Miner wrote to the *Sentinel* with the following questions:

First—Have we as colored men the right to pre-empt ground for mining purposes?
Second—Have we any rights in common with White men?
Third—Why were our interests taken from us and given to White men?[140]

With these three questions, Colored Miner cut to the heart of the contradiction of a racially divided colonial society that espoused a doctrine of colorblindness. By questioning Begbie's decision through an explicitly racial lens, Colored Miner highlighted the effects of race within the supposedly equitable community of miners. The questions evidently struck a nerve, and they elicited an immediate response.

Directly below Colored Miner's letter, the editor of the *Sentinel* made it clear that as far as the paper was concerned, the issue at stake was a violation of miners' rights, not racism. The *Sentinel* felt that it was "unnecessary to state in answer of Colored Miner's first and second questions, that the mining laws of this colony make no distinction as to the color of a man's skin." In responding to Colored Miner's third question, the *Sentinel* merely restated Begbie's justification that the Davis Company supposedly knew they were "jumping" the claim, and did not question this reasoning beyond the fact that it was not accepted by the jury.[141]

A week later, the *Sentinel* carried another response to Colored Miner. D. L., a black man, stressed that "whatever might appear wrong in that judgment let it not be attached to any bias, feeling, or prejudice, so far as English justice is concerned." D. L. went on to state that he did "not think that one holding the position that Hon. Chief Justice does could be biased with any feeling respecting color."[142] While disagreeing with Begbie's decision, D. L. felt it necessary to defend the institution of British law, in the face of Colored Miner's attack on the law's symbolic cornerstone, equality. In D. L.'s estimation, Begbie could not be biased, because that would undercut the system that, theoretically at least, gave African Canadians equality.[143] D. L. also voiced criticism of Laumeister's comments at the Richfield courthouse meeting, saying that the "word (darkies I mean) should not be used by any gentleman."[144] Under a guise of English civility, D. L. attempted to minimize the role of race in the dispute because of the way it threatened the rhetoric of equality in British law.

Ultimately, though, the Davis dispute in the Cariboo would prove to be the last gasp of African Canadian attempts to seek racial equality in British Columbia. Since the heyday of their activism and power in the early 1860s, the position of people of African descent in the colony had steadily worsened. On Vancouver Island, the 1864 election had split the African Canadian population, with a majority of black British subjects proving decisive in defeating a measure that would have allowed black Americans to become British subjects. The motivations of the black British subjects are opaque, but they might have been acting to deflect growing antiblack hostility by opposing a bill that did not directly benefit them. In response, black

Americans labeled the British-born blacks traitors to their race and viciously attacked them in the press.[145] Torn apart by internal divisions, the African Canadian community never again exercised the decisive influence they had in 1860. At the same time, a growing racism, implicitly supported by Governor Kennedy, contributed to the exclusion of the black rifle company from official ceremonies.[146]

As racial categories continued to consolidate and grow in significance in British Columbia, events in the United States contributed to the end of widespread participation by people of African descent in colonial society. The end of the Civil War in 1865, and the years of reconstruction that followed, convinced most African Americans to return to the United States, depriving the community in British Columbia of both numbers and leadership.[147] The remaining population of African descent was scattered, politically divided, and largely irrelevant to the discourse of race and gender in the final years before British Columbia joined the confederation in 1871.

CONCLUSION

By the time British Columbia joined Canada in 1871, the definition of white manliness had shifted considerably from what it was in 1858. In the early years of the rush, the British population, and in particular the powerful colonial elite, strove to create a colonial society predicated on what they saw as uniquely British principles: male equality, colorblindness, and order, largely in reaction to the perceived threat represented by the large numbers of white American immigrants. By the middle years of the 1860s, as the British population and government of the colony became more comfortable with the white American population, their commitment to colorblindness became increasingly rhetorical and ineffectual on the ground, replaced with a growing sense of shared white manhood and white supremacy.

But while the creation of the colonial regime in British Columbia, as in California, was a crucial aspect of the development of ideas of white manliness, it was not the only factor. Instead, ideas of white manliness were also powerfully shaped in both locations by cultural, social, and economic forces that, in the goldfields of the Pacific slope, concentrated most forcefully on ideas of risk and gambling.

CHAPTER 4

Pursuing Dame Fortune

Risk and Reward during the Gold Rushes

IN THE MID-NINETEENTH CENTURY, ANGLO-AMERICAN gold rushers came from a society that espoused a belief that hard work and dogged perseverance would result in success.[1] Financial success was a key measure of an individual's character; but in California and in British Columbia, gold seekers discovered that "the success of the miner depends a great deal upon luck. He may be industrious, economical, possessed of good morals, labor perseveringly for months, and sometimes years, and still be poor." Conversely, "an unprincipled spendthrift in a few months may realize a fortune."[2] Settlers had come face to face with one of the main ways that gold rushes upset the assumed relationship between work, reward, and character that was integral to ideologies of white and male supremacy. In an environment where risk and chance seemed to permeate all of society, these concepts shaped, and were shaped by, claims to white manliness. These ideas informed how white men conceptualized and justified a social order predicated on their domination of others and preferential access to political, social, and economic resources.

The concept of risk in the nineteenth century and its links to race and gender remain largely unexplored.[3] Although scholars of modernity have paid some attention to risk, they have (unsurprisingly, given their topic) located the origins of risk later, particularly in the emergence of large bureaucracies.[4] But the white men who participated in gold rushes also sought to assess risk, to predict outcomes of risky behavior, and to establish ways of controlling risk. Though the gold rushers examined and discussed risk and chance incessantly, they did so in an unscientific way. They relied on personal and anecdotal evidence rather than statistical analysis, and their understanding of causation often identified factors, such as God or Fortuna, at which many in the twenty-first century would scoff. Gold rushers generated and propagated understandings of how to ameliorate, avoid, or explain risk through the way they talked about and performed white manliness.

For Anglo-Americans of the early and mid-nineteenth century, risk and chance (often called "gamble," "fortune," or "luck") were related but not interchangeable concepts. While chance was "an event that happens, falls out, or takes place, without being contrived, intended, expected, or foreseen" and was therefore independent of human influence, risk entailed human agency.[5] Risk involved the decision "to hazard; to put to chance; to endanger" one's health, finances, reputation, even sanity, in pursuit of "striking it rich" in California.[6] While chance or luck could strike randomly, risk was the result of a deliberate decision and could be controlled, avoided, or mitigated. For gold rushers, the luck perceived as inherent in the primary economic activity, mining, and the most talked about leisure activity, gambling, pointed to a perceived disjuncture between work and reward.[7] In their own ways, both gambling and mining undercut received wisdom about the relationship between hard work, self-control, and success; indeed, it often seemed that success attended the lazy or impulsive. While this alone would have been troubling enough, the concerns of Anglo-Americans were compounded because ideas about work and leisure did more than shape how they spent their time: they also defined who respectable white men were. The presence of agency in the concept of risk gave white settlers a way to reconcile life in the gold rushes with expectations of society in the East about how respectable white men were supposed to work and play.

By the mid-nineteenth century, work and leisure were central to middle-class Anglo-American concepts of character and identity. Working and playing in certain ways marked Anglo-American men as both manly and white, in explicit opposition to nonwhites, off-whites, women, and children. Middle-class white men from the Northeast believed that, as white men, they exemplified the virtues of bravery, determination, and self-control—attributes manifested in the truism that dogged determination would be rewarded by economic independence. This would, in turn, allow a white man to participate, on his own terms, in the market and politics while sustaining a domestic "hearth" with a wife and children. While financial success was the goal, just as important was how he attained that goal. Anglo-American men were supposed to demonstrate their status as paragons of restrained manhood through financial independence and respectable leisure pursuits. The rough culture of the laboring class, centered on the tavern, card table, and physicality, was explicitly juxtaposed against "proper" forms of leisure, such as lectures, visits, and balls.[8]

In California, however, the dominant forms of work and leisure, especially before 1852, explicitly challenged these paths to white manhood. On the one hand, much of Californian society mirrored the rough working-class culture of the East, with its emphasis on manual labor, drink, and gambling. On the other hand, work and leisure in California were bound up with chance and risk, further undermining the ability of white settlers vested in middle-class values to use these activities as paths to becoming proper, as opposed to degraded, white men. Yet, lured by the promise of wealth, thousands of gold rushers struggled with the riskiness of work and leisure in California. To bolster their claims to an identity as white men, they linked the concept of risk, with its assumption of human agency, to the forms and practices of work and leisure in California. White settlers thus sought in part to protect what seemed to be at risk in California: their status as white men.

"LIFE'S PRIZES ARE BY LABOR GOT":
RISK AND WORK IN CALIFORNIA

Eastern audiences were particularly crucial for performances of white manliness. The vast majority of gold rushers viewed the gold rush as a means of securing the wealth that would allow them to return to the East and establish themselves as independent farmers or businessmen surrounded by supportive and dependent families.[9] This shaped how gold rushers talked about their experiences to eastern audiences. Letters and accounts published for audiences in the East attest to the fact that *how* a man got his money in California mattered just as much as, if not more than, actually getting it. Understood in the idea that dogged determination eventually led to success was the assumption that Anglo-American men would be faced with multiple setbacks in life. For a white man, a momentary failure was of little importance, because the ultimate outcome was ensured by undaunted resolve. A failure of character was far more serious, since it revealed his fundamental inability to ever be a respectable white man. This helps explain why some gold rushers were willing to discuss their financial setbacks, while most denied gambling (even though they assured their audiences that everyone else did it).[10] In the mid-nineteenth century, wealth could indicate a male's status as a white man but was not a determiner of it. Great wealth gathered through unsuitable means would mark a man as off-white and disreputable.

Even with a preexisting ideology that helped account for, and sometimes excuse, failure, gold rushers had to overcome two major discursive obstacles to make mining an acceptable form of work for white men vested in middle-class values. First, mining was much like the rough, dirty work characteristic of the working class in the East; second the "gamble" of mining challenged the relationship between work and reward. Indeed, not only did the physical nature of mining challenge received notions of what sort of labor middle-class white men should do, but also gold rushers worried that they were not particularly well suited for it. Letter after letter remarked on the hardships and sickness in the mines. According to one correspondent, it was only "the hard-working men, those who are accustomed to exposure and who know how to use the pick and the crowbar—the men of muscle and robust constitution—who can be certain of improving their condition by coming to the mines."[11] As many gold rushers learned, they would have to "harden" themselves to manual labor and the physical dangers of mining in California.[12] Some gold rushers also advocated avoiding work in the "*heat of the day . . . & the chill of the night.*"[13] According to commentators like these, the labor was rough, but because miners worked for themselves and worked with the energy and vigor that characterized the "go ahead" attitude of California, that labor served to ennoble, not degrade, them.[14] "There is," opined William Taylor, "as much difference between the muscular action of a California miner and that of a man hired by the month to work on a farm, as between the agonizing, aimless movements of the sloth and the pounce of the panther."[15]

The role of luck posed another challenge to mining as a path to respectable white manhood. If mid-nineteenth-century Anglo-Americans held that hard work, perseverance, and determination led to success, then a man's character, as manifested by his actions, had a direct causal link to his success or failure in life. While men might be "embarrassed" in their fortunes temporarily, outright failure came from a lack of willpower, from laziness, or from other aspects of a corrupted character that made an individual's status as a white man suspect.[16] In the mines, however, major discoveries of gold seemed to happen at random, rewarding undeserving as often as deserving miners. Given that Greek and Roman historical and mythological references permeated the culture of the early republic, it is perhaps not surprising that some came to talk of Fortuna, or Dame Fortune, as influencing their fates in the gold mines.[17] It is significant that gold rushers not only came to at least partly reject the truism of the day, that determination led to success, but also, when they did, resorted to the imagery of a fickle and capricious female deity. By doing so, they drew on a convention linking chance, irrationality, and femininity that had deep roots in the Western intellectual tradition. The ancient Greek word *Tyché* and the Latin *Fortuna* are both feminine nouns; from Plutarch to the present, the deity has been consistently depicted as female in written and visual representations.[18] The use of Dame Fortune allowed gold rushers to blame a woman for their failures. When miners spoke of individuals as having good luck, especially unusually good luck, they often identified nonwhite or off-white men as the beneficiaries. As J. D. Borthwick commented, "There was a common saying, of the truth of which I saw myself many examples, that sailors, niggers, and Dutchmen, were the luckiest men in the mines: a very drunken old salt was always particularly lucky."[19] Dame Fortune allowed gold rushers to attribute the success of off-white and nonwhite men not to their own actions but to the agency of an outside force.

In contrast, when gold rushers spoke of white men and Dame Fortune, they talked of winning Dame Fortune's "favor" through hard work and determination, thereby reestablishing the relationship between work and reward through the exercise of manly attributes.[20] As Timothy Osborn remarked, "Faint heart never will win fair lady."[21] Charles Pancoast, a Quaker, followed this logic to its extreme:

> If golden Fortune be your goal,
> Take off your coat, your sleeves uproll;
> Though Fortune is a fickle Dame
> She smiles upon the brave of Soul.
> But if she frown, still hoe your row,

Pursue her, no surrender make,
The favors she will not bestow
Upon you, you by force may take.
Life's prizes are by Labor got,
They come to those who toil and spin;
Strike, strike the Iron while 'tis hot,
    Go in and win![22]

For Pancoast, the reestablishment of the work-reward relationship would be completed even if it required the metaphorical rape of Dame Fortune. Pancoast was unusual in his assertion that a sufficient application of masculine energy could force "Life's prizes" from Dame Fortune. Instead, most gold seekers viewed their relationship with Dame Fortune as a courting ritual, one of the few occasions in nineteenth-century American society when a woman could not be compelled by a man.[23] This allowed gold rushers to assert their agency and, therefore, their manliness, while leaving room for failure to be attributed to the capriciousness of a feminized understanding of luck.

Despite the fact that the luck of gold mining could be explained away, accounted for, or embraced, the letters from gold rushers to audiences at home reveal how many warned others not to try their luck in California. Their accounts stressed physical dangers, crime, and the doubtful odds of accumulating a fortune.[24] These letters were part of a gold rusher performance of white manhood for eastern audiences. By exposing themselves to the gamble of life in California, these men, even if financial failures, asserted that they, unlike their readers, had actually gone to California and "seen the elephant."

When these warnings listed the dangers of life in California, they provided an easy explanation for the failure of a gold rusher and underscored the "anomalous condition" of California. In California, many correspondents argued, normal rules did not apply. A job that in the East would have marked a man as a laborer did no such thing in California.[25] An aversion to laboring in California could expose a man to charges of thinking himself, in the words of Timothy Osborn, "'to[o] delicate' to dig in the mines and too consequential to turn his labor into a plebeann channel."[26] Many a gold rusher went to California at least partly to prove he was not a "dandy."[27] California was, as forty-niner J. W. L. Brown put it, "A place to try a mans grit."[28] By portraying themselves as courageous, firm, and undaunted in the face of the risks of mining, gold rushers believed that they revealed essential aspects of their character to each other and to family and friends back East.[29]

Of course, many Anglo-Americans "tried their hand" at mining before moving on to take part in that other California gold rush: mining the miners. As miners-turned-merchants, such men could lay claim to both the rough physicality of mining and employment in a properly middle-class profession. Gold rushers could not fully resolve the tension between the middle-class identities they aspired to and the nature of the work they were doing, but they largely succeeded in depicting their actions as indicative of the essential respectability of their characters, albeit shaped by the demands of life in the anomalous society of California. The result was a way for white settlers to differentiate themselves from an array of racialized and gendered others.

Beginning around 1851, explicit references to the gamble of mining decreased in the accounts of gold rushers, corresponding with the increasing dominance of wage work in the mines.[30] Employment as wage laborers disconnected gold rushers from the gamble of trying to "strike it rich," except to the extent that someone had to find gold in order to ensure that wages were paid. Presumably, the discourse of mining-as-gamble had less relevance to these workers. In the popular imagination however, the trope of mining-as-gamble was, by 1851, firmly cemented to ideas of white manliness. This is why Frank Soulé, writing in 1855, could still talk about the gold miners' business being "closely allied to gambling, with its rare chances of suddenly making a great fortune."[31] Three years later William Taylor asserted that the success of miners was due to "chance . . . [and] some hav[ing] better health than others," despite the overwhelming dominance of wage labor in the mines by that date.[32] The image of the risky business of mining was exciting (which helped sell copies of newspapers and published accounts from the goldfields) and suggested that California, despite the "progress" inevitably cited elsewhere in these accounts, retained something of its earlier character, a character that positioned it in contrast to a rapidly industrializing, urbanizing, and wage-oriented Northeast.[33]

Even as the mining-as-gamble trope faded in importance in California correspondence and firsthand accounts, two related tropes that had more relevance in the emerging wage-labor economy gained traction. The figure of the prospector reflected the assumption that prospecting was riskier than mining known deposits for low but consistent wages, since it involved moving to new and unknown locations, multiple hardships, and the increased potential of encountering Native Americans.[34] As such, prospecting perpetuated the sense of individual opportunity, an opportunity that was explicitly linked to white manliness. Anglo-Americans believed that they, more than any other group, had a drive to seek out the newest and richest diggings.[35] While the figure of the prospector was present throughout the gold rush period, after 1852 he became romanticized as the embodiment of a type of risk-taking and independent white manliness that represented a similarly romanticized period before the growth of wage labor.[36] The figure of the prospector served a dual purpose: as a link between white men and high-risk, high-reward forms of mining, and as an embodiment of a continued discomfiture with wage labor among middle-class white men in California. This was given particular meaning when juxtaposed against a second trope, that of "Chinaman's wages."

According to many white settlers, Chinese mining ideally took place on claims that had already been worked, with the largest and richest deposits removed, where they would make low but consistent "Chinaman's wages."[37] When working in large groups for low pay on the discarded claims of others, Chinese miners conformed to gold rushers' expectations of feminized nonwhites engaging in a form of mining that involved little risk and little chance of striking it rich.[38] Gold rushers identified with the perceived traits of the prospector—his courage, his self-reliance, and his right to rich diggings— juxtaposed with what they perceived as Chinese miners' cowardice.[39] These ideas suggested that not only were the supposedly timid Chinese unsuited for political participation, but they also deserved to be excluded from or driven out of mining areas. Ideas about risk and mining, therefore, directly supported the emerging colonial order in California.

The growth of wage labor and the large influx of Chinese in the early 1850s hardened these attitudes, a cycle that, in turn, helped justify a racially divided workforce and, in some cases, the exclusion of nonwhite laborers from the mines, by suggesting that white men deserved the lion's share of the wealth.[40] Racial understandings of risk that developed in the early years of the gold rush informed the creation of a system of racially divided labor in the mines, even as the day-to-day experience of gold rushers was increasingly removed from the experience of mining as a gamble. As attitudes toward risk and work began to shift, so too did attitudes toward risk in leisure pursuits.

MEN WITH "CLEAN, WHITE, SOFT HANDS": RISK AND LEISURE IN CALIFORNIA

Ideas of risk were as critical to Anglo-American understandings of leisure as they were to their understandings of work. Middle-class white men saw that they had to take ungentlemanly risks in order to go after gold, and so they rationalized this by reworking their characterizations of the risky things they were doing—superimposing admirable "white male" traits on gold rush activities. While taking risks in work could bolster a claim to being a white man, recreational risk-taking, or gambling, threatened the integrity of white manliness, either by blurring the distinction between "white" and "nonwhite" behavior or by creating situations in which the Anglo-American man was equal or inferior to the nonwhite men with whom he associated. However, unlike with mining, middle-class white men in California made little or no attempt to reframe gambling as indicative of white manliness. By defining white manhood against this activity, middle-class white men sought to differentiate themselves from nonwhite and off-white others in a manner that would be legible to audiences in the East.

That gambling was the defining leisure pursuit of the early years of the gold rush is not a coincidence. California was the latest in a series of peripheral areas whose "unsettled" nature allowed gambling to take place openly. Gold mining directly fueled the growth of gambling by providing gambling saloons with an inexhaustible source of income. The risks of the gambling hall also seemed to mirror the risks of gold mining, and some have argued that this relationship "encouraged people's trust in luck and speculation."[41] To be sure, there were some like John Wilson Palmer, who arrived in California broke. Luckily for Palmer, one man wished to pay a debt owed by his father to Palmer's father, a proposition with which Palmer was uncomfortable. Palmer and the man then hit upon a compromise: Palmer told the man he would stake the "three rascally ounces . . . on a card; if they are lost, there will be an end of our dispute, and you can tell your father you paid me. If they win, we will divide the spoils." To this the acquaintance agreed, noting, "You will be sure to win—the Devil is always kind to the green gamester." Sure enough, Palmer won repeatedly, eventually walking away with $384 that, when combined with a loan of a "dozen or so" ounces of gold from his friend, allowed him to open a shop the next day.[42] Palmer's tale is unusual for the way it legitimized gambling as a path to middle-class respectability.

Revulsion at gambling's moral implications, mixed with attraction to its excitement and potential, was the most common response of Anglo-American men. When gold rushers sent accounts home to family and friends, they tended to downplay the attraction of gambling because they recognized that those in the East would not approve.

By 1850, Anglo-American men perceived California as a place of exceptional social dangers. The lack of social restraints in the form of family, churches, and most importantly, white women meant that many who in the East had apparently behaved in a socially acceptable manner now engaged in activities such as drinking, swearing, prostitution, interracial sex, and gambling.[43] The most commented-on of these, and the focus of the greatest attempts at regulation, were gambling and drinking to excess, which often went hand in hand.[44] Interracial sex did not seem to concern commentators in 1849 and 1850 as much as gambling, because colonized women were expected to be sexually available; and in the context of California, such couplings were minimized as prostitution and conducted somewhat discreetly.[45] Perhaps even more importantly, these relationships were understood as temporary arrangements pending the arrival of white women in the West or the return of white men to the East. Gambling, drinking, and swearing, on the other hand, were very public and common; and they indicated the potential degradation of white men in a manner that imperiled their ability to return to the East as white men or to "advance" California from its primitive state to a civilized one.[46] The risk of gambling, drinking, and swearing lay in the way these activities threatened to collapse the distinctions between white and nonwhite manliness. The image of the gambler seemed to embody this threat.

To understand the meaning of gambling to settlers in California, it is necessary to understand how most of them thought of the figure of the gambler. In California, gambling did not make a person a gambler; it simply denoted a person as someone who gambled.[47] Gamblers, also known as blacklegs and sharps, had a number of characteristics that differentiated them from casual players. The major difference was that gamblers treated the game as their employment, not as a leisure activity. By the middle of the nineteenth century, gamblers had become firmly associated with criminals in the public mind in America, but in California the preponderance of wealth meant that gamblers increasingly turned to volume and house odds instead of trickery to secure their incomes.[48] Despite this shift, many miners continued to associate gamblers with trickery and deception.[49] In California, gamblers were further distinguished by their functional role as dealers or hosts of the games; setting up a game and inviting others to play was seen as marking oneself as a gambler.[50] If such actions defined gamblers, then their bodies and demeanor also set them apart. While miners embraced a dirty, unkempt, "hardened" body and appearance, gamblers were often described as dressing in "foppish" clothes reminiscent of the dandies of the East or as having "delicate" or "clean, white, soft hands."[51] The gamblers' character, as reflected by their faces, also underscored their difference from white men. Whereas gamblers' faces betrayed no emotion when confronting enormous losses or gains, Anglo-Americans frequently grew visibly excited, demonstrating the threat gambling posed to the self-control that was a vital part of white manliness.[52] That gamblers, especially nonwhite gamblers such as Mexicans, could risk huge sums of money without becoming excited only underscored for Anglo-American men the idea that these groups did not properly value money or work. For middle-class white men, these physical traits and attitudes marked gamblers as degraded, in contrast to the miners' manly natures.

Gold rushers had much the same problem with gambling as they did with the "lottery" of mining: They wanted skill and effort, not luck, to be the determiners of success. If skill determined success at cards, then it could be used as a way to evaluate the character of the player. In the rare instances where middle-class white men who gambled were depicted positively, their character was reflected in their skill at card playing.[53] Mostly, though, gold rushers denigrated gambling as "mere game[s] of chance," denying that any games, but especially those associated with Mexicans, required skill.[54] Instead, they attributed the success of gamblers to the influence of alcohol, cheating, or odds that favored the dealer.[55]

Erotic pictures, female bartenders and dealers, alcohol, displays of wealth, the lure of the unknown, a lack of social controls, and an admitted dearth of alternative social outlets all conspired to draw middle-class white men into the gambling halls.[56] Once there, the long odds of success in mining and the evident wealth piled on the tables "seduced" these men and encouraged them to gamble.[57] In some cases, a miner felt "*assured* he *knew* the card" and, now that it was not a game of chance but of skill, "took out his bag of dust" before inevitably losing.[58] Perhaps most importantly, it may have seemed to some gold rushers that the gaming tables presented a chance to assert their dominance, and therefore their white manliness, over women, gamblers, and other subordinates. Gambling offered the potential to enact white manliness by converting a game of chance to a demonstration of character. This may help explain why, despite the opprobrium heaped upon gambling and gamblers, so many gold rushers tried their hands at the card table.

Once a gold rusher started betting, he needed to win in order to assert his dominance over the gambler in front of spectators. In one example provided by John Letts, a miner was "too *shrewd* to let the gambler have his money. He doubles the bet, putting the money on the same card, thinking that a card must, at least, win every other time." By making his status as a white man dependent upon his winning the game, the miner essentially wagered his identity. As "the other betters and bystanders now begin to manifest an interest in the affair," the miner became "excited; he sees that others are looking at him, and displays the greatest amount of courage by taking another drink, and calling for another deal."[59] Once he started losing, the miner found himself trapped at the table, unable to withdraw and admit that he had been beaten, until he was, as Letts colorfully put it, "immolated upon the altar of avarice."[60] Therein lay gambling's gravest threat to white manliness: its potential to exploit contradictions in the discourse of white manliness to cause Anglo-American men to be degraded and dominated.

The spaces in which gambling occurred also underscored the danger that it posed to the boundaries between white men and others. From 1849 to at least 1852, gambling halls were, by most accounts, the most opulent buildings in whatever town they happened to be in. Only in the middle years of the 1850s did gambling halls lose their premier standing in San Francisco, as a combination of mounting social opprobrium, fires, and legal measures moved them off the major thoroughfares, where they were replaced by more "respectable" businesses.[61] But in San Francisco in 1849 and 1850, the gambling halls occupied an uncomfortable position as the "best" buildings in town.[62] For many, the solution was to depict the gambling halls as degraded spaces and their opulence as a trap to lure unwary, weak, or careless men.[63]

To these observers, the occupants of the gambling halls proved the degraded nature of the space. Inside, as Hinton Helper colorfully described, "octogenarians, youthful and middle-aged men, married and unmarried women, boys and girls, white and black, brown and copper-colored, the

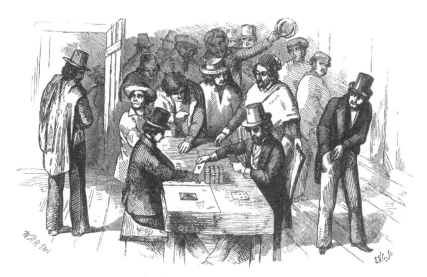

GAMBLING SCENE IN SAN FRANCISCO.

Public gambling encouraged men to wager not only their fortunes but also their identities. Source: Ryan, *Personal Adventures*, 2:213.

quarrelsome and the peaceable, all associate together; and, at times, as might be expected, fight, maim, and kill each other with the same indifference with which people generally pursue their daily occupations."[64] In other words, gambling halls were degraded not just because of the gambling that occurred there but also because of the way they collapsed boundaries between people.[65] As Frank Marryat put it, just to get inside such a hall you had to push through "Mexicans, Miners, Niggers, and Irish brick-layers."[66] For a social and political order predicated on maintaining differ-ence, the apparent leveling that occurred in the gambling halls made them deeply threatening.

While some hard-liners, often devout Christians, found any form of gam-bling to be profane, certain forms met with widespread tolerance, and it is illuminating to examine these for what they reveal about ideas of white man-liness and risk in California.[67] For many middle-class white men, a private game, either in the mines or in the cities, was acceptable.[68] Without gamblers, these games lacked the threat of a degraded other who used women, alcohol, and trickery to extract money. The very discreetness of these games suggests that they were not about public displays of white manliness and attempts to establish dominance over a degraded other. They therefore reduced the chance a white man would be publically bested by a supposed inferior. Both the literal and metaphorical stakes of these games were lower.

One of the most frequent topics in letters and accounts written for audiences in the East was the prevalence of gambling in California. Accounts commented on the pervasiveness of gambling and that it was "common with all classes."[69] Account after account suggested that the author, nearly alone among the throngs of humanity in California, was only an observer of gambling, not a participant.[70] It is easy to believe Charles Thompson's claim that "if you hear any of them [men who had been in California] ever saying that when he was in California he did not drink, did not gamble & did not dissipate to a greater or less[er] degree you may take my word for it, that he is lying & that in the strongest sense of the term."[71] Unlike Thompson, who was unusual in his honesty with his uncle, most gold rushers were probably more like Chauncey Canfield's fictional miner, who recorded his dalliances with gambling and the resulting guilt in his "diary." Canfield's miner started gambling to try and meet a Frenchwoman who was dealing cards. After losing seventy dollars and failing to get her attention, the miner worried about what his sweetheart back East would think of his gambling. That she might have objected to his reason for gambling did not seem to cross his mind. Several days later, the miner's guilt was compounded when he received a letter from his father informing him that his mother was worried about him being in such "an awful wicked place," but that "he isn't afraid of his boy not coming out all right."[72] Frequent discussions about gambling in letters home indicate the central role it played in both the social and the symbolic worlds of the miners. Gambling was one of the most popular leisure activities and seemed to represent a core "truth" about Californian society. That correspondents evinced, despite the popularity of gambling, little interest in reshaping the discourse surrounding it to make it a positive indicator of character suggests their own ambivalence toward the activity and their awareness of the attitudes of their audience.

Unlike mining, gambling could not be redefined to fit the "proper" relationship between work and reward. While individual miners might convince themselves that betting was a test of skill, for the middle-class audience in the East this flawed logic reflected a mind and character weakened by drink and excitement. Many of the accounts of miners' gambling underscored this interpretation, stressing the loss of control, even madness, and ultimate ruin of the man who gambled.[73] Additionally, while mining seemed to provide a solution for deep-seated concerns about "dandyism" and economic dependence, gambling was never able to shake its preexisting disreputable reputation as a peripheral, socially dangerous activity.[74] Even Anglo-American men in California, who gambled extensively, had conflicted feelings about the activity. They were simultaneously attracted to the thrill of gambling, especially the instant wealth it could grant, and guilt-ridden because they knew family and friends back home (and indeed many of their fellow miners) would see their participation as calling into question their character as calm and rational white men.

RISK AND WHITE MANLINESS IN CALIFORNIA

Faced with the prevalence of gambling in Californian society, white settlers found numerous ways to explain and excuse gambling's presence. One of the main ways they explained gambling in California was by pointing to the "anomalous" condition of the state. The unsettled nature of Californian society, its fluid, mobile, and overwhelmingly male society, combined with a dearth of alternative sources of entertainment, meant that, as William Olden explained to his sister, "the great trouble here is where to spend ones evening[;] there is no recourse except the gambling saloon's."[75] If gambling was not excusable, then its presence in California was at least understandable, even desirable in a way. Historian Brian Roberts has argued that, for many middle-class white men who went to California, the gold rush offered an opportunity to "slum," a chance to move temporarily "down into the real depths and spaces occupied by lower classes and ethnic others."[76] Depictions of gambling fit this motif. Middle-class white men used descriptions of gambling to stress the differences between their world and that of their audience. The success of this rhetorical strategy lay in their ability to position themselves for their eastern audiences as outside observers of gambling, rather than as participants. As outside observers, each laid claim to an identity as a white man slumming among gamblers and their marks. Unlike the people they observed, these correspondents seemingly chose to risk neither their money nor their status in a game of chance. Implicit in each of these accounts was the assumption that, as a white man, the author could be trusted because he had more in common with his readers than with the people he described.

In reading and reproducing these accounts, eastern audiences legitimated the white manliness of these observers of gambling.

After 1850 the perceived danger represented by gambling and gambling halls meant that local, civic, and state governments all moved to regulate gambling. Although gambling had been given official sanction in October 1849 with the issuance of licenses to dealers in San Francisco, as early as August 1850 a grand jury was already discussing how to suppress "gambling, bull baiting, and prize fighting at any time, and theatrical and other exhibitions for public amusement on Sundays."[77] By 1851 gambling had been prohibited on Sundays, but with mixed results, and it would take until 1855 for a more comprehensive law to be passed.[78] Initially, reformers seemed satisfied to drive gambling underground, but by 1858 even this was considered a threat to public order and safety in San Francisco.[79] Some mining districts followed suit, banning gambling or driving out professional gamblers; but enforcement, always a problem in California, remained sporadic throughout the gold rush period.[80]

These developing regulations point to a shift in public toleration of gambling in California. There are several reasons for this shift, not least of which was an increasing diversity of venues for leisure and sources of income for government.[81] Arguably the most important reason was that as gold rushers became permanent residents and were joined by an increasing number of white women, they began to articulate their white manliness not by observing gambling but by suppressing it, by seeking to "civilize" California. The voyeuristic attraction of "slumming" in gambling halls diminished as gold rushers began to worry that gambling represented a fundamental disorder in Californian society and therefore indicated a weakness in the character of the white men there. For attitudes toward risk in both work and leisure, the years from 1850 to 1852 represent a period of transition.

In the first two years of the California gold rush, risk, particularly the risks involved in mining and gambling, had emerged as a way for middle-class white men to describe and enforce the bounds of white manliness and, at the same time, a racial and gender hierarchy in California. It was in part through their understanding of risk that Anglo-American men conceptualized and justified their domination of certain areas of the gold mines on the basis of their claims to be white men. Risk also shaped how gold rushers thought of social dangers, particularly the threat that gambling represented to what they thought of as the core characteristics of white men—their self-control, coolness, rationality, and separation from a spectrum of "degraded" others. Ultimately, the discourses and practices surrounding risk were crucial to the formation and maintenance of a form of white manhood in California that was related to, but distinct from, the white manhood articulated in the East. These understandings of the relationship between risk and white manliness would continue to evolve in the subsequent gold rush in British Columbia.

"SCALING FORTUNE'S HEIGHT" IN BRITISH COLUMBIA

Sometime in the mid-1860s, James Anderson, the Cariboo poet, penned a few lines strongly reminiscent of attitudes that had prevailed a decade earlier in California:

> The sailor braves the stormy sea,
> And dares the angry wave—
> And the soldier fights for glory,
> That finds him in the grave.
> More daring still, the miner's strife,
> In scaling Fortune's height—
> For in the "battle-field of life,"
> His is the hardest fight.[82]

Anderson's poem demonstrates the continuity of ideas of risk, gender, and race between the two gold rushes. As in California, the figure of the miner remained closely linked to martial, manly figures and to the vicissitudes of Fortune. But while risk remained important to gold rushers' self-identification as white men, differences in the social, political, and physical environments, as well as the passage of ten years between the two rushes, meant that the specifics of the interaction between risk, gender, and race in British Columbia differed from what had preceded them in California. The differences between the gold rushes in British Columbia and California also permitted other concerns to move to the forefront of public discourse about white manliness.

Especially in 1858, men with experience in California dominated in British Columbia, and they brought with them the hope that the discovery of gold marked a return to the "days of '49." A return to the days of '49 meant abundant, easily accessible placer deposits that would provide opportunities for individual prospectors to get rich instead of working for wages.[83] But while these men talked of returning to the days of '49, in reality they neither fully desired to turn back the passage of time completely, nor were capable of returning to earlier understandings of the meaning of white manliness. Instead, a variety of factors, including geography, economics, and changing cultural understandings of the meaning of white manliness, shaped how Anglo-Americans in British Columbia perceived the relationship between white manliness, risk, and reward.

By 1858, wage labor dominated gold mining in California; and a hope that British Columbia represented a return to the days of '49 helps explain the magnitude of the initial rush to British Columbia.[84] A movement away from wage work also suggested that risk might again become central to Anglo-American understandings of the relationship between mining and manliness. Of course, most gold rushers also wanted the new gold discovery to be a "sure thing," a way to avoid wage work and failure, as many of them now believed had been the case in the first years of the California gold rush.[85] These dreams of re-creating the idealized days of '49 in British Columbia collided with the reality of mining in the colony, the most significant aspect of which was the nature and distribution of gold deposits.

The initial gold discoveries and mining in 1858 took place largely on the relatively accessible bars that lined the lower Fraser River. These placer deposits were soon depleted, and miners were faced with the choice of either heading home or farther upstream, hoping to find the area from which the placer deposits had been eroded. The minority of miners who headed upstream eventually discovered large deposits in the Cariboo Mountains as early as 1859. However, the most significant gold deposits tended to be located meters below the surface, often under layers of hard clay and gravel.[86] Extracting these deposits required the formation of partnerships or share-holder-owned companies using wage labor to reroute rivers, dig mining shafts, and apply hydraulic pressure on a massive scale.[87] Large private companies with professional managers, of the sort that characterized the Comstock Lode and later mining rushes, were comparatively rare, though not unheard of. [88]

Crucially, the gold region of the Cariboo was far more remote and less accessible than any gold deposits in California. With few exceptions, Governor Douglas succeeded in forcing miners to enter the colony via the capital,

Victoria. Miners had little alternative to journeying by steamboat to Fort Yale or Fort Hope and then undertaking "the tallest kind of walking" up the Fraser River to the various diggings.[89] With the discovery of gold in the Cariboo, this process was extended far into the interior of the province. The eventual development of the Cariboo Wagon Road and the Douglas Route somewhat diversified the paths to the mines; but with the exception of the mining area in the Cariboo Mountains (which formed an interconnected web of settlement and transportation routes more akin to that of California), settlement and travel in British Columbia took place along a few routes between Forts Hope and Yale and the gold districts. As a result, simply getting to the gold mines entailed considerable time and expense, often leaving new arrivals in the Cariboo with little choice but to take wage work, especially when they discovered that most of the good claims had already been staked off.[90]

Although many settlers worked at one time or another for wages, there is little evidence to suggest the formation of a stable class structure. Instead, there was a fair degree of economic mobility. As James Anderson remarked,

> Minin's 's like the country here,
> has mony an up an' doon;
> Ane day ye're stannin' on ye're feet,
> The next day on your croon![91]

Laborers were themselves often former or future owners of mining claims who used wage labor to sustain themselves while waiting for a better opportunity.[92] With few exceptions, mine owners could not afford to avoid working alongside their employees, and they performed much of the same work and encountered the same risks of cave-ins, flooding, exposure, and exhaustion as their employees.[93] The ability to move up (or down), combined with a greater expectation that wage work and mining were compatible, seems to have taken much of the sting out of wage labor. Indeed, instead of protesting the existence of wage work, many settlers complained that there was not enough of it.[94]

Without a permanent or coherent class structure among miners in the colony, ideas about work, risk, and manliness seem to have been widely shared among settlers, even as the prevalence of wage labor made it difficult to revert to the logic of chance and fortune that had characterized the early years of mining in California. However comfortable settlers might have been with wage labor, it still challenged how they thought about themselves as miners. As in California, middle-class white men in British Columbia linked the figure of the miner to a variety of other figures of martial manhood, such as the sailor and soldier.[95] However, miners were well aware that a combination of heavy physical labor and wages could make them appear like the rough working class of the cities to friends and family in the East. To distinguish what they did from wage work found in the East, miners emphasized the danger of mining. In account after account, middle-class white men stressed the physical danger posed by traveling, living, and mining in British Columbia.

Although Vancouver Island had a moderate climate, mainland British Columbia during the 1860s experienced a series of bitterly cold winters, with the Fraser River freezing almost to the ocean in 1862 and again in 1864.[96] Seasonal flooding posed a danger and was largely responsible for the perception of the Fraser River mines as a "humbug" in 1858.[97] The trails from the lower Fraser Canyon north were also arduous. As John Wilkinson put it, "The foot trail through the canions is really an awful one up and down mountains over and under rocks until you really have a doubt in your own mind which you perfer going up or coming down."[98] W. Champness provided one of the more vivid and detailed accounts of the journey, in which he encountered "swarms of mosquitoes," dangerous river crossings, mountain ranges, "frightful precipices," "awful gorges," "narrow defiles," waist-deep swamps and mud, "dead and fallen trees," and, as if that were not enough, bears. Champness felt justified in stating that "every one capable of giving an opinion agrees that no country in the world can be compared with British Columbia."[99] Especially in the early years of the Cariboo rush, the physical danger encountered traversing the "most wretched and miserable country" was unparalleled by anything in the California experience, save perhaps for those miners who traveled overland.[100] It was, claimed Champness, "utterly useless for persons of weak constitution, or feeble powers of endurance to attempt the expedition to the up-country mines of Cariboo and the creeks."[101] The increasing focus on physical danger and, not coincidentally, on the body, in the accounts of miners in British Columbia is an early movement toward the shift from manliness to masculinity that occurred more widely at the end of the century.[102] Focusing on the physical dangers and hardships of gold mining gave gold rushers a way to differentiate their labor from that of the working classes in the East and provided a way to rhetorically tie themselves to other figures of martial manhood, such as pioneers.

Descriptions of the physical hardships of traveling to the mines began to shift in the late 1860s with the building of the Cariboo Wagon Road, the opening of the Douglas Route, and the establishment of stagecoach lines from New Westminster to Barkerville. In 1861, Francis Barnard began offering the first coach rides to the Cariboo from Lillooet. By 1868, Barnard's Express had over two thousand horses stationed at roadhouses every sixteen miles on the route and ran frequent and affordable stagecoaches.[103] With faster, easier, and cheaper travel between the Cariboo and the coast, the trip ceased to be a stage for the performance of courageous and hardy white manhood.[104] Obviously, dangers such as the cold snap that injured several men in the winter of 1868 still occurred; but for the most part, the population of the gold mines was increasingly made up of residents who lived year-round in the interior, were familiar with the environment, and knew how to deal with it.[105] But while the trip to the Cariboo became easier, residents still believed that living and working in the Cariboo required greater toughness than in the lower mainland.

Risk did not completely disappear from the discourse of white manliness in British Columbia. Some miners still talked of trying to entice "Dame Fortune . . . to smile upon us" and of the same "hard gambling profession of a gold miner" as they had in California.[106] For these men, mining remained subject to a capricious, feminized understanding of luck, but they were an ever-shrinking minority.[107] The risk that most men talked about in British Columbia differed subtly from the risk talked about in California. By 1862, mining was still a gamble, but luck was increasingly becoming something you made, and risk, something to be managed through the application of knowledge.[108] John Evans, arguably the most famous of the large mine owners in the Cariboo, reflected this new attitude when he secured several claims on both sides of one river, so as not to miss a seam, and several smaller claims on other rivers. Evans sought to manage risk by diversifying, or as he put it, by looking to have "several strings to my bow."[109] Speaking in this way, Evans literally marked himself as a "fortune-hunter," linking mining to another manly, martial activity, hunting, while simultaneously demonstrating his manly ability to manage the risk of mining.

After this shift in attitude toward luck, the outcome of mining increasingly became an indicator of skill, and white manliness was increasingly
tied to knowledge and expertise. Whereas in California, the bar for entry
into white manliness had largely been how a person mined, in British
Columbia a man's success at mining increasingly indicated his status
because it signaled knowledge and mastery. The *Cariboo Sentinel*, in addition to listing lectures by experts and disseminating technical knowledge
of local geology, called for "a higher degree of mining . . . [in which] the pick
and the shovel need to be supplanted by the steam engine, reservoirs, and
aqueducts."[110] While incipient, this trend toward specialization and education, occurring in conjunction with the development of wage labor and
large mining companies, presaged the eventual development of ideas of
white manliness characterized by greater social stratification and the development of a managerial class.[111]

By bringing skill back into the equation of mining-as-gamble, settlers
in British Columbia sought to undercut the element of chance that had so
severely strained the work-reward relationship in the mines of California.
In British Columbia, white manliness could be measured by besting physical dangers and by succeeding in mining, often through the application
of knowledge. This emphasis on knowledge indicates greater economic
and cultural integration with the East and speaks to the increasing stan-
dardization of cultural perspectives on work, race, and gender across the
continent.[112]

The persistence of older notions of risk was most evident in the continuing celebration of the prospector. As in California, middle-class white men
believed that the new and presumably rich gold deposits were the right of
the white man. Nonwhite miners, such as the Chinese, were more properly
confined to working already-mined areas for "Chinamen's wages" or serving as wage labor for Anglo-American employers.[113] As they had in California, these attitudes occasionally manifested as attempts to drive out or
exclude Chinese miners from the gold region.[114] Also as in California,
Anglo-American prospectors, surveyors, and explorers emerged as some of
the major cultural heroes of the gold rush in British Columbia.[115] Indeed,
the colonial government gave official sanction to the exceptional and admirable status of these men. In addition to providing material support for
expeditions, the government also legislated "discovery claims." A discovery
claim allowed the first miner, or party of miners, in a new mining area to

record a claim double the usual size.[116] These discovery claims, in combination with the various movements to exclude nonwhites from new or rich diggings, were concrete manifestations of the widespread assumption that the social and political order of the colony should support white men as the primary beneficiaries of the gold rush. As in California, attitudes toward risk served to organize society and inform the implementation of a colonial hierarchy designed to benefit those who were believed to act like white men. Linking a tendency to be risk averse in mining with effeminacy allowed these measures to be easily justified even in the supposedly colorblind colonial society of British Columbia.

In sum, the dreams of returning to the days of '49, with their abundant gold and lack of wage work, died soon after the first wave of Californian miners arrived in 1858. After that, the main gold areas were found in the interior of the colony, where geography and economics conspired to make wage labor commonplace. By 1862, with the rush fully under way in the Cariboo Mountains, settlers now celebrated the management of risk and the braving of physical danger as key markers of white manliness in the mines. At the same time, settlers also continued, somewhat nostalgically, to celebrate the gamble of mining, most notably in their celebration and support of prospectors. In so doing, Anglo-Americans reaffirmed the link between mining and manly, martial, white frontier figures. Middle-class whites' ideas about risk in the mines of British Columbia therefore indicate that this was a period of transition, not only from older ways of explaining and managing risk to more modern methods, but also from ideas of white manliness to white masculinity.

MINERS WILL GAMBLE: GAMBLING IN BRITISH COLUMBIA

Although gambling in British Columbia never occupied the central position in public discourse that it did in California, it was still a matter of concern. Although tolerated to a greater extent than in California, gambling was socially problematic to some gold rushers in British Columbia. Legally, British Columbia relied on the Gaming Act (1845) passed by Parliament for guidance in suppressing undesirable forms of gambling.[117] The most innovative portion of this act, section 18, reversed precedent and made wagers unenforceable contracts, thereby making it legal for gamblers to avoid paying any lost bets. Additionally, British Columbia occasionally enforced an earlier law "proscribing common gaming houses." These laws functioned in much the same manner as they did in England: they linked the legitimacy of gambling to social class by regulating public gaming but condoning private gaming among elites.[118] None other than Chief Justice of the Supreme Court Matthew Begbie, well known as a "man who loved whist," lost $1.25 to Peter O'Reilly, Gold Commissioner, in September 1864.[119] Nor were all the games low stakes. On August 11, 1865, Henry Ball, magistrate, "foolishly lost $1000" at poker and loo. A thousand dollars lost while gambling was an astronomical loss, more than most men saw in an entire year.[120] While the Gaming Act had made wagers unenforceable as legal contracts, this may have added to the aura of honor surrounding wagers among elites, as a player was now obligated only by honor and reputation to pay the bet. Bets between colonial elites, much as those between the English elites whom they emulated, validated claims to respectable white manhood.

At the same time that the colonial elites gambled among themselves, they also enforced the Gaming Act and closed down gambling establishments throughout the colony. The result was a fair bit of confusion in the lower echelons of society over the legitimacy of gambling in the colony. George Blake, a police sergeant in the Cariboo, claimed that he had not laid charges against certain gambling houses because he "thought they would be protected by the government." Indeed, Blake claimed his superiors had told him that "Governor Douglas and Mr. [Joseph] Pemberton [a close associate of Douglas] were perfectly aware of [the gambling] going on."[121] Blake's confusion is understandable given the elite's practices and the fact that saloons openly advertised "whist, freeze-out, and other games."[122] While these ads claimed that the stakes were "apples," the prosecution records for the colonies reveal that cash was more common than fruit. Gambling was not conducted on the sly. Despite official prohibition and occasional enforcement, gambling, in common gaming houses or not, was a widely practiced and condoned social vice. Some of the resistance to enforcing the antigambling laws may have come from economic pragmatism, as when Pemberton said "that miners would gamble[,] mining itself being a sort of gambling[;] and if they could not do it here they would go elsewhere and take much of the money out of the country." But it is telling that the only games that were never suppressed were those of the elites.[123]

In choosing when to suppress gambling, and which games to suppress, the authorities revealed something about the threat they perceived from some types of gambling. For example, games run by and for the Chinese were particular targets of enforcement. This was consistent with widespread understandings of Chinese urban spaces as dangerous and in need of regulation.[124] Interracial mixing at games of skill and chance was also discouraged or derided.[125] As in California, the elites worried some games of chance could allow white men to be corrupted by or taken advantage of by non- or off-whites. Games played in saloons, between white men and nonwhites or degraded whites, were too public to go without regulation.

English miner Philip Hankin recognized the effects of public perception on one's standing as a white man suitable for employment. As he put it, "One does not, as a rule, feel inclined to give a young man a place in your office, with whom you have been playing cards, or Billiards[,] . . . so I took very good care never to be seen in any of the Saloons either by day or night."[126] As in California, gambling in British Columbia had repercussions for a gold rusher's status as a white man; but in British Columbia, who an individual gambled with and the public visibility of that gambling were more important than whether an individual hosted the game or not. Conversely, if a man gambled in a respectable (and presumably at least semiprivate) manner, gambling might not affect his standing as a white man at all. Indeed, if a man conducted himself properly, paid his debts, and did not ruin himself, it could even enhance his claim to white manliness.

The symbolic importance of gambling to gold rush society and to white manliness in British Columbia was considerably less than what it had been in California, and this shift reveals the way in which ideas of white manliness changed between the two rushes. Whereas gambling had arguably attracted significant attention from social commentators in California, the primary area of concern in British Columbia was sexually based social dangers. As historian Adele Perry has observed, "Sex lay at the heart of both British Columbia's colonial project and critiques of it."[127] In particular, settlers in British Columbia worried about the repercussions of mixed-race sexual relationships between white men and indigenous women.[128] While some settlers, notably missionaries and Hudson's Bay Company employees, saw a potential for the uplift of indigenous women through these relationships, the tide of public opinion shifted, and most saw these relationships as a threat to white manhood.[129] According to Reverend T. Derrick, even speaking the Chinook jargon could endanger a man's manliness. It is easy to infer Derrick's thoughts about mixed-race relationships.[130] The reasons for this shift have been studied in detail elsewhere, but suffice it to say that hardening attitudes toward race and the arrival of small, but significant, numbers of white women fueled an increasing trend to see mixed-race sexual relationships as potential sites of degradation.[131]

Another major factor in focusing social concern on sex in British Columbia was the fear of permanency. In California, mixed-race sexual unions were perceived as part of the larger act of "slumming" and were, therefore, by definition temporary, ephemeral conquests that could actually reinforce the white manliness of Anglo-American men. The massive demographic decline of the indigenous population, combined with the continued influx of white women and the determination of most bachelors to return to the East to wed, minimized the potential social disruption represented by mixed-race sexual relationships. In British Columbia, in contrast, the demographic and geopolitical situation moved concerns regarding mixed-race sexual relationships to the forefront of colonial discourse. The gold rush in British Columbia, despite the hopes of its boosters, never brought the same scale of immigration that California experienced. Even at the peak, immigrants numbered in the thousands, not the tens of thousands as in California.[132] Additionally, while the indigenous population did suffer some decline resulting from increased contact with settlers during the gold rush, it was never as severe as in California.[133] Indeed, until the closing years of the nineteenth century, the indigenous population of British Columbia outnumbered the nonindigenous population, which remained largely confined to Vancouver Island, to the Lower Mainland, and along the Fraser River.[134] This persistent indigenous population, combined with the limited immigration of white women, occurring within the context of consolidating ideas of race and biological determinism, meant that mixed-race sexual relationships appeared to pose a much more significant threat to white manliness in British Columbia than in California.

In the eyes of observers, the threat of mixed-race sexual relationships was that Anglo-American men risked becoming "squaw men."[135] The very term *squaw man* is revealing. In it, the white male, usually the dominant subject, has been reduced to secondary importance beside the identifier *squaw*, a racialized image strongly linked to disease, laziness, and prostitution.[136] Symbolically, then, in mainstream public discourse, a white man who chose to engage in a sexual relationship with an indigenous female stood to lose any claim to white manliness. In response to this threat, social reformers in British Columbia tried to protect white manhood through the development of surrogate white families in bachelors' halls, YMCAs, literary and mechanics institutes, and the church until white women, that ultimate colonial panacea, arrived in force.[137]

CONCLUSION

Though risk never completely disappeared, its importance to understandings of white manliness diminished from 1848 to 1871 in California and British Columbia, largely owing to the growth of wage work and an increasing emphasis on the physical body. Throughout the period, however, risk helped conceptualize and justify a social order in California and in British Columbia in which settlers who identified as white men believed they should dominate colonial society. Risk did this by giving meaning to white manliness. What defined white men in both California and British Columbia was that they knew when to take a risk and when and how to avoid it.

The attitudes of gold rushers toward risk cannot be cleanly dissociated from their attitudes toward the body and appearance. On the one hand, as the emphasis on the clean, soft hands of the gambler attests, the body was always important for Anglo-American understandings of the people involved in risky work or leisure. On the other hand, the rise of wage work in California and British Columbia was accompanied by a broader transformation in the European world of the mid-nineteenth century, which now placed greater emphasis on the body and on biological notions of race.

CHAPTER 5

Dirty Clothes, Clean Bodies

The Body and Costume of White Manliness

"I HAVE LIVED LONG ENOUGH IN CALIFORNIA," remarked D. B. Bates in 1858, "to learn from experience never to judge a person by his apparel," a sentiment echoed by participants in the British Columbia gold rush.[1] This was a disturbing trend to Anglo-Americans, as appearances mattered in British and American society in the mid-nineteenth century. Appearance was, most commentators held, the key to understanding a person's character. Outward decay marked inner corruption; likewise, beauty marked inner purity. But while clothes and other outward trappings should reveal a person's inner character, they could also obscure it, as most Anglo-Americans realized. If matters were confused enough in the urban centers of the East, where con men and prostitutes sought to mislead the unwary, then they were positively chaotic in the goldfields of California and British Columbia.[2] This uncertainty was especially problematic because most of the participants in the gold rushes were strangers to each other and could not rely on reputation or experience to inform their perceptions of their neighbors. It was, therefore, necessary for them to evaluate an individual's character through his or her appearance.

Middle-class white men tried two strategies to make order out of chaos in the goldfields. First, they relied on stereotypes, paying particular attention to how behavior and dress should reflect each other. Second, sensing the ways in which dress could be a disguise, they placed increasing emphasis on "knowing" the nature and characteristics of the body. Dress and body became two of the key ways they evaluated character and worth. These two aspects were not static, however, and as ideas about biological difference became more widespread, and the problems of judging people by their clothes and outward appearance more apparent, a gradual shift to emphasize the body over clothing became apparent by the end of the British Columbia gold rush.

THE MINER'S COSTUME AND OTHER DRESS

Common economic, social, and cultural forces created parallel concerns about the meaning of appearances in California and British Columbia. In both societies, new arrivals quickly adopted clothes suitable for mining and discarded clothes suited to a more settled existence in the East. Practical considerations were not the only factor shaping the choice of clothes. Accounts often referred to a red flannel shirt, blue pants tucked into rubber boots, and a slouch hat as the "miner's costume."[3] These clothes signified that the wearer was an experienced miner, hardened to the deprivations and challenges of mining. Indeed, to John Borthwick, it seemed as if "old miners" on their way home "were jealous . . . of every bit of California mud which adhered to their ragged old shirts and patch-work pantaloons, as evidences that they, at least, had 'seen the elephant.'"[4] Donning mining clothes was part of a larger performance of a type of white manliness strongly tied to the particular context of the gold rush. Notably, while Anglo-Americans in other colonial contexts steadfastly clung to clothing that was more appropriate to London or New York, in California and British Columbia the vast majority of the immigrants embraced a radically different appearance.[5] This discrepancy is explained by the meaning of the mining costume, aside from its practicality and availability.

Two accessories to the miner's costume confirmed the wearers' status as experienced and hardened: weapons and facial hair. In California and British Columbia, miners frequently wore guns and knives in their belts, concealed them on their persons, or kept them close at hand. With these, the miner likened himself to other frontier figures, such as the soldier, the filibuster, and the pioneer, and signaled to himself and others that he would not be dominated by other men, that he would, if provoked, defend himself with deadly force. Though gold rushers tended to emphasize the danger of Native American attacks and other violent crimes, in actuality, with the exception of Indian warfare in California, populations during both gold rushes experienced crime rates comparable those in the East.[6] The profusion of weaponry was more the product of middle-class white men's desire to mark themselves as manly, martial men than it was a response to actual conditions.[7]

One of the most striking ways that Anglo-American men in California and British Columbia presented themselves as manly, tough, and experienced miners was through the cultivation of facial hair. This was more revolutionary than might be immediately evident. The growth of facial hair in mainstream society during the mid-nineteenth century was largely an attempt to embrace a natural manliness in response to the increasingly unnatural industrialized world.[8] In Britain, at least, the suppression of the revolutions of 1848 weakened the linkage between beards and radical ideology, making facial hair acceptable to the mainstream of British society. As a result, the adoption of beards in Britain seems to date from the 1850s.[9] However, facial hair in California dates from the earliest days of the rush, when, for example, Alonzo Rathbun sat for three photographs before he shaved and remarked that his "mustash come up to my eyes. My whiskers hung down on my breast."[10] Not only was facial hair common in California, but also the special mention many gold rushers made of it in letters, and the pictures that were sent home, testify to its adoption in California in advance of mainstream adoption in either the United States or Britain.[11]

Early adoption suggests that facial hair had a special meaning in California that subsequently carried over to British Columbia. Again, the British history of facial hair is suggestive. Some of the early adopters had been army, police, and naval officers, with civilians following suit to lay claim to what was becoming a marker of manly martial virtue.[12] Anglo-Americans, too, believed that there was a practical rationale for growing beards. Commentators argued that beards provided protection for miners in the harsh conditions of the mines, a justification that suggested the appearance of gold rushers reflected a tough, martial manhood suited to the rough conditions of the goldfields.[13] While the facial hair that gold rushers grew linked them to military officers, the beards of the former were generally unkempt and bushy, tying the beards and the beard-wearers to another group of icons of martial manliness: frontiersmen and mountain men.[14] By the mid-1850s, the linking of the bearded faces of miners with manly toughness developed to the point that an article in the *Alta California* could contrast the "full manly growth of beard" with "faces made smooth and girl-like by the continued use of the razor."[15]

By the time the gold rush in British Columbia started in 1858, not only had the wearing of facial hair become less controversial in Britain, but also the precedent of California powerfully conditioned new and old gold rushers alike to link the wearing of facial hair to an identity as a tough, manly miner. As a result, there was far less commentary on the wearing of beards, though their ubiquity is attested to in the visual records of the gold rush.[16] The prevalence of facial hair in the British Columbia gold rush speaks to the way the linkage between facial hair and tough, natural manliness had become thoroughly normalized by the 1860s in gold rush societies. In the mining societies of California and British Columbia, a mining costume, consisting of clothes, weapons, and facial hair, came to mark an individual as tough and experienced, the key traits that distinguished the manly miner from his opposite, the urbanized and effeminate dandy.

Just as the rugged miner's character was reflected in his appearance, the dandy's complete unsuitability for the mines was reflected in his. The dandy, with his "kid gloves that covered lily white hands, small walking stick, hair usually long, and soaped down until his head shines like a junk bottle, feet encased in patent leather boots, [and] speaking a sweet little language of his own . . . was never known to have done an hour's work in his life."[17] The dandy's appearance reflected his weakness of character—specifically, his inability to suffer hardships and hard work in the pursuit of reward. Instead, the dandy "mincingly" picked his way through the mud, searching for "ah very rich hole, whah a gentlemen could procure an agreeable shade to work under."[18] Account after account described encounters with dandies, focused on their clothes and unrealistic expectations, and concluded by noting their ultimate failure.[19]

In many ways the figure of the dandy bore a marked resemblance to that of the gambler.[20] Soft hands, fancy clothes, and a desire to reap rewards without having to work hard characterized both. Tellingly, both dandies and gamblers purportedly often lacked beards, although they might have ornamental and showy moustaches that did not imply rugged manliness.[21] Where the figures of the dandy and the gambler diverged was in the threat they posed to white men. The gambler was a figure of corruption, luring foolish and gullible miners to waste their money; but the dandy was so effeminate that he was a danger only to himself as he proceeded, woefully unprepared, to the mines.

By the time of the British Columbia gold rush, the image of the dandy had faded in importance as something for white men to define themselves against. Instead, that concern had been replaced by a more general concern about "persons of weak constitution, or feeble powers of endurance," "city friends," or "sons of independent gentlemen, attorneys and bankers' clerks, doctors, . . . lawyers, magistrates, . . . and many others of the same stamp" who would be unable to make it as gold miners, as they were "incompetent to perform skilled labour."[22] Belief in the unsuitability of the dandy lived on, transformed and generalized into a disdain for city professionals, part of the same reaction against the increasingly urbanized and industrialized world that gave gold mining much of its symbolic meaning. Criticism of dandyism also helped justify the labor of middle-class white men in the mines. Gold rushers went to great lengths to explain to audiences at home why they were doing manual labor and how it strengthened their character.[23] By attack-

An African American dandy.
Source: Soulé, *The Annals of San Francisco*, 506.

ing the dandy and his successors, these men underscored the idea that not everyone was suited to gold mining, that only men with the right characters and bodies could make a go of it.

Dandies posed not only a gendered challenge but also a racial challenge to white manliness. Their traits, and especially their love of ostentatious display, linked them rhetorically to images of Native Americans and African Americans in California. Benjamin Wingate claimed that, having made a necklace out of buttons, some indigenous men were "as much pleased with themselves as a New York dandy with his white kids and mustache," while others noticed African Americans "strutting along in a dandified manner."[24] Throughout the nineteenth century both Native Americans and African Americans were the subject of rebuke and ridicule for attempting to dress like whites and either looking ridiculous (as in the case of indigenous peoples) or being pretentious (as in the case of African Americans). The behavior and dress of the dandy implied degradation and a dangerous confusion about the boundary separating white men from nonwhites.

Another figure who closely resembled the dandy was the greenhorn, the newly arrived, or inexperienced, miner. Like the dandy, the greenhorn was often clothed in "city style, with sack coat, flashy vest, and pantaloons with straps on."[25] Also, like the dandy, the greenhorn was the subject of derision by the experienced miner. As Charles Thompson remarked on his first encounter with miners in California, "They looked at our fine dresses, our delicate complexions, our *verdant* questions, and still more verdant plans as if they had a supreme contempt for us."[26] Underscoring their unpreparedness, greenhorns were singled out as easy marks for gamblers and prostitutes.[27] But unlike the dandy, the greenhorn was prepared to work hard to become a miner. Where the dandy became frustrated at the first disappointment and hard labor, the greenhorn persevered.[28] Being a greenhorn was a transitional stage through which middle-class white men from the East passed en route to becoming manly white miners. Unlike the dandy, whose character was reflected in the tenacity with which he clung to his foppish clothes and manner, the greenhorn had a latent manly character that became manifest over time and with experience through a hardened body, lengthening facial hair, and the increasingly worn clothes of a miner.

The term *greenhorn* appears only infrequently in accounts of the British Columbia gold rush. At least two trends discouraged its widespread usage. First, the percentage of inexperienced miners in British Columbia was far lower than it had been in California, especially in the first year of the rush, when the vast majority of the migrants came from California or Australia. Additionally, a small, but still significant number of newly arrived miners in British Columbia, most notably the Welsh, were experienced miners.[29] Second, the term *greenhorn* was an Americanism unfamiliar to most British

A greenhorn asks for advice from a hardened miner. Source: Delano, *Pen Knife Sketches*, opp. p. 9.

subjects and unlikely to find its way into official correspondence.[30] Though the figure of the greenhorn appeared explicitly only very rarely in British Columbia, it continued to resonate.

In British Columbia, as in California, middle-class white men believed the key to success would be perseverance, hard work, and a corresponding

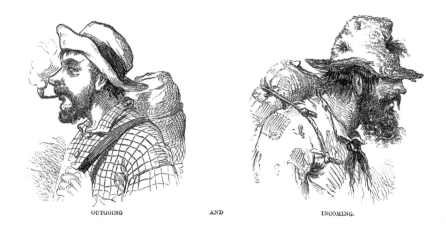

OUTGOING   AND   INCOMING.

The transition from greenhorn to experienced miner. "Before" and "after" images were common in both gold rushes. Source: Browne, *Crusoe's Island*, 419.

toughening of the body into the hardened miner's physique, usually garbed in ragged and worn clothes. This trajectory was exemplified in W. Champness's serialized account of his journey to and from the gold mines. Champness described the rigors of the journey and his party's perseverance in the face of natural obstacles while other men with their "pale, pinched faces and tattered rags" failed.[31] Though facing extreme challenges, new arrivals could become miners if they had "physical strength, patience, and good temper."[32] In British Columbia a person either arrived with the physical ability to succeed in the mines or he failed. In contrast, in California, a person's character enabled his body to develop in order to handle the labor of the mines. This is also partly why accounts in British Columbia de-emphasized the figure of the dandy and narrowed the category of suitable miners to exclude an array of people who had fine characters but who were physically unprepared for the mines.[33] This was part of a larger cultural trend that increasingly emphasized the importance of the body to ideas of white manliness.

A large part of what made these figures so important in the gold rushes was the way that gold rush society upset traditional ways of knowing a person's character. Most young settlers arrived with only tenuous connections to their fellow gold rushers. The family and community social networks that had largely defined them in the East did not exist in the goldfields. Among other things, this situation encouraged the widespread use of nicknames.[34] The anonymity of gold rush society provided an opportunity for men to re-create and redefine themselves.

For some commentators, this lack of restraint allowed a person's true character to be revealed. As John Borthwick noted, with the "outside pressure of society being removed, men assumed their natural shape, and showed what they really were, following their unchecked impulses and inclinations."[35] In this light, the costume of the dandy, gambler, or miner became a reflection of a person's true character. But for others, anonymity fostered deception. Mary Megquier, for instance, found California "a complete farce. . . . [T]he greatest dandies wear their beard long, their hair uncombed."[36] To commentators like Megquier, a lack of social restraints allowed people to assume false appearances with relative ease. The tension between these two views of men's appearances during the gold rush would not—indeed, could not—be resolved, and these questions about the integrity of appearances were further challenged by the on-again, off-again relationship some miners had with the mining costume.

Middle-class white miners sometimes removed their mining costumes by shaving their faces, washing their clothes, or even putting on special suits. There were many reasons for this transformation. It often occurred on Sunday, and for some religious miners the link between cleanliness and godliness may have been foremost in their minds.[37] For others, dressing up in what Prentice Mulford tellingly called his "dandy outfit" had to do with a rare visit to a larger town or city.[38] Alternatively, miners might shave, wash, or change their clothes to impress white women.[39] Most miners returning to the East resumed wearing clothes more appropriate to that region shortly after their arrival. In each case, the change in appearance signaled that, to a certain degree, the miner's costume, like that of the westerner or the pioneer, was a herald of, but ultimately unsuited to, the white man's "civilization."[40] But there was more going on than a transitory embrace of a rough, martial manhood, as becomes apparent when tracking the shifting meanings of appearance between California and British Columbia.

In going to and from California, and at certain moments in California, Anglo-Americans moved between embracing the appearance and identity of the urban denizen (whose clothes were rapidly becoming the marker of the emergent middle class) and assuming the appearance and identity of the gold miner on the edge of civilization.[41] In so doing, these men also moved between identities as restrained white men and martial white men.[42] Middle-class white men celebrated becoming miners and looked back at their eastern counterparts with a fair degree of disdain; but at the same time they also envied aspects of the latter's lifestyle, most notably access to women and families. These men never fully rejected either the restrained, urban aspect of their manhood or the martial, frontier aspect. Instead, in California they took the first tentative steps toward reconciling standards of restrained manhood and martial manhood in a new synthesis.

This process was far more pronounced by the time of the British Columbia gold rush, aided by two major cultural developments in the Anglo-American world. The first was the increasing traction of biological racism in general society. Biological racism encouraged Anglo-Americans to think of their bodies as fundamentally different from, and superior to, nonwhite bodies. Though Charles Darwin's *On the Origin of Species* was not published until 1859, the idea that physical differences explained seemingly innate differences between different groups of humans had been growing in popularity since the early years of the century. Even before being linked to the theory of evolution, biological racism was an increasingly popular way of understanding society, one that heavily emphasized the immutability of bodies. As the body became more important for signifying identity, Anglo-Americans also perceived it as being more stable than it had been in the past.[43] As just one example of this trend, theories of environmentalism, which posited that the body changed to reflect its environment, fell out of favor.[44] In their place was a growing conviction among Anglo-Americans that distinct races had inherent and essential characteristics—characteristics that were supposedly identifiable from the study of the body and behavior of individuals.

The second trend that promoted the reconciliation of restrained manliness and martial manliness was the growing acceptance of facial hair in British and American society.[45] As a result, settlers in British Columbia could change their clothes without quite the same effect on their sense of identity. This is nicely demonstrated in the photographs of the Cariboo gold rush. These photographs show that whether wearing a mining or a town outfit, middle-class white men wore their beards.[46] One can presume that these same bearded middle-class white men made up the membership in organizations symbolizing restrained manliness, such as the Burrard Inlet Mechanic's Institute's Reading Room, Barkerville's Cariboo Library, and the YMCA in Victoria.[47] This indicates a growing degree of Anglo-American comfort with combining aspects of martial manhood and restrained manhood into a new synthesis, where the natural manliness of the beard could coexist with the cultivated and civilized manliness of the suit.

But while middle-class white men came to celebrate a changing approach to appearance that affirmed a practical, natural manliness, they remained ambivalent or hostile when individuals crossed gender lines, as frequently happened in California and British Columbia.[48] For example, the extreme dearth of white women sometimes presented middle-class white men at dances with little choice but to dance with each other. While settlers sometimes wore a cloth patch or other item that symbolized their being "ladies" for the dance, it was understood that this was a pragmatic, temporary measure.[49] Although some individuals playing the part of women undoubtedly enjoyed the transgressive and homoerotic aspects of the act, there is no indication that the majority of participants thought of these men as effeminate or transgressive.[50]

A man actually donning women's clothes appears to have been a rarer occurrence, but two instances suggest broader attitudes. The first occurred in July 1855, when, after losing a court case and perhaps a little drunk, Charles DeLong and Gus Lewis "dressed up in woman's *clothes* and cut a swell, rode through town [near Camptonville, California] and fooled all the boys."[51] The second was in November 1857, when two police officers arrested Thomas Brady, a black man, for "parading about the street" while "dressed like a woman." Though Brady claimed that he had been attending an all-male, or "stag," dance and had only stepped out to get some crackers and cheese, the officers asserted that "for the last five or six years, the negro has been in the habit of dressing like a man in the day time and like a woman at night."[52] As long as the cross-dressing was temporary, as for a stag dance or joke, it was acceptable; but permanency suggested deviancy that needed to be regulated, and it evoked fears of overfeminine men.[53] That Brady was African American certainly did not help his claim that he was not being transgressive.

Women dressing as men could raise similar concerns about gender roles, permanence, and behavior. A number of women passing as men were "discovered" in the gold rushes of California and British Columbia;

and sometimes men, like David Higgins, "felt strongly and unaccountably drawn" to the disguised female, moved by "a strange emotion."[54] George Payson echoed these sentiments when he noticed "a handsome young man . . . drest in the height of the fashion, with a superabundance of jewelry, and a pair of the very smallest boots, which I thought partially accounted for his peculiar mincing gait." Payson soon found the sight of the man aroused in him feelings of "painful aversion." But when the "handsome young man" was revealed to be a woman, "her mincing gait became a swimming walk—her love of ornament, her little simpering ways, her downcast lids, were her hereditary, inalienable right, with which I had no more reason nor inclination to find fault than with her slight figure and delicate complexion."[55]

The cases where men admitted to being attracted to women in disguise share a key similarity: the woman's disguise was temporary, supposedly motivated by a desire not to draw attention from the overwhelmingly male population of the goldfields. As Madame Gregoire put it, "Sometimes it is necessary for someone like me to disguise myself as a boy and to trick men, despite all of my good intentions. That is the way things are here in California." Even more importantly, these women purportedly did not relish wearing men's clothes, nor did they make any claim that men's clothes represented their true selves. Gregoire referred to herself in women's clothes as "myself . . . as I really am, as Madame Gregoire," while Madame Gremiere, another cross-dressing Frenchwoman, "turned bright red" when her disguise was publically revealed.[56] The wearing of male clothes by these women was acceptable because it was presented as a disguise used to protect them from the male population of the mines. That many of these women and men assuredly wore clothes associated with the other sex as a way to express gender and sexual nonconformity went unnoticed.

But when women adorned themselves with men's clothes as an assertion of alternative forms of femininity, the reaction by most Anglo-American men ranged from skepticism to antipathy. And no article of women's clothing caused more debate than the bloomer.[57] The bloomer first achieved prominence in 1851 in New York and emerged out of a trans-Atlantic movement for women's rights and private experimentation with dress reform. The bloomer consisted of baggy pants worn under a knee- or calf-length skirt. Though the outfit initially met with widespread acclaim, public opinion hardened against it within a matter of months.[58] Among gold rushers, debate over the wearing of bloomers appeared only in California, which is unsurprising given that the new fashion had largely disappeared from the streets and public debate by the time of the British Columbia gold rush.[59] To its California promoters, the bloomer represented a return to a more natural form, with corresponding benefits for mobility, decency (as it would not ride up to expose skin), cleanliness, and health.[60] According to its detractors, however, not only were most of these benefits a sham, but the bloomer also represented a dangerous move toward female social and political equality.[61]

In the middle years of the nineteenth century, men's clothes were mass-produced and functional, suited to participation in an active and democratic public world. In contrast, women's clothes were customized and deliberately ornate, reflecting women's proper location in the private and domestic world.[62] Even though bloomer promoters seldom explicitly made the case that the garment could lead to greater equality, its popularity among, and promotion by, early suffragists was telling.[63] Critics, including "Dame Shirley" of California, ridiculed the bloomer because it represented a substantial movement away from not only traditional female dress but also traditional female roles and behaviors.[64] Ironically, the half-dress of the bloomer constituted a greater threat than cross-dressing women to the integrity of the relationship between male clothes and male roles in the goldfields.

The gender threat of the bloomer was reflected in the apolitical figure of the prostitute, and it was here that the threat of the transgressive woman would achieve its greatest longevity in the goldfields.[65] The imagined link between prostitution and male attire was a class-based assumption imported from the East, where lower-class working women, more likely to wear pants, were presumed to be sexually available for cash.[66] As the political threat of the bloomer faded, the figure of the pants-wearing prostitute continued to represent not only a physical danger (they were often described as armed or violent) but also a threat to the morality of middle-class white men. Instead of taking up with pants-wearing prostitutes, respectable white men should seek unions with proper white women, whose appropriate clothing reflected their commitment to maintaining the gender division upon which white male privilege rested.

In California, however, the wearing of pants or bloomers threatened more than just gender boundaries. It also threatened claims to white racial superiority. In the nineteenth century, the supposed superiority of white women played a key role in justifying colonial domination of off- and non-white others, and one of the key markers of that superiority was white women's dress.[67] To commentators, the collapsing of gender divisions represented by the bloomer was mirrored in the clothing of the Chinese. As the *Alta* argued on July 7, 1851, Californians did not have to go all the way to Turkey to acquire a bloomer costume; instead, "our neighbors of . . . Celestial birth, can furnish the fashions . . . and show us how they are worn, virtually 'setting the fashions.' We saw one a day or two since. . . . It was worn by a young Chinese girl who resides here."[68] Indeed, a lack of clear gender divisions was one of the most common critiques of Chinese society, with Hinton Helper claiming that "you would be puzzled to distinguish the women from the men, so inconsiderable are the differences in dress and figure."[69] The supposed lack of gender divisions reinforced settler perceptions that Chinese men were weak and Chinese women unattractive.[70] By seeming to break down the division between male and female, white and nonwhite, bloomers represented a threat to the logic of difference that underscored the claims of middle-class white men to superiority and rightful dominance in colonial society.

The clothing and appearance of nonwhites were also important for defining who was a white man and for affirming the superiority of men's bodies and the clothes men wore in the colonial contexts of California and British Columbia. The Chinese and indigenous populations were particularly significant to this process. The importance of these two groups derived not only from their numbers but also from the way that both (though in different ways) fell well outside the bounds of whiteness. While the status of Irish, German, Spanish, and even Mexican and Chilean peoples was debated within colonial societies on the West Coast, comparatively rare were those who believed that Native Americans and Chinese could ever become full participants in colonial society. In colonial societies filled with eye-catching foreigners, the Chinese and Native Americans were the two most remarked upon groups, and their ubiquity in the historical record speaks to their importance as referents for ideas of white manliness.

Descriptions of indigenous Californians were particularly negative. The label applied by settlers to indigenous Californians, *digger* (an echo of *nigger*), reflected the strong parallels gold rushers drew between indigenous Californians and African Americans. As William Ryan put it, indigenous Californians were "very dark, indeed I may almost say black, with a slight tinge of copper colour; the features are, in all other respects, as purely African in their cast, the nose being large and flat, the cheek-bones salient, the lips thick and wide and the forehead as low as is consistent with a faint supposition of the existence of a brain, to which their pretensions are miserably small."[71] For Theodore Johnson, the "complexion" of indigenous Californians was "a dark mahogany, or often nearly black, their faces round or square, with features approximating nearer to the African than the Indian."[72] The bodies of indigenous Californians suggested to some gold rushers that they shared traits attributed to African Americans—namely, submissiveness, laziness, and suitability to coerced labor. In some ways, this link is surprising, given that for much of American history, Native Americans were considered separate from, and superior to, African Americans.[73] The widespread understanding of indigenous Californians as similar to African Americans may have helped justify a peculiarly Californian system of Native American enslavement.

This negative perception of indigenous Californians seems to have been influenced by three main factors. First, many indigenous Californians were enslaved by the Spanish and Mexicans in all but name, a practice continued under American control.[74] Second, because indigenous Californians ate berries, bugs, and roots and did not ride horses or hunt big game as did the indigenous people of the Plains, and because they had lived under Spanish and Mexican colonialism for so long, many settlers wrongly assumed that they did not know how to fight, and that they were naturally submissive and degraded.[75] These two factors, in turn, influenced the third. Middle-class white men, particularly those who had crossed the Plains, drew an unflattering comparison between indigenous Californians and the Sioux (who had already emerged as iconic warriors) or with Native Americans of story and memory.[76] Supposedly, while other Native Americans were honorable, physically imposing, and imbued with a savage manhood, indigenous Californians were degraded, physically weak, and naturally cowardly and submissive. These traits, when contrasted with those of gold rushers, justified middle-class white male domination of colonial society.

A decade later, white settlers only rarely drew similar parallels between Native Americans in British Columbia and people of African descent.[77] Instead, gold rushers fixated on what they saw as the misshapen bodies of the indigenous peoples of British Columbia. On the one hand, gold rushers focused considerable attention on the practice of head-flattening, seeing in it "a grotesque foil for Western ideals of womanhood."[78] In the eyes of middle-class white men, head-flattening was linked to their presumed decreased intelligence and degraded sexual practices, such as polygamy, and directly contrasted with the purity of white women.[79] Gold rushers also criticized Native Americans for having "stunted and mis-shapen" lower limbs, supposedly from spending so much time in canoes.[80] In both cases, settlers saw these distorted bodies as the result of the lifestyle choices of Native Americans, a fact reinforced when the coastal fishing tribes were compared unfavorably with the supposedly more active and athletic "*hunting tribes* of the interior."[81] Again, as in California, the appearance (and hence lifestyles and character) of indigenous peoples was judged against standards of whiteness and an idealized representation of what indigenous people should be like. In both cases, most Native Americans in British Columbia, but especially those along the coast, were deemed to be inferior, and as in California, this had the practical effect of further justifying colonialism in British Columbia. Unlike in California, however, the colonial project in British Columbia did not involve the enslavement of the indigenous population, so there was far less incentive to link the appearance of Native Americans to that of African Americans, especially so because the treatment of people of African descent was a marker of supposedly superior British principles.

Besides justifying the colonial project in both rushes, the appearance of indigenous peoples served Anglo-Americans as a form of shorthand with which to articulate and understand the meaning of whiteness. One way they did this was by spending considerable time focusing on the features and characteristics of indigenous women. In doing so, Anglo-Americans relied heavily on the image of the "princess" and her "darker twin," the squaw, so adroitly analyzed by Rayna Green.[82] Green argues that Anglo-Americans understood indigenous women through twinned figures, the princess and the squaw. Where princesses were lighter skinned, with European features, and civilized despite their savage surroundings, squaws were "too fat, and unlike their Princess sisters, dark and possessed of cruder, more Indian features." While the princess lived in the untouched wilderness, the squaw lived near the white man's settlements, where she, like her male counterparts, became degraded through contact with "civilization."[83] In both California and British Columbia, the image of the squaw dominated accounts of indigenous women, with descriptions focusing on their supposedly distorted and dark features, their lack of "proper" clothes, and their perceived sexual availability.[84]

But whereas indigenous women (and, for that matter men) became degraded through contact with civilization, white women flourished in it. Indeed, the link between white women and the idea of civilization was such that they were often used, along with the market economy and Christianity, as the metric for measuring an area's "advancement."[85] As the *Alta* put it in 1851, "It looks civilized and christianlike to see ladies daily passing along our streets, amusing themselves in that never-tiring occupation of shopping."[86] "Dame Shirley" believed that the "sweet restraining influences of pure womanhood" could cause even the roughest miners to act in a dignified and proper manner, and a lack of respectable white women explained the disorder of the gold mines.[87] In California and British Columbia, as in other colonial projects throughout the globe in the mid-nineteenth century, Christianity, capitalism, and respectable white women made up three interlocking aspects of colonial domination.[88]

As reflected in white settlers' perceptions of indigenous women's dress, indigenous women could not substitute for white women. In California, the former seemed incapable of dressing like white women; in British Columbia, where many indigenous women, at least near white settlements, wore the clothes of white women, gold rushers saw their choice of dress as akin to putting on airs.[89] To settlers, indigenous women could never be ladies, because they could never completely shed their association with the image of the squaw.[90] Their presence, especially when they attempted to dress like white women, justified the colonial project and served as a visible reminder of the advantages of white women.

Settlers also understood the Chinese as remarkably visually different from themselves in dress and body. Both the way they perceived these differences, and their reactions to them, underscore how they thought about white manliness in the goldfields. As they did with all groups, Anglo-Americans measured Chinese men and women against a standard of beauty that saw any deviation from the ideal of whiteness as degradation. To middle-class white men in California, the "portentous ugliness" of the Chinese suggested their "lying, knavery, and natural cowardice," while in British Columbia the "odd-looking, almond-eyed" Chinese were "a disagreeable, thievish lot."[91] By extension, only Anglo-American men and women had the appearance of proper members of each colonial society. Where Chinese faces and bodies suggested criminality and cowardice, Anglo-American faces and bodies (when properly attired) suggested honesty and bravery.

There was one aspect of Chinese appearance that drew more commentary and reaction from Anglo-Americans than any other, and that was Chinese men's practice of shaving the front of the head while wearing the rest of the hair in a long braid, or queue. The queue originated as a method of social control introduced by the Manchu in 1644. It served as a public marker of loyalty and subservience, and cutting it off was an act of rebellion against Manchu rule.[92] Few Anglo-Americans were aware of this, however, and saw in the queue only a strange and anachronistic sign of China's backwardness.[93] While a few pro-Chinese voices argued that the Chinese would make ideal citizens and were fast adapting to American ways, even the most optimistic of these noted, as did an article in the *Alta California* in 1851, that there seemed to be distinct limitations on their assimilation, foremost among which were the Chinese "language and costume," particularly the queue.[94] Most gold rushers saw in the queue the manifestation of Chinese resistance to "civilized" standards and values. Given this, it is not surprising that Chinese queues sometimes came in for violent attention. In several instances in California and British Columbia, settlers either dragged Chinese men by their queues or cut them off.[95] The attacks were a way to force the Chinese to conform to Anglo-American norms and, simultaneously, underscored the claim that Chinese men were weak and effeminate and would never actually be equal to middle-class white men.

The Native American and Chinese population shared another key characteristic according to settlers in California and British Columbia: both were allegedly reservoirs of disease. In California, attention soon came to focus on the Chinese population, and specifically upon San Francisco's Chinatown, as a source of possible contagion. In British Columbia, the focus was more on Native Americans, especially the Songhee village adjacent to Victoria. In both cases, concerns focused on nonwhites whose population concentrations directly abutted significant concentrations of white settlers. Ultimately, concerns about illness in nonwhites were actually concerns for Anglo-American health. At the same time, constructing nonwhites' spaces as sources of contagion that could affect whites' spaces suggested that disease in nonwhite bodies was a normative condition, while for whites disease was an abnormal status.

Disease and health were of paramount concern to Anglo-Americans in both gold rushes. Gold rushers recognized the hardships and dangers involved in mining, but they also believed that their experiences in the gold mines would toughen them and make them stronger.[96] Sickness threatened to undercut all of that, revealing the weakness of their bodies and possibly denying them a "good death," surrounded by loved ones.[97] As William Taylor put it, with "no kind sister's hand to wipe the death-sweat from the brow; nor affectionate wife to impress on the pallid cheek the parting kiss[,] . . . no gathering of the children around the departing father to receive his last, solemn charge, catch his last smile and lingering look," "death . . . seemed clothed with extraordinary terrors."[98]

Anglo-Americans believed that both the environment and a person's habits could cause sickness by disrupting the delicate balance inside the body. Disease and ill-health, therefore, had two interlocking causes. Men got sick because of the environment or because something in their characters or bodies made them susceptible.[99] It was this second understanding that had particular bearing on understandings of white manliness in the gold rushes. To some commentators, it seemed as if disease among gold rushers was almost wholly attributable to moral failings. For example, in British Columbia, Matthew Macfie claimed, "most of the diseases I have witnessed have been brought on by imprudence in the way of exposure or excess," while Thomas Allsop asserted that "the greatest cause of illness here [in California] is, excessive drinking. . . . Of the deaths here, three out of four are directly owing to drunkenness and its consequences."[100] But most Anglo-Americans shied away from identifying moral failings as the cause of so much disease among gold rushers and instead preferred to blame "the sickly season" and other environmental causes, thereby removing their own morality from the discussion.[101] In stark contrast, Anglo-American discussions about disease among nonwhites almost exclusively focused on moral failings as the causative, or decisive, factor. Of special concern was the perceived propensity of nonwhites, and especially the Chinese and indigenous populations, to live in filth. The mid-nineteenth century saw the earliest rumblings of the sanitation concerns that would come to be omnipresent during the latter part of the century and would provide a key justification for imperialism.[102] During the California and British Columbia gold rushes, concerns over filth and disease among nonwhites could become almost hysterical.

The newspapers in California and British Columbia played the key role in disseminating an understanding of the spaces of nonwhites as diseased.[103] Under the heading "Still the Celestials Come," the *Alta California* reported in 1854 that "it is a notorious fact that the domicils of this singular race, are generally filthy beyond all description," and that it was "exceedingly probable that San Francisco will not be exempted from the scourge [cholera]" unless "some prompt measures [are] adopted to make them keep their habitations in a cleanly state."[104] However, dire warnings such as these from California newspapers paled in comparison to the dozens of articles printed in British Columbia papers warning of the threat posed by indigenous populations. As the *British Columbian* claimed in 1862, "That the filthy habits of these Indians engenders contagion, and that generally of the most fatal type, is sufficiently known by everybody"; and with the advent of smallpox among the Native Americans, "the immediate removal of the poor creatures . . . admits of neither argument or delay."[105] By locating disease in spaces occupied by nonwhites, settlers asserted not only the unsuitability of those people to govern themselves but also the necessity for the colonial government to take ever-more invasive measures to regulate and control nonwhites and their living areas.

Fear about preserving the health of white bodies and spaces led to sometimes drastic actions. In California, fire hoses were turned on Chinatowns throughout the state. Though weakly condemned as "savor[ing] somewhat of rowdyism," the action was generally applauded for both washing out the "notoriously filthy" Chinese residences and for encouraging the Chinese to relocate to a safe distance from white residences.[106] In British Columbia, a long-standing push by some settlers to relocate indigenous populations away from towns such as Victoria and New Westminster found new traction in the context of the smallpox epidemic of 1862.[107] To settlers in British Columbia, it was unsurprising that smallpox spread rapidly in the "nest[s] of filth and crime" that were Native American settlements. The solution, offered in late April, was simple: "The entire Indian population should be removed from the reservation to a place remote from communication with the whites; whilst the infected houses with all their trumpery should be burned to ashes."[108] By mid-May, this policy was put into effect near Victoria, with the police burning over one hundred indigenous homes and forcing the residents to leave.[109] These actions had a disastrous effect on the indigenous population, spreading smallpox throughout the colony and precipitating a massive demographic decline.[110] Though some middle-class whites expressed concern for sick Chinese or Native Americans, most commentators seemed content to preserve the health of white bodies and spaces.

Medical examinations also emerged as a particularly powerful way of knowing various types of racialized bodies. Medical examinations confirmed for some gold rushers that non- and off-whites were physically inferior to whites. Even if the results of these medical examinations were not widely distributed, they are important as manifestations of popular attitudes.[111] One of the most startling cases occurred in California where, in the *California State Medical Journal*, R. Bell presented his 1855 autopsy of a young Native American male. Diagnosing death from intussusception (where part of the intestine collapses in on the other), Bell went on to draw far-reaching conclusions about the nature of indigenous bodies. "Indulg[ing] in the luxuries enjoyed by civilized people," according to Bell, caused obesity, laziness, vascular and lymphatic disorders, and fatty disease in the indigenous brain. On the nature of the Native American brain, Bell spent considerable time, detailing not only its allegedly inferior size but also its "deficiency of the superior, or intellectual portions" that could be found in white brains.[112] Like Bell, many Anglo-Americans in California and British Columbia drew inspiration from thinkers like Samuel Morton and Josiah Nott and concluded that humankind existed in a biologically determined hierarchy in which middle-class white men occupied the very peak, and people such as the Native Americans and Chinese, the very bottom.[113]

Medical examinations not only confirmed Anglo-American perceptions that non- and off-whites were inferior to whites, but they also confirmed the nature of that inferiority. For instance, medical testimony in British Columbia held that mixed-race girls developed sexually earlier than their white counterparts, helping confirm the image of indigenous and other nonwhite women as lascivious and sexually available.[114] In another instance, during a trial where two white men stood accused of getting a young Native American woman, Sophie, drunk and then raping and killing her, David

Brown, the coroner, testified that "if [the body was of] a white girl of the same age [I] would say she had been raped[,] but [I] could not say in the case of an Indian girl." The two men were eventually found guilty only of supplying Sophie with the liquor that led to her death.[115] Medical testimony seemed to offer objective evidence that nonwhite women were sexual objects while simultaneously setting white women apart as sacrosanct.

Physical examinations could also provide proof of the natural character of non- and off-whites in other ways. Diseases, and especially sexually transmitted diseases, were used on several occasions to prove the degraded and criminal nature of Italian, Chinese, and indigenous men charged with felonies.[116] In each of these cases, the alleged presence of sexually transmitted disease in the victim was enough to convict the men. The case of an indigenous man named Kar-le, also known as "Charley," illustrates this point and deserves further consideration. On the last day of 1862, Kar-le was arraigned on charges of having either drugged or physically assaulted a young white child, Caroline Estol, and then sexually assaulting her near Esquimalt, on Vancouver Island. Despite Kar-le's testimony that the girl had choked on a nut and passed out, and the testimony of the woman who employed him that she continued to trust him with her daughter, the case quickly came to focus on the child's apparent suffering from gonorrhea. If Kar-le could be proven to have gonorrhea, this would be enough evidence for a conviction.

However, a dispute soon arose between various doctors about whether or not Kar-le did, in fact, have gonorrhea. Joseph Haggin found signs of gonorrhea on his first inspection, but failed to do so on his second, while James Dickson was unsure whether it was gonorrhea at all, and John Helmcken failed to find any symptoms of the disease whatsoever. Alleging that Kar-le must have wiped away the discharged pus, Haggin and Dickson ordered the guard to keep Kar-le standing in the court yard for four hours. They then returned and squeezed his genitals to produce pus, proving to their satisfaction, if not to Helmcken's, that Kar-le was in fact diseased.[117] Whether such evidence was enough to convict Kar-le was not recorded. This episode reveals the degree to which Anglo-American men felt both the need and the authority to probe nonwhite bodies in order to know their true character. Tellingly, although there are multiple cases of white men committing sexual assault and rape, sexually transmitted diseases do not appear to have been at issue in those cases.[118] Once again, the discourse surrounding disease served to establish nonwhite bodies as threatening and different, a difference that required colonial authorities to observe not only the behavior but also the bodies of nonwhite colonial subjects.

For middle-class white men, observations of death and rituals of grieving were, like medical examinations, a way of confirming appearances. In the mid-nineteenth century, Anglo-Americans believed that death was a crucial moment in a man's life, as it revealed his true nature and path forward through the afterlife.[119] Maintaining control during, and sometimes over, his death marked an individual as a proper, respectable white man.[120] It was also crucial that he be surrounded by loved ones as he died, so that the family could "assess the state of the dying person's soul" and "evaluate the family's chances for a reunion in heaven."[121] A good death was one in which the man, surrounded by family, met death quietly but bravely, showing neither fear nor unbecoming levity. At the same time, the behavior of the grievers also reflected on their own characters, and the entire nexus of rituals surrounding death and grieving could be juxtaposed against the less restrained and supposedly illegitimate death and grieving rituals of nonwhites in order to show the superiority of white men.

In California and British Columbia, of course, the man who had family, let alone friends, to surround him and witness his death was rare indeed. As it would during the American Civil War, the prospect of dying away from home raised profound concerns for many gold rushers.[122] The fear of dying alone was such that many men, fearing that they were near death or that they would die if they stayed, returned home to be with loved ones.[123] Even more common were the lamentations for men who were dying, or who had died, alone.[124] Though the prospect of being denied a good death was profoundly disturbing, most gold rushers did not seem to dwell on it, believing, in the time-honored tradition of young men everywhere, that it was not going to happen to them.

Care for the sick, dying, and dead was one way that middle-class whites were supposed to be able to demonstrate their assumed innate superiority over non- and off-white others. William Ryan observed one such scene in California as he watched Mr. Larkins, rumored to have killed his wife, being tended on his deathbed by his young daughter. Despite the presumed guilt of the father, she cared for him with "the tenderness so peculiar to the female sex" and "gentle affection."[125] Larkins, as it turns out, was lucky. Most white men who died in the gold rushes did not have family to care for them and died "poor and friendless[,] . . . alone, without hope."[126] Nevertheless, the ideal remained, and in the gold rushes it often fell to white friends, often male but preferably female, to provide succor and comfort.[127] This ideal contrasted greatly with the perceived reaction of nonwhites to death and suffering. To W. Champness, the reaction of nonwhites to sickness and death presented a "beautiful contrast" with the "abundant instances where pestilence and death have been fearlessly braved even by tender and delicate Christian women."[128] Native Americans came in for special condemnation on this point, being accused of abandoning their sick out of fear of becoming infected themselves.

Further separating nonwhites from whites were the ways in which they mourned the dead. In both California and British Columbia, white settlers tended to express disgust or annoyance at nonwhite burial and mourning rituals. For instance, typical judgments from California contemptuously noted the "continuous howling" and the wearing of a mixture of pitch and charcoal to mark the period of mourning in indigenous death and mourning rituals.[129] Typical, too, is the claim in the fictional biography of Alfred Jackson that the Native Americans simply chose one woman to be the chief mourner, regardless of her relationship with the deceased.[130] Other nonwhites, such as the Chinese, were also singled out for their unfamiliar rituals—in particular, their funeral parades and preference for shipping the deceased back to China.[131] In each case, nonwhites' rituals surrounding illness, death, and grief were set apart as inferior and antithetical to the idealized qualities of Anglo-American grieving and burial rituals.

Less common, but more visible, was the behavior of individuals faced with execution. Public deaths provided a highly observable way to judge an individual's character. The behavior of the condemned never solely reflected their character but instead had wider gender and racial repercussions. The simultaneous executions of two white men, Joseph Hetherington and Philander Brace, in California demonstrate the difference between supposedly manly and unmanly ways to die. The *Alta California* reported minutely on the appearance and actions of Hetherington and Brace after their sentencing by the Vigilance Committee of 1856. Entering Hetherington's cell, the *Alta* reporter found him "cool and collected" and "ready and prepared for the fate that awaited him." On the scaffold, Hetherington gave a speech proclaiming his innocence and stating that he was ready to meet his God.

All in all, Hetherington acted with restraint, dignity, and a fitting degree of solemnity. The same could not be said for Brace, however. The reporter found that Brace manifested "no penitence or dread," and that he treated the priest to "the most obscene and vulgar language" and threatened to kick him out. On the scaffold, Brace continually interrupted Hetherington's speech, referred to the crowd as "ignoramuses," and claimed he did not need religion as he was already drunk. Needless to say, in the eyes of respectable middle-class whites, the "wonderful and revolting performances" of Brace tied him to the lack of self-restraint and cowardice expected of condemned nonwhites, whereas Hetherington met a manly death.[132]

Just over a decade later, a similarly twinned execution in British Columbia would also seemingly reveal the link between an individual's identity and his behavior on the scaffold. In 1867, James Barry, a white man, and Nikel Palsk, an indigenous man, were hanged for separate acts of murder in the Cariboo.[133] During the trials, the *Cariboo Sentinel* drew an interesting distinction between the two men's actions. Palsk's act of murder was "less revolting to humanity" than Barry's because "the perpetrator was an unenlightened savage," while Barry was a white man who could be found "in our midst."[134] But although Barry's racial identity made his act of murder more unexpected and appalling, it also provided the means by which he, and white men in general, could ultimately be redeemed on the scaffold. During his execution, Barry, like Hetherington, "betrayed no signs of trepidation, but sustained himself throughout the trying scene with the utmost fortitude and courage." Palsk, on the other hand, struggled as he was led to the scaffold and "behaved in a very excited manner, and indulg[ed] in the most foul and blasphemous language[,] . . . endeavouring all the while to extricate himself from his pinions."[135] In their deaths both Hetherington and Barry demonstrated essential characteristics of white manliness. They were brave, solemn, and prepared. In life, the alleged criminal behavior of both men meant that respectable Anglo-Americans would have viewed them as off-white and unmanly; but in the moments before their deaths, both men were able to somewhat rehabilitate themselves and demonstrate that, whatever their flaws, they remained, to some degree, white men. This was never an option for Palsk. Even had he met his death in keeping with Anglo-American ideals, this would likely have been attributed to savage nobility, admirable in its own way, but never the equal of white manliness.[136] The connections between

Palsk and Brace reveal the ways that perceptions of bodies, character, and white manliness intersected even at the moment of death.

CONCLUSION

For middle-class white men in California and British Columbia, appearance was one of the key ways they came to understand themselves, their neighbors, and the society they shared. In particular, middle-class white men read dress and bodies in order to categorize their world. Their understandings of dress and bodies remained remarkably consistent between the two rushes. This is not, of course, to say that developments in each gold rush mirrored the other. As just one example, key figures such as the dandy and greenhorn ceased to be cultural touchstones, while the ideas they represented were transmitted and transformed into a discourse about suitability for mining that placed a heavier emphasis on the body.

Ultimately, in both California and British Columbia, white settlers used their understanding of clothes and of bodies to justify and explain the dominance of white men over an array of non- and off-whites. While this logic remained consistent, the specific meanings attached to clothes and bodies shifted subtly but significantly from 1848 to 1871. In California, middle-class white men relied on clothes to determine an individual's character more than they would in British Columbia. Part of the reason for this shift was the growing awareness that clothes could be worn as a disguise. Over time, gold rushers became increasingly concerned both with disreputable whites passing themselves off as respectable, and with the challenge that non- and off-whites who dressed like miners posed. Additionally, in California, middle-class white men's emphasis on clothes reflected an understanding of their identity as contextual. In other words, gold rushers in California believed that the way they acted and dressed reflected an aspect of their identity, one that might not be wholly appropriate in the East they had left. By the time of the British Columbia rush, however, middle-class white men saw their behavior and actions in the gold mines as an intensification of values that had been repressed in the East, and they seem to have come to believe that the rush represented an opportunity to fully realize their true character. By the time of the British Columbia rush, in other words, a middle-class white man generally felt little compulsion to switch back and forth between an appearance as a civilized urbanite and an appearance as a rough miner, preferring to combine both into a new synthesis. Though Anglo-Americans did not disregard clothing completely, this new synthesis encouraged them to emphasize the body. As a result, the ability of nonwhites to claim status as respectable members of gold rush society, regardless of their dress, became increasingly limited.

Endings and Beginnings

THE GOLD RUSHES OF CALIFORNIA AND BRITISH COLUM-
bia could not last. Eventually the gold ran out or remained only in deep
veins that required machinery and capital to extract. Where mining continued, it was done by large companies with men working for wages. Some
miners stuck around, working in the cities and farms that came to dominate
the landscape, but many more left, looking for fortune elsewhere or returning home. Behind them, they left silted rivers and bare, eroded hills. But
as widespread and lasting as these environmental consequences were, they
paled in comparison to the scope and impact of the social orders the gold
miners created.

The massive and diverse wave of gold rushers swept away the existing
societies and replaced them with new ones. In both locations, the indigenous population was killed, displaced, or confined to reservations. In California, the land was also wrested away from the Mexican population. The
end result in California and British Columbia was the same: a colonial
landscape in which self-professed white men tended to own the biggest and
best parcels of land. Gold mining also stimulated the building of cities and
the farms with which to feed them.[1] But while mining camps and towns had
provided the first major markets for the farms, the widespread use of
hydraulic mining in the Sierra Nevada caused massive siltation and flooding in the downstream farmlands. In 1884, Judge Lorenzo Sawyer, a former

miner who had stayed to practice law, ruled that mining companies were no longer allowed to discharge debris into the Yuba River, effectively ending hydraulic mining.[2] The way was now clear for agriculture to become the dominant industry in California.

In British Columbia a somewhat different transition occurred. British Columbia never saw the genocidal level of violence against Native Americans that characterized the California experience. Nevertheless, in the decades following the gold rush, Native Americans were forced out of a variety of industries and confined to poverty-stricken reservations.[3] Fishing, logging, and coal mining quickly emerged as the major industries in most areas of the province.[4] At the same time, British Columbia joined Canada in 1871, transitioning from an HBC-dominated colonial society to a more democratic form of government. In both California and British Columbia, therefore, the gold rushes dramatically reshaped the political, demographic, and environmental landscape, accelerating both regions' integration into their respective nations.

While the gold rushes died out, their effects on ideas of white manliness persisted. To explore white manliness in the context of the gold rushes of the West Coast is to do more than interrogate two key interwoven normative identities of the mid-nineteenth century: it is to trace how these identities were fundamentally bound up in the understanding and exercise of authority. Though it was never a given, strong cultural currents made it very likely that middle-class white men from the eastern United States and Great Britain would define white manliness as the key identifier of who should rule in the colonial societies of California and British Columbia. But because gender and race are social constructions, the diverse and unruly social and political situations in both gold rushes meant that the boundaries of white manliness were never solidified, never fully agreed upon, and instead were constantly negotiated.

Despite these disagreements, a general trend between 1848 and 1871 is evident in how Anglo-Americans in the goldfields talked about white manliness. For gold rushers, part of the appeal of the California gold rush was that it gave them a chance to articulate a reactionary form of martial manhood that rejected many of the assumptions of the then-dominant restrained manhood of the eastern United States and Great Britain. At the same time, however, many of these men sought to establish a more "civilized" social order and worried about how friends and family in the East viewed them. As what had usually been intended to be short sojourns in the goldfields turned into permanent settlement, middle-class white men grew increasingly uncomfortable with some of the more radical rejections of eastern standards. But they also did not want to give up the claim that the new forms of white manliness in the West were distinct from, and in some ways superior to, older forms of white manliness in the East. This began a process of reconciling the two forms of white manliness into something new, a process that continued in British Columbia. In British Columbia, middle-class white men generally stopped switching between behaviors and dress that marked them as either restrained white men or martial white men and, instead, began combining the two into a nascent hybrid form of white manhood. This combination of martial manhood and restrained manhood anticipated in many ways the development of white masculinity that historian Gail Bederman has identified as emerging in the late nineteenth century.

Bederman has argued that between 1880 and 1917, ideas of manliness and middle-class identity came under pressure originating from large-scale socioeconomic changes that virtually eliminated "small-scale, competitive capitalism."[5] These changing conditions encouraged middle-class men to articulate a new concept, "masculinity," which emphasized the strength and authority of the white male body, but did so without the moral component of both martial manliness and restrained manliness. Bederman argues that the development of masculinity encouraged middle-class men to see themselves as "a little bit 'barbarous,'" combining the strengths of civilization and savagery in one body.[6]

Gold rushers in California and British Columbia would never claim to be savage, but in their embrace of a blended martial white manhood and restrained white manhood, they were taking the first steps in that direction. Functionally, both forms of white manhood linked particular bodies and behaviors with a colonial arrangement of authority and power. Additionally, from the 1840s to the early 1870s, ideas of biological determinism became increasingly pronounced as modern forms of racialist discourse emerged full-blown in the aftermath of Darwin's and Herbert Spencer's publications and events like the American Civil War and the rebellion in India. When these factors combined with the desire of gold rushers to more closely conform to eastern standards of white manliness, while also maintaining their sense of difference, it was relatively easy for many

Anglo-Americans in the West to blend ideas of martial manhood and restrained manhood in a way that increasingly stressed physical bodies.

This is not to say that the process was smooth or predetermined. In California, republican ideas about the proper virtues necessary for citizenship, and about who could embody those virtues, framed a debate over how to define white manliness in the California gold rush. While some groups, such as Native Americans and the Chinese, were too alien to be considered either white or manly, there was greater debate about the status of African Americans and Latin Americans. For their part, African Americans, Chinese, and Latin Americans all contested their status.[7] Even the behaviors that marked an individual as a white man were contested between a rougher, more diverse segment of society grouped together under the banner of the Democratic Party and their predominately middle-class opponents. In this multiway contest over the definition of white manliness in California, colonial authority gradually moved to support a narrow understanding of white manliness characterized by ethnic origins from western and northern Europe and the values and behaviors emphasized by middle-class white men.

In British Columbia, the debate and trajectory were somewhat different, largely because of the persistence of British colonial authority. Concern over American influence led colonial authorities to advocate a "colorblind" colonial policy, in which they claimed that nationality was the single most important defining characteristic. In practice however, this "colorblind" colonial policy was contentious and uneven. The rhetoric of colorblindness was never intended to suggest an egalitarian society but to buttress a class- and nationality-based hierarchy while obscuring how race and gender actually functioned in the colony. Nevertheless, the rhetoric of colorblindness did create opportunities for non-Europeans, especially those of African descent, to participate more equally in colonial society. These limited gains relied on the continuing perception by the British colonial elites that the American population was the real threat; and when this apparent threat receded, the policy of colorblindness was quietly jettisoned in favor of a growing belief that a common bond of white manliness linked British and American men of European descent.

That ideas of white manliness increasingly unified rather than divided men of European descent stemmed, at least in part, from the way that white manliness gradually came to combine aspects of restrained manliness and martial manliness. In the early 1800s, both forms of manhood relied heavily on appearance and behavior to signify whether an individual was, in fact, manly. But as ideas of biological difference consolidated into modern conceptions of race over the middle decades of the 1800s, it became increasingly possible for middle-class men to reconcile the different behaviors attached to each form of manliness by insisting that, while behaviors changed to suit the situation, their core identities as white men were rooted in their bodies.

Central to the emergence of this hybrid form of white manhood was the goldfield system that connected disparate gold rushes through flows of ideas, people, money, and goods. The connections led to widely shared assumptions about how white men should act in, and react to, the conditions of a gold rush. The goldfield system maintained not only the reality of actual connections between the gold rushes but also the perception of middle-class white men that gold rush society differed from the world they had left. It was only when middle-class white men began to see their society as incorporated into the larger Anglo-American society that the goldfield system finally faded. Crucially, for many settlers the turning point was the arrival of significant numbers of white women. The arrival of white women did not stop mining or change economic connections between mining areas, but it did mean that one of the main ways middle-class white men justified their difference from easterners (a lack of white women) became less believable. This, combined with the economic transformation of the surviving mines into sites of wage labor, undercut the justifications used by middle-class white men to explain why both their society and western white men looked so different from their eastern counterparts.

It might seem inevitable that as the gold rushes ended, the distinctive version of white manliness there would fade as well. But while it did fade, it did not disappear completely. The memory of gold rush society—of California and British Columbia as lands of opportunity, but only to those with the strength of character and body to see it through—continued to inform a regional variant of white manliness long after the rush had passed.

In the same vein, the gold rushes of the Pacific slope seem to have had an impact on the development of ideas of white masculinity in the East. Between 1848 and 1920, America's fascination with the myth of the frontier as a place of manly rebirth and opportunity exploded into a national obsession (most notably with the groundbreaking publication of Owen Wister's *The Virginian* in 1902). Though the Great Plains and Southwest dominated this imaginary West and elevated the cowboy to masculine folk-hero status, the mines of the Pacific slope and the figure of the miner also emerged as popular touchstones for the new masculinity.[8] The image of the masculine white miner conquering both the landscape and nonwhite peoples reoccurred again and again in popular works of art and literature.[9] With the discovery of gold in the Klondike in 1896, the image of the masculine white miner enjoyed an even greater popularity. Tellingly, many of the novels about the Klondike featured grizzled old forty-niners handing the mantle of masculinity to a new generation. Such is the case in Jack London's 1912 novel *Smoke Bellew*, in which a young urban dandy accompanies his uncle, a veteran of California, to the Klondike, where he, too, becomes as "tough as rawhide."[10] The same time period also saw the publication of early histories of the gold rushes and the formation of pioneer societies dedicated to commemorating and celebrating the rushes and heroizing the participants.[11] No less an embodiment of the new masculinity and the West than President Teddy Roosevelt read Bret Harte and other celebratory accounts of the California gold rush as a child and young man.[12]

While more work is necessary in order to understand the extent of the influence, it is clear that ideas that emerged in California and British Columbia anticipated and helped shape the concept of white masculinity that emerged at the dawn of the twentieth century. This concept continues to be manifested in innumerable current contexts, from stand-your-ground laws, to attitudes about police violence, to opinions about the place of immigrants in both societies. In the United States, the Tea Party seems like a reformulation of the San Francisco Vigilance Committee of 1856 (whose members also tied themselves explicitly to the supposed values of the Founding Fathers), in that both are steeped in ideas of American exceptionalism, popular (but racially exclusive) republicanism, and the belief that they are "the people" rising up against corrupt government. We see it also in modern efforts to narrowly define citizenship by restricting voting among African Americans, or by restricting the immigration of Muslims, in the name of protecting the republic from corruption. In the 2015 Canadian federal election, the Conservative Party attempted to mobilize voters by banning the wearing of the niqab at citizenship ceremonies, proposing to establish a hotline to report "barbaric cultural practices," and extolling the virtues of "old stock" (meaning white or western European) immigrants. We see it also in the way American and Canadian men today are often contrasted—in light of ideas about white masculinity—with Middle Eastern men, who supposedly lack the courage and martial abilities of white men, and who, like Native Americans in the nineteenth century, resort to strategies (such as ambushes, planting IEDs, or killing women and children) that reveal their lack of moral character. In short, the notions of white manhood established in the nineteenth century persist today, and their legacies can be seen everywhere, from the least-threatening rituals of male practical joking to the most menacing expressions of white male superiority. The gold rush roots of modern North American white masculinity are crucial to understanding our current epoch.

NOTES

INTRODUCTION

1   Jacob Fisher to Frederick Fisher, 21 September 1850, Mss C-B 547: 2, in Gold
    Rush Letters, Bancroft Library, Berkeley, California (hereafter BANC).
2   E. G. B., "From the Mines," *Alta California*, 10 May 1849.
3   Azariah Smith, *The Gold Discovery Journal of Azariah Smith*, ed. David Bigler
    (Logan: Utah State University Press, 1996), 108–9. On the Mexican-American
    War, see Robert Walter Johannsen, *To the Halls of the Montezumas: The Mexi-
    can War in the American Imagination* (New York: Oxford University Press,
    1985). On the demographic composition of pre-rush California, see Rodman W.
    Paul, *California Gold: The Beginning of Mining in the Far West* (Cambridge,
    Mass.: Harvard University Press, 1947), 23–29; Sucheng Chan, "A People of
    Exceptional Character: Ethnic Diversity, Nativism, and Racism in the Califor-
    nia Gold Rush," in *Rooted in Barbarous Soil: People, Culture, and Community
    in Gold Rush California*, ed. Kevin Starr and Richard J. Orsi (Berkeley: Univer-
    sity of California Press), 50–57.
4   Rodman Paul, *Mining Frontiers of the Far West, 1848–1880* (New York: Holt,
    Reinhart and Winston, 1963); Charlene Porsild, *Gamblers and Dreamers: Women,
    Men, and Community in the Klondike* (Vancouver: University of British Colum-
    bia Press, 1988).
5   John Kasson, *Rudeness and Civility: Manners in Nineteenth-Century Urban
    America* (New York: Hill and Wang, 1990), 71. To put this growth in perspec-
    tive: it still meant that by 1860, only one in five Americans lived in an urban
    center. See Charles Nelson Glaab and A. Theodore Brown, *A History of Urban
    America* (New York: Macmillan, 1967), 26.
6   On this see Marcus Cunliffe, *Chattel Slavery and Wage Slavery: The Anglo
    American Context, 1830–1860* (Athens: University of Georgia Press, 1979);
    Eric Foner, *Free Soil, Free Labor, Free Men: The Ideology of the Republican
    Party before the Civil War* (New York: Oxford University Press, 1995), esp.
    introduction; Thomas Augst, *The Clerk's Tale: Young Men and Moral Life in*

Nineteenth-Century America (Chicago: University of Chicago Press, 2003); Christopher Clark, "The Consequences of the Market Revolution in the American North," in *The Market Revolution in America: Social, Political, and Religious Expressions, 1800–1880*, ed. Melvyn Stokes and Stephen Conway (Charlottesville: University Press of Virginia, 1996), 26–30. These changes affected the countryside as well. See Hal S. Barron, *Those Who Stayed Behind: Rural Society in Nineteenth-Century New England* (New York: Cambridge University Press, 1984), 16–31.

7   Robert Woods, *The Demography of Victorian England and Wales* (Cambridge: Cambridge University Press, 2000), 360–62. The best account of what life was like in London during this period is Liza Picard, *Victorian London: The Life of a City, 1840–1870* (New York: St. Martin's Press, 2006). On reactions to urbanization, see David Newsome, *The Victorian World Picture: Perceptions and Introspections in an Age of Change* (New Brunswick, N.J.: Rutgers University Press, 1997), 7–8, 15–49.

8   Newsome, *The Victorian World Picture*, 74–75; David Alderson, *Mansex Fine: Religion, Manliness and Imperialism in Nineteenth-Century British Culture* (New York: Manchester University Press, 1998), 10–11.

9   Cunliffe, *Chattel Slavery and Wage Slavery*; William Van Vugt, *Britain to America: Mid-Nineteenth-Century Immigrants to the United States* (Urbana: University of Illinois Press, 1999), 3–4; Daniel Walker Howe, "Victorian Culture in America," in *Victorian America*, ed. Daniel Walker Howe ([Philadelphia]: University of Pennsylvania Press, 1976), 3–10; Blake McKelvey, *American Urbanization: A Comparative History* (Glenview, Ill.: Scott, Foresman, 1973), 27–28, 40.

10 Gertrude Himmelfarb, *Victorian Minds* (New York: Knopf, 1968), 276–77; Howe, "Victorian Culture in America," 14–16; Brian Roberts, *American Alchemy: The California Gold Rush and Middle-Class Culture* (Chapel Hill: University of North Carolina Press, 2000), 2–15; Susan Lee Johnson, *Roaring Camp: The Social World of the California Gold Rush* (New York: W. W. Norton, 2000), 135, 279–80.

11 Amy S. Greenberg, *Manifest Manhood and the Antebellum American Empire* (New York: Cambridge University Press, 2005), 11.

12 Howe, "Victorian Culture in America," 10, 17. See also Himmelfarb, *Victorian Minds*, 277; Christopher Lane, *Hatred and Civility: The Antisocial Life in Victorian England* (New York: Columbia University Press, 2006), 2.

13 Newsome, *The Victorian World Picture*, 7–12; Himmelfarb, *Victorian Minds*, 276–77; Howe, "Victorian Culture in America," 4–5, 14–15; Roberts, *American Alchemy*, 121–29; Susan Thorne, "The Conversion of Englishmen and the

Conversion of the World Inseparable: Missionary Imperialism and the Language of Class in Early Industrial Britain," in *Tensions of Empire: Colonial Cultures in a Bourgeois World*, ed. Frederick Cooper and Ann Laura Stoler (Berkeley: University of California Press, 1997), 238–39.

14   Greenberg, *Manifest Manhood*, 12.

15   Ray Allen Billington, *Land of Savagery / Land of Promise: The European Image of the American Frontier in the Nineteenth Century* (New York: Norton, 1981), 130, 151–52; Reginald Horsman, *Race and Manifest Destiny: The Origins of American Racial Anglo-Saxonism* (Cambridge, Mass.: Harvard University Press, 1981), 83–85; John David Unruh, *The Plains Across: The Overland Emigrants and the Trans-Mississippi West, 1840–1860* (Urbana: University of Illinois Press, 1979), 14, 30.

16   Greenberg, *Manifest Manhood*, 12–13; John Tosh, *A Man's Place: Masculinity and the Middle-Class Home in Victorian England* (New Haven, Conn.: Yale University Press, 1999), 125; Roberts, *American Alchemy*. On the South, see Craig Thompson Friend and Lorri Glover, *Southern Manhood: Perspectives on Masculinity in the Old South* (Athens: University of Georgia Press, 2004).

17   See, for example, Thorne, "The Conversion of Englishmen," 238–62; Anne McClintock, *Imperial Leather: Race, Gender, and Sexuality in the Colonial Contest* (New York: Routledge, 1995); Philippa Levine, *Prostitution, Race, and Politics: Policing Venereal Disease in the British Empire* (New York: Routledge, 2003).

18   The term *off-white* refers to a range of peoples occupying what María DeGuzmán calls the "critically unacknowledged third position" between a black-white binary in the understanding of race. Off-white peoples were often of European or mixed-European descent, but were sometimes understood by people of Anglo-Saxon descent as problematic, occupying a blurry middle ground between white and nonwhite. See María DeGuzmán, *Spain's Long Shadow: The Black Legend, Off-Whiteness, and Anglo American Empire* (Minneapolis: University of Minnesota Press, 2005), xxvii. See also David R. Roediger, *Working toward Whiteness: How America's Immigrants Became White; The Strange Journey from Ellis Island to the Suburbs* (New York: Basic Books, 2005), 4; McClintock, *Imperial Leather*, 132–80.

19   Robert F. Berkhofer, *The White Man's Indian: Images of the American Indian from Columbus to the Present* (New York: Knopf, 1978), 28.

20   J. A. Banks and Olive Banks, *Feminism and Family Planning in Victorian England* (Liverpool, U.K.: Liverpool University Press, 1964), 58–61, 71–82; Richard Dyer, *White* (New York: Routledge, 1997), 57; Catherine Hall, *Civilising Subjects: Colony and Metropole in the English Imagination, 1830–1867* (Chicago: University of Chicago Press, 2002), 141–42; Fredrick B. Pike, *The United States*

and Latin America: Myths and Stereotypes of Civilization and Nature (Austin: University of Texas Press, 1992), xiiv, 6; Tosh, A Man's Place, 2–6, 103–11; Winthrop Jordan, White over Black: American Attitudes toward the Negro, 1550–1812 (Chapel Hill: University of North Carolina Press, 1968); Berkhofer, The White Man's Indian; Cunliffe, Chattel Slavery and Wage Slavery; Hazel Waters, Racism on the Victorian Stage: Representation of Slavery and the Black Character (Cambridge: Cambridge University Press, 2007), 89–130, passim; Christine Bolt, Victorian Attitudes to Race (Toronto: University of Toronto Press, 1971), 37–42, 75–86.

21   Newsome, The Victorian World Picture, 3–49; Foner, Free Soil, xi–xxxi.

22   Newsome, The Victorian World Picture, 26; G. M. Young, Victorian England: Portrait of an Age, 2nd ed. (New York: Oxford University Press, 1953), 53–54; Robert Bernard Martin, Enter Rumour: Four Early Victorian Scandals (London: Faber and Faber, 1962), 190–220.

23   For two suggestive works on the partial transmission of eastern values during the California gold rush, see Roberts, American Alchemy; Lewis O. Saum, The Popular Mood of Pre–Civil War America (Westport, Conn.: Greenwood Press, 1980), 200–24.

24   Ann Laura Stoler and Frederick Cooper, "Between Metropole and Colony: Rethinking a Research Agenda," in Cooper and Stoler, Tensions of Empire, 27. All quotes are as found in the sources, except where modified for clarity by ellipses or by text enclosed in square brackets.

25   See J. S. Holliday, Rush for Riches: Gold Fever and the Making of California (Oakland: Oakland Museum of California, 1999); H. W. Brands, The Age of Gold: The California Gold Rush and the New American Dream (New York: Doubleday, 2002); Malcolm J. Rohrbough, Days of Gold: The California Gold Rush and the American Nation (Berkeley: University of California Press, 1997); Adele Perry, On the Edge of Empire: Gender, Race, and the Making of British Columbia, 1849–1871 (Toronto: University of Toronto Press, 2001).

26   Some exceptions are Paul, Mining Frontiers of the Far West; Jay Monaghan, Australians and the Gold Rush: California and Down Under, 1848–1854 (Berkeley: University of California Press, 1966); David Goodman, Gold Seeking: Victoria and California in the 1850s (Stanford, Calif.: Stanford University Press, 1994).

27   Lorenzo Veracini, Settler Colonialism: A Theoretical Overview (New York: Palgrave Macmillan, 2010), 3; Patrick Wolfe, Settler Colonialism and the Transformation of Anthropology: The Politics and Poetics of an Ethnographic Event (New York: Cassell, 1999), 1–3.

28   In other words, from the start of the California gold rush and ending with the last major gold rush in the lower forty-eight states, in the Black Hills. The

Klondike gold rush, starting in 1896, looked back nostalgically to the earlier gold rushes but was not really part of the system. For an excellent discussion of the Klondike, see Porsild, *Gamblers and Dreamers*.

29 Scott Sandage, *Born Losers: A History of Failure in America* (Cambridge, Mass.: Harvard University Press, 2005).

30 See Paul Spickard, *Almost All Aliens: Immigration, Race, and Colonialism in American History and Identity* (New York: Routledge, 2007), 23–25; Catherine Hall and Sonya O. Rose, eds., *At Home with the Empire: Metropolitan Culture and the Imperial World* (New York: Cambridge University Press, 2006); Hall, *Civilising Subjects*; Paul Kramer, *The Blood of Government: Race, Empire, the United States, and the Philippines* (Chapel Hill: University of North Carolina Press, 2006).

31 See R. A. Burchell, *The San Francisco Irish, 1848–1880* (Manchester, U.K.: Manchester University Press, 1979), 3–13; Matthew Frye Jacobson, *Whiteness of a Different Color: European Immigrants and the Alchemy of Race* (Cambridge, Mass.: Harvard University Press, 1998), 5; Jason Pierce, *Making the White Man's West: Whiteness and the Creation of the American West* (Boulder: University of Colorado Press, 2016), 12–13.

32 Burchell, *The San Francisco Irish*, 3.

33 McClintock, *Imperial Leather*, 6–7.

34 Hubert Howe Bancroft, *History of California* (San Francisco: History Co., 1886), 6:116–17; Elisha Oscar Crosby, *Memoirs of Elisha Oscar Crosby: Reminiscences of California and Guatemala from 1849 to 1864*, ed. Charles A. Barker (San Marino, Calif.: Huntington Library, 1945), 4–6; Johannsen, *To the Halls of the Montezumas*.

35 Sean Wilentz, *Chants Democratic: New York City and the Rise of the American Working Class, 1788–1850* (New York: Oxford University Press, 1986), 317–21; Ray Allen Billington, *The Protestant Crusade, 1800–1860: A Study of the Origins of American Nativism* (Chicago: Quadrangle Books, 1964), 1–16, 33, 39, 41, 118–20.

36 Bancroft, *History of California*, 6:116–17; Ava Fran Khan, *Jewish Voices of the California Gold Rush: A Documentary History, 1849–1880* (Detroit: Wayne State University Press, 2002), 36; Yonatan Eyal, *The Young America Movement and the Transformation of the Democratic Party, 1828–61* (New York: Cambridge University Press, 2007), 94–104; Tim Roberts, "The United States and the European Revolutions of 1848," in *The European Revolutions of 1848 and the Americas*, ed. Guy P. C. Thomson (London: Latin America Studies, 2002), 76–93; Newsome, *The Victorian World Picture*, 45–50.

37 John Charles Frémont, John Torrey, and James Hall, *Report of the Exploring Expedition to the Rocky Mountains in the Year 1842, and to Oregon and North*

California in the Years 1843–44 (Washington, D.C.: Gales and Seaton, printers, 1845); Richard Henry Dana, *Two Years before the Mast and Other Voyages* (New York: Library of America, 2005); Richard T. Stillson, *Spreading the Word: A History of Information in the California Gold Rush* (Lincoln: University of Nebraska Press, 2006), 4–15.

38 Stillson, *Spreading the Word*, 13–15.

39 James Polk, "Message to Congress, 5 December, 1848," in *Journal of the Senate of the United States of America, 1789–1873*, 13th Cong., 2nd sess., 5 December 1848.

40 Malcolm Rohrbough, "No Boy's Play: Migration and Settlement in Early Gold Rush California," in Starr and Orsi, eds. *Rooted in Barbarous Soil*, 28.

CHAPTER 1: GETTING TO GOLD

1   Peter Decker, *The Diaries of Peter Decker: Overland to California in 1849 and Life in the Mines, 1850–1851*, ed. Helen S. Giffen (Georgetown, Calif.: Talisman Press, 1966), 40.

2   Population estimates for California are the source of some contention. My numbers are derived from Clifford E. Trafzer and Joel H. Hyer, eds., *Exterminate Them: Written Accounts of the Murder, Rape, and Slavery of Native Americans during the Gold Rush, 1848–1868* (East Lansing: Michigan State University Press, 1999), xxiii; Rodman Paul, *Mining Frontiers of the Far West, 1848–1880* (New York: Holt, Rinehart and Winston, 1963), 15. For population counts that differ in specifics but show approximately the same ratios, see Albert L. Hurtado, *Indian Survival on the California Frontier* (New Haven, Conn.: Yale University Press, 1988), 1; Sucheng Chan, "A People of Exceptional Character: Ethnic Diversity, Nativism, and Racism in the California Gold Rush," in *Rooted in Barbarous Soil: People, Culture, and Community in Gold Rush California*, ed. Kevin Starr and Richard J. Orsi (Berkeley: University of California Press, 2000), 50; Benjamin Madley, *An American Genocide: The United States and the California Indian Catastrophe, 1846–1873* (New Haven, Conn.: Yale University Press, 2016), 347.

3   Rodman Paul, *California Gold; The Beginning of Mining in the Far West* (Cambridge, Mass.: Harvard University Press, 1947), 117–19; Gray Brechin, *Imperial San Francisco: Urban Power, Earthly Ruin* (Berkeley: University of California Press, 1999), 32–39, 64; D. W. Meinig, *The Shaping of America: A Geographical Perspective on 500 Years of History* (New Haven, Conn.: Yale University Press, 1993), 2:6–55.

4   Hubert Howe Bancroft, *The History of British Columbia* (San Francisco: History Co., 1887), 32:361.

5   "Remarks on the Fraser River Gold Mines and Washington Territory," *San Francisco Bulletin*, 1 May 1858. The most expensive tickets were fifty dollars, but tickets could be had for under twenty dollars on a sailing vessel. "The Rush for Fraser River," *Alta California*, 21 April 1858; "Letter from Victoria," *Alta California*, 9 July 1858.

6   Paul, *California Gold*, 117–19.

7   John Mack Faragher, *Women and Men on the Overland Trail* (New Haven, Conn.: Yale University Press, 1979), 16, 18, 20.

8   Brian Roberts, *American Alchemy: The California Gold Rush and Middle-Class Culture* (Chapel Hill: University of North Carolina Press, 2000), 12–15, 25.

9   Faragher, *Women and Men on the Overland Trail*, 36; Roberts, *American Alchemy*, 71–79, 264.

10   Reginald Horsman, *Race and Manifest Destiny: The Origins of American Racial Anglo-Saxonism* (Cambridge, Mass.: Harvard University Press, 1981).

11   Ray Allen Billington, *Land of Savagery / Land of Promise: The European Image of the American Frontier in the Nineteenth Century* (New York: Norton, 1981), 130, 151–52; Horsman, *Race and Manifest Destiny*, 83–85.

12   Amy S. Greenberg, *Manifest Manhood and the Antebellum American Empire* (New York: Cambridge University Press, 2005), 11–13. For contemporary Britain, see Bruce Haley, *The Healthy Body and Victorian Culture* (Cambridge, Mass.: Harvard University Press, 1978), 123–25.

13   Billington, *Land of Savagery*, 130, 151–52; Greenberg, *Manifest Manhood*, 92–93; Aims McGuinness, *Path of Empire: Panama and the California Gold Rush* (Ithaca, N.Y.: Cornell University Press, 2008), 37–38; Faragher, *Men and Women on the Overland Trail*, 14, 85–90, 178.

14   John David Unruh, *The Plains Across: The Overland Emigrants and the Trans-Mississippi West, 1840–1860* (Urbana: University of Illinois Press, 1979), 14, 30.

15   Daniel Defoe, *The Life and Strange Surprising Adventures of Robinson Crusoe* (1719; repr., New York: Grossett & Dunlap, 1946); Roberts, *American Alchemy*, 53; George Payson, *Golden Dreams and Leaden Realities* (New York: G. P. Putnam, 1853), 21, 106–7, 133; Charles Ellis, "Journal of a Voyage from Boston, Mass. to San Francisco, California in the Brig *North Bend*, Captain Higgins," in *California Gold Rush Voyages, 1848–1849: Three Original Narratives*, ed. John E. Pomfret, Charles Henry Ellis, and John N. Stone (San Marino, Calif.: Huntington Library, 1954), 68; John David Borthwick, *The Gold Hunters: A First Hand Picture of Life in California Mining Camps in the Early Fifties*, ed. Horace Kephart (1857; repr., New York: International Fiction Library, 1917), 23; J. W. L. Brown to Mrs. A. G. Brown, 24 February 1854, Brown Family Papers, 1830–98, folder 3, box 1524, California Room of the California State Library,

Sacramento (hereafter CRCSL); Richard Lunt Hale, *The Log of a Forty-Niner: Journal of a Voyage from Newburyport to San Francisco in the Brig. Genl. Worth, Commanded by Captain Samuel Walton*, ed. Carolyn Ernestine Hale Russ (Boston: B. J. Brimmer 1923), 49.

16   Payson, *Golden Dreams and Leaden Realities*, 21.

17   Michael Tate, *Indians and Emigrants: Encounters on the Overland Trails* (Norman: University of Oklahoma Press, 2006), 4–12, 19; Unruh, *The Plains Across*, 3–4.

18   Rayna Green, "The Pocahontas Perplex: The Image of Indian Women in American Culture," *Massachusetts Review* 16, no. 4 (Autumn 1975): 698–714; Andrea Smith, *Conquest: Sexual Violence and American Indian Genocide* (Cambridge, Mass.: South End Press, 2005), 10, 23, 55; Berkhofer, *The White Man's Indian*, 88–90, 113–65.

19   Tate, *Indians and Emigrants*, 13–19; Richard T. Stillson, *Spreading the Word: A History of Information in the California Gold Rush* (Lincoln: University of Nebraska Press, 2006), 9–10, 75, 83; Unruh, *The Plains Across*, 45–46.

20   Franklin Langworthy, *Scenery of the Plains, Mountains and Mines* (Princeton, N.J.: Princeton University Press, 1932), 2; Theodore T. Johnson, *Sights in the Gold Region, and Scenes by the Way* (New York: Baker and Scribner, 1849), 3; Tate, *Indians and Emigrants*, 18–19.

21   Elisha Oscar Crosby, *Memoirs of Elisha Oscar Crosby: Reminiscences of California and Guatemala from 1849 to 1864*, ed. Charles A. Barker (San Marino, Calif.: Huntington Library, 1945), 10–11. See also Oscar Lewis, *Sea Routes to the Gold Fields: The Migration by Water to California in 1849–1852* (New York: A. A. Knopf, 1949), 51.

22   María DeGuzmán, *Spain's Long Shadow: The Black Legend, Off-Whiteness, and Anglo-American Empire* (Minneapolis: University of Minnesota Press, 2005), xxvii–xxix, 5–6, 42, 69, 70–72; Lyman Beecher, *A Plea for the West* (1835; repr., New York: Arno Press, 1977); Samuel Morse, *Foreign Conspiracy against the Liberties of the United States: The Numbers of Brutus* (1835; repr., New York: Arno Press, 1977); David Bennett, *The Party of Fear: From Nativist Movements to the New Right in American History* (Chapel Hill: University of North Carolina Press, 1988), 37–48.

23   Morse, *Foreign Conspiracy*, 45.

24   Fredrick B. Pike, *The United States and Latin America: Myths and Stereotypes of Civilization and Nature* (Austin: University of Texas, 1992), 54–55.

25   Horsman, *Race and Manifest Destiny*, 98–99; Linda Nash, *Inescapable Ecologies: A History of Environment, Disease, and Knowledge* (Berkeley: University of California Press, 2006), 13–14, 28–29; Pike, *The United States and Latin America*, xiiv, 22, 51–72.

26 John Lloyd Stephens, *Incidents of Travel in Central America, Chiapas and Yucatan* (1841; repr., New York: Dover, 1969); Richard Henry Dana, *Two Years before the Mast and Other Voyages* (New York: Library of America, 2005).

27 Dana, *Two Years before the Mast*, 369.

28 Stephens, *Incidents of Travel in Central America*, 193; Dana, *Two Years before the Mast*, 45, 73, 75–77, 230; see also DeGuzmán, *Spain's Long Shadow*, xxviii, 66–69, 74–76.

29 Robert Walter Johannsen, *To the Halls of the Montezumas: The Mexican War in the American Imagination* (New York: Oxford University Press, 1985), 21–23, 30, 45, 116, 167–70.

30 Johannsen, *To the Halls of the Montezumas*, 16, 21–30, 40–45; Horsman, *Race and Manifest Destiny*, 208–47.

31 Horsman, *Race and Manifest Destiny*, 1–6, 59–62, 99–100, 208–49; Johannsen, *To the Halls of the Montezumas*, 40, 170.

32 Ralph J. Roske, "The World Impact of the California Gold Rush, 1849–1857," *Arizona and the West* 5, no. 3 (Autumn 1963): 211–17. For Britain, see Frank Marryat, *Mountains and Molehills; or, Recollections of a Burnt Journal* (1855; repr., Philadelphia: Lippincott, 1962) and the *London Times*.

33 Faragher, *Men and Women on the Overland Trail*, 24; William A. Bowen, *The Willamette Valley: Migration and Settlement on the Oregon Frontier* (Seattle: University of Washington Press, 1978), 53–57.

34 Unruh, *The Plains Across*, 45–46, 73–80; Tate, *Indians and Emigrants*, 19; Langworthy, *Scenery of the Plains*, 2.

35 Unruh, *The Plains Across*, 72–74, 328–29; Langworthy, *Scenery of the Plains*, 11; Decker, *The Diaries of Peter Decker*, 1.

36 Unruh, *The Plains Across*, 328–29.

37 Lewis, *Sea Routes to the Gold Fields*, 24.

38 Lewis, 21–29.

39 James Delgado, *To California by Sea: A Maritime History of the California Gold Rush* (Columbia: University of South Carolina Press, 1990), 35–36, 41; Frank Soulé, *The Annals of San Francisco: Containing a Summary of the History of . . . California, and a Complete History of . . . Its Great City* (New York: Appleton, 1855), 352; Charles Thompson to uncle, 10 September 1851, Mss C-B 547: 8, in Gold Rush Letters, BANC; Eliza W. Farnham, *California, In-doors and Out; or, How We Farm, Mine, and Live Generally in the Golden State* (New York: Dix, Edwards, 1856), 4–18.

40 A. J. McCall, *The Great California Trail in 1849, Wayside Notes of an Argonaut . . . Reprinted from the Steuben Courier* (Bath, N.Y.: Steuben Courier Print, 1882), 12–13.

41 Records are sparse, but what there is from the Argonaut migration to British Columbia does not mention companies, only the purchase of tickets. See, for example, Cecil Williams Buckley, Journal, 17 April 1862, E/B/B85, British Columbia Archives, Victoria (hereafter BCARS).

42 Buckley, Journal, 17 April 1862.

43 R. Byron Johnson, *Very Far West Indeed: A Few Rough Experiences on the North-West Pacific Coast* (London: S. Low, Martson, Low & Searle, 1872), 2–3.

44 Buckley, Journal, 4 May 1862.

45 Decker, *The Diaries of Peter Decker*, 115.

46 D. A. Millington, Journal of a California Miner, 11 April 1850, CRCSL.

47 Nelson Kingsley, *Diary of Nelson Kingsley, a California Argonaut of 1849*, ed. Frederick Teggart (Berkeley: University of California, 1914), 259–62.

48 William Henry Harrison Hall, *The Private Letters and Diaries of Captain Hall: An Epic of an Argonaut in the California Gold Rush, Oregon Territory, Civil War, and Oil City*, ed. Eric Schneirsohn (Glendale, Calif.: London Book Company, 1974), 14; Ellis, "Journal of a Voyage," 95; Bayard Taylor, *Eldorado; or, Adventures in the Path of Empire, Comprising a Voyage to California, via Panama; Life in San Francisco and Monterey; Pictures of the Gold Region, and Experiences of Mexican Travel* (New York: G. P. Putnam's Sons, 1879), 44; Joseph Benton, Journal 1849 Jan. 11–1856 Dec. 31, 14 January 1849, CRCSL.

49 Benton, Journal, 13 February 1849.

50 Hale, *The Log of a Forty-Niner*, 46. A droger is a heavy, slow cargo vessel.

51 For more on greenhorns, see chapter 5.

52 Hale, *The Log of a Forty-Niner*, 19; Kingsley, *Diary of Nelson Kingsley*, 284, 290; Delgado, *To California by Sea*, 35–36.

53 Edwin Waite, Reminiscences, 22, CRCSL.

54 Byron McKinstry, *The California Gold Rush Overland Diary of Byron McKinstry, 1850–1852* (Glendale, Calif.: A. H. Clark, 1975), 92–100; Decker, *The Diaries of Peter Decker*, 55.

55 John Carr, *Pioneer Days in California: Historical and Personal Sketches* (Eureka, Calif.: Times Publishing, 1891), 35.

56 Alfred Doten, *The Journals of Alfred Doten, 1849–1903*, ed. Walter Van Tilburg Clark (Reno: University of Nevada Press, 1973), 4; Benjamin Wingate, *Uncertain Country: The Wingate Letters, San Francisco, California—Meriden, New Hampshire, 1851–1854*, ed. Stephen Vincent (Berkeley, Calif.: Friends of the Bancroft Library, 2000), 13; Johnson, *Sights in the Gold Region*, 3.

57 John Tosh, *A Man's Place: Masculinity and the Middle-Class Home in Victorian England* (New Haven, Conn.: Yale University Press, 1999), 103, 111, 117–18; Elliott West, *Growing Up with the Country: Childhood on the Far-Western Frontier*

(Albuquerque: University of New Mexico Press, 1989), 101–17. For another discussion of "play" among gold rushers, see Roberts, *American Alchemy*, 108, 117.

58 Kingsley, *Diary of Nelson Kingsley*, 239, 262–64; Doten, *The Journals of Alfred Doten*, 6, 9; Alexander Barrington, *A California Gold Rush Miscellany Comprising: The Original Journal of Alexander Barrington, Nine Unpublished Letters from the Gold Mines, Reproductions of Early Maps and Towns from California Lithographs; Broadsides, &c.* (San Francisco: Grabhorn Press, 1934), 4.

59 For a diminutive definition of *boy*, see Noah Webster, *An American Dictionary of the English Language: Containing the Whole Vocabulary of the First Edition in Two Volumes Quarto; the Entire Corrections and Improvements of the Second Edition in Two Volumes Royal Octavo; to Which Is Prefixed an Introductory Dissertation on the Origin, History, and Connection, of the Languages of Western Asia and Europe, with an Explanation of the Principles on Which Languages Are Formed* (Springfield, Mass.: George and Charles Merriam, 1855), 145.

60 Doten, *The Journals of Alfred Doten*, 4, 6, 8, 9, 11–12; John N. Stone, "Brief Notes of a Cape Horn Voyage in 1849," in *California Gold Rush Voyages, 1848–1849: Three Original Narratives*, ed. John E. Pomfret, Charles Henry Ellis, and John N. Stone (San Marino, Calif.: Huntington Library, 1954), 133.

61 McCall, *The Great California Trail in 1849*, 13.

62 Doten, *The Journals of Alfred Doten* 12; Lewis, *Sea Routes to the Gold Fields*, 54–57.

63 Hale, *The Log of a Forty-Niner*, 46.

64 Hale, 50–54. For British Columbia, see Arthur Thomas Bushby, "The Journal of Arthur Thomas Bushby, 1858–1859," *British Columbia Historical Quarterly* 21, no. 1 (January 1957): 101.

65 This shift anticipates the shift from manliness to masculinity later in the nineteenth century identified by Gail Bederman. Gail Bederman, *Manliness and Civilization: A Cultural History of Gender and Race in the United States, 1880–1917* (Chicago: University of Chicago Press, 1995).

66 Bushby, "Journal," 101

67 William S. M'Collum, *California as I Saw It: Correspondence, Manuscript, Prospectuses; Sherwood Anderson, a Bibliography: Manuscript, 1 letter; Western Reaches: Misc. Items; Early Day Letters from Aurora: Correspondence, Manuscript* (Buffalo, N.Y.: George H. Derby, 1850), 6. See also Johnson, *Sights in the Gold Region*, 3.

68 Faragher, *Women and Men on the Overland*, 178.

69 Washington Peck, *On the Western Trails: The Overland Diaries of Washington Peck*, ed. Susan M. Erb (Norman, Okla.: Arthur H. Clark, 2009), 68.

70   Alonzo Rathbun, Alonzo W. Rathbun Diary 1849–51, 109, 113, Mss 2006/199, BANC.

71   Tate, *Indians and Emigrants*, 183; Unruh, *The Plains Across*, 127–29, 134.

72   Wingate, *Uncertain Country*, 13; Doten, *The Journals of Alfred Doten*, 4, 12.

73   Stephen Chapin Davis, *California Gold Rush Merchant: The Journal of Stephen Chapin Davis* (San Marino, Calif.: Huntington Library, 1956), 41. On the conflict see McGuinness, *Path of Empire*, 57.

74   Lewis, *Sea Routes to the Gold Fields*, 61.

75   Of course, posing as Native Americans attacking a wagon train could end very badly as well. See Tate, *Indians and Emigrants*, 149–51.

76   Lewis, *Sea Routes to the Gold Fields*, 58–59.

77   Taylor, *Eldorado*, 44–45.

78   Roberts, *American Alchemy*, 3–24.

79   Nash, *Inescapable Ecologies*, 13–25, 28–29, 40–41.

80   M'Collum, *California as I Saw It*, 8. See also Elisha Smith Capron, *History of California, from Its Discovery to the Present Time: Comprising also a Full Description of Its Climate, Surface, Soil, Rivers, Towns . . . Agriculture, Commerce, Mines, Mining, &c., with a Journal of the Voyage from New York, via Nicaragua, to San Francisco, and Back, via Panama . . .* (Cleveland, Ohio: Jewett, Proctor and Worthington, 1854), 259; James Morison, *By Sea to San Francisco: 1849–1850: The Journal of Dr. James Morison* (Memphis, Tenn.: Memphis State University Press, 1977), 9; Borthwick, *The Gold Hunters*, 24; G. B. Worden to Ira Brown, 23 April 1849, Mss C-B 547:138, BANC; John Marsh Smith, manuscript 308, John Marsh Smith Collection, CRCSL.

81   W. Champness, *To Cariboo and Back* (London: Religious Tract Society, 1865), 203; Macfie, *Vancouver Island and British Columbia*, 8; Johnson, *Very Far West Indeed*, 11–12.

82   Samuel Bowles, *Our New West: Records of Travel between the Mississippi River and the Pacific Ocean; over the Plains—over the Mountains—through the Great Interior Basin—over the Sierra Nevada—to and Up and Down the Pacific Coast; with Details of the Wonderful Natural Scenery, Agriculture, Mines, Business, Social Life, Progress, and Prospects . . . Including a Full Description of the Pacific Railroad; and of the Life of the Mormons, Indians, and Chinese; with Map, Portraits, and Twelve Full Page Illustrations* (Hartford, Conn.: Hartford Publishing, 1869), 520.

83   Bowles, 518. See also Champness, *To Cariboo and Back*, 204.

84   William King, Diary, 4, A01000, BCARS. The "pestering" comment comes from John Cowley, Diary 1862, 30 April 1862, E/B/C832, BCARS.

85   In reality, the situation in Panama was partly the result of collaboration between
      Panamanian authorities and U.S. citizens. However, the average visitor seems
      to have been unaware of this. See McGuinness, *Path of Empire*, 10, 11, 42, 73–77.
      For a discussion of American filibustering campaigns, see Greenberg, *Manifest
      Manhood*.

86   Errol Wayne Stevens, *Incidents of a Voyage to California, 1849: A Diary Aboard
      the Bark Hersilia, and in Sacramento, 1850* (Los Angeles: Western History Asso-
      ciation, 1987), 24.

87   Faragher, *Women and Men on the Overland Trail*, 85; McKinstry, *The California
      Gold Rush Overland Diary of Byron McKinstry*, 107; Peck, *On the Western Trails*,
      68; Herman Reinhart, *The Golden Frontier: The Recollections of Herman Fran-
      cis Reinhart, 1851–1869* (Austin: University of Texas Press, 1962), 11; Lorenzo
      Sawyer, *Way Sketches: Containing Incidents of Travel across the Plains from
      St. Joseph to California in 1850, with Letters Describing Life and Conditions in
      the Gold Region* (New York: E. Eberstadt, 1926), 35–36.

88   Hurtado, *Indian Survival*, 172; James J. Rawls, *Indians of California: The Chang-
      ing Image* (Norman: University of Oklahoma Press), 1984, 28–30, 49, 69, 186–
      200.

89   Joseph Goldsborough Bruff, *Gold Rush: The Journals, Drawings and Other
      Papers of J. Goldsborough Bruff, Captain, Washington City and California Min-
      ing Association, April 2, 1849–July 20, 1851*, ed. Georgia Willis Read, Ruth Louise
      Gaines, and Frederick Webb Hodge (New York: Columbia University Press,
      1949), 17.

90   John Bidwell, Journey to California, 3, Mss C-E 65:47, BANC; Hubert Howe
      Bancroft, *History of California* (San Francisco: History Co., 1886), 6:149. Gaub
      is a misspelling of gob, a slang term meaning "a lot of."

91   Sarah Bayliss Royce, *A Frontier Lady: Recollections of the Gold Rush and Early
      California*, ed. Ralph Henry Gabriel (New Haven, Conn.: Yale University Press,
      1932), 13–14.

92   Glenda Riley, *Confronting Race: Women and Indians on the Frontier, 1815–1915*
      (Albuquerque: University of New Mexico Press, 2004), 216.

93   Rathbun, Diary, 113.

94   John M. Letts, *A Pictorial View of California: Including a Description of the
      Panama and Nicaragua Routes, with Information and Advice Interesting to All,
      Particularly Those Who Intend to Visit the Golden Region, by a Returned Cali-
      fornian* (New York: H. Bill, 1853), 33.

95   Borthwick, *The Gold Hunters*, 24; Mary Jane Megquier, *Apron Full of Gold: The
      Letters of Mary Jane Megquier from San Francisco, 1849–1856*, ed. Robert Glass

Cleland (San Marino, Calif.: Huntington Library, 1949), 10–12; Wingate, *Uncertain Country*, 14; William R. Olden from Panama to identified recipient, 13 May 1849, William R. Olden Gold Rush Letters; Pioneer Letters, 1849–77, CRCSL; Johnson, *Sights in the Gold Region*, 12–13; Taylor, *Eldorado*, 28.

96   M'Collum, *California as I Saw It*, 22. See also Doten, *The Journals of Alfred Doten*, 31.

97   Ellis, "Journal of a Voyage," 48.

98   Stone, "Brief Notes," 109–110.

99   M'Collum, *California as I Saw It*, 19.

100   Doten, *The Journals of Alfred Doten*, 33; Hale, *The Log of a Forty-Niner*, 40; Benton, Journal, 29 April 1849.

101   Davis, *California Gold Rush Merchant*, 37–43.

102   McGuinness, *Path of Empire*, 1–2, 37, 128–35.

103   W. Champness, *To Cariboo and Back* (London: Religious Tract Society, 1865), 203.

104   W. M. Mark, *Cariboo: A True and Correct Narrative* (Stockton, U.K.: W. M. Wright, 1863), 3, 10. For similar comments, see Bushby, "Journal," 105–6; George Blair, Diary, 5–9, Mss 0816, BCARS; John Emmerson, "British Columbia and Vancouver Island: Voyages, Travels and Adventures," 13–14, 16–17, B188, CRCSL; E., Gold Rush Letter, 22 April 1854, folder 12, box 17, CRCSL; Bowles, *Our New West*, 518, 520–21; Matthew Macfie, *Vancouver Island and British Columbia: Their History, Resources, and Prospects* (1865; repr., New York: Arno Press, 1973), 8.

105   The best discussion of the impact of colonialism in Panama during this period is McGuinness, *Path of Empire*.

106   Johnson, *Sights in the Gold Region*, 152, 201, 204; Borthwick, *The Gold Hunters*, 135–36; M'Collum, *California as I Saw It*, 51–52; George Holbrook Baker, Personal Papers, Diaries May 1849–Aug 1850, 28 June 1849, George Holbrook Baker Collection, folder 6, box 1844, CRCSL; "From the Sacramento—Difficulties at the Mines between the Americans and Chilians," *New York Tribune*, 2 August 1849, in Material for Proposed Publication of Gold Rush Letters, Carbons of Letters from Newspapers, folder 1, box 2170, CRCSL; "The Indian Massacre in California," *New York Tribune*, 15 August 1849, in Material for Proposed Publication of Gold Rush Letters, Carbons of Letters from Newspapers, folder 1, box 2169, CRCSL; "Description of Sutter's Fort—Washing—A Model Gold-Washer—Prices of Provisions at the Mills—The Oregonians and the Indians—Forty Indian Girls Killed, to Save Them from the Whites—Mining Association Formed—Expedition Four Months Too Early," in Material for Proposed Publication of Gold Rush Letters, Carbons of Letters from Newspapers, box 2169, folder 1,

CRCSL; Bancroft, History of California, 6:72–73; Madley, *American Genocide*; Brendan Lindsay, *Murder State: California's Native American Genocide, 1846–1873* (Lincoln: University of Nebraska Press, 2012), esp. 110–23.

107 Bowles, *Our New West*, 517–20.

108 Reginald Pidcock, "Adventures in Vancouver 1862–1868," p. 3, vol. 4b, box 2, Mss 0728, BCARS.

109 Buckley, Journal, 10, 14 May 1862.

110 Emmerson, "British Columbia and Vancouver Island," 26.

111 Buckley, Journal, 10 May, 14 May 1862.

112 Johnson, *Very Far West Indeed*, 8.

113 Gunther Barth, *Instant Cities: Urbanization and the Rise of San Francisco and Denver* (New York: Oxford University Press, 1975), xxii.

114 Borthwick, *The Gold Hunters*, 54.

115 "San Francisco as It Is: Manuscript," 1, folder 1, box 2140, CRCSL.

116 Letts, *A Pictorial View of California*, 47.

117 Soulé, *The Annals of San Francisco*, 216.

118 "San Francisco as It Is: Manuscript," 1.

119 Stone, "Brief Notes," 142; Marryat, *Mountains and Molehills*, 9.

120 Pringle Shaw, *Ramblings in California: Containing a Description of the Country, Life at the Mines, State of Society, &c.; Interspersed with Characteristic Anecdotes, and Sketches from Life* (Toronto: J. Bain, [1856?]), 26. See also Soulé, *The Annals of San Francisco*, 25–30, 258; William Redmond Ryan, *Personal Adventures in Upper and Lower California, in 1848–9* (New York: Arno Press, 1973), 2:173–75, 250; Farnham, *California, In-doors and Out*, 257–52; Alonzo Delano, *Pen Knife Sketches; or, Chips of the Old Block, a Series of Original Illustrated Letters, Written by One of California's Pioneer Miners* (Sacramento, Calif.: Published at The Union office, 1853), 43.

121 Farnham, *California, In-doors and Out*, 257.

122 Hale, *The Log of a Forty-Niner*, 120.

123 Borthwick, *The Gold Hunters*, 54. See also Marryat, *Mountains and Molehills*, 13.

124 Hale, *The Log of a Forty-Niner*, 64. Borthwick described "the great majority [of the buildings as] nondescript, shapeless, patchwork concerns." Borthwick, *The Gold Hunters*, 54.

125 Soulé, *The Annals of San Francisco*, 160–61, 245; Thomas Allsop, *California and Its Gold Mines: Being a Series of Recent Communications from the Mining Districts, upon the Present Condition and Future Prospects of Quartz Mining; with an Account of the Richer Deposits, and Incidental Notices of the Climate, Scenery, and Mode of Life in California* (London: Groombridge and Sons, 1853), 18–19; "Have We a Grumbler among Us?" *Alta California*, 1 June 1853.

126 M'Collum, *California as I Saw It*, 33.

127 Macfie, *Vancouver Island and British Columbia*, 21.

128 George Styles, Diary, 22 June 1862, Mss 0536, BCARS. John Cowley, for instance, echoes these sentiments. See Cowley, Diary 1862, 20 May 1862.

129 Johnson, *Very Far West Indeed*, 21.

130 Arthur Birch, Victorian Odyssey, 85, A00272, BCARS.

131 Champness, *To Cariboo and Back*, 206.

132 Francis Poole, *Queen Charlotte Islands: A Narrative of Discovery and Adventure in the North Pacific* (London: Hurst and Blackett, 1872), 50.

133 James Nelles, Diary 1862, 20 February 1862, Barkerville Archive (hereafter BA).

134 Poole, *Queen Charlotte Islands*, 44.

135 Champness, *To Cariboo and Back*, 207; Johnson, *Very Far West Indeed*, 28–29; Poole, *Queen Charlotte Islands*, 50–51; Mark, *Cariboo*, 16–17; Blair, Diary, 3; King, Diary, 13–15; Styles, Diary, 22 June 1863; Cowley, Diary 1862, 19, 22 May 1862; Emmerson, "British Columbia and Vancouver Island," 31.

136 Mark, *Cariboo*, 16.

137 Emmerson, "British Columbia and Vancouver Island," 50–51.

138 Stuart Creighton Miller, *The Unwelcome Immigrant: The American Image of the Chinese, 1785–1882* (Berkeley: University of California Press, 1969), 168–69. For a detailed account of Chinese experiences of San Francisco during this period, see Yong Chen, *Chinese San Francisco, 1850–1943: A Trans-Pacific Community* (Stanford, Calif.: Stanford University Press, 2000), 55–75.

139 See, for example, Noman Asing, "To His Excellency Governor Bigler," *Alta California*, 5 May 1852; Reverend William Speer, "China and California, Their Relations Past and Present: A Lecture in Conclusion of a Series in Relation to the Chinese People, Delivered in the Stockton Street Presbyterian Church, San Francisco, June 28, 1853," CRCSL; Joshua Paddison, *American Heathens: Religion, Race, and Reconstruction in California* (Berkeley: University of California Press, 2012), 28; D. Michael Bottoms, *An Aristocracy of Color: Race and Reconstruction in California and the West, 1850–1890* (Norman: University of Oklahoma Press, 2013), 34–38.

140 Langworthy, *Scenery of the Plains*, 151.

141 Bernard J. Reid, *Overland to California with the Pioneer Line: The Gold Rush Diary of Bernard J. Reid*, ed. Mary McDougall Gordon (Stanford, Calif.: Stanford University Press, 1983), 145. Both italics and quote marks are original.

142 Carr, *Pioneer Days*, 60–61. The quote is from page 60.

143 Finely McDiarmid, *Letters to My Wife* (Fairfield, Wash.: Ye Galleon Press, 1997), 61.

144 Adele Perry, *On the Edge of Empire: Gender, Race, and the Making of British Columbia, 1849–1871* (Toronto: University of Toronto Press, 2001), 124–66.

145 See, for example, "The Gold Diggings on Frazer River," *London Times*, 30 June 1858; Donald Frazer, "Our Correspondent," *London Times*, 4 August 1858; Donald Frazer, "British Columbia," *London Times*, 5 August 1858. On overall migration numbers, see William E. Van Vugt, *Britain to America: Mid-Nineteenth-Century Immigrants to the United States* (Urbana: University of Illinois Press, 1999), 7.

146 Van Vugt is interested in immigration to the United States, but in terms of push and pull factors affecting British emigrants, his work is applicable to British Columbia. Van Vugt, *Britain to America*, 3, 7, 11–13, 155.

147 Van Vugt, 89–90. Some colonial officials worried about American immigration. See Matthew Begbie to Governor Douglas, 18 May 1859, Colonial Correspondence, file 142b1, B0137, BCARS.

148 This is especially true for African Canadians who emigrated from the United States and who opted to return to reunite with family and take part in the hopeful atmosphere of Reconstruction. See James Pilton, "Negro Settlement in British Columbia, 1858–1871" (master's thesis, University of British Columbia, 1951), 196–200.

149 Bancroft, *History of British Columbia*, 388–90.

150 "San Francisco Rivals in the North—Victoria and Its Denizens," *San Francisco Evening Bulletin*, 20 July 1858. See also "A Sanctum Talk with a Passenger by the *Sierra Nevada*," *Alta California*, 8 July 1858; "Letter from Victoria," *Alta California*, 9 July 1858.

151 William Nixon, "Letter to Robert Nixon," *San Francisco Evening Bulletin*, 20 July 1858.

152 A Returned Miner, "The Difficulty of Access to the Fraz Mines [*sic*]," *Alta California*, 7 June 1858; W. V. W., "Letter from Our Special Fraser River Correspondent," *Alta California*, 5 October 1858; George Wilbur, "Further Information from a Frazer River Miner—Difficulties of Travel There," *San Francisco Evening Bulletin*, 9 June 1858.

153 For criticism of the HBC, see Independent, "Letter from Victoria, V.I.," *San Francisco Evening Bulletin*, 6 June 1858; "The Fraser River News," *Alta California*, 6 June 1858; "The Rights of the Hudson's Bay Company," *Alta California*, 9 June 1858; "The Exactions of the Hudson's Bay Company," *Alta California*, 7 July 1858; W. T. Ballou, "Letter from Fort Hope," *Alta California*, 8 July 1858. For positive accounts, see C. Aubrey Angelo, "Letter from C. Aubrey Angelo," *Alta California*, 8 July 1858; "Letter from Victoria," *Alta California*, 9 July 1858; "Letters from Victoria, V.I.," *San Francisco Evening Bulletin*, 8 July 1858.

154   Independent, "Letter from Victoria, V.I.," *San Francisco Evening Bulletin*, 31 May 1858; "The Rights of the Hudson's Bay Company," *Alta California*, 9 June 1858; W. V. W., "Our Special Victoria Correspondence," *Alta California*, 19 July 1858.

155   F. F. Davis, "The 'Bostons' and the Indians in the North," *San Francisco Evening Bulletin*, 8 May 1858, italics in the original; Independent, "Letter from Victoria, Vancouver Island," *San Francisco Evening Bulletin*, 7 May 1858; "Matters at Victoria, V.I.," *San Francisco Evening Bulletin*, 9 July 1858; "San Francisco Rivals in the North," *San Francisco Evening Bulletin*, 20 July 1858.

156   Henry Fitch, "Other Letters from Victoria," *San Francisco Evening Bulletin*, 15 July 1858; "Favorable Reports from the Mines" and "Further from the New Gold Mines," *Alta California*, 6 May 1858; Independent, "Letter from Victoria, Vancouver Island," *Alta California*, 7 May 1858; "Later from the North," *Alta California*, 23 May 1858.

157   "Letter from Victoria, V.I.," *San Francisco Evening Bulletin*, 15 July 1858.

158   Poole, *Queen Charlotte Islands*, 55; Sophia Cracroft, *Extracts from the Letters of Miss Sophia Cracroft, Sir John Franklin's Niece, February to April 1861 and April to July 1870* (Victoria, B.C.: [Provincial Archives of British Columbia], 1974), 2, emphasis original.

159   Perry, *On the Edge of Empire*, 110, 112–23; Cracroft, *Extracts from the Letters of Miss Sophia Cracroft*, 19–21.

160   Chuen-yan David Lai, *Chinatowns: Towns within Cities in Canada* (Vancouver: University of British Columbia Press, 1988), 10–11, 184–87.

161   Mark, *Cariboo*, 18–19.

CHAPTER 2: A WHITE MAN'S REPUBLIC

1   The job of alcalde was a government position that combined the offices of mayor and justice. Americans came to see it largely as synonymous with the position of "justice of the peace." David Alan Johnson, *Founding the Far West: California, Oregon, and Nevada, 1840–1890* (Berkeley: University of California Press, 1992), 28–29.

2   Walter Colton, *Three Years in California [1846–49]* (New York: A. S. Barnes, 1850), 246–52.

3   Bayard Taylor, *Eldorado; or, Adventures in the Path of Empire, Comprising a Voyage to California, via Panama; Life in San Francisco and Monterey; Pictures of the Gold Region, and Experiences of Mexican Travel* (New York: G. P. Putnam's Sons, 1879), 146.

4   Native studies and the academic studies of new western history have proven more willing to pay attention to the impact of colonial forces on the West,

yet they tend to focus on the material aspects of colonialism and minimize the social and cultural aspects. See, for example, Patricia Limerick, *The Legacy of Conquest: The Unbroken Past of the American West* (New York: Norton, 1987) and Richard White, *"It's Your Misfortune and None of My Own": A History of the American West* (Norman: University of Oklahoma Press, 1991).

5   See John David Unruh, *The Plains Across: The Overland Emigrants and the Trans-Mississippi West, 1840–1860* (Urbana: University of Illinois Press, 1979), 340–43; Malcolm J. Rohrbough, *Days of Gold: The California Gold Rush and the American Nation* (Berkeley: University of California Press, 1997), 41; Oscar Lewis, *Sea Routes to the Gold Fields: The Migration by Water to California in 1849–1852* (New York: A. A. Knopf, 1949), 10.

6   María DeGuzmán, *Spain's Long Shadow: The Black Legend, Off-Whiteness, and Anglo-American Empire* (Minneapolis: University of Minnesota Press, 2005), xxvii. See also David Roediger, *Working toward Whiteness: How America's Immigrants Became White; The Strange Journey from Ellis Island to the Suburbs* (New York: Basic Books, 2005), 4. As Stacey Smith and Joshua Paddison have shown, this process continued into the period of Reconstruction. Stacey Smith, *Freedom's Frontier: California and the Struggle over Unfree Labor, Emancipation, and Reconstruction* (Chapel Hill: University of North Carolina Press, 2013); Joshua Paddison, *American Heathens: Religion, Race, and Reconstruction in California* (Berkeley: University of California Press, 2012).

7   Rodman W. Paul, *California Gold: The Beginning of Mining in the Far West* (Cambridge, Mass.: Harvard University Press, 1947), 22–23.

8   Timothy Coffin Osborn, Timothy Coffin Osborn Journal: ms., 1850 June 14–1855 Jan. 1, 39, Mss C-F 81, BANC; Eliza W. Farnham, *California, In-doors and Out; or, How We Farm, Mine, and Live Generally in the Golden State* (New York: Dix, Edwards, 1856), 181.

9   Eric Foner, *Free Soil, Free Labor, Free Men: The Ideology of the Republican Party before the Civil War* (New York: Oxford University Press, 1995), xi–xxvi; Brian Roberts, *American Alchemy: The California Gold Rush and Middle-Class Culture* (Chapel Hill: University of North Carolina Press, 2000), 25, 183; David Roediger, *The Wages of Whiteness: Race and the Making of the American Working Class* (New York: Verso, 1999), 65–80.

10 Joseph Benton, Journal 1849 Jan. 11–1856 Dec. 31, 5 August 1849, vol. 1, CRCSL (emphasis as underlining in original); William Taylor, *California Life Illustrated* (New York: Carlton & Porter, 1860), 286.

11 Charles White, *St. Joseph (MO) Gazette*, 28 July 1848, folder 1, box 2168, CRCSL; "The Execution of Jenkins," *Alta California*, 12 June 1851; "Mssrs. Editors," *Alta*

California, 10 June 1851; "Incendiarism in San Francisco," *Alta California*, 24 January 1850; Robert M. Senkewicz, *Vigilantes in Gold Rush San Francisco* (Stanford, Calif.: Stanford University Press, 1985), 75–78; Albert Benard de Russailh, *Last Adventure: San Francisco in 1851; Translated from the Original Journal of Albert Benard de Russailh by Clarkson Crane*, ed. Clarkson Crane (San Francisco: Westgate Press, 1931), 33. On nineteenth-century America's love-hate relationship with secret societies in a republic, see Mark C. Carnes, *Secret Ritual and Manhood in Victorian America* (New Haven, Conn.: Yale University Press, 1989).

12   D. Michael Bottoms, *An Aristocracy of Color: Race and Reconstruction in California and the West, 1850–1890* (Norman: University of Oklahoma Press, 2013), 3–4; Jason Pierce, *Making the White Man's West: Whiteness and the Creation of the American West* (Boulder: University of Colorado Press, 2016), 9; Kevin Starr and Richard J. Orsi, eds., *Rooted in Barbarous Soil: People, Culture, and Community in Gold Rush California* (Berkeley: University of California Press, 2000), viii; Sucheng Chan, "A People of Exceptional Character: Ethnic Diversity, Nativism, and Racism in the California Gold Rush," in *Rooted in Barbarous Soil: People, Culture, and Community in Gold Rush California* (Berkeley: University of California Press, 2000), 57–58.

13   Colton, *Three Years in California*, 247–48.

14   Foner, *Free Soil*, xi–xxvi. On the pervasiveness of republican ideology, see Roediger, *The Wages of Whiteness*, 27–36, 43–44, 50–51, 66–74; Sean Wilentz, *Chants Democratic: New York City and the Rise of the American Working Class, 1788–1850* (New York: Oxford University Press, 1986), 61–63, 92–94; Drew Gilpin Faust, *James Henry Hammond and the Old South: A Design for Mastery* (Baton Rouge: Louisiana State University Press, 1982), 40–42. On race and citizenship, see Dana Nelson, *National Manhood: Capitalist Citizenship and the Imagined Fraternity of White Men* (Durham, N.C.: Duke University Press, 1998).

15   Johnson, *Founding the Far West*, x, 9.

16   Elisha Smith Capron, *History of California, from Its Discovery to the Present Time: Comprising Also a Full Description of Its Climate, Surface, Soil, Rivers, Towns . . . Agriculture, Commerce, Mines, Mining, &c, with a Journal of the Voyage from New York, via Nicaragua, to San Francisco, and Back, via Panama . . .* (Cleveland, Ohio: Jewett, Proctor and Worthington, 1854), 171.

17   Paul R. Spickard, *Almost All Aliens: Immigration, Race, and Colonialism in American History and Identity* (New York: Routledge, 2007), 5–6.

18   William Henry Ellison, *A Self-Governing Dominion: California, 1849–1860* (Berkeley: University of California Press, 1950), 25–27.

19   Johnson, *Founding the Far West*, 125, 129; Ellison, *A Self-Governing Dominion*, 30.

20 Ellison, *A Self-Governing Dominion*, 75.

21 Roediger, *The Wages of Whiteness*, esp. 35–36; Bruce R. Dain, *A Hideous Monster of the Mind: American Race Theory in the Early Republic* (Cambridge, Mass.: Harvard University Press, 2002), viii.

22 Johnson, *Founding the Far West*, 126, quote is from 128. The best treatment of Northern whites' fears of slave labor remains Foner, *Free Soil*, esp. xi–xxxi.

23 Johnson, *Founding the Far West*, 128–29.

24 Johnson, *Founding the Far West*, 126–27.

25 California State Legislature, "An Act for the Government and Protection of the Indians," in *The Statutes of California, First Session of the Legislature, 1849–1850* (San Jose: J. Winchester, State Printer, 1850), chap. 133, 408–9. See also Albert Hurtado, *Indian Survival on the California Frontier* (New Haven, Conn.: Yale University Press, 1988), 5.

26 Treaty of Guadalupe Hidalgo [exchange copy], February 2, 1848 [Electronic Records], Perfected Treaties, 1778–1945, Record Group 11, General Records of the United States Government, 1778–1992, National Archives.

27 J. Ross Browne, *Report of the Debates in the Convention of California on the Formation of the State Constitution in September and October, 1849* (Washington, D.C.: Jon T. Towers, 1850), 62–74; Johnson, *Founding the Far West*, 125–26.

28 Browne, *Report of the Debates*, 63. Californios were California residents of at least some Spanish descent, born before the American conquest.

29 California Constitution (1849), art. 2, sec. 1.

30 Browne, *Report of the Debates*, 62.

31 Browne, *Report of the Debates*, 62–73; Johnson, *Founding the Far West*, 125; Ellison, *A Self-Governing Dominion*, 30.

32 Charles Edward Pancoast, *A Quaker Forty-Niner: The Adventures of Charles Edward Pancoast on the American Frontier*, ed. Anna Paschall Hannum (Philadelphia: University of Pennsylvania Press, 1930), 289–90; William Downie, *Hunting for Gold: Reminisences [sic] of Personal Experience and Research in the Early Days of the Pacific Coast from Alaska to Panama* (San Francisco: California Publishing, 1893), 81; Rodman W. Paul, *Mining Frontiers of the Far West, 1848–1880* (New York: Holt, Rinehart, and Winston, 1963), 23–27.

33 Charles Howard Shinn, *Mining Camps: A Study in American Frontier Government* (New York: Charles Scribner Sons, 1885), 206–7.

34 Alfred T. Jackson, *The Diary of a Forty-Niner* (Boston: Houghton Mifflin, 1930), 222, 232.

35 Downie, *Hunting for Gold*, 21–23; Shinn, *Mining Camps*, 243.

36 Even as Americans debated the racial attributes of various Europeans, they set them apart from foreigners from outside Europe. See Ian Haney López, *White*

by Law: The Legal Construction of Race (New York: New York University Press, 2006); Mae M. Ngai, "The Architecture of Race in American Immigration Law: A Reexamination of the Immigration Act of 1924," *Journal of American History* 86, no. 1 (June 1999): 67–92; Spickard, *Almost All Aliens*, esp. 5–11, 89–130, 169.

37   Fernando Purcell, "'Too Many Foreigners for My Taste': Law, Race and Ethnicity in California, 1848–1852," in *Evil, Law and the State: Perspectives on State Power and Violence*, ed. John T. Parry (Amsterdam: Rodopi, 2006), 18; Ken Gonzales-Day, *Lynching in the West, 1850–1935* (Durham, N.C.: Duke University Press, 2006), 9.

38   Earl Pomeroy, *The Pacific Slope: A History of California, Oregon, Washington, Idaho, Utah, and Nevada* (New York: Knopf, 1965), 43–46; Johnson, *Founding the Far West*, 76, 122.

39   Downie, *Hunting for Gold*, 81.

40   Charles Thompson to uncle, 10 September 1850, Mss C-B 547:8, in Gold Rush Letters, BANC.

41   Thomas J. Green, "Report," *Alta California*, 5 April 1850.

42   Green. *Peon* referred to bound labor, often from eastern or southern Europe. *Chinean* meant "Chinese," *Canacker* meant "Hawaiian," while *convict gold digger* referred to Australians.

43   Gunther Peck, *Reinventing Free Labor: Padrones and Immigrant Workers in the North American West, 1880–1930* (New York: Cambridge University Press, 2000).

44   Alfred Doten, *The Journals of Alfred Doten, 1849–1903*, ed. Walter Van Tilburg Clark (Reno: University of Nevada Press, 1973), 76; Susan Lee Johnson, *Roaring Camp: The Social World of the California Gold Rush* (New York: W. W. Norton, 2000), 240–54.

45   Ramón Gil Navarro, *The Gold Rush Diary of Ramón Gil Navarro*, ed. Maria del Carmen Ferreyra and David Sven Reher (Lincoln: University of Nebraska Press, 2000), 92, 97; Leo, "Sonora—Disturbances in the Mines," *Alta California*, 27 May 1850; Robert Wilson, "San Joaquin and Placer Intelligence," *Alta California*, 3 June 1850.

46   Friedrich Gerstäcker, *Scenes of Life in California*, trans. George Cosgrave and Gustave Revilliod (1856; repr., San Francisco: J. Howell, 1942), 51–52; Leo, "Sonora," 27 May 1850.

47   Leo, "Sonora," *Alta California*, 27 May 1850.

48   Benjamin Butler Harris, journal of B. B. Harris, 11–12, Microfilm 10, CRCSL.

49   Leo, "Sonora," *Alta California*, 27 May 1850.

50   Navarro, *Gold Rush Diary*, 119.

51   Johnson, *Roaring Camp*, 210–15.

52   Hubert Howe Bancroft, *History of California* (San Francisco: History Co., 1886), 6:404–6; "Latest from Stockton," *Alta California*, 4 June, 1850; "Foreign Miners Tax," *Alta California*, 7 March 1851.

53   Shinn, *Mining Camps*, 246.

54   Downie, *Hunting for Gold*, 21–23; J. M. E., "A Letter from the Mines," *Alta California*, 31 August 1849; Murder and Lynching," *Alta California*, 5 May 1852; Ben Bowen, Ben Bowen Diary and Notebook: Mss, 1854–59, 50–51, Mss C-F 192, BANC; Jackson, *The Diary of a Forty-Niner*, 232; William Redmond Ryan, *Personal Adventures in Upper and Lower California, in 1848–9* (New York: Arno Press, 1973) 2:296–99; Ernest de Massey, *A Frenchman in the Gold Rush: The Journal of Ernest de Massey, Argonaut of 1849*, ed. Marguerite Eyer Wilber (San Francisco: California Historical Society, 1927), 36.

55   See, for example, William Stacy, "The Difficulties in Tuolumne County," *Alta California*, 22 July 1852; Peregrine Pilgrim, "Sonora Correspondent," *Alta California*, 23 February 1853. See also Smith, *Freedom's Frontier*, 10–12, 81–85; Peck, *Reinventing Free Labor*.

56   Foner, *Free Soil*, xi–xxvi; Marcus Cunliffe, *Chattel Slavery and Wage Slavery: The Anglo American Context, 1830–1860* (Athens: University of Georgia Press, 1979), xv, 3–6, 20, 29; Roediger, *The Wages of Whiteness*.

57   J. M. E., "A Letter from the Mines," *Alta California*, 31 August 1849.

58   Jackson, *The Diary of a Forty-Niner*, 232.

59   Bowen, Diary and Notebook, 50–51.

60   John Hovey, quoted in Johnson, *Roaring Camp*, 199; James J. Ayers, *Gold and Sunshine, Reminiscences of Early California* (Boston: R. G. Badger, 1922), 46. For a detailed analysis of the events of the "Chilean War" and a close reading of the biases of the source texts, see Johnson, *Roaring Camp*, 196–207.

61   Navarro, *Gold Rush Diary*, 68–69.

62   Navarro, *Gold Rush Diary*, 74.

63   Robert Wilson, "The Disturbance at the Mines," *Alta California*, 2 January 1850; Ayers, *Gold and Sunshine*, 48–49; Navarro, *Gold Rush Diary*, 75–76.

64   Ayers, *Gold and Sunshine*, 48–55; Wilson, "The Disturbance at the Mines."

65   Ayers, *Gold and Sunshine*, 54–56; Navarro, *Gold Rush Diary*, 78–79; Wilson, "The Disturbance at the Mines."

66   Robert Wilson, "The Chilean Disturbance," *Alta California*, 7 January 1850.

67   Wilson; Navarro, *Gold Rush Diary*, 79.

68   Navarro, *Gold Rush Diary*, 79; Wilson, "The Disturbance at the Mines"; Wilson, "The Chilean Disturbance."

69   Navarro notes that one of the men hanged was actually Mexican. Navarro, *Gold Rush Diary*, 82–84; Ayers, *Gold and Sunshine*, 58.

70 Navarro, *Gold Rush Diary*, 68–69.

71 Ryan, *Personal Adventures*, 2:296. *Californians* here refers to Hispanic residents of California, sometimes called Californios.

72 "The Tax on Foreign Miners and the Policy of Expulsion," *Alta California*, 12 May 1852.

73 "The Tax on Foreign Miners."

74 Stuart Creighton Miller, *The Unwelcome Immigrant: The American Image of the Chinese, 1785–1882* (Berkeley: University of California Press, 1969).

75 "Our Population," *Alta California*, 8 March 1850. See also "Celestial," *Alta California*, 11 May 1850; "Latest from the Celestials," *Alta California*, 11 August 1850; "More Murder and Robbery," *Alta California*, 7 October 1850.

76 "More Murder and Robbery," *Alta California*, 7 October 1850; "Celestial" *Alta California*, 11 May 1850; "The China Boys," *Alta California*, 12 May 1851; "Asiatic Immigration," *Alta California*, 16 May 1851; Reverend William Speer, "China and California, Their Relations Past and Present: A Lecture in Conclusion of a Series in Relation to the Chinese People, Delivered in the Stockton Street Presbyterian Church, San Francisco, June 28, 1853," CRCSL.

77 See, for example, Osborn, Timothy Coffin Osborn Journal, 191.

78 "Foreign Immigration," *Alta California*, 20 February 1850.

79 John David Borthwick, *The Gold Hunters: A First-Hand Picture of Life in California Mining Camps in the Early Fifties*, ed. Horace Kephart (1857; repr., New York: International Fiction Library, 1917), 253; Capron, *History of California*, 146. On the problematic nature of the term and category of "coolie," see Moon-ho Jung, *Coolies and Cane: Race, Labor, and Sugar in the Age of Emancipation* (Baltimore: Johns Hopkins University Press, 2006), 5.

80 Paul, *California Gold*, 101, 117–19; "Legislative Intelligence," *Alta California*, 14 April 1852; "The Chinese Immigration," *Alta California*, 26 April 1852; "Legislative Intelligence," *Alta California*, 30 April 1852; Peregrine Pilgrim, "The Chinese in California," *Alta California*, 29 July 1853.

81 "The Chinese and Their Assumption of Jurisdiction in San Francisco," *Alta California*, 8 June 1853; Mountaineer, "Letter from the Mountains," *Alta California*, 15 June 1853; "Chinese Vigilant Committee," *Alta California*, 26 August 1853.

82 "Difficulties among the Chinese," *Alta California*, 13 August 1852; "The Chinese and Their Assumption of Jurisdiction," *Alta California*, 8 June 1853; Mountaineer, "Letter from the Mountains"; "Chinese Vigilant Committee," *Alta California*, 26 August 1853; "The Chinese Case," *Alta California*, 5 January 1854; "Chinese Villainy," *Alta California*, 12 March 1854.

83 J. E. Clayton, "Remarks of the Hon. J. E. Clayton, on the Chinese Question: Delivered in the Assembly Chamber, on the 18th of April, 1855," 3, CRCSL.

84 Wilson Flint, "Speech of Hon. Wilson Flint, in the Senate of California, March 21, 1856: on the Bill to Reduce the Chinese Mining License Tax," 3, CRCSL. Pro-Chinese voices were increasingly limited to the missionary and merchant classes. See, for example, Californian, "The Chinese," *Alta California*, 11 July 1857; "The Chinese Population," *Alta California*, 7 December 1857.

85 On the emerging racial hierarchy of California in the late 1850s, but especially during the period of Reconstruction, see Paddison, *American Heathens*; Bottoms, *An Aristocracy of Color.*

86 Hurtado, *Indian Survival*, 23–26, 32–35; James J. Rawls, *Indians of California: The Changing Image* (Norman: University of Oklahoma Press, 1984), 3–6, 13–21.

87 California State Legislature, "An Act for the Government and Protection of the Indians," 408–9. See also Hurtado, *Indian Survival*, 5.

88 California State Legislature, "An Act for the Government and Protection of the Indians"; Benjamin Madley, *An American Genocide: The United States and the California Indian Catastrophe, 1846–1873* (New Haven, Conn.: Yale University Press, 2016); Brendan C. Lindsay, *Murder State: California's Native American Genocide, 1846–1873* (Lincoln: University of Nebraska Press, 2012); Clifford Trafzer and Joel Hyer, eds., *Exterminate Them: Written Accounts of the Murder, Rape, and Slavery of Native Americans during the California Gold Rush, 1848–1868* (East Lansing: Michigan State University Press, 1999); Hurtado, *Indian Survival*, 107–23.

89 Theodore Johnson, *Sights in the Gold Region, and Scenes by the Way* (New York: Baker and Scribner, 1849), 152, 201, 204. See also Borthwick, *The Gold Hunters*, 135–36; William S. M'Collum, *California as I Saw It* (Buffalo, N.Y.: George H. Derby, 1850), 51–52; George Holbrook Baker, Personal Papers, Diaries May 1849–Aug. 1850, 28 June 1849, George Holbrook Baker Collection, folder 6, box 1844, CRCSL; "From the Sacramento—Difficulties at the Mines between the Americans and Chilians," *New York Tribune*, 2 August 1849, in Material for Proposed Publication of Gold Rush Letters, Carbons of Letters from Newspapers, folder 1, box 2170, CRCSL; "The Indian Massacre in California," *New York Tribune*, 15 August 1849, in Material for Proposed Publication of Gold Rush Letters, Carbons of Letters from Newspapers, folder 1, box 2169, CRCSL; "Description of Sutter's Fort—Washing—A Model Gold-Washer—Prices of Provisions at the Mills—The Oregonians and the Indians—Forty Indian Girls Killed, to Save Them From the Whites—Mining Association Formed—Expedition Four Months Too Early," *New York Tribune*, 1 September 1849, in Material for Proposed Publication of Gold Rush Letters, Carbons of Letters from Newspapers, folder 1, box 2169, CRCSL.

90 On the critical role of Oregonians in fostering genocide in California, see Madley, *An American Genocide*, 76–77.

91 "Indian Affairs on the Pacific," *San Francisco Bulletin*, 1 September 1856, quoted in Trafzer and Hyer, *Exterminate Them*, 49–52. On the contours of the national debate at this time, see Francis Paul Prucha, *The Great Father: The United States Government and the American Indians* (Lincoln: University of Nebraska Press, 1984), 1:184–410, esp. 381–92.

92 For the extermination perspective, see "Indian Difficulties," *Alta California*, 11 May 1850; "Indian Affairs on the Pacific," *San Francisco Bulletin*, 1 September 1856, quoted in Trafzer and Hyer, *Exterminate Them*, 49–52; Herman Francis Reinhart, *The Golden Frontier: The Recollections of Herman Francis Reinhart, 1851–1869* (Austin: University of Texas Press, 1962), 32. For the protection perspective, see Pancoast, *A Quaker Forty-Niner*, 298–99; Hurtado, *Indian Survival*, 127–28; Rawls, *Indians of California*, 144–46, 183.

93 Trafzer and Hyer, *Exterminate Them*, xxiii; Hurtado, *Indian Survival*, 100; Rawls, *Indians of California*, 171; Madley, *American Genocide*, 347.

94 Frank Soulé, *Annals of San Francisco: Containing a Summary of the History of . . . California, and a Complete History of . . . Its Great City* (New York: Appleton, 1855), 188, 301, 413. Soulé charts the growth of San Francisco from 375 inhabitants "without reckoning the Indians," in 1847, to between 36,000 and 42,000 by 1852. See also Gray Brechin, *Imperial San Francisco: Urban Power, Earthly Ruin* (Berkeley: University of California Press, 1999), 16–64.

95 Ellison, *A Self-Governing Dominion*, 11–12; Johnson, *Founding the Far West*, 24–25, 28–30.

96 Ellison, *A Self-Governing Dominion*, 11–14, 16–21, 66; Neal Harlow, *California Conquered: War and Peace on the Pacific, 1846–1850* (Berkeley: University of California Press, 1982), 265–85; Soulé, *Annals of San Francisco*, 205, 208, 218–19.

97 Nancy Taniguchi, *Dirty Deeds: Land, Violence, and the 1856 San Francisco Vigilance Committee* (Norman: University of Oklahoma Press, 2016), 59.

98 Capron, *History of California*, 171.

99 George Holbrook Baker to mother, 20 June 1849, file 5, box 1844, CRCSL; James H. Carson, *Early Recollections of the Mines, and a Description of the Great Tulare Valley* (Stockton, Calif.: published to accompany the steamer edition of the "San Joaquin Republican," 1852), 19. Modern scholars have confirmed that crime was not out of control in San Francisco. Taniguchi, *Dirty Deeds*, 9.

100 Senkewicz, *Vigilantes*, 75, 78.

101 The First Regiment of the New York Volunteers consisted of 917 farmers, mechanics, artisans, and petty criminals who agreed to fight Mexico in exchange for free passage to California. By the time they arrived, the war was over and they disbanded. Joshua Paddison, *A World Transformed: Firsthand*

Accounts of California before the Gold Rush (Berkeley, Calif.: Heyday Books, 1998), 311n1; "The Chilenos and Other Foreigners in the City of San Francisco Attacked by an Armed Party of Americans—Great Excitement—Meeting of the Citizens—Formation of a Citizen Armed Police—Arrest of the Rioters—Their Trial and Sentence," *Alta California*, 2 August 1849, steamer edition; Bancroft, *History of California*, 6:211–12.

102 "More News from California—Illegal Assembly—Governor's Proclamation—Politics and the Gold Digging—Prospects for Emigrants—Goods for a Song, &c., &c.," *New York Herald*, 17 September 1849.

103 "More News from California."

104 "The Chilenos and Other Foreigners," *Alta California*, 2 August 1849; "More News from California," *New York Herald*, 17 September 1849.

105 David T. Courtwright, *Violent Land: Single Men and Social Disorder from the Frontier to the Inner City* (Cambridge, Mass: Harvard University Press, 1996), 121; Linda Gordon, *The Great Arizona Orphan Abduction* (Cambridge, Mass.: Harvard University Press, 1999), 255; Paddison, *A World Transformed*, 331n1.

106 "The Chilenos and Other Foreigners," *Alta California*, 2 August 1849.

107 Ryan, *Personal Adventures*, 1:260; Palmer described the Hounds as dressing in "carnival attire, mixed of Mexican, Chinese, and Indian garments, snatched with impunity from the nearest shop." John Williamson Palmer, *The New and the Old; or, California and India in Romantic Aspects* (New York: Rudd & Carleton, 1859), 79.

108 Ryan, *Personal Adventures*, 2:260.

109 "The Chilenos and Other Foreigners," *Alta California*, 2 August 1849.

110 "The Chilenos and Other Foreigners"; "More News from California," *New York Herald*, 17 September 1849; Bancroft, *History of California*, 6:211–12.

111 "More News from California," *New York Herald*, 17 September 1849.

112 "The Chilenos and Other Foreigners," *Alta California*, 2 August 1849.

113 "The Chilenos and Other Foreigners."

114 Bancroft, *History of California*, 6:211–12; Ryan, *Personal Adventures*, 2:257–63; "The Riots in California—Arrest and Trial of the Rioters—Their Punishment—The Election—The Mines—Sickness—Deaths &c., &c.," *New York Herald*, 14 September 1849.

115 "More News from California," *New York Herald*, 17 September 1849.

116 "The Chilenos and Other Foreigners," *Alta California*, 2 August 1849. Brigadier General Persifor Smith was a short-lived military governor of California. On the proclamation, see Aims McGuinness, *Path of Empire: Panama and the California Gold Rush* (Ithaca, N.Y.: Cornell University Press, 2008), 34.

117 Ryan, *Personal Adventures*, 2:257–58.

118 "The Chilenos and Other Foreigners," *Alta California*, 2 August 1849.

119 John M. Letts, *A Pictorial View of California: Including a Description of the Panama and Nicaragua Routes, with Information and Advice Interesting to All, Particularly Those Who Intend to Visit the Golden Region, by a Returned Californian* (New York: H. Bill, 1853), 52.

120 Susan Lee Johnson has identified a similar phenomenon in the southern mines, with the Chinese as effeminate victims and Joaquin Murrieta as the unmanly aggressor. See Johnson, *Roaring Camp*, 35.

121 The term *Sydney Duck* referred to their point of origin (Sydney, Australia) and ocean voyage to California.

122 Peter Decker, Diaries of Peter Decker: Manuscripts, Galleys, Ill[ustrations], 2 February 1851, 29 April 1851, Talisman Press Collection, Box 2127, CRCSL; John Carr, *Pioneer Days in California: Historical and Personal Sketches* (Eureka, Calif.: Times Publishing, 1891), 82.

123 The *Alta* complained of the universality of equating "South Pacific islanders" with criminals or "Sydney Birds." See "Crime among Us," *Alta California*, 28 October 1850. Of course, just under a month later, the *Alta* did exactly that and identified immigrants from Australia as criminals in spirit, if not in fact. "Immigration of Convicts," *Alta California*, 20 November 1850. See "Local Matters," *Alta California*, 16 March 1850; "Marital Rights," *Alta California*, 28 April 1851; "The Same Old Drunk," *Alta California*, 12 August 1851. On the migration and acceptance of Australian Irish in California, see Malcolm Campbell, *Ireland's New Worlds: Immigrants, Politics, and Society in the United States and Australia, 1815–1922* (Madison: University of Wisconsin Press, 2007), 86–91, 95–103.

124 Downie, *Hunting for Gold*, 11–12.

125 C. Sam to Willie, 27 February 1851, Mss C-B 547:53, BANC; "A Coward's Weapon," *Alta California*, 27 May 1850. A slung-shot was a heavy object tied with a length of rope to the wrist. This allowed the attacker to throw it at an opponent and pull it back to throw again.

126 "Immigration of Convicts," *Alta California*, 20 November 1850; see also Alonzo Rathbun, Alonzo W. Rathbun Diary 1849–1851, 9 May 1851, BANC; de Russailh, *Last Adventure*, 17–18.

127 "Immigration of Convicts," *Alta California*, 20 November, 1850.

128 "Law and Order," *Alta California*, 16 July 1850.

129 "The Excitement Yesterday," *Alta California*, 23 February 1851; "Incidents of Yesterday—Trial of Jas. Stuart," *Alta California*, 24 February 1851.

130 "What Should Our Citizens Do?" *Alta California*, 23 February 1851.

131 "Secret Organization," *Alta California*, 11 June 1851.

132 "The Excitement Yesterday," *Alta California*, 23 February 1851; "Incidents of Yesterday," *Alta California*, 24 February 1851.

133 "Incidents of Yesterday," *Alta California*, 24 February 1851; "City Intelligence—Yesterday," *Alta California*, 25 February 1851.

134 "The Excitement Yesterday," *Alta California*, 23 February 1851; "What Should Our Citizens Do?" *Alta California*, 23 February 1851; "Incidents of Yesterday," *Alta California*, 24 February 1851; "The Courts and the People," *Alta California*, 24 February 1851.

135 "Incidents of Yesterday," *Alta California*, 24 February 1851.

136 Letts, *A Pictorial View of California*, 54; Senkewicz, *Vigilantes*, 81.

137 "San Francisco as It Is: Manuscript," 181.

138 "The Vigilance Committee," *Alta California*, 13 June 1851; "City Intelligence—The Coroner's Inquest Continued," *Alta California*, 13 June 1851.

139 "Secret Organization," Alta California, 11 June 1851; "San Francisco as It Is: Manuscript," 181.

140 "Arrest of a Robber! Trial and Sentence by the Citizen Police; Execution on the Plaza!" Alta California, 11 June 1851; "San Francisco as It Is: Manuscript," 180–81.

141 "Arrest of a Robber!" *Alta California*, 11 June 1851; "City Intelligence-Coroner's Inquest" *Alta California*, 12 June 1851.

142 "Arrest of a Robber!" *Alta California*, 11 June 1851.

143 "San Francisco as It Is: Manuscript," 181.

144 Palmer, *The New and the Old*, 73; "City Intelligence—Coroner's Inquest," *Alta California*, 12 June 1851; "City Intelligence—the Coroner's Inquest Continued," *Alta California*, 13 June, 1851.

145 "The Verdict of the Coroner's Jury in the Case of Jenkins," *Alta California*, 14 June 1851.

146 "Law and Order," *Alta California*, 14 June 1851; "Organization of the Vigilance Committee," *Alta California*, 12 June 1851; "The Execution of Jenkins," *Alta California*, 12 June 1851.

147 "Law and Order," *Alta California*, 14 June 1851.

148 "Secret Organization," *Alta California*, 11 June 1851.

149 "Law and Order," *Alta California*, 14 June 1851.

150 "The Execution of Jenkins," *Alta California*, 12 June 1851; "Law and Order," *Alta California*, 14 June 1851.

151 "The Execution of Jenkins," *Alta California*, 12 June 1851; "[Title illegible]," *Alta California*, 19 June 1851.

152 The Execution of Jenkins," *Alta California*, 12 June 1851; "Public Meeting," *Alta California*, 12 June 1851.

153 "Law and Order," 14 June 1851; "San Francisco as It Is: Manuscript," 185–86.

154 In 1851 and 1856, crime rates in San Francisco were on a par with the national average. Senkewicz, *Vigilantes*, 75–77; Kevin Mullen, *Dangerous Strangers: Minority Newcomers and Criminal Violence in the Urban West, 1850-2000* (New York: Palgrave, 2005), 14, 50; Taniguchi, *Dirty Deeds*, 9–10.

155 "The First Legal Execution," *Alta California*, 21 November 1855; "Progress of Civilization," *Alta California*, 28 January 1856. The most comprehensive account of the second Vigilance Committee is Taniguchi, *Dirty Deeds*.

156 John M. Findlay, *People of Chance: Gambling in American Society, from Jamestown to Las Vegas* (New York: Oxford University Press, 1986), 96; Frank F. Fargo, A True and Minute History of the Assassination of James King of Wm. at San Francisco, Cal: Also Remarks of the Press Concerning the Outrage; an Account of the Formation and Action of the Vigilance Committee; Meetings and Resolutions of the Citizens of Sacramento, Marysville and Stockton; Funeral Ceremonies of Mr. King, with the Addresses of Rev. Messrs. Cutler and Lacy over the Body; and the Execution of Casey and Cora / Carefully Compiled from Various Sources, p. 2, CRCSL.

157 Fargo, A True and Minute History of the Assassination of James King of Wm., 2–3.

158 "Incidents of Wednesday's Occurrence," *Alta California*, 16 May 1856; Senkewicz, *Vigilantes*, 134, 170.

159 "Events of Yesterday—Rescue of the Prisoners, Casey and Cora, without Resistance," *Alta California*, 19 May 1856; "Incidents of Wednesday's Occurrence," *Alta California*, 16 May 1856; Senkewicz, *Vigilantes*, 134, 170.

160 "Events of Yesterday—Death of Mr. King—A Wonderful Sensation in the Community—The Whole City Draped in Mourning," *Alta California*, 21 May 1856; "Events of Yesterday—Funeral of Mr. James King of Wm.—Execution of Casey and Cora by the Vigilance Committee!!—The Day," *Alta California*, 23 May 1856.

161 "Events of Yesterday," *Alta California*, 21 June 1856.

162 Christopher Waldrep, *The Many Faces of Judge Lynch: Extralegal Violence and Punishment in America* (New York: Palgrave Macmillan, 2002), 55–56.

163 Senkewicz, *Vigilantes*, 186–87; Taniguchi, *Dirty Deeds*.

164 "Constitution of the Committee of Vigilance, San Francisco—Adopted May 15th, 1856," *Alta California*, 14 June 1856.

165 Foner, *Free Soil*, xi–xxvi; Roediger, *The Wages of Whiteness*, 50–51, 66–74; Philip J. Ethington, *The Public City: The Political Construction of Urban Life in San Francisco, 1850–1900* (New York: Cambridge University Press, 1994), 55–58; Wilentz, *Chants Democratic*, 61–63, 92–94.

166 Johnson, *Founding the Far West*, 127–30.

167 On the rhetoric of slavery for white Americans, see Roediger, *The Wages of Whiteness*, 36, 55–60, 66, and Edmund S. Morgan, "Slavery and Freedom: The American Paradox," *Journal of American History* 59, no. 1 (June 1972): 5–29.

168 Untitled article, Alta California, 16 May 1856; untitled article, Alta California, 20 May 1856; "The Law of the People Is Supreme," Alta California, 6 June 1856; "The Address of the Vigilance Committee," Alta California, 9 June 1856.

169 A Looker On, "Thoughts from a Looker-On, to Those in the Distance—No. 2," *Alta California*, 22 July 1856.

170 "The Ultimate Result," *Alta California*, 16 July, 1856.

171 "Constitution of the Committee of Vigilance," *Alta California*, 14 June 1856.

172 "Mass Meeting of the Citizens," *Alta California*, 15 June 1856; "Fort Vigilance," *Alta California*, 13 June 1856; "The Mass Meeting Last Night—A Concourse of 10,000 People!—A Terrible Rebuke to Ballot-Box Stuffing!—Great Unanimity of Action!—Speeches, Resolutions, Incidents, &c. &c.," *Alta California*, 13 July 1856; "Banner Presentation—the Vigilance Committee Endorsed by the Ladies," *Alta California*, 19 July 1856; "Events of Yesterday—Grand Parade and Review of the Vigilance Committee!—5,000 Men Bearing Arms!—Immense Concourse of Citizens!—Particulars, Incidents, and Reflections," *Alta California*, 19 August 1856.

173 "Banner Presentation," *Alta California*, 19 July 1856.

174 Taniguchi, *Dirty Deeds*, 32, 53. Belle Ryan married Charles Cora shortly before his execution, allowing him a Catholic burial. Afterward, Belle Cora ran a brothel in San Francisco until her death from pneumonia in 1862.

175 The class-laden rhetoric, too, is important here. "The Law of the People Is Supreme," *Alta California*, 6 June 1856.

176 "The Address of the Vigilance Committee," *Alta California*, 9 June 1856.

177 "To the People of California," *Alta California*, 9 June 1856.

178 "To the People of California."

179 "The Address of the Committee," *Alta California*, 10 June 1856; Senkewicz, *Vigilantes*, 171–72; Bancroft, *History of California*, 6:744; Johnson, *Founding the Far West*, 200, 247–48; H. Brett Melendy and Benjamin Gilbert, *The Governors of California: Peter H. Burnett to Edmund G. Brown* (Georgetown, Calif.: Talisman Press, 1965), 67–73.

180 For a discussion of the invisibility of English immigrants in American immigration, see Spickard, *Almost All Aliens*, 97–100. In a telling example, Borthwick noted that the post office had two windows: one for foreigners, one for Americans and Englishmen. See Borthwick, *The Gold Hunters*, 91–92. Also, see Pringle Shaw, *Ramblings in California: Containing a Description of the Country,*

Life at the Mines, State of Society, &c.; Interspersed with Characteristic Anec-dotes, and Sketches from Life (Toronto: J. Bain, [1856?]), 25.

181 Shaw, *Ramblings in California*, 16, 18. For similar descriptions of Germans, see Farnham, *California, In-doors and Out*, 264–65; William Shaw, *Golden Dreams and Waking Realities: Being the Adventures of a Gold-Seeker in California and the Pacific Islands* (London: Smith, Elder, 1851), 20; Hinton Rowan Helper, *The Land of Gold, Reality versus Fiction* (Baltimore: H. Taylor, 1855), 33.

182 "The French Citizens of the Vigilance Committee," *Alta California*, 27 May 1856; "Adopted Citizens and the Vigilance Committee," *Alta California*, 29 June 1856.

183 *San Francisco Daily Herald*, 12 June 1856; Senkewicz, *Vigilantes*, 169–70; Rohrbough, *Days of Gold*, 142–43; Ethington, *The Public City*, 96–97. Both the Germans and French were praised for contributing a company of men to the committee. "Events of Yesterday—Rescue of the Prisoners," *Alta California*, 19 May 1856; Taniguchi, *Dirty Deeds*, 47, 102, 170.

184 Senkewicz, *Vigilantes*, 137.

185 R. A. Burchell, *The San Francisco Irish, 1848–1880* (Manchester, U.K.: Manchester University Press, 1979), 3, 34; Steven P. Erie, *Rainbow's End: Irish-Americans and the Dilemmas of Urban Machine Politics, 1840–1985* (Berkeley: University of California Press, 1988), 26–30, 33–35.

186 "Those Notified to Leave," *Alta California*, 19 June 1856; A Looker On, "Thoughts from a Looker-On," *Alta California*, 22 July 1856.

187 "The Executive Committee of the General Committee of Vigilance," *Alta California*, 27 August 1856; "Adopted Citizens and the Vigilance Committee," *Alta California*, 29 June 1856.

188 "The Effect in the East," *Alta California*, 20 June 1856; "Revolution in San Francisco," *New York Times*, 14 June 1856; F. W. H., "News from California—the Revolution in San Francisco," *Alta California*, 30 June 1856.

189 "Martial Law," *Alta California*, 4 June 1856; "Rumors of an Attack on the Vigilance Committee by the U.S. Authorities," *Alta California*, 24 July 1856; "An Anticipated Collision," *Alta California*, 25 July 1856; "The Committee and the U.S. Officers," *Alta California*, 28 July 1856; E. B. Boutwell to Governor Johnson, 29 June 1856, Vigilance Collection 1856, folder 27, CRCSL.

190 "Report of Maj. Gen. Volney E. Howard," *Alta California*, 26 June 1856; "The Vigilance Committee Correspondence—Interesting Documents—Gov. Johnson's Letter to the President—The President's Reply—Letters of Gov. Johnson, Gen. West, Wool, Capt. Farragut, Capt. Bentwell, Judge Terry, &c.," *Alta California*, 6 September 1856; Waldrep, *The Many Faces of Judge Lynch*, 55–58.

191 "The Origin of Lynch Law," *Alta California*, 3 August 1856.

192 Untitled article, *Alta California*, 16 May 1856; "Events of Yesterday—Rescue of the Prisoners," *Alta California*, 19 May 1856; untitled article, *Alta California*, 21 May 1856; "The Necessity of a Vigilance Committee," *Alta California*, 29 May 1856; "Gone," *Alta California*, 6 June 1856; "The Address of the Vigilance Committee," *Alta California*, 9 June 1856; "The Address of the Committee," *Alta California*, 10 June 1856; "Revolution," *Alta California*, 10 June, 1856.

193 Joseph Benton, Sermon [Vigilance and Reform], 18 May 1856, Joseph Augustine Benton Collection, box 28, CRCSL.

194 "The Effect in the East," *Alta California*, 20 June 1856.

195 Joseph Benton, Sermon [Vigilance and Reform].

196 "Events of Yesterday—Murderous Attack upon S. A. Hopkins, of the Vigilance Committee! by D. S. Terry, of the Supreme Court—Arrest of Terry and Maloney by the Committee—Surrender of the "Law and Order" Forces!—One Hundred Prisoners Taken!—2,000 Arms Secured—Vigilance Committee Triumphant!—Condition of the Wounded Man—Particulars and Incidents," *Alta California*, 22 June 1856; "Events of Yesterday—The Day after the Surrender—Release of the Prisoners of War—Arrest of J. L. Durkee by the U.S. Marshal—Condition of Mr. Hopkins—Further Particulars and Incidents," *Alta California*, 23 June 1856; "Report of Maj. Gen. Volney E. Howard," 26 June 1856; Vigilance Collection, 1856, box 324, unnumbered folder, CRCSL.

197 "The Vigilance Committee Correspondence," *Alta California*, 6 September 1856; E. B. Boutwell to Governor Johnson, 29 June 1856; William Kibbe to J. Neely Johnson, Governor, Vigilance Collection 1856, 14 August 1856, folder 18, CRCSL.

198 "The Vigilance Committee Correspondence," *Alta California*, 6 September 1856.

199 "The Vigilance Committee," *Alta California*, 13 August 1856; "The Vigilance Committee," *Alta California*, 16 August 1856.

200 David Terry, *Trial of David S. Terry by the Committee of Vigilance, San Francisco* (San Francisco: R. C. Moore, 1856), 1–73.

201 "The Executive Committee to the General Committee of Vigilance," *Alta California*, 27 August 1856.

202 Browne, *Report of the Debates*, 62.

CHAPTER 3: ENGLISH PRINCIPLES ENCOUNTER AMERICAN REPUBLICANISM

1 W. D. Moses, "A Letter from Brother Moses," *San Francisco Evening Bulletin*, 7 May 1858.

2 James Pilton, "Negro Settlement in British Columbia, 1858–1871" (master's thesis, University of British Columbia, 1951), 30; Edward Cridge, Diary 6 June 1853–19 October 1854; 10 February, 1858–3 June 1859, Cridge Papers, 91, Mss

0320, BCARS; Crawford Kilian, *Go Do Some Great Thing: The Black Pioneers of British Columbia* (Vancouver, B.C.: Douglas & McIntyre, 1978), 23–25.

3   I take the term *English principles* from "Political Meeting," *Victoria Gazette*, 9 January 1860. For British perceptions of American versus British social order, see Tina Loo, *Making Law, Order, and Authority in British Columbia, 1821–1871* (Toronto: University of Toronto Press, 1994), 150–51.

4   This was not a standard attitude throughout the British empire. See David Killingray, "'A Good West Indian, a Good African, and, in Short, a Good Britisher': Blacks and British in a Colour-Conscious Empire," in *Ambiguities of Empire: Essays in Honour of Andrew Porter*, ed. R. F. Holland, S. E. Stockwell, and A. N. Porter (London: Routledge, 2008), 23–25.

5   Frederick Cooper and Ann Laura Stoler, *Tensions of Empire: Colonial Culture in a Bourgeois World* (Berkeley: University of California Press, 1997); Amy S. Greenberg, *Manifest Manhood and the Antebellum American Empire* (New York: Cambridge University Press, 2005); Catherine Hall, *Civilising Subjects: Colony and Metropole in the English Imagination, 1830–1867* (Chicago: University of Chicago Press, 2002); Philippa Levine, ed., *Gender and Empire* (New York: Oxford University Press, 2004); Ann Laura Stoler, *Carnal Knowledge and Imperial Power: Race and the Intimate in Colonial Rule* (Berkeley: University of California Press, 2002); Adele Perry, *On the Edge of Empire: Gender, Race, and the Making of British Columbia, 1849–1871* (Toronto: University of Toronto Press, 2001).

6   Perry, *On the Edge of Empire*, 17–21, 51–56.

7   For other instances where British colonial authorities claimed to be less racist to justify colonialism, see Christine Bolt, "Race and the Victorians," *British Imperialism in the Nineteenth Century*, ed. C. C. Eldridge (London: Macmillan, 1984), 144. These assertions existed alongside of, and were intertwined with, British racist beliefs. Paula Krebbs, *Gender, Race, and the Writing of Empire: Public Discourse and the Boer War* (New York: Cambridge University Press, 1999), 116.

8   Perry, *On the Edge of Empire*.

9   Perry, *On the Edge of Empire*, 9.

10 Robin Fisher, *Contact and Conflict: Indian-European Relations in British Columbia, 1774–1890* (Vancouver: University of British Columbia Press, 1992), 25.

11 Loo, *Making Law, Order, and Authority*, 20; Richard Mackie, *Trading beyond the Mountains: The British Fur Trade on the Pacific, 1793–1843* (Vancouver: University of British Columbia Press, 1997), 326.

12 Richard Mackie, "The Colonization of Vancouver Island, 1849–1858," *BC Studies* 96 (Winter 1992–93): 4–6.

13 The history of colonial British Columbia governance is complicated. In 1849, the colony of Vancouver Island was created first under Governor Richard

Blanshard, then James Douglas. The mainland, known as British Columbia, was left as the domain of the HBC. In 1858, British Columbia became a colony, and Douglas was appointed governor of both Vancouver Island and British Columbia, though they were technically separate colonies. In 1864, Governor Arthur Kennedy was appointed to Vancouver Island and Governor Frederick Seymour to British Columbia. Largely for financial reasons, the colonies were amalgamated in 1866 to form a new colony, also called British Columbia, under Governor Seymour. This continued until British Columbia joined the Canadian confederation in 1871.

14   Loo, *Making Law, Order, and Authority*, 36–37; Sylvia Van Kirk, "Tracing the Fortunes of Five Founding Families of Victoria," *BC Studies*, 115–16 (Autumn–Winter 1997–98): 149–52.

15   Edward Wakefield, *A View of the Art of Colonization, with Present Reference to the British Empire: In Letters between a Statesman and a Colonist* (Kitchener, Ont.: Batoche Books, 2001), 18, 24–25, 28, 44, 94–103.

16   Wakefield, *A View of the Art of Colonization*, 115.

17   Mackie, "The Colonization of Vancouver Island," 25; Fisher, *Contact and Conflict*, 58. While cheap compared to Europe, land in British Columbia was considerably more expensive and remote than land in the United States.

18   Loo, *Making Law, Order, and Authority*, 39.

19   Perry, *On the Edge of Empire*, 127–28, 131–38, 146–66.

20   Edward Wakefield, *The Collected Works of Edward Gibbon Wakefield*, ed. Muriel F. Lloyd Prichard (Glasgow: Colins, 1968), 151–52.

21   Jean Barman, *The West beyond the West: A History of British Columbia*, 3rd ed. (Toronto: University of Toronto Press, 1991), 64–67.

22   Governor Douglas, "Letter to Colonial Secretary," 8 May 1858, Great Britain, Colonial Office, GR-0326, BCARS.

23   Matthew Begbie to Governor Douglas, 18 May 1859, Colonial Correspondence, file 142b1, B0137, BCARS. See also Kinahan Cornwallis, *The New Eldorado, or, British Columbia* (London: Thomas Cautley Newby, 1858), xvi.

24   Cornwallis, *The New Eldorado*, xv–xvii, 157–59, 205–6; T. G. Price, "Letter from Victoria," in *The Merthyr Telegraph*, 31 May 1862; Returned Digger, *Cariboo: The Newly Discovered Gold Fields of British Columbia* (Fairfield, Wash: Ye Galleon Press, 1975), 7.

25   Although it is anachronistic, I apply *African Canadian* to all people of African descent in what would become Canada. It is used interchangeably with *black settlers* and *people* (or *settlers*) *of African descent*.

26   Matthew Begbie, "Letter to Douglas, 30 April, 1860," Colonial Correspondence, file 142c, B01308, BCARS, emphasis original.

27 John Gibson, "Letter to Mother, 12 October, 1858," in John C. Gibson Letters, box 206, CRCSL.

28 Quote is from Cornwallis, *The New El Dorado*, 283; Kilian, *Go Do Some Great Thing*, 47.

29 Pilton, "Negro Settlement," 177.

30 Kilian, *Go Do Some Great Thing*, 47.

31 Fisher, *Contact and Conflict*, 2–3.

32 For an analysis of the relationship between the HBC and the indigenous population, see Fisher, *Contact and Conflict*, 24–72.

33 Daniel Marshall, "Claiming the Land: Indians, Goldseekers, and the Rush to British Columbia" (PhD diss., University of British Columbia, 2000), 87–88.

34 T. A. Rickard, "Indian Participation in the Gold Discoveries," *British Columbia Historical Quarterly* 2, no. 1 (January 1938): 13; James Douglas, letter to Edward Henry, Lord Stanley, 15 June, 1858, in "Colonial Despatches of British Columbia: 1858," ed. James Hendrickson, vol. 1a (March 1988), University of Victoria Library, Victoria, British Columbia (hereafter UVIC); James Moore, "The Discovery of Hill's Bar in 1858," *British Columbia Historical Quarterly* 3, no. 3 (July 1939): 219. Hill's Bar is right at the border of the Sto:lo and Nlaka'pamux nations, and the specific natives at Hill's Bar were never clearly identified in the original sources.

35 Moore, "The Discovery of Hill's Bar," 219. *Bluejackets* refers to enlisted sailors.

36 Douglas, letter to Edward Henry, Lord Stanley, 15 June 1858.

37 Douglas, letter. James Moore also claimed that Douglas gave the Native Americans "a blowout of hard tack and malasses" which would be in keeping with HBC practices. (A "blowout" is a lavish party.) See Moore, "The Discovery of Hill's Bar," 219.

38 Marshall, "Claiming the Land," 33, 124, 141, 199–200, 244.

39 Sewell, "Letter from Fraser River," *Alta California*, 3 September 1858. For more details, see Hubert Bancroft, *History of British Columbia* (San Francisco: History Co., 1887), 395; "Indian Difficulties," *Victoria Gazette*, 20 August 1858; H. M. Snyder, "The Indian Difficulties," in *Victoria Gazette*, 24 August 1858; "Account of Captain Snyder's Expedition," in *Victoria Gazette*, 1 September 1858.

40 Sewell, "Letter from Fraser River"; Bancroft, *History of British Columbia*, 395; Snyder, "The Indian Difficulties."

41 Marshall, "Claiming the Land," 206–20.

42 "Selling Liquor to the Indians," *Victoria Gazette*, 10 August 1858; H. M Snyder, "Letter from Captain Snyder," *Victoria Gazette*, 24 August 1858; "Account of Captain Snyder's Expedition," *Victoria Gazette*, 1 September 1858.

43 "Account of Captain Snyder's Expedition," *Victoria Gazette*, 1 September 1858. Graham and Galloway were not identified by first name.

44 Sewell, "Letter from Fraser River"; Bancroft, *History of British Columbia*, 395; Snyder, "The Indian Difficulties," *Victoria Gazette*, 24 August 1858; "Letter from Fort Yale," *Victoria Gazette*, 24 August 1858; E. O. S. Scholefield, *British Columbia from the Earliest Times to the Present* (Vancouver, B.C.: S. J. Clarke., 1914), 35.

45 The identities of these men were not recorded, so their status as "chiefs" is debatable given the tendency of whites to use that term loosely. T. W. G., "Letter from Fort Yale," *Victoria Gazette*, 1 September 1858; "Account of Captain Snyder's Expedition," *Victoria Gazette*, 1 September 1858; Richard Hicks, "Official Correspondence Relative to the Indian Difficulties on the Upper Fraser— Letter to Governor Douglas, 22 August, 1858," in *Victoria Gazette*, 27 August 1858.

46 "Selling Liquor to the Indians," *Victoria Gazette*, 10 August 1858; Snyder, "Letter from Captain Snyder," *Victoria Gazette*, 24 August, 1858; "Account of Captain Snyder's Expedition," *Victoria Gazette*, 1 September 1858.

47 James Douglas, letter to Edward Henry, Lord Stanley, 27 August 1858, in "Colonial Despatches of British Columbia: 1858," ed. James Hendrickson, vol. 1a (March 1988), UVIC; Rickard, "Indian Participation," 16.

48 James Douglas, letter to Edward Henry, Lord Stanley, 12 October 1858, quoted in Rickard, "Indian Participation," 16–17.

49 Snyder, "The Indian Difficulties"; H. M. Snyder, "Latest News Direct from the Fraser River," *San Francisco Bulletin*, 25 September 1858, quoted in Marshall, "Claiming the Land," 243.

50 "Meeting of Miners and Residents at Fort Hope," *Victoria Gazette*, 24 August 1858.

51 T. W. G., "Mining Correspondence," *Victoria Gazette*, 25 August 1858; Snyder, "The Indian Difficulties," *Victoria Gazette*, 24 August 1858.

52 Scholefield, *British Columbia*, 36.

53 Edward M'Gowan, "Reminiscences: Unpublished Incidents in the Life of the 'Ubiquitous,'" *San Francisco Argonaut*, 18 May 1878, 25 May 1878, 1 June 1878.

54 Matthew Begbie, "Letter to Douglas, 3 February, 1859," quoted in Frederic Howay, *Early History of the Fraser River Mines* (Victoria, B.C.: C. F. Banfield, 1926), 32–40.

55 Whannell, "Letter to Douglas, 31 December, 1858," quoted in Howay, *Early History*, 57.

56 Kilian, *Go Do Some Great Thing*, 88. For similar sentiments, see Edward F. Miller, *Ned McGowan's War* (Don Mills, Ont.: Burns and MacEachern, 1968), 4;

Donald Hauka, *McGowan's War* (Vancouver, B.C.: New Star Books, 2003), 2, 99; Mark Forsythe and Greg Dickson, *The Trail of 1858: British Columbia's Gold Rush Past* (Madeira Park, B.C.: Harbour Publishing, 2007), 43. Other works reflect a similar stereotypical view of American and British relations in the colony. See George Fetherling, *The Gold Crusades: A Social History of Gold Rushes, 1849–1929* (Toronto: University of Toronto Press, 1997), 7, 72.

57   Matthew Begbie, "Letter to Douglas, 3 February, 1859," quoted in Howay, *Early History*, 32–40; David Higgins, *The Mystic Spring, and Other Tales of Western Life* (Toronto: W. Briggs, 1904), 51.

58   Begbie, "Letter to Douglas, 3 February, 1859" quoted in Howay, *Early History*, 32–40; Whannell, "Letter to Douglas, 31 December, 1858," quoted in Howay, *Early History*, 56–57.

59   Douglas, letter to Edward Henry, Lord Stanley, 15 June 1858, in "Colonial Despatches of British Columbia: 1858," ed. James Hendrickson, vol. 1a (March 1988), UVIC; "Miners' Meeting at Hill's Bar," *Victoria Gazette*, 6 November 1858.

60   Bancroft, *History of British Columbia*, 402; Whannell, "Letter to Brew, 8 Feb, 1859," quoted in Howay, *Early History*, 71–76; Colonial Secretary, "Letter to Brew, 18 January, 1859," file 186, Chartres Brew Correspondence, B01310, BCARS.

61   Matthew Begbie, "Letter to Governor, 3 Feb, 1859," Colonial Correspondence, file f142a, B01307, BCARS.

62   Carl I. Wheat, "Ned, the Ubiquitous," in *California Historical Quarterly* 6, no. 1 (March 1927), 26; James H. Ross, "Letter to Governor Douglas, 9 May, 1859," quoted in Howay, *Early History*, 58–59. The Royal Victoria Yeomanry Corps was an Australian unit.

63   Higgins, *The Mystic Spring*, 52–54; George Perrier, "Letter from Justice Perrier," *Victoria Gazette*, 1 February 1859.

64   Begbie, "Letter to Douglas, 3 February, 1859," quoted in Howay, *Early History*, 39.

65   David Goodman, *Gold Seeking: Victoria and California in the 1850s* (Stanford, Calif.: Stanford University Press, 1994), 96, 104.

66   Richard Moody, "Letter to Arthur Blackwood, 1 February, 1859," *British Columbia Historical Quarterly* 25, nos. 1–2 (January–April 1951): 97, 99. McGowan's account, written to justify his actions to an American audience, gives a different version of events, one not supported by other sources. See Edward M'Gowan, "Reminiscences: Unpublished Incidents in the Life of the 'Ubiquitous,'" in *San Francisco Argonaut*, 1 June 1878.

67   Begbie, "Letter to Douglas, 18 January, 1859," quoted in Howay, *Early History*, 28.

68   Begbie, "Letter to Douglas, 3 February, 1859," quoted in Howay, *Early History*, 37.

69 Richard Mayne, *Four Years in British Columbia and Vancouver Island: An Account of Their Forests, Rivers, Coasts, Gold Fields and Resources for Colonisation* (London: John Murray, 1862), 70; Moody, "Letter to Arthur Blackwood," 103.

70 Moody, "Letter to Arthur Blackwood," 103, emphasis original.

71 Margaret Ormsby, *British Columbia, a History* (Toronto: Macmillan, 1958), 159, 184; Perry, *On the Edge of Empire*, 14, 132–33. On the changing demographics of the colony, see A. C. Elliott, "Lillooet, B.C. Census 1862," in Colonial Correspondence, B01327, BCARS; "Mining Intelligence," *British Columbian*, 10 August 1865.

72 Matthew Begbie, "Letter to Douglas, 30 April, 1860," Colonial Correspondence, file 142c, B01308, BCARS, emphasis original.

73 Passenger, "Letter from Victoria," *Alta California*, 6 May 1858.

74 Cridge, Diary, 91–95.

75 Sharpstone, "An Earnest Appeal," *Victoria Gazette*, 24 August 1858, emphasis original. "Aromatic luxury" is a code phase for the perceived body odor of people of African descent and was a common racist trope at the time.

76 Mifflin Gibbs, "An Answer to 'An Earnest Appeal,'" *Victoria Gazette*, 25 August 1858.

77 Matthew Macfie, *Vancouver Island and British Columbia; Their History, Resources, and Prospects* (1865; repr., New York: Arno Press, 1973), 389; Edward Cridge, "Letter from Rev. Cridge," *Victoria Gazette*, 26 August 1858.

78 "Religious Feud," *British Colonist*, 21 October 1859; Kilian, *Go Do Some Great Thing*, 59.

79 "Religious Feud," *British Colonist*, 21 October 1859.

80 William Clarke, quoted in Kilian, *Go Do Some Great Thing*, 57.

81 Kilian, *Go Do Some Great Thing*, 57–58; Robin Winks, *The Blacks in Canada: A History* (Buffalo, N.Y.: McGill-Queen's University Press, 1997), 282.

82 Further complicating the debate, the supporters of integration were often associated with the HBC elite, who were already viewed suspiciously by the reform faction for their attitudes toward mixed-race relationships with Native Americans. See Perry, *On the Edge of Empire*, 58–78; Van Kirk, "Tracing the Fortunes of Five Founding Families of Victoria," 149–79.

83 Pilton, "Negro Settlement," 112–14; Edgar Fawcett, *Some Reminiscences of Old Victoria* (Toronto: W. Briggs, 1912), 219.

84 Edmund Hope Verney, *Vancouver Island Letters of Edmund Hope Verney, 1862–65* (Vancouver: University of British Columbia Press, 1996), 193; Pilton, "Negro Settlement," 112–25.

85   British Columbia, Attorney General, 7 November 1860, file 1860/17, Box 1, GR-0419, BCARS. No white men were charged.

86   Pilton, "Negro Settlement," 196–200.

87   Pilton, 92.

88   Amor De Cosmos, quoted in H. Robert Kendrick, "Amor De Cosmos and Confederation," in *British Columbia and Confederation*, ed. W. George Shelton (Victoria, B.C.: published for the University of Victoria by the Morriss Print Co., 1967), 69.

89   Untitled editorial, *British Colonist*, 18 December 1858.

90   "Aliens and the Franchise," *British Colonist*, 29 November 1859.

91   "Mr. Cary's Meeting," *British Colonist*, 21 May 1861, emphasis original.

92   Pilton, "Negro Settlement," 94; "A Trap," *British Colonist*, 21 November 1859.

93   "Smith for Victory—but no Victory for Smith," *Victoria Gazette*, 2 January 1860; "Political Meeting," *Victoria Gazette*, 9 January 1860; "Mr. Amor De Cosmos," *British Colonist*, 3 January 1860.

94   Shears, "The Election and the Colored People," *British Colonist*, 12 January 1860, emphasis original.

95   Untitled editorial, *Victoria Gazette*, 13 January 1860.

96   "Political Meeting," *Victoria Gazette*, 9 January 1860.

97   Pilton, "Negro Settlement," 100.

98   Douglas, also known as Port Douglas, was located at the north end of Harrison Lake and was a major waypoint on the Douglas Road to the goldfields. The town and road were named for Governor Douglas.

99   Pilton, "Negro Settlement," 202; "First Provincial Legislative Assembly—First Session," *British Colonist*, 7 March, 1872; "First Provincial Legislative Assembly—First Session," *British Colonist*, 21 March 1872.

100 Vancouver Island, "An Act to Provide for the Naturalization of Aliens, 1861," in *A Collection of the Public General Statues of the Colony of Vancouver Island, Passed in the Year 1859, 1860, 1861, 1862, and 1863* (Victoria: British Colonist Office, 1866).

101 Matthew Begbie, *Journey into the Interior of British Columbia* (London: Royal Geographic Society Journal, 1861), 3:243; Matthew Begbie to Governor Douglas, Colonial Correspondence, 30 April 1860, file 142B1, B01307, BCARS; Matthew Begbie to William Young, Colonial Correspondence, 29 June 1860, file 142c, B01308, BCARS.

102 Untitled editorial, *Victoria Gazette*, 18 May 1860; John McLaren, Hamar Foster, and Chet Orloff, eds., *Law for the Elephant, Law for the Beaver: Essays in the Legal History of the American West* (Regina, Sask.: Canadian Plains Research Center, 1992), 36.

103 Also known as the Bute Inlet massacre, Chilcotin Uprising, Chilcotin Resistance, and Chilcotin War. I use *Tsilhqot'in* instead of *Chilcotin* because it more accurately reflects proper pronunciation and the wishes of the Tsilhqot'in people.

104 In the Tsilhqot'in language *Klatsassin* means: "We do not know his name." See "Klatsassin and the Chilcotin War" on "We Do Not Know His Name," www.canadianmysteries.ca/sites/klatsassin/home/indexen.html#.

105 "Dreadful Massacre—Murder of 14 of the Bute Inlet Road Party by Indians—Miraculous Escape of 3 of the Men," *British Colonist*, 12 May 1864.

106 "More Indian Murders!—McDonald and Two of His Party Killed—Several Others Severely Wounded—The Volunteers, with Indian Allies, on the Track of the Murderers—Marines from the Sutlej to Be Landed," *British Colonist*, 27 June 1864.

107 Great Britain Colonial Office, B.C., Executive Council Minutes, 1864, 14, 16 May 1864, GR-1224, BCARS; Arthur Birch to George Cox, Colonial Correspondence, 14 May 1864, file 379, B01321, BCARS; "The Bute Massacre," *British Colonist*, 23 May 1864; "An Indian Policy," *British Colonist*, 30 May 1864; "The Bute Massacre," *British Colonist*, 18 May 1864.

108 "The Chilcoaten Expeditions," *British Colonist*, 8 September 1864; "The Expedition against the Indians," *British Columbian*, 7 September 1864; "Later from the Chilacoten Country," *British Columbian*, 7 September 1864.

109 Matthew Begbie to Governor Seymour, Colonial Correspondence, 30 September 1864, file 142f, B01308, BCARS.

110 Peter O'Reilly, Diary 1864, 100, file 3, box 6, A01913, BCARS.

111 "The Last Indian Atrocity," *British Colonist*, 12 May 1864. On the emerging consensus see "Dreadful Massacre," *British Colonist*, 12 May 1864; "The Bute Massacre," *British Colonist*, 18 May 1864; "An Indian Policy," *British Colonist*, 30 May 1864.

112 "Emergency Meeting," *British Colonist*, 2 June 1864.

113 "An Indian Policy," *British Columbian*, 21 May 1864.

114 "The Way Our Neighbors Settle Indian Difficulties," *British Colonist*, 17 September 1864; "An Indian Policy," *British Columbian*, 21 May 1864.

115 "An Indian Policy," *British Columbian*, 21 May 1864; "Our Relations with the Indians," *British Columbian*, 13 June 1863.

116 "Sir James Douglas and the Indians," *British Columbian*, 8 June 1864; "An Indian Policy," *British Colonist*, 30 May 1864.

117 "Sir James Douglas and the Indians," *British Columbian*, 8 June 1864.

118 "An Indian Policy," *British Columbian*, 21 May 1864.

119 "An Indian Policy."

120 "Later from the Chilacoten Country," *British Colonist*, 7 September 1864; "The Chilcoaten Expeditions," *British Colonist*, 8 September 1864; Matthew Begbie to Governor Seymour, Colonial Correspondence, 30 September 1864, file 142f, B01308, BCARS.

121 Henry Ball, Journal of Henry Maynard Ball, 3–4, Mss 0750, BCARS; on the racial and gender implications of mixed-race relationships, see Perry, *On the Edge of Empire*, 58–79.

122 "Later from the Chilacoten Country," *British Colonist*, 7 September 1864; "The Chilcoaten Expeditions," *British Colonist*, 8 September 1864; "The Expedition against the Indians," *British Columbian*, 7 September 1864.

123 Arthur Birch to George Cox, Colonial Correspondence, 14 May 1864, file 379, B01321, BCARS.

124 Great Britain Colonial Office, B.C., "Executive Council Minutes, 1864," 16 October 1864, GR-1224, BCARS.

125 Matthew Begbie to Governor Seymour, Colonial Correspondence, 30 September 1864, file 142f, B01308, BCARS.

126 Great Britain Colonial Office, B.C., "Executive Council Minutes, 1864," 16 October, 1864, GR-1224, BCARS.

127 See, for example, British Columbia Gold Commissioner, Cariboo, Mining Licenses, 1, 28 May 1866; 6 June 1866; 29 May 1867; 6, 20, 26 July 1867; 5 July 1868; 23 May 1870; 26 July 1870; 23 May 1871; 2 October 1871, file 5, box 1, GR-0255, BCARS; W. D. Moses, Diary #2 1869, 9 January 1869; 9 May 1869, BA.

128 "Arrival of the Enterprise—$250,000 in Gold Dust," *British Colonist*, 20 October 1862; "Later from Cariboo," *British Colonist*, 20 July 1864; "Mining Intelligence," *British Colonist*, 17 October 1865; "British Columbia," *British Colonist*, 4 December 1865; "Cariboo," *British Colonist*, 30 July 1863; "British Columbia," *Victoria Daily Chronicle*, 10 July 1863; "British Columbia," *Victoria Daily Chronicle*, 12 July 1863; "British Columbia," *Victoria Daily Chronicle*, 18 September 1865; "British Columbia," *Victoria Daily Chronicle*, 28 September 1865; "News from Cariboo," *British Columbian*, 15 July 1863; "Correspondence," *British Columbian*, 5 August 1863; "Accident," *Cariboo Sentinel*, 25 June 1870.

129 Pilton, "Negro Settlement," 157.

130 Pilton, "Negro Settlement," 154.

131 "Gold Commissioner's Court," *Cariboo Sentinel*, 24 May 1866.

132 "Gold Commissioner's Court"; "Irresponsible Deputies: Decisive Stand Taken by Judge Cox," *Cariboo Sentinel*, 31 May 1866; "Davis Co'y vs. Aurora," *Cariboo Sentinel*, 7 June 1866.

133 "Supreme Court," *Cariboo Sentinel*, 21 June 1866.

134 Judge Begbie, quoted in "Supreme Court," *Cariboo Sentinel*, 21 June 1866; untitled article, *Cariboo Sentinel*, 18 June 1866.

135 "Supreme Court," *Cariboo Sentinel*, 21 June 1866.

136 "Supreme Court."

137 "Mass Meeting," *Cariboo Sentinel*, 25 June 1866.

138 Loo, *Making Law, Order, and Authority*, 128; "Mass Meeting," *Cariboo Sentinel*, 5 June 1866.

139 "Mass Meeting," *Cariboo Sentinel*, 25 June 1866.

140 Colored Miner, "To the Editor of the 'Cariboo Sentinel,'" *Cariboo Sentinel*, 25 June 1866.

141 Colored Miner, "To the Editor."

142 D. L., "To the Editor of the 'Cariboo Sentinel,'" *Cariboo Sentinel*, 2 July 1866.

143 D. L., "New Advertisements," *Cariboo Sentinel*, 23 July 1870.

144 D. L., "To the Editor," *Cariboo Sentinel*, 2 July 1866.

145 Pilton, "Negro Settlement," 107.

146 Pilton, "Negro Settlement," 117–25.

147 Mifflin W. Gibbs, *Shadow and Light: An Autobiography* (New York: Arno Press and the New York Times, 1968), 108; Pilton, "Negro Settlement," 200.

CHAPTER 4: PURSUING DAME FORTUNE

1 E. Anthony Rotundo, *American Manhood: Transformations in Masculinity from the Revolution to the Modern Era* (New York: Basic Books, 1993), 179–81; and E. Anthony Rotundo, "Learning about Manhood: Gender Ideals and the Middle-Class Family in Nineteenth-Century America," in *Manliness and Morality: Middle-Class Masculinity in Britain and America, 1800–1940*, ed. J. A. Mangan and James Walvin (New York: St. Martin's Press, 1987), 37; Thomas Augst, *The Clerk's Tale: Young Men and Moral Life in Nineteenth-Century America* (Chicago: University of Chicago Press, 2003), 4.

2 D. B. Bates, *Incidents on Land and Water* (1857; repr., New York: Arno Press, 1974), 187. The clash between the "Culture of Control" and the "Culture of Chance" identified by Lears occurred in magnified form in California. T. J. Jackson Lears, *Something for Nothing: Luck in America* (New York: Penguin Group, 2004), 7.

3 Histories of gambling, such as John M. Findlay, *People of Chance: Gambling in American Society, from Jamestown to Las Vegas* (New York: Oxford University Press, 1986); Ann Fabian, *Card Sharps and Bucket Shops: Gambling in Nineteenth-Century America* (New York: Routledge, 1999); and Lears, *Something for Nothing*, are some of the most detailed studies of the social and

cultural attitudes and practices surrounding risk in the nineteenth century, even if they do not interrogate the concept itself.

4   Historians of modernity actively engage with risk as a concept. See Christopher Dummitt, *The Manly Modern: Masculinity in Postwar Canada* (Vancouver: University of British Columbia Press, 2007), 13; and Ulrich Beck, *World Risk Society* (Malden, Mass.: Polity Press, 1999), 3–4.

5   Noah Webster and Noah Parker, *An American Dictionary of the English Language: Containing the Whole Vocabulary of the First Edition . . . the Entire Corrections and Improvements of the Second Edition . . . to Which Is Prefixed an Introductory Dissertation on the Origin, History, and Connection, of the Languages of Western Asia and Europe, with an Explanation of the Principles on Which Languages Are Formed* (Springfield, Mass.: George and Charles Merriam, 1856), 190.

6   Samuel Johnson, *A Dictionary of the English Language: In Which the Words Are Deduced from Their Originals, Explained in Their Different Meanings, and Authorized by the Names of the Writers in Whose Works They Are Found* (London: Printed for F. C. and J. Rivington, 1815), s.v. "risk."

7   Rotundo, *American Manhood*, 179–81; and Rotundo, "Learning about Manhood," 37; Augst, *The Clerk's Tale*, 4.

8   Rotundo, *American Manhood*, ix, 3, 20–22. The most influential group shaping attitudes toward manhood in California and elsewhere in the nation were from the Northeast.

9   Different groups came to equate whiteness with financial independence and control over the domestic sphere. See Eric Foner, *Free Soil, Free Labor, Free Men: The Ideology of the Republican Party before the Civil War* (New York: Oxford University Press, 1995), xi–xxvi; David Roediger, *The Wages of Whiteness: Race and the Making of the American Working Class* (New York: Verso, 1999), 27–36, 43–44, 50–51, 66–74; and Sean Wilentz, *Chants Democratic: New York City and the Rise of the American Working Class, 1788–1850* (New York: Oxford University Press, 1986), 61–63, 92–94. See also John Tosh, *A Man's Place: Masculinity and the Middle-Class Home in Victorian England* (New Haven, Conn.: Yale University Press, 1999). On the intention of most gold rushers to make their fortune and return to the East, see Brian Roberts, *American Alchemy: The California Gold Rush and Middle-Class Culture* (Chapel Hill: University of North Carolina Press, 2000), 23–24, 36, 218–19, 227–28, 256–62; Susan Lee Johnson, *Roaring Camp: The Social World of the California Gold Rush* (New York: W. W. Norton, 2000), 196; and Malcolm J. Rohrbough, *Days of Gold: The California Gold Rush and the American Nation* (Berkeley: University of California Press, 1997), 36, 256–59.

10 "Gold Digging in California—the Other Side of the Picture . . . ," 27 December 1849, *New York Herald*, folder 1, box 2170, Gold Rush Letters for Proposed Publication, CRCSL; Henry Packer Billington to Mary Judkins, 20 July 1857, Henry Packer Billington Letters (hereafter Billington Letters), BANC; John N. Stone, "Brief Notes of a Cape Horn Voyage in 1849," in *California Gold Rush Voyages, 1848–1849: Three Original Narratives*, ed. John E. Pomfret, Charles Henry Ellis, and John N. Stone (San Marino, Calif.: Huntington Library, 1954), 167–69; Charles Edward Pancoast, *A Quaker Forty-Niner: The Adventures of Charles Edward Pancoast on the American Frontier*, ed. Anna Paschall Hannum (Philadelphia: University of Pennsylvania Press, 1930), 109; H. Darlington to parents, 26–27 October 1849, Mss C-B 547:137, Gold Rush Letters, BANC.

11 "Advice to Gold Diggers," *New York Tribune*, 30 August 1849, folder 1, box 2170, Gold Rush Letters, CRCSL. See also E. Gould Buffum, *Six Months in the Gold Mines* (1850; repr., Ann Arbor: University of Michigan Press, 1966), 132; Felix Paul Wierzbicki, *California as It Is and as It May Be; or, A Guide to the Gold Region* (1849; repr., New York: Grabhorn Press, 1970), 42.

12 James J. Ayers, *Gold and Sunshine, Reminiscences of Early California* (Boston: R. G. Badger, 1922), 34; James Duffy to Jenny, 20 June 1853, Mss C-B 547: 128, Gold Rush Letters, BANC; Jacob Fisher to Frederick Fisher, 21 September 1850, Mss C-B 547: 11, Gold Rush Letters, BANC; Thomass [sic] Nosseter to John Bell, 20 December 1849, Mss C-B 547: 115, Gold Rush Letters, BANC.

13 Joseph Benton to Dr. I. Linsly, February 27, 1850, Joseph Augustine Benton Collection, box 29, CRCSL.

14 Frank Soulé, *Annals of San Francisco: Containing a Summary of the History of . . . California, and a Complete History of . . . Its Great City* (New York: Appleton, 1855), 258; William Redmond Ryan, *Personal Adventures in Upper and Lower California, in 1848–9* (New York: Arno Press, 1973), 2:173–75; Eliza W. Farnham, *California, In-doors and Out; or, How We Farm, Mine, and Live Generally in the Golden State* (New York: Dix, Edwards, 1856), 257–52; Pringle Shaw, *Ramblings in California: Containing a Description of the Country, Life at the Mines, State of Society, &c.; Interspersed with Characteristic Anecdotes, and Sketches from Life* (Toronto: J. Bain, [1856?]), 25–30; Alonzo Delano, *Pen Knife Sketches; or, Chips of the Old Block, a Series of Original Illustrated Letters, Written by One of California's Pioneer Miners* (Sacramento, Calif.: Published at the Union office, 1853), 43.

15 William Taylor, *California Life Illustrated* (New York: Carlton & Porter, 1860), 278.

16 Rotundo, *American Manhood*, 179–81, and Rotundo, "Learning about Manhood," 37; Augst, *The Clerk's Tale*, 4; Karen Halttunen, *Confidence Men and Painted*

Women: A Study of Middle-Class Culture in America, 1830–1870 (New Haven, Conn.: Yale University Press, 1982), 4–6, 40; Amy Greenberg, *Manifest Manhood and the Antebellum American Empire* (New York: Cambridge University Press, 2005), 139–47.

17   Meyer Reinhold, *Classica Americana: The Greek and Roman Heritage in the United States* (Detroit: Wayne State University Press, 1984), 18, 175, 180–86, 193, 250; John Pullman, *History of Education in America* (Columbus, Ohio: Merrill, 1982), 65, 74–75; Margaret Malamud, *Ancient Rome and Modern America* (Malden, Mass.: Wiley-Blackwell, 2009), especially chapters 1–3.

18   Henry George Lidell, Robert Scott, Henry Stuart Jones, Roderick McKenzie, and Eric Arthur Barber, *A Greek-English Lexicon* (Oxford: Oxford University Press, 1968), 1839; G. W. Glare, *Oxford Latin Dictionary* (Oxford: Oxford University Press, 2007), 727.

19   John Borthwick, *The Gold Hunters: A First Hand Picture of Life in California Mining Camps in the Early Fifties*, ed. Horace Kephart (1857; repr., New York: International Fiction Library, 1917), 74, 162–63. See also Howard C. Gardiner, *In Pursuit of the Golden Dream: Reminiscences of San Francisco and the Northern and Southern Mines, 1849–1857*, ed. Dale Lowell Morgan (Stoughton, Mass.: Western Hemisphere, 1970), 81–82, 95; Pancoast, *A Quaker Forty-Niner*, 281, 290.

20   Pancoast, *A Quaker Forty-Niner*, 306; John Marsh Smith to William George, Aug. 9, 1850, Manuscript 308, CRCSL; "Persevere," *Alta California*, 17 October 1850.

21   Timothy Coffin Osborn, Timothy Coffin Osborn Journal: ms., 1850 June 14–1855 Jan. 1, 148, Mss C-F 81, BANC.

22   Pancoast, *A Quaker Forty-Niner*, 306.

23   For the gender dynamics of courting, see Rotundo, *American Manhood*, 104.

24   Lorenzo Sawyer, *Way Sketches: Containing Incidents of Travel across the Plains from St. Joseph to California in 1850, with Letters Describing Life and Conditions in the Gold Region*, ed. Edward Eberstadt (New York: E. Eberstadt, 1926), 120; "Advice to Gold-Diggers," 30 August 1849, *New York Tribune*, Gold Rush Letters, folder 1, box 2170, CRCSL; Lucius Anson Booth to Newton Booth, July 16, 1849, in William Benemann, ed., *A Year of Mud and Gold: San Francisco in Letters and Diaries, 1849–1850* (Lincoln: University of Nebraska Press, 1999), 20.

25   Roberts, *American Alchemy*, 145–46; Ayers, *Gold and Sunshine*, 34.

26   Osborn, Journal, 65.

27   Roberts, *American Alchemy*, 1–15.

28   J. W. L. Brown to Mrs. A. G. Brown, 6 March 1853, Brown Family Papers, folder 1, box 1524, CRCSL.

29   Roberts, *American Alchemy*, 3.

30 Rodman W. Paul, *California Gold: The Beginning of Mining in the Far West* (Cambridge, Mass.: Harvard University Press, 1947), 116–19, 171–73; Findlay, *People of Chance*, 79–89, 95.

31 Soulé, *The Annals of San Francisco*, 403.

32 Taylor, *California Life Illustrated*, 279.

33 Roberts, *American Alchemy*, 5, 13, 121–29.

34 I use the term *prospectors* to refer to a class of men whom gold rushers understood to perpetually seek new diggings, often in indigenous territory. In contrast, most gold rushers looked for "prospects" along whatever creek or gulch they happened to find as they followed the crowd from digging to digging. See Taylor, *California Life Illustrated*, 281–84, and Paul, *California Gold*, 56–58.

35 Soulé, *The Annals of San Francisco*, 402–3; Charles Thompson to uncle, Gold Rush Letters, 10 September 1850, Mss C-B 547: 8, BANC; A. L. Baker, Diary in the California Mines: M.S., 1849–50, 25 March 1850, Mss 2003/195c, BANC; Farnham, *California, in-Doors and Out*, 264; Buffum, *Six Months in the Gold Mines*, 35, 73; Taylor, *California Life Illustrated*, 281–84; Paul, *California Gold*, 117–31; Edna Bryan Buckbee, *The Saga of Old Tuolumne* (New York: Press of the Pioneers, 1935), 89–91. For criticism of rushing from digging to digging (which simultaneously suggests its prevalence), see Ayers, *Gold and Sunshine*, 70; and Gardiner, *In Pursuit of the Golden Dream*, 81, 87.

36 Soulé, *The Annals of San Francisco*, 402–3; Taylor, *California Life Illustrated*, 281–84; "The Gold Diggings on the Fraser River," *London Times*, 20 July 1858; Donald Frazer, "A Trip to Vancouver," *London Times*, 27 August 1858; and "Letter from Victoria," *Alta California*, 9 July 1858.

37 Borthwick, *The Gold Hunters*, 253; Frank Marryat, *Mountains and Molehills; or, Recollections of a Burnt Journal* (1855; repr. Philadelphia: Lippincott, 1962), 172; Shaw, *Ramblings in California*, 21–22.

38 The link between the Chinese and low-risk activity extended to white settler's perceptions of their gambling. See Marryat, *Mountains and Molehills*, 172.

39 Johnson, *Roaring Camp*, 35; "The Outrages in the Mines," *Alta California*, 17 July 1850; "More Murder and Robbery," *Alta California*, 7 October 1850; "Murders in the Mines," *Alta California*, 12 October 1850; and "A Row," *Alta California*, 15 May 1851.

40 While a racial division of labor existed from the earliest days of the Gold Rush, the move to capital-intensive mining and the growing dominance of wage labor exacerbated the debate over nonwhite labor. See Soulé, *Annals of San Francisco*, 378, 380–81; "The Chinese," *Alta California*, 12 September 1853; "No Mercy to Chinamen," *Alta California*, 30 November 1857; Albert L. Hurtado, *Indian Survival on the California Frontier* (New Haven, Conn.: Yale University Press, 1988),

5, 104–7; Johnson, *Roaring Camp*, 240–54, 260–70; Rohrbough, *Days of Gold*, 12–13; Daniel Cornford, "We All Live More Like Brutes Than Humans: Labor and Capital in the Gold Rush," in *A Golden State: Mining and Economic Development in Gold Rush California*, ed. James J. Rawls, Richard J. Orsi, and Marlene Smith-Baranzini (Berkeley: University of California Press, 1999), 85–86, 97; Paul, *California Gold*, 322, 329, 349–52.

41 Findlay, *People of Chance*, 87.

42 John Williamson Palmer, *The New and the Old; or, California and India in Romantic Aspects* (New York: Rudd & Carleton, 1859), 22–31.

43 Borthwick, *The Gold Hunters*, 74; Brian Roberts used the term *slumming* to describe these behaviors and intention of the majority to reintegrate back into proper society. Roberts, *American Alchemy*, 219.

44 See, for example, "Doings of the Grand Jury," *Alta California*, 30 November 1850; "Disgraceful Row," *Alta California*, 26 January 1851; "Report of the Special and Judiciary Committee, upon Houses of Ill Fame," *Alta California*, 27 November 1855; "From the Gold Region," 22 April 1849, *New York Tribune*, Gold Rush Letters, folder 1, box 2170, CRCSL.

45 Osborn, Journal, 58, 85–86, 101–2, 114–15, 121–22, 197, 208, 213; Ayers, *Gold and Sunshine*, 36; William Shaw, *Golden Dreams and Waking Realities: Being the Adventures of a Gold-Seeker in California and the Pacific Islands* (London: Smith, Elder, 1851), 20; Hinton Rowan Helper, *The Land of Gold, Reality versus Fiction* (Baltimore: H. Taylor, 1855), 41–43; Greenberg, *Manifest Manhood*, 90–91, 123–29.

46 Helper, *The Land of Gold*, 36–44, 64–74, 109, 114; George Payson, *Golden Dreams and Leaden Realities* (New York: G. Putnam, 1853), 75–77; Taylor, *California Life Illustrated*, 285–86; Louise Amelia Knapp Clappe, *The Shirley Letters from California Mines in 1851–52; Being a Series of Twenty-Three Letters from Dame Shirley (Mrs. Louise Amelia Knapp Smith Clappe) to Her Sister in Massachusetts, and Now Reprinted from the Pioneer Magazine of 1854–55; with Synopses of the Letters, a Foreword, and Many Typographical and Other Corrections and Emendations, by Thomas C. Russell* (San Francisco: Thomas C. Russell, 1922), 52, 79–81, 228; Chauncey L. Canfield, *The Diary of a Forty-Niner* (Boston: Houghton Mifflin, 1920), 39. Frank Soulé halfheartedly defended some of these practices while revealing a general awareness among Californians of how the gambling, drinking, and swearing in their society was perceived in the East. Soulé, *The Annals of San Francisco*, 503.

47 Herman Reinhart, *The Golden Frontier: The Recollections of Herman Francis Reinhart, 1851–1869* (Austin: University of Texas Press, 1962), 27.

48 Findlay, *People of Chance*, 48–50, 83; David Dustin to John K. Dustin, 14 August 1850, Mss C-B 547:40, Gold Rush Letters, BANC.

49   For examples of suspicions about cheating gamblers, see Marryat, *Mountains and Molehills*, 17; Pancoast, *A Quaker Forty-Niner*, 300–301; Payson, *Golden Dreams and Leaden Realities*, 76; Silas Weston, *Life in the Mountains; or, Four Months in the Mines of California* (Providence, R.I.: B. T. Albro, 1854), 27–31; "San Joaquin Intelligence," *Alta California*, 14 August 1850; "Shooting Affray at Shasta—the Murderer Hung by the People," *Alta California*, 10 April 1853. Of course, sometimes these stereotypes were right. John Pierce, a gambler, recorded in his diary the key to his marked deck. See John Pierce, "Diary, 1863–1873," 106, California State Library, Sacramento.

50   For an example of a man being marked as a gambler by setting up a game, see Borthwick, *The Gold Hunters*, 70. For examples of men gambling but not becoming gamblers, see Ryan, *Personal Adventures*, 2:205; Friedrich Ger-stäcker, *Scenes of Life in California*, trans. George Cosgrave and Gustave Revil-liod (1856; repr., San Francisco: J. Howell, 1942), 80–86; Shaw, *Golden Dreams and Waking Realities*, 44–46. On the different perception of gambling in California, see James H. Carson, *Early Recollections of the Mines, and a Description of the Great Tulare Valley* (Stockton, Calif.: published to accompany the steamer edition of the "San Joaquin Republican," 1852), 15–16, 40–41.

51   Hubert Howe Bancroft, *History of California* (San Francisco: History Co., 1886), 6:224; Delano, *Pen Knife Sketches*, 31; Carson, *Early Recollections of the Mines*, 19; Ayers, *Gold and Sunshine*, 35.

52   Findlay, *People of Chance*, 94; Bayard Taylor, *Eldorado; or, Adventures in the Path of Empire, Comprising a Voyage to California, via Panama; Life in San Francisco and Monterey; Pictures of the Gold Region, and Experiences of Mexican Travel* (New York: G. Putnam's Sons, 1879), 119; Marryat, *Mountains and Molehills*, 18; Ryan, *Personal Adventures*, 2:210–12; Theodore T. Johnson, *Sights in the Gold Region, and Scenes by the Way* (New York: Baker and Scribner, 1849), 197; John Letts, *A Pictorial View of California: Including a Description of the Panama and Nicaragua Routes, with Information and Advice Interesting to All, Particularly Those Who Intend to Visit the Golden Region, by a Returned Californian* (New York: H. Bill, 1853), 48–50. Indeed, Charles Thompson described himself as going "half-mad" while gambling. Thompson to uncle, 10 September 1850.

53   "Letter from San Francisco, Alto [*sic*] California, April 1, 1848," *New York Herald*, 19 August 1848; Ayers, *Gold and Sunshine*, 74–78; Palmer, *The New and the Old*, 22–30.

54   "Interesting Narrative of the Voyage to California, by a New York Volunteer . . . &c.," *New York Herald*, 19 August 1848.

55   Letts, *A Pictorial View of California*, 48–50; Shaw, *Ramblings in California*, 35; Borthwick, *The Gold Hunters*, 68–69.

56 Albert Benard de Russailh, *Last Adventure: San Francisco in 1851; Translated from the Original Journal of Albert Benard de Russailh by Clarkson Crane*, ed. Clarkson Crane (San Francisco: Westgate Press, 1931), 12–16; Ryan, *Personal Adventures*, 2:164–65, 176; Elisha Smith Capron, *History of California, from Its Discovery to the Present Time: Comprising Also a Full Description of Its Climate, Surface, Soil, Rivers, Towns . . . Agriculture, Commerce, Mines, Mining, &c., with a Journal of the Voyage from New York, via Nicaragua, to San Francisco, and Back, via Panama . . .* (Cleveland, Ohio: Jewett, Proctor, and Worthington, 1854), 148–50.

57 Gerstäcker, *Scenes of Life in California*, 71; untitled article, *Alta California*, 8 January 1855; de Russailh, *Last Adventure*, 13–14; H. B. Lum to brother, 16 July 1850, Mss C-B 547:35, Gold Rush Letters, BANC; John Carr, *Pioneer Days in California: Historical and Personal Sketches* (Eureka, Calif.: Times Publishing, 1891), 60–61.

58 Osborn, Journal, 197. See also Carr, *Pioneer Days in California*, 79; Borthwick, *The Gold Hunters*, 61–62.

59 Letts, *A Pictorial View of California*, 48–49.

60 Letts, 49. For similar examples, see Capron, *History of California*, 150; Gerstäcker, Scenes of Life in California, 90–92; "The Man Who Wanted to Be Broke," *Alta California*, 7 September 1850.

61 Soulé, *The Annals of San Francisco*, 308, 368, 399–400, 423, 501–2; Bancroft, *History of California*, 6:240–41.

62 E. Phelps to J. C. Ray, 23 November 1850, Mss C-B 547:136, Gold Rush Letters, BANC; Ayers, *Gold and Sunshine*, 37, 93; Capron, *History of California*, 148–50; Bates, *Incidents on Land and Water*, 202–3; Borthwick, *The Gold Hunters*, 64; Payson, *Golden Dreams and Leaden Realities*, 75–77; Marryat, *Mountains and Molehills*, 13, 17–18.

63 Borthwick, *The Gold Hunters*, 66–68; Ryan, *Personal Adventures*, 2:216, 275–76; James Lansing to M. L. Pitly, 14 January 1851, Mss C-B 547:288, Gold Rush Letters, BANC; Capron, *History of California*, 148–50; Bates, *Incidents on Land and Water*, 199–203.

64 Helper, *The Land of Gold*, 73.

65 Ryan, *Personal Adventures*, 2:216; Borthwick, *The Gold Hunters*, 66.

66 Marryat, *Mountains and Molehills*, 18.

67 For views of Californian gambling as profane, see Capron, *History of California*, 145–51; Carson, *Early Recollections of the Mines*, 40; Pancoast, *A Quaker Forty-Niner*, 300–301.

68 "Dance Houses and Female Saloons," *Alta California*, 28 March 1853; "Gambling," *Alta California*, 2 February 1855; Reinhart, *The Golden Frontier*, 33;

Bancroft, *History of California*, 6:461; Stone, "Brief Notes of a Cape Horn Voyage," 133; Findlay, *People of Chance*, 100.

69 "Gold Digging in California," 27 December 1849, *New York Herald*, Gold Rush Letters, folder 1, box 2170, CRCSL.

70 Billington, 20 July 1857; H. B. Lum to brother, 26 July 1850, Mss C-B 547:35, Gold Rush Letters, BANC; Stone, "Brief Notes of a Cape Horn Voyage," 167–69; Pancoast, *A Quaker Forty-Niner*, 109; H. Darlington to parents, 26–27 October 1849, Mss C-B 547:137, Gold Rush Letters, BANC; Charles Ross Parke, *Dreams to Dust: A Diary of the California Gold Rush, 1849–1850*, ed. James Davis (Lincoln: University of Nebraska Press, 1989), 102.

71 Thompson to uncle, 10 September 1850, Mss C-B 547: 8, Gold Rush Letters, BANC.

72 Canfield, *The Diary of a Forty-Niner*, 7–8. On guilt and gambling, see also Payson, *Golden Dreams and Leaden Realities*, 76–77.

73 Thompson to uncle, Gold Rush Letters, 10 September 1850, Mss C-B 547: 8, BANC; Taylor, *Eldorado*, 120; Stone, "Brief Notes of a Cape Horn Voyage," 167–69; Pancoast, *A Quaker Forty-Niner*, 109.

74 I differ slightly from John Findlay, who saw a shift in attitudes toward gambling in the mid-1850s. I suggest that a focus on legal measures obscures the underlying, extremely conflicted attitudes toward gambling. See Findlay, *People of Chance*, 79–89, 95; and Fabian, *Card Sharps and Bucket Shops*.

75 William Olden to sister, William R. Olden Gold Rush Letters, May 1850, folder 10, box 11, CRCSL.

76 Roberts, *American Alchemy*, 218–19.

77 "Ordinance for Revenue," *Alta California*, 11 October 1849; "Local Matters—Report of the Grand Jury," *Alta California*, 22 August 1850; Soulé, *The Annals of San Francisco*, 231.

78 "Sunday in San Francisco," *Alta California*, 2 February 1851; "Licensed Gambling," *Alta California*, 8 November 1857; Gary Kurutz, "Popular Culture on the Golden Shores," in *Rooted in Barbarous Soil: People, Culture, and Community in Gold Rush California*, ed. Kevin Starr and Richard J. Orsi (Berkeley: University of California Press, 2000), 284–89.

79 "Gambling," *Alta California*, 2 February 1855; "A Nuisance," *Alta California*, 2 August 1856; "Descent on a Gambling Institution, and Arrest of the Offenders," *Alta California*, 8 March 1858.

80 "San Joaquin Intelligence," *Alta California*, 26 January 1852; "Gambling Law in the Mountains," *Alta California*, 1 May 1856; Weston, *Life in the Mountains*, 26–31; Findlay, *People of Chance*, 89, 95–100.

81 Findlay, *People of Chance*, 95.

82   James Anderson, *Sawney's Letters and Cariboo Rhymes* (Toronto: W. S. Johnson & Co'y, 1895), 54, BA.

83   "The Rush for Fraser River," *Alta California*, 21 April 1858; "Letter from Victoria," *Alta California*, 9 July 1858.

84   Paul, *California Gold*, 117–19.

85   "The Rush for Fraser River," *Alta California*, 21 April 1858; "Letter from Victoria," *Alta California*, 9 July 1858.

86   Robert M. Galois, "Gold Mining and Its Effects on Landscapes of the Cariboo" (master's thesis, University of Calgary, 1972), 3, 34.

87   "Forks of Quesnelle," *British Columbian*, 13 February 1864; "British Columbia," *British Colonist*, 31 December 1864.

88   "Bedrock Drain," 28 June 1864, BA; W. D. Moses, "Diary #2, 1869," 9 January 1869, A01046, BCARS; John Evans, "Diary of John Evans: The British Columbia Mining Adventure, 1862–1864," ms. 2111, BCARS.

89   John B. Wilkinson to his brother, Letters from Victoria and Cariboo, 1860–65, 22 September 1860, BA; Tina Loo, *Making Law, Order, and Authority in British Columbia, 1821–1871* (Toronto: University of Toronto Press, 1994), 56–57. A very small group of Canadians attempted an ill-fated overland journey to the goldfields. More concerning to colonial authorities was the constant trickle of American migrants from Washington Territory, but this route was slow and dangerous, making the trip to Victoria preferable for the vast majority of migrants. See Reinhart, *The Golden Frontier*, 120–30 and Joanne Leduc, *Overland from Canada to British Columbia* (Vancouver: University of British Columbia Press, 1981).

90   Amos Wright to brother, 16 November 1865, Mss 1976, BCARS; Cecil Williams Buckley, Journal, 4, 7 August 1862, E/B/B85, BCARS; Philip Hankin, Memoirs, 55–56, E-B-H19A, BCARS; W. M. Mark, *Cariboo: A True and Correct Narrative* (Stockton, U.K.: W. M. Wright, 1863), 29–34.

91   Anderson, *Sawney's Letters*, 22, BA.

92   Lucius A. Edelblute, *A True Story of the Adventures of Cariboo Ed in the Far West* (Bountiful, Utah: Family History Publishers, 1998), 52–105; Roger Harkness to Sabrina Harkness, Harkness Papers, 10 June 1863, BCARS; Loo, *Making Law, Order, and Authority*, 77.

93   Newspapers of the day rarely mention mine owners separately from the act of mining. Also, in the court cases analyzed by Loo, no evidence of a worker-management split is evident. Loo, *Making Law, Order, and Authority*, 93–133.

94   "Mining Intelligence," *Cariboo Sentinel*, 8 July 1867; "A Hint to the Unemployed," *Cariboo Sentinel*, 21 October 1867; W. M. Smithe, "Editor Cariboo Sentinel," *Cariboo Sentinel*, 1 June 1868.

95   Anderson, *Sawney's Letters*, 54, BA.
96   W. Champness, *To Cariboo and Back* (London: Religious Tract Society, 1865), 234; Edmund Hope Verney to father, 5 May 1863, in Edmund Hope Verney, *Vancouver Island Letters of Edmund Hope Verney, 1862–65*, ed. Allan Pritchard (Vancouver: University of British Columbia Press, 1996), 137, 184.
97   Charles C. Gardiner, "Letter to Editor of *The Islander*, 17 Nov., 1858," *British Columbia Historical Quarterly* 1 (October 1937), 252; Champness, *To Cariboo and Back*, 234.
98   Wilkinson to his brother, 22 September 1860.
99   Champness, *To Cariboo and Back*, 219, 231–34.
100   E. J. Neal to brother, 2 September 1862, 1, BA.
101   Champness, *To Cariboo and Back*, 259.
102   Gail Bederman, *Manliness and Civilization: A Cultural History of Gender and Race in the United States, 1880–1917* (Chicago: University of Chicago Press, 1995).
103   Francis Jones Barnard, "Barnard's Express," BA; "Fare Reduced," *Cariboo Sentinel*, 6 May 1867; "Later from the Interior," *British Columbian*, 4 January 1865.
104   "Traveling," *Cariboo Sentinel*, 5 May 1868.
105   Alexander Allan to Thomas Dearberg, Alexander Allan Letterbook: 2 January 1868–20 October 1876, 2 January 1868, 1, BA.
106   The first quote is from Mark, *Cariboo*, 26. The second quote is from John B. Wilkinson to his parents, Letters from Victoria and Cariboo, 1860–65, 11 June 1862, BA. See also James Wilson Nelles, Diary, 7 June 1862, BA.
107   This is part of a broader cultural shift. See Lears, *Something for Nothing*, 138–201.
108   "The Scientific American," *Cariboo Sentinel*, 22 January 1870; "Letter from Victoria, No. 5," *Cariboo Sentinel*, 28 June 1866.
109   Evans, Diary, 17.
110   "Prospects of Cariboo," *Cariboo Sentinel*, 17 April 1869; "The Yield of Gold," *Cariboo Sentinel*, 30 June 1869. See also "Mining Intelligence," *Cariboo Sentinel*, 28 May 1866; 29 July, 30 September 1867.
111   David Montgomery, *The Fall of the House of Labor: The Workplace, the State, and American Labor Activism, 1865–1925* (New York: Cambridge University Press, 1987). See especially chapters 2 and 5.
112   Roberts, *American Alchemy*, 5, 15, 24–27.
113   Argus, "Letter from Cayoosh," *British Colonist*, 2 May 1861; "News from Above," *British Columbian*, 30 May 1861; "Mining Intelligence," *Cariboo Sentinel*, 30 September 1867; W. M. Smithe, "Editor Cariboo Sentinel," 1 June 1868; Alexander Allan to Mr. Suter (editor of the *Mainland Guardian*), Alexander Letterbook, 2 January 1868–20 October 1876, 6 January 1870, BA.

114 "News from Above," *British Columbian*, 30 May 1861; "Arrivals from the River," *British Colonist*, 10 June 1861; Argus, "Letter from Cariboo," *British Colonist*, 7 October 1861; Vialor, "En Route to Cariboo," *British Colonist*, 1 June 1863.

115 "A Fine Prospect," *Cariboo Sentinel*, 12 May 1869.

116 British Columbia, Gold Fields Act 1859; "Prospecting Willow River," *Cariboo Sentinel*, 6 March 1869; Explorer, "Peace River Expedition," *Cariboo Sentinel*, 1 May 1869; "Peace River Expedition," *Cariboo Sentinel*, 12 May 1869; "Exploration," *Cariboo Sentinel*, 1 September 1869.

117 British Columbia, Attorney General, 14 November 1865, file 1865/37, box 4, GR-0419, BCARS.

118 David Miers, *Regulating Commercial Gambling: Past, Present, and Future* (New York: Oxford University Press, 2004), 9, 21–24.

119 Arthur Birch, *Victorian Odyssey*, Birch Family Papers, 90, BCARS; Peter O'Reilly, 8 September 1864, O'Reilly Family Papers, box 6, file 3, BCARS.

120 Henry Ball, Journal of Henry Ball, 18 August 1864–27 October 1865, Mss 0750, Ball Papers, 167, BCARS, emphasis original. Loo is a trick-taking game, similar to whist and contract bridge. The loss is so large, I suspect that Ball might have forgotten a decimal, and that the actual loss was a still-significant ten dollars.

121 British Columbia, Attorney General, 1 January 1864, box 3, file 1864/17, GR-0419, BCARS.

122 Arcade Billiard and Bowling Saloon, BA; Adelphi Saloon, BA.

123 British Columbia, Attorney General, 1 January 1864, box 3, file 1864/17, GR-0419, BCARS.

124 British Columbia, Attorney General, 11 March 1865, box 4, file 1865/15, GR-0419, BCARS; Richfield Police, Court Case Book, 1862–71, 8 February 1868, GR-0598, BCARS. On attitudes toward the Chinese in British Columbia, see Kay Anderson, *Vancouver's Chinatown: Racial Discourse in Canada, 1875–1980* (Montreal: McGill-Queen's University Press, 1991); and W. Peter Ward, *White Canada Forever: Popular Attitudes and Public Policy toward Orientals in British Columbia* (Montreal: McGill-Queen's University Press, 1978).

125 Richfield Police, Court Case Book 1862–71, 8 February 1868, GR-0598, BCARS; D. L., "D. L. to the Editor," *Cariboo Sentinel*, 23 July 1870.

126 Hankin, Memoirs, 56.

127 Adele Perry, *On the Edge of Empire: Gender, Race, and the Making of British Columbia, 1849–1871* (Toronto: University of Toronto Press, 2001), 48.

128 Perry, 68; "Profits of Agriculture," Cariboo Sentinel, 24 July 1869; Thomas Robert Mitchell to his parents, 25 May, 16 June, 1862, Mss 0838, BCARS.

129 Perry, *Edge of Empire*, 106.

130 "Lecture on Manliness," *Cariboo Sentinel*, 21 August 1869.

131 Perry, *Edge of Empire*; Loo, *Making Law, Order, and Authority*. For a broader context, see Ann Laura Stoler, *Carnal Knowledge and Imperial Power: Race and the Intimate in Colonial Rule* (Berkeley: University of California Press, 2002).

132 Robin Fisher, *Contact and Conflict: Indian-European Relations in British Columbia, 1774–1890* (Vancouver: University of British Columbia Press, 1977), 95–98; Jean Barman, *The West beyond the West: A History of British Columbia*, 3rd ed. (Toronto: University of Toronto Press, 1991), 66.

133 Robert Stevenson, *Rose Expedition of 1862*, 2, Mss 0315, BCARS; William George Cox, Colonial Correspondence, 8 January 1863, file 378, B1312, BCARS; Elizabeth Furniss, *Dakelh Keyoh: The Southern Carrier in Earlier Times* (Quesnel, B.C.: Quesnel School District no. 28, 1993), 6.

134 Perry, *Edge of Empire*, 4.

135 "Profits of Agriculture," *Cariboo Sentinel*, 24 July 1869; Mitchell to his parents, 25 May 1862.

136 Rayna Green, "The Pocahontas Perplex: The Image of Indian Women in American Culture," *Massachusetts Review* 16, no. 4 (Autumn 1975): 700–711; Mark, *Cariboo*, 20.

137 Perry, *Edge of Empire*, 83–90, 124–66.

CHAPTER 5: DIRTY CLOTHES, CLEAN BODIES

1 D. B. Bates, *Incidents on Land and Water* (1857; repr., New York: Arno Press, 1974), 118. For British Columbia, see R. George Cowley, Diary, 1, E/B/C831A, BCARS; Matthew Macfie, *Vancouver Island and British Columbia: Their History, Resources, and Prospects* (1865; repr. New York: Arno Press, 1973), 414.

2 On the relationship between appearance and character, especially in the urbanizing East, see Karen Halttunen, *Confidence Men and Painted Women: A Study of Middle-Class Culture in America, 1830–1870* (New Haven, Conn.: Yale University Press, 1982), esp. 2–72; Amy Greenberg, *Manifest Manhood and the Antebellum American Empire* (New York: Cambridge University Press, 2005), 138–41; John Kasson, *Rudeness and Civility: Manners in Nineteenth-Century Urban America* (New York: Hill and Wang, 1990), 93–98; Thomas Augst, *The Clerk's Tale: Young Men and Moral Life in Nineteenth-Century America* (Chicago: University of Chicago Press, 2003), 261.

3 James Ayers, *Gold and Sunshine, Reminiscences of Early California* (Boston: R. G. Badger, 1922), 35–36; J. K. Osgood, "Letter to George Strang, 20 August, 1849," in William Benemann, ed., *A Year of Mud and Gold: San Francisco in Letters and Diaries, 1849–1850* (Lincoln: University of Nebraska Press, 1999), 33; Robert Smith Lammot, "Letter to His Brother Dan, 15 January, 1850," in

Benemann, *A Year of Mud and Gold*, 126; Bayard Taylor, *Eldorado; or, Adventures in the Path of Empire, Comprising a Voyage to California, via Panama; Life in San Francisco and Monterey; Pictures of the Gold Region, and Experiences of Mexican Travel* (New York: G. Putnam's Sons, 1879), 62; G. W. M., "San Francisco," in *Alta California*, 30 October 1853. For British Columbia see R. Byron Johnson, *Very Far West Indeed: A Few Rough Experiences on the North-West Pacific Coast*, 3rd ed. (London: S. Low, Martson, Low & Searle, 1872), 118; Kinahan Cornwallis, *The New El Dorado; or, British Columbia* (London: Thomas Cautley Newby, 1858), 2; Society for the Propagation of the Gospel in Foreign Parts, "Letter from Richard Dowson, Victoria, 3 May, 1859," in Letters Received Columbia, 1858–74, vol. 1, H/A/S02, BCARS; Sophia Cracroft, *Lady Franklin Visits the Pacific Northwest: Being Extracts from the Letters of Miss Sophia Cracroft, Sir John Franklin's Niece, February to April 1861 and April to July 1870* (Victoria, B.C.: [Provincial Archives of British Columbia], 1974), 38–39.

4   John Borthwick, *The Gold Hunters: A First Hand Picture of Life in California Mining Camps in the Early Fifties*, ed. Horace Kephart (1857; repr., New York: International Fiction Library, 1917), 59–60, 64. See also Paschal Mack to sister, 20 August 1853, Mss C-B 547:61, BANC.

5   On contemporary styles of dress in the East, see Kasson, *Rudeness and Civility*, 121. On colonial dress, see Bernard Cohn, *Colonialism and Its Forms of Knowledge: The British in India* (Princeton, N.J.: Princeton University Press, 1996), 149–60.

6   For California, see Robert M. Senkewicz, *Vigilantes in Gold Rush San Francisco* (Stanford, Calif.: Stanford University Press, 1985), 75–77. There are no easily accessible statistics for British Columbia, but local newspapers are noticeably devoid of any crime wave hysteria.

7   On the ubiquity of guns in the gold rushes, see Howard Gardiner, *In Pursuit of the Golden Dream: Reminiscences of San Francisco and the Northern and Southern Mines, 1849–1857* (Stoughton, Mass: Western Hemisphere, 1970), 15; "San Francisco As It Is: Manuscript," 288, folder 1, box 2140, CRCSL. On British Columbia, see "The Gold Diggings on Fraser River," *London Times*, 30 July 1858; British Columbia, Attorney General, "Inquisitions, Vancouver Island (Colony), 1859–Nov. 18, 1866," 11 August 1864, BCARS; Chartres Brew to Colonial Secretary, 28 July 1868, Colonial Correspondence, file 197, B01311, BCARS.

8   Christopher Oldstone-Moore, "The Beard Movement in Victorian Britain" *Victorian Studies* 48, no. 1 (Autumn 2005): 7–34.

9   Unfortunately, little has been written about facial hair in the American context. Oldstone-Moore, 10.

10   Alonzo Rathbun, Alonzo W. Rathbun Diary 1849–51, 183, BANC.

11   Hinton Helper, *The Land of Gold, Reality versus Fiction* (Baltimore: H. Taylor, 1855), 180; Mary Megquier, *Apron Full of Gold: The Letters of Mary Jane Megquier from San Francisco, 1849–1856*, ed. Robert Glass Cleland (San Marino, Calif.: Huntington Library, 1949), 37; S. S. L. to Sister Mary, 13 August 1858, Mss 2007 62, BANC; Mack to Sister, 20 August 1853. On California's role as a trendsetter in the wearing of facial hair, see "Wearing the Beard," *Alta California*, 29 September 1853.

12   Oldstone-Moore, "The Beard Movement in Victorian Britain," 13.

13   "Mustachios," *Alta California*, 19 March 1854; "Wearing the Beard," *Alta California*, 29 September 1853; Oldstone-Moore, "The Beard Movement in Victorian Britain," 12.

14   On the unusual nature of Californian beards, see Rathbun, Diary, 183; Helper, *The Land of Gold*, 180; J. H. Mankin, "Recollections of Early Days," SMCII, folder 6, box 24, CRCSL. On the linkage between gold miners, beards, and frontiersmen, see Borthwick, *The Gold Hunters*, 135.

15   "Wearing the Beard," *Alta California*, 29 September 1853.

16   See, for example, "Gold Escort Leaving Barkerville, 1865," A03148, BCARS; "Wedding of John A. Cameron, Also Known as Cariboo Cameron, 1860," A01158, BCARS; Louis Blanc, "Tin Shop, Barkerville; Decorated for Visit of Governor Anthony Musgrave, 1869," A03774, BCARS; Louis Blanc, "Firemen's Arch; William's Creek Fire Brigade Welcoming Governor Musgrave, Barkerville," A03762, BCARS. See also Cracroft, *Lady Franklin Visits the Pacific Northwest*, 39.

17   James Carson, *Early Recollections of the Mines: And a Description of the Great Tulare Valley* (Stockton, Calif.: published to accompany the steamer edition of the "San Joaquin Republican," 1852), 28.

18   For the "mincing" comment, see William Redmond Ryan, *Personal Adventures in Upper and Lower California, in 1848–9* (New York: Arno Press, 1973), 2:173. For the mocking imitation of a dandy's speech, see Carson, *Early Recollections of the Mines*, 27–28.

19   For California dandies, see Carson, *Early Recollections of the Mines*, 27–29; Ryan, *Personal Adventures*, 2:173; George Payson, *Golden Dreams and Leaden Realities* (New York: G. Putnam, 1853), 105–7. For British Columbia dandies, see "Letter to Father," *Abedare Times*, 6 December 1862, in Welsh, Barkerville Files, BA; Tit for Tat, "The Mines—Loafers—Indian Mustering on the Sound," *Alta California*, 22 June 1858; "Our Return Miners," *British Columbian*, 5 July 1862.

20   The figure of the gambler is dealt with in chapter 4.

21   For gamblers, see Hubert Howe Bancroft, *History of California* (San Francisco, 1886), 6:224; Alonzo Delano, *Pen Knife Sketches; or, Chips of the Old Block, a*

Series of Original Illustrated Letters, Written by One of California's Pioneer Miners (Sacramento, Calif.: published at The Union office, 1853), 31. For dandies, see Megquier, *Apron Full of Gold*, 37; Prentice Mulford, *Prentice Mulford's Story*, ed. Frederic Remington (1889; repr. Oakland, Calif.: Biobooks, 1953), 57–58.

22   The first two quotes are from W. Champness, *To Cariboo and Back* (London: Religious Tract Society, 1865), 259. The latter two quotes are from John Emmerson, "British Columbia and Vancouver Island: Voyages, Travels, and Adventures," B188, CRCSL, 148.

23   See, in particular, chapter 4.

24   *Kids* refers to kid gloves, made of goatskin. Benjamin Wingate, *Uncertain Country: The Wingate Letters, San Francisco, California—Meriden, New Hampshire, 1851–1854*, ed. Stephen Vincent (Berkeley, Calif.: Friends of the Bancroft Library, 2000), 72; Stanton Coblentz, *Villains and Vigilantes: The Story of James King, of William, and Pioneer Justice in California* (New York: Wilson-Erickson, 1936), 12; Frank Soulé, *The Annals of San Francisco: Containing a Summary of the History of . . . California, and a Complete History of . . . Its Great City* (New York: Appleton, 1855), 257–58; Timothy Coffin Osborn, Timothy Coffin Osborn Journal: ms., 14 June 1850–1 January 1855, 131, Mss C-F 81, BANC.

25   E. G. B., "From the Mines," *Alta California*, 10 May 1849.

26   Charles Thompson to uncle, 10 September 1851, Mss C-B 547:8, Gold Rush Letters, BANC.

27   For California, see Alonzo Delano's play *A Live Woman in the Mines, or, Pike County Ahead!* ([1857, purporting to represent 1850]; repr., Cambridge: ProQuest Information and Learning Company, 2003; "Arrest of Mrs. Yates," *Alta California*, 14 September 1851; "ABC Game," *Alta California*, 27 March 1853. For British Columbia, see Macfie, *Vancouver Island and British Columbia*, 407. This fit with the broader cultural concern with inexperienced men in unfamiliar urban environments being easily misled. See Halttunen, *Confidence Men and Painted Women*.

28   On the evolution of the greenhorn into the miner, see Delano, *Pen Knife Sketches*, 10–14. See also E. G. B., "From the Mines," *Alta California*, 10 May 1849.

29   For the account by the leader of one the largest groups of Welsh miners, see John Evans, "Diary of John Evans: The British Columbia Mining Adventure, 1862–1864," ms. 2111, BCARS.

30   John Bartlett, *Dictionary of Americanisms: A Glossary of Words and Phrases Usually Regarded as Peculiar to the United States* (Boston: Little, Brown, 1859), 180. Bartlett identifies green as an Americanism and defines it as "uncouth, raw, inexperienced, applied to persons. . . . [I]t answers to the English use of the

word verdant." Greenhorn does make an appearance in Johnson's 1827 dictionary, though it is noted as being "a low expression," suggesting that it was not in
common circulation in middle- and upper-class Britain. See Samuel Johnson,
*A Dictionary of the English Language: In Which Words Are Deduced from Their
Originals; and Illustrated in Their Different Significations, by Examples from
the Best Writers; Together with a History of the Language, and an English Grammar*, vol. 2 (London: printed for Longman, Rees, Orme, Brown, and Green et al.,
1827), unpaginated. In one of the few cases where the term greenhorn is used
in British Columbia, it is in quotation marks. See Macfie, *Vancouver Island and
British Columbia*, 407.

31   Champness, *To Cariboo and Back*, 233, 249.

32   Champness, *To Cariboo and Back*, 259.

33   One unknown author disagreed with most of his contemporaries, saying,
"Nine out of ten men have been well enough used by nature to become strong
men" so long as they had a "stout" enough heart to keep at. In this way the
author more clearly harkens back to a Californian-style emphasis on character,
but in conjunction with a strong body. *Cariboo: The Newly Discovered Gold
Fields of British Columbia* (Fairfield, Wash.: Ye Galleon Press, 1975), 3–5.

34   Henry Packer, 11 May 1852, Mss 84/90c, Henry Billington Packer Letters, 1849–
58, BANC. For British Columbia, see Macfie, *Vancouver Island and British
Columbia*, 414.

35   Borthwick, *The Gold Hunters*, 74–75. See also Charles Ross Parke, *Dreams to
Dust: A Diary of the California Gold Rush, 1849–1850*, ed. James Davis (Lincoln:
University of Nebraska Press, 1989), 101; Taylor, *Eldorado*, 32; Richard Lunt
Hale, *The Log of a Forty-Niner: Journal of a Voyage from Newburyport to San
Francisco in the Brig. Genl. Worth, Commanded by Samuel Walton* (Boston:
B. J. Brimmer, 1923), 65.

36   Megquier, *Apron Full of Gold*, 37. For a claim that both traders and gamblers
donned the miner's costume in order to mislead them, see Delano, *Pen Knife
Sketches*, 23, 31.

37   For instance, Alfred Doten clearly established this link on his way to California. See Alfred Doten, *The Journals of Alfred Doten, 1849–1903*, ed. Walter Van
Tilburg Clark (Reno: University of Nevada Press, 1973), 6.

38   Mulford, *Prentice Mulford's Story*, 57–58; Osborn, Journal, 192–93.

39   John Carr, *Pioneer Days in California: Historical and Personal Sketches*
(Eureka, Calif.: Times Publishing, 1891), 279; Osborn, Journal, 203; Charles
Bridgen to his cousin, Mary A. Cushing, 11 March 1852, Mss C-B 547 100,
BANC.

40   For a discussion of the westerner and the pioneer, see chapter 4.

41   On clothes and the emergent middle class, see Kasson, *Rudeness and Civility*, 118–21; Michael Zakim, *Ready-Made Democracy: A History of Men's Dress in the American Republic, 1760–1860* (Chicago: University of Chicago Press, 2003), esp. 188–93, 203, 210.

42   On martial and restrained manhood, see Greenberg, *Manifest Manhood*, 11–13.

43   On the increasing importance of biological racism in the mid-nineteenth century, see Nancy Stepan, *The Idea of Race in Science: Great Britain, 1800–1960* (Hamden, Conn.: Archon Books, 1982), 20–82; Robert F. Berkhofer, *The White Man's Indian: Images of the American Indian from Columbus to the Present* (New York: Knopf, 1978), 55–61.

44   Stepan, *The Idea of Race in Science*, 36–39, 45–46. On the lingering impact of environmentalism, see Linda Lorraine Nash, *Inescapable Ecologies: A History of Environment, Disease, and Knowledge* (Berkeley: University of California Press, 2006).

45   Oldstone-Moore, "The Beard Movement in Victorian Britain."

46   See, for example "Gold Escort Leaving Barkerville, 1865," A03148, BCARS; "Wedding of John A. Cameron, Also Known as Cariboo Cameron, 1860," A01158, BCARS; Louis Blanc, "Tin Shop, Barkerville; Decorated for Visit of Governor Anthony Musgrave, 1869," A03774, BCARS; Louis Blanc, "Firemen's Arch; William's Creek Fire Brigade Welcoming Governor Musgrave, Barkerville," A03762, BCARS.

47   Adele Perry, *On the Edge of Empire: Gender, Race, and the Making of British Columbia, 1849–1871* (Toronto: University of Toronto Press, 2001), 79–83; Burrard Inlet Mechanic's Institute, Minute Book, 17 September 1868 to 12 April 1884, Mss E/C/B94, BCARS; Alexander Allan to Thomas Dearberg, 2 January 1868, Alexander Allan Letterbook, BA.

48   As Peter Boag has shown, cross-dressing was a frequent occurrence throughout the West. Peter Boag, *Re-dressing America's Frontier Past* (Berkeley: University of California Press, 2011), 1.

49   Susan Lee Johnson, *Roaring Camp: The Social World of the California Gold Rush* (New York: W. W. Norton, 2000), 173; Clare Sears, "All That Glitters: Trans-ing California's Gold Rush Migrations," *GLQ: A Journal of Lesbian and Gay Studies* 14, nos. 2–3 (2008): 387–88. It is not known if similar events occurred in British Columbia, but given the isolation of the mining camps and a dearth of white women, it certainly seems probable.

50   In the eyes of most observers, cross-dressing individuals conformed to what Boag has termed the "progress narrative" of cross-dressing in the West. Boag, *Re-dressing America's Frontier Past*, 10, 30, 57–58.

51   Charles DeLong, Diary 1856, 10 July 1856, box 212, folder 5, CRCSL.

52 "Both Sides," *Alta California*, 4 November 1857.

53 For criticisms of effeminate men, see the discourse surrounding the dandy, in Carson, *Early Recollections of the Mines*, 27–28; Ryan, *Personal Adventures*, 2:173. See also Kasson, *Rudeness and Civility*, 118–21; Zakim, *Ready-Made Democracy*, 192–203.

54 I use the term *disguised female* to signify the juxtaposition of costume and what the observers would have understood as the person's "true" sex. I am not making a claim about the gender identity of the subject. The quote is from David Higgins, *The Mystic Spring, and Other Tales of Western Life* (Toronto: W. Briggs, 1904), 35. For an example from California, see Ramón Gil Navarro, *The Gold Rush Diary of Ramón Gil Navarro*, ed. Maria del Carmen Ferreyra and David Sven Reher (Lincoln: University of Nebraska Press, 2000), 83.

55 Payson, *Golden Dreams and Leaden Realities*, 271–72.

56 Navarro, *Gold Rush Diary*, 83, 103. See also Higgins, *The Mystic Spring*, 35–40; Mary Seacole, *Wonderful Adventures of Mrs. Seacole in Many Lands* (1857; repr., New York: Oxford University Press, 1988), 18; Taylor, *Eldorado*, 27; "Female Labor in the Mines," *Alta California*, 14 December 1850.

57 For the bloomer costume in public debate, see "[Illegible] and Bloomer Fashions," *Alta California*, 7 July 1851; "Female Costume," *Alta California*, 5 August 1851; A Reformer, "Female Costume—a Lady's Opinion," *Alta California*, 7 August 1851; A Conservative, "A New Costume—a Lady's Opinion," *Alta California*, 10 August 1851; A Reformer, "The New Costume—a Reply to 'Conservative,'" *Alta California*, 11 August 1851; "More 'Bloomers,'" *Alta California*, 17 August 1851; E. C. S., "A Spirited Bloomer," *Alta California*, 16 September 1851.

58 For a history of dress reform in the nineteenth-century, see Gayle V. Fischer, *Pantaloons and Power: Nineteenth-Century Dress Reform in the United States* (Kent, Ohio: Kent State University, 2001), 80–109 and Carol Mattingly, *Appropriate[ing] Dress: Women's Rhetorical Style in Nineteenth-Century America* (Carbondale: Southern Illinois University Press, 2002), 40–81.

59 Fischer, *Pantaloons and Power*, 102.

60 A Reformer, "Female Costume—a Lady's Opinion," *Alta California*, 7 August 1851.

61 A Conservative, "A New Costume—a Lady's Opinion," *Alta California*, 10 August 1851; Louise Amelia Knapp Clappe, *California in 1851: The Letters of Dame Shirley*, ed. Carl Wheat (San Francisco: Grabhorn Press, 1933), 114–16.

62 Zakim, *Ready-Made Democracy*, 7, 187–88, 200–203.

63 Fischer, *Pantaloons and Power*, 91; Zakim, *Ready-Made Democracy*, 200–203; Mattingly, *Appropriate[ing] Dress*.

64   Clappe, *California in 1851*, 114–16; A Conservative, "A New Costume—a Lady's Opinion," *Alta California*, 10 August 1851.

65   On cross-dressing and prostitution in California, see Friedrich Gerstäcker, *Scenes of Life in California*, trans. George Cosgrave and Gustave Revilliod (1856; reprint, San Francisco: J. Howell, 1942), 38. For British Columbia, see George Blair, Diary of George Blair: Feb. 17 1862–Dec. 29 1863, 65, Mss 0186, BCARS; "News from Williams Creek," in *Daily British Colonist*, 10 September 1862.

66   Anne McClintock, *Imperial Leather: Race, Gender, and Sexuality in the Colonial Contest* (New York: Routledge, 1995), 132–77; Catherine Smith and Cynthia Greig, *Women in Pants: Manly Maidens, Cowgirls, and Other Renegades* (New York: H. N. Abrams, 2003), 10–11, 44–51; Gerstäcker, *Scenes of Life in California*, 38.

67   On the critical role of white women in colonialism see, for example, Perry, *On the Edge of Empire*, 139–93; Philippa Levine, *Prostitution, Race, and Politics: Policing Venereal Disease in the British Empire* (New York: Routledge, 2003); Nupur Chaudhuri and Margaret Strobel, eds., *Western Women and Imperialism: Complicity and Resistance* (Bloomington: Indiana University Press, 1992); Ann Laura Stoler, *Carnal Knowledge and Imperial Power: Race and the Intimate in Colonial Rule* (Berkeley: University of California Press, 2002); Mattingly, *Appropriate[ing] Dress*, 10.

68   "[Illegible] and Bloomer Fashions," *Alta California*, 7 July 1851

69   Helper, *The Land of Gold*, 86, 88, 89. See also Carr, *Pioneer Days in California*, 69–70; Elisha Smith Capron, *History of California, from its Discovery to the Present Time: Comprising Also a Full Description of Its Climate, Surface, Soil, Rivers, Towns . . . Agriculture, Commerce, Mines, Mining, &c., with a Journal of the Voyage from New York, via Nicaragua, to San Francisco, and Back, via Panama . . .* (Cleveland, Ohio: Jewett, Proctor and Worthington, 1854), 152–53.

70   Soulé, *The Annals of San Francisco*, 368–69, 378–79, 384–86; Payson, *Golden Dreams and Leaden Realities*, 237; Capron, *History of California*, 152. For British Columbia, see J. Monroe Thoington, *The Cariboo Journal of John Macoun*, 202, BA. This is in keeping with a pattern throughout the U.S. West. See Boag, *Redressing America's Frontier Past*, 140–46.

71   Ryan, *Personal Adventures*, 1: 92–93.

72   Theodore Johnson, *Sights in the Gold Region, and Scenes by the Way* (New York: Baker and Scribner, 1849), 155–56. See also Lucius A. Edelblute, *A True Story of the Adventures of Cariboo Ed in the Far West* (Bountiful, Utah: Family History Publishers, 1998), 15; Bates, *Incidents on Land and Water*, 130–31, 150–51, 166; Doten, *The Journals of Alfred Doten*, 207–8; Helper, *The Land of Gold*, 270–71; Frank Marryat, *Mountains and Molehills; or, Recollections of a Burnt Journal*

(1855; repr., Philadelphia: Lippincott, 1962), 41–42; Albert Benard de Russailh, *Last Adventure: San Francisco in 1851; Translated from the Original Journal of Albert Benard de Russailh by Clarkson Crane*, ed. Clarkson Crane (San Francisco: Westgate Press, 1931), 90–91; William Shaw, *Golden Dreams and Waking Realities: Being the Adventures of a Gold-Seeker in California and the Pacific Islands* (London: Smith, Elder., 1851), 15–16, 108; Edwin Waite, "Reminiscences," 76–77, CRCSL; Capron, *History of California*, 19–20.

73 Allan Gallay, *The Indian Slave Trade: The Rise of the English Empire in the American South, 1670–1717* (New Haven, Conn.: Yale University Press, 2002), 47, 312–13; Winthrop Jordan, *White over Black: American Attitudes toward the Negro, 1550–1812* (Chapel Hill: University of North Carolina Press, 1968), 89–91.

74 Albert Hurtado, *Indian Survival on the California Frontier* (New Haven, Conn.: Yale University Press, 1988), 5.

75 Shaw, *Golden Dreams*, 15–16; Bates, *Incidents on Land and Water*, 166; Marryat, *Mountains and Molehills*, 41–42; Capron, *History of California*, 19–20.

76 Doten, *The Journals of Alfred Doten*, 207; Bates, *Incidents on Land and Water*, 150–51; Helper, *The Land of Gold*, 268; Osborn, Journal, 131; Johnson, *Sights in the Gold Region*, 155–56; Charles Edward Pancoast, *A Quaker Forty-Niner: The Adventures of Charles Edward Pancoast on the American Frontier*, ed. Anna Paschall Hannum (Philadelphia: University of Pennsylvania Press, 1930), 342; Capron, *History of California*, 19–20.

77 Cracroft, *Lady Franklin Visits the Pacific Northwest*, 12; Attorney General of British Columbia, "Assault on Shaynuk," 10 June 1864, file 1864/36, box 4, GR-0419, BCARS; M. Stannard, *Memoirs of a Professional Lady Nurse* (London: Simpkin, Marshall, 1873), 186.

78 Perry, *On the Edge of Empire*, 52–53.

79 Johnson, *Very Far West Indeed*, 84; John Domer, *New British Gold Fields: A Guide to British Columbia and Vancouver with Coloured Map Showing the Gold and Coal Fields, Constructed from Authentic Sources* (London: Hugh Barclay, 1858), 24. On white women in British Columbia, see Perry, *On the Edge of Empire*, 125–93.

80 Domer, *New British Gold Fields*, 24. See also Richard Mayne, *Four Years in British Columbia and Vancouver Island: An Account of Their Forests, Rivers, Coasts, Gold Fields and Resources for Colonisation* (London: John Murray, 1862), 242–43.

81 Johnson, *Very Far West Indeed*, 86, quote is from 428, emphasis original. See also Mayne, *Four Years in British Columbia*, 242–43.

82 Rayna Green, "The Pocahontas Perplex: The Image of Indian Women in American Culture," *Massachusetts Review* 16, no. 4 (Autumn 1975): 698–714.

83 Green, "The Pocahontas Perplex," 704–11.

84 For California, see Bates, *Incidents on Land and Water*, 152–53; Joseph Golds-borough Bruff, *Gold Rush: The Journals, Drawings and Other Papers of J. Golds-borough Bruff, Captain, Washington City and California Mining Association, April 2, 1849–July 20, 1851*, ed. Georgia Willis Read, Ruth Louise Gaines, and Frederick Webb Hodge (New York: Columbia University Press, 1949), 78, 83; E. Gould Buffum, *Six Months in the Gold Mines* (1850; repr., Ann Arbor: University of Michigan Press, 1966), 43; Doten, *The Journals of Alfred Doten*, 125–26; Osborn, Journal, 57–58, 101–2, 121–22. For British Columbia, the imagery of indigenous women has been given considerable attention by Perry in *On the Edge of Empire*, 49–74. See also Blair, Diary, 17–18; Emmerson, "British Columbia and Vancouver Island," 49–50; Champness, *To Cariboo and Back*, 248.

85 Frank [Pearl] to [his sister Theresa], 8 July 1850, Mss C-B 547:21, BANC; Charles T. Brigden to his cousin, Mary A. Cushing, 11 March 1852, Mss C-B 547:100, BANC; "Ladies in San Francisco," *Alta California*, 4 February 1851; "Arrival of Ladies," *Alta California*, 17 October 1853; "Cheering News from Cariboo," *British Colonist*, 10 June 1861; "Columbian Immigration Society," *British Columbian*, 21 June 1862; Brian Roberts, *American Alchemy: The California Gold Rush and Middle-Class Culture* (Chapel Hill: University of North Carolina Press, 2000), 219–29; Perry, *On the Edge of Empire*, 139–46.

86 "Ladies in San Francisco," *Alta California*, 4 February 1851.

87 Clappe, *California in 1851*, 31–34.

88 See, for example, Levine, *Prostitution, Race, and Politics*; Chaudhuri and Strobel, eds., *Western Women and Imperialism*; Stoler, *Carnal Knowledge and Imperial Power*.

89 Bates, *Incidents on Land and Water*, 154–56; Buffum, *Six Months in the Gold Mines*, 43; Philip Hankin, Memoirs, 53–54, E-B-H19A, BCARS; "Arrest of Street Walkers," in *British Colonist*, 8 May 1860.

90 One of the few exceptions would be Arthur Bushby, who was smitten with one of James Douglas's mixed-race daughters. See Arthur Thomas Bushby, "The Journal of Arthur Thomas Bushby, 1858–1859," *British Columbia Historical Quarterly* 21, no. 1 (January 1957): 122.

91 The first quote is from Payson, *Golden Dreams and Leaden Realities*, 237. The second is from Soulé, *The Annals of San Francisco*, 378. The British Columbia quote is from William Mark, *Cariboo: A True and Correct Narrative* (Stockton, U.K.: W. M. Wright, 1863), 16.

92 Weikun Cheng, "Politics of the Queue: Agitation and Resistance in the Beginning and End of Qing China," in *Hair: Its Power and Meanings in Asian*

Cultures, ed. Alf Hiltebeitel and Barbara D. Miller (Albany: State University of New York Press, 1998), 123–38; Patricia Ebrey, *The Cambridge Illustrated History of China* (New York: Cambridge University Press, 2010), 221; Jonathan Spence, *The Search for Modern China* (New York: Norton, 1990), 28, 38–39, 50–53.

93 One of the few commentators to understand the importance of the queue was Mark, *Cariboo*, 17. On the history of the queue, see Cheng, "Politics of the Queue," 123–28; Ebrey, *History of China*, 221.

94 "Foreign Miners," *Alta California*, 2 May 1851.

95 DeLong, Diary 1855, 23 October 1855; "Cutting Off a Tail," *Alta California*, 25 May 1851; Police and Prisons Department Esquimalt, Charge Book, 15 April 1863–23 December 1864, 2 July 1863, vol. 2, GR-0428, BCARS; British Columbia Attorney General, Indecent Assault, 16, 25 July 1866, file 1866, box 4, BCARS.

96 Jacob Fisher to Frederick Fisher, 21 September 1850, Mss C-B 547:11, Gold Rush Letters, BANC; David Dustin to John K. Dustin, 14 August 1850, Mss C-B 547:40, Gold Rush Letters, BANC; Champness, *To Cariboo and Back*, 259; Ayers, *Gold and Sunshine*, 34; James Duffy to Jenny, 20 June 1853, Mss C-B 547: 128, Gold Rush Letters, BANC; Fisher to Fisher, 21 September 1850, Gold Rush Letters, BANC; Thomass [*sic*] Nosseter to John Bell, 20 December 1849, Mss C-B 547:115, Gold Rush Letters, BANC.

97 Drew Gilpin Faust, *This Republic of Suffering: Death and the American Civil War* (New York: Alfred A. Knopf, 2008), 6–17.

98 William Taylor, *California Life Illustrated* (New York: Carlton & Porter, 1860), 143. See also Stephen Chapin Davis, *California Gold Rush Merchant: The Journal of Stephen Chapin Davis* (San Marino, Calif.: Huntington Library, 1956), 16; Shaw, *Golden Dreams*, 95, 99; Anonymous, "Journal of a Voyage from New Bedford to San Francisco," in *A Year of Mud and Gold: San Francisco in Letters and Diaries, 1849–1850*, ed. William Benemann (Lincoln: University of Nebraska Press, 1999), 30; Anne Wilson Booth, "Journal," in Benemann, *A Year of Mud and Gold*, 93. For British Columbia, see Thomas Mitchell to parents, 7 October 1862, Mss 0838, BCARS.

99 Nash, *Inescapable Ecologies*, 13–14, 18–29, 38–40.

100 Macfie, *Vancouver Island and British Columbia*, 181; Thomas Allsop, *California and Its Gold Mines: Being a Series of Recent Communications from the Mining Districts, upon the Present Condition and Future Prospects of Quartz Mining; with an Account of the Richer Deposits, and Incidental Notices of the Climate, Scenery, and Mode of Life in California* (London: Groombridge and Sons, 1853), 73–74.

101 Soulé, *The Annals of San Francisco*, 211.

102 McClintock, *Imperial Leather*, 207–31.

103   See, for example Nayan Shah, *Contagious Divides: Epidemics and Race in San Francisco's Chinatown* (Berkeley: University of California Press, 2001), esp. 20–44; Glenda Gilmore, *Gender and Jim Crow: Women and the Politics of White Supremacy in North Carolina, 1896–1920* (Chapel Hill: University of North Carolina Press, 1996), 168–73; Perry, *On the Edge of Empire*, 110–23.

104   "Still the Celestials Come," *Alta California*, 19 August 1854.

105   "The Indian Question Again," *British Columbian*, 3 May 1862.

106   Untitled editorial, *Alta California*, 22 August 1854.

107   See, for example, "Small Pox amongst the Indians," *British Columbian*, 30 April 1862; "The Small Pox among the Indians," *British Colonist*, 28 April 1862; "How to Get Rid of a Troublesome Question," *British Colonist*, 29 May 1862.

108   "The Small Pox among the Indians," *British Colonist*, 28 April 1862.

109   "The Small Pox," *British Colonist*, 14 May, 1862.

110   On the effect of the small pox epidemic on British Columbia's indigenous population, see "Small Pox," *British Colonist*, 5 January 1863; "British Columbia— Latest News," *British Colonist*, 17 January 1863; "Latest from British Columbia," *British Colonist*, 23 January 1863; "Important from Cariboo," *British Colonist*, 30 January 1863; "Important from Cariboo," *British Colonist*, 25 February 1863; "News from Cariboo!" *British Colonist*, 27 February 1863; "Important from Cariboo!" *British Colonist*, 12 March 1863; "Lightning Creek," *British Colonist*, 28 March 1863; "The Interior," *British Columbian*, 31 January 1863; "Latest from Richfield," *British Colonist*, 21 February 1863; "Lillooet," *British Colonist*, 25 February 1863.

111   On the way that science, particularly race science, has been influenced by pre-existing cultural beliefs, see Stephen Jay Gould, *The Mismeasure of Man* (New York: W. W. Norton, 1981), 31–39, 50–54, 69–72.

112   R. Bell, "A Case of Intussusception, with Remarks," *California State Medical Journal* (1856): 203–10.

113   Bell, 210; Macfie, Vancouver Island and British Columbia, 379–83. Gould, *The Mismeasure of Man*, 31–39, 50–54, 69–72.

114   Vancouver Island, Supreme Court of Civil Justice, "Ah Yan Carnally Abusing a Child under 10 Yrs of Age," 2 August 1866, B09802(1), BCARS.

115   Henry Crease, British Columbia, District of Quesnellemouth, 11 March 1865, file 1, box 3, Mss 0054, BCARS.

116   "Outrage upon a Child," *Alta California*, 13 October 1855; British Columbia, Attorney General, 31 December 1862, file 1862, box 2, GR-0419, BCARS; Vancouver Island, Supreme Court of Civil Justice, "Ah Yan Carnally Abusing a Child under 10 Yrs of Age," 2 August 1866, B09802(1), BCARS; British Columbia Attorney General, Indecent Assault, 16, 25 July 1866, file 1866, box 4, BCARS.

117 British Columbia, Attorney General, 31 December 1862, file 1862, box 2, GR-0419, BCARS.

118 See, for example, "Rape," *Alta California*, 4 February 1851; "Outrageous," *Alta California*, 25 February 1851; "Rape," *Alta California*, 2 April 1852; British Columbia Attorney General, Indecent Assault, 3 April 1865, file 1865/21, box 4, GR0419, BCARS; British Columbia Attorney General, Rape of Esther Meiss, 31 May 1864, file 1864/38, box 4, GR0419, BCARS; British Columbia Attorney General, Rape, 25 September 1866, file 1866/28, box 6, GR0419, BCARS.

119 Faust, *This Republic of Suffering*, 8.

120 Greenberg's example from the South is linked to a broader belief that had resonance throughout the Anglo-American world. Kenneth S. Greenberg, *Honor and Slavery: Lies, Duels, Noses, Masks, Dressing as a Woman, Gifts, Strangers, Humanitarianism, Death, Slave Rebellions, the Proslavery Argument, Baseball, Hunting, and Gambling in the Old South* (Princeton, N.J.: Princeton University Press, 1996), 87–114.

121 Faust, *This Republic of Suffering*, 10.

122 Faust, *This Republic of Suffering*, 10; Taylor, *California Life Illustrated*, 143; Davis, *California Gold Rush Merchant*, 16; Shaw, *Golden Dreams*, 95, 99; Anonymous, "Journal of a Voyage from New Bedford to San Francisco," 30; Booth, "Journal," 93. For British Columbia, see Thomas Mitchell to parents, 7 October 1862, Mss 0838, BCARS.

123 Soulé, *The Annals of San Francisco*, 631–32; Taylor, *Eldorado*, 36–37; Robert Stevenson, Diary and Memo Book 1863–76, Mss 0315, BCARS; Cecil Williams Buckley, Journal, 12 July 1862, E/B/B85, BCARS.

124 Taylor, *California Life Illustrated*, 143; Davis, *California Gold Rush Merchant*, 16; Shaw, *Golden Dreams*, 95, 99; Anonymous, "Journal of a Voyage from New Bedford to San Francisco," 30; Booth, "Journal," 93. For British Columbia, see Thomas Mitchell to parents, 7 October 1862, Mss 0838, BCARS.

125 Ryan, *Personal Adventures*, 2:134–36.

126 "The Dying and the Dead," *Alta California*, 29 September 1856.

127 Wingate, *Uncertain Country*, 20–21; Anonymous, "Journal of a Voyage from New Bedford to San Francisco," 30; Walter Colton, *Three Years in California [1846–49]* (New York: A. S. Barnes, 1850), 360–61. On the unsuitability of non-whites to care for whites, see "Hospital," *Cariboo Sentinel*, 20 August 1866; "Mining Board Meeting," *Cariboo Sentinel*, 27 August 1866.

128 Champness, *To Cariboo and Back*, 258–59.

129 Ben Bowen, Ben Bowen Diary and Notebook: Mss, 1854–59, 50–51, Mss C-F 192, BANC; J. H. Mankin, Recollections of Early Days, 2–7, folder 6, box 24, CRCSL; "The Diggings—Indian Difficulties," *Alta California*, 25 May 1850; "City Items,"

Alta California, 18 February 1858. For British Columbia, see John Cowley, Diary, 1862, 29, 33, E-B-C832, BCARS. Indeed, British Columbia passed a law to protect Indian graves from plundering by curiosity-seekers. See Great Britain Colonial Office, "An Ordinance to Prevent the Violation of Indian Graves," 30 March 1865, in "Preconfederation Statues of British Columbia (V.I.) 1859–71, D8, BCARS.

130 Chauncey L. Canfield, *The Diary of a Forty-Niner* (Boston: Houghton Mifflin, 1920), 10–11.

131 See, for example, California Legislature, Senate, "Speech of Hon. Wilson Flint, in the Senate of California, March 21, 1856: On the Bill to Reduce the Chinese Mining Tax," 5, CRCSL; and "A Chinese Washerman," *Cariboo Sentinel*, 19 July 1866.

132 "Events of Yesterday," *Alta California*, 30 July 1856.

133 "Execution of the Murderers—James Barry and the Indian Nikel Palsk," *Cariboo Sentinel*, 12 August 1867.

134 "Criminal Trials," *Cariboo Sentinel*, 4 July 1867.

135 "Execution of the Murderers—James Barry and the Indian Nikel Palsk."

136 For an example of a Native American acting like the ideal white man, but still being seen as different, see "Trial of Antonio Garra, the Hostile Indian Chief," *San Diego Herald*, 17 January 1852, quoted in Clifford Trafzer and Joel Hyer, eds., *Exterminate Them: Written Accounts of the Murder, Rape, and Slavery of Native Americans during the California Gold Rush, 1848–1868* (East Lansing: Michigan State University Press, 1999), 111. For a contemporary example, see Greenberg's comparison of the executions of Nat Turner and John Brown in Greenberg, *Honor and Slavery*, 87–91, 99–107.

EPILOGUE

1 On the legacy of the California gold rush, and especially of the transition to agriculture, see Larry M. Dilsaver, "After the Gold Rush," *Geographical Review* 75, no. 1 (January 1985): 1–18; Ralph Mann, *After the Gold Rush: Society in Grass Valley and Nevada City, California, 1849–1870* (Stanford, Calif.: Stanford University Press, 1982).

2 Robert Kelley, "The Mining Debris Controversy in the Sacramento Valley," *Pacific Historical Review* 25, no. 4 (November 1956): 344–45.

3 Diane Newell, *Tangled Webs of History: Indians and the Law in Canada's Pacific Coast Fisheries* (Toronto: University of Toronto Press, 1999); Robin Fisher, *Contact and Conflict: Indian-European Relations in British Columbia, 1774–1890* (Vancouver: University of British Columbia Press, 1977), esp. 146–211; Cole Harris, *Making Native Space: Colonialism, Resistance, and Reserves in British Columbia* (Vancouver: University of British Columbia Press, 2002).

4   On the economic and social development of British Columbia after the gold
     rush, see Jean Barman, *The West beyond the West: A History of British Colum-
     bia*, 3rd ed. (Toronto: University of Toronto Press, 2007), 114–28

5   Gail Bederman, *Manliness and Civilization: A Cultural History of Gender and
     Race in the United States, 1880–1917* (Chicago: University of Chicago Press, 1995),
     5–12.

6   Bederman, *Manliness and Civilization*, 18–19, 74.

7   See, for example, the literature on the State Conventions of Colored Citizens,
     including Quintard Taylor, *In Search of the Racial Frontier: African Americans
     in the American West, 1528–1990*. (New York: W. W. Norton, 1998), 91–92; Miff-
     lin W. Gibbs, *Shadow and Light: An Autobiography* (New York: Arno Press and
     New York Times, 1968), 15. See also "State Convention of the Colored Citizens
     of California," *Pacific Appeal* (San Francisco), 1, no. 2 (12 April 1862): 2; "Pro-
     ceedings of the California State Convention of Colored Citizens," *Elevator* (San
     Francisco), 1, no. 31–33 (17 November 1865).

8   Bederman, *Manliness and Civilization*.

9   Janice Tolhurst Driesbach et al., *Art of the Gold Rush* (Berkeley: University of
     California Press, 1998); Bayard Taylor, *Eldorado; or, Adventures in the Path of
     Empire, Comprising a Voyage to California, via Panama; Life in San Francisco
     and Monterey; Pictures of the Gold Region, and Experiences of Mexican Travel*
     (New York: G. Putnam's Sons, 1879); A. J. McCall, *The Great California Trail
     in 1849, Wayside Notes of an Argonaut . . . Reprinted from the Steuben Courier*
     (Bath, N.Y.: Steuben Courier Print, 1882); William Downie, *Hunting for Gold:
     Reminiscences [sic] of Personal Experience and Research in the Early Days of the
     Pacific Coast from Alaska to Panama* (San Francisco: California Publishing,
     1893); John Carr, *Pioneer Days in California: Historical and Personal Sketches*
     (Eureka, Calif.: Times Publishing, 1891); John David Borthwick, *The Gold Hunt-
     ers: A First Hand Picture of Life in California Mining Camps in the Early Fifties*,
     ed. Horace Kephart (1857; repr., New York: International Fiction Library, 1917).

10   Jack London, *Smoke Bellew* (New York: Century Company, 1912), 181.

11   Peter Blodgett, "Worlds of Wonder and Ambition: Gold Rush California and
     the Culture of Mining Bonanzas in the North American West," in *A Com-
     panion to the Literature and Culture of the American West*, ed. Nicolas Witschi
     (Malden, Mass.: Wiley-Blackwell, 2011), 39–40; Hubert Howe Bancroft, *History
     of California* (San Francisco: History Co., 1886) and *History of British Columbia*
     (San Francisco: History Co., 1887); E. O. S. Scholefield, *British Columbia from
     the Earliest Times to the Present* (Vancouver: S. J. Clarke, 1914); Charles Howard
     Shinn, *Mining Camps: A Study in American Frontier Government* (New York:
     Charles Scribner's Sons, 1885).

12   Teddy Roosevelt's favorite childhood magazine, *Our Young Folks*, edited by J. T. Trowbridge, Lucy Larcom, and Gail Hamilton, contained a number of stories about gold rush California that generally presented gold miners as tough and hardy embodiments of moral virtue. See, for example, A. Hartlie, "A Birthday Box: A Parlor Drama," *Our Young Folks* 2 (1866): 744; Rose Terry, "Polly Sylvester's Dream," *Our Young Folks* 6 (1870): 51–55; J. T. Trowbridge, "One Good Turn Deserves Another: A Play for Boys," *Our Young Folks* 8 (1872): 119–22; see also Theodore Roosevelt, *Ranch Life and the Hunting-Trail* (1888; repr., Ann Arbor, Mich.: University Microfilms, 1966), 95, 97.

BIBLIOGRAPHY

ARCHIVES

BA   Barkerville Archives, Barkerville, British Columbia
BANC   Bancroft Library, Berkeley, California
BCARS   British Columbia Archives, Victoria
CRCSL   California Room of the California State Library, Sacramento
UVIC   University of Victoria Library, Victoria, British Columbia

NEWSPAPERS

Titles vary slightly over time.

Alta California (San Francisco), 1849–60
British Colonist and Victoria Chronicle, 1859–71
British Columbian (New Westminster), 1861–69
Cariboo Sentinel (Barkerville), 1865–71
Elevator (San Francisco), 1865–69
Herald (New York), 1849
Mainland Guardian (New Westminster), 1870
Merthyr Telegraph (Wales), 1862
Mirror of the Times (San Francisco), 1857
New York Times, 1856
Pacific Appeal (San Francisco), 1862–67
San Francisco Argonaut, 1878
San Francisco Evening Bulletin, 1858–59
Times (London), 1849–64
Victoria Daily Chronicle, 1863–66
Victoria Gazette, 1858–60

OTHER SOURCES

Alderson, David. *Mansex Fine: Religion, Manliness and Imperialism in Nineteenth-Century British Culture*. New York: Manchester University Press, 1998.

Allen, Robert. *Horrible Prettiness: Burlesque and American Culture*. Chapel Hill:
University of North Carolina Press, 1991.

Allsop, Thomas. *California and Its Gold Mines: Being a Series of Recent Communications from the Mining Districts, upon the Present Condition and Future Prospects of Quartz Mining; with an Account of the Richer Deposits, and Incidental Notices of the Climate, Scenery, and Mode of Life in California*. London: Groombridge and Sons, 1853.

Anderson, David, and David Killingray. *Policing the Empire: Government, Authority, and Control, 1830–1940*. Manchester, U.K.: Manchester University Press, 1991.

Anderson, Kay. *Vancouver's Chinatown: Racial Discourse in Canada, 1875–1980*. Montreal, Quebec: McGill-Queen's University Press, 1991.

Anderson, Warwick. *Colonial Pathologies: American Tropical Medicine, Race, and Hygiene in the Philippines*. Durham, N.C.: Duke University Press, 2006.

Augst, Thomas. *The Clerk's Tale: Young Men and Moral Life in Nineteenth-Century America*. Chicago: University of Chicago Press, 2003.

Ayers, James J. *Gold and Sunshine, Reminiscences of Early California*. Boston: R. G. Badger, 1922.

Bancroft, Hubert Howe. *The History of British Columbia*. San Francisco: History Co., 1887.

———. *History of California*. Vol. 6. San Francisco: History Co., 1886.

Banks, J. A., and Olive Banks. *Feminism and Family Planning in Victorian England*. Liverpool, U.K.: Liverpool University Press, 1964.

Barman, Jean. *The West beyond the West: A History of British Columbia*. 3rd ed. Toronto: University of Toronto Press, 2007.

Barrington, Alexander. *A California Gold Rush Miscellany Comprising: The Original Journal of Alexander Barrington, Nine Unpublished Letters from the Gold Mines, Reproductions of Early Maps and Towns from California Lithographs; Broadsides, &c*. San Francisco: Grabhorn Press, 1934.

Barron, Hal S. *Those Who Stayed Behind: Rural Society in Nineteenth-Century New England*. New York: Cambridge University Press, 1984.

Barth, Gunther Paul. *Instant Cities: Urbanization and the Rise of San Francisco and Denver*. New York: Oxford University Press, 1975.

Bartlett, John. *Dictionary of Americanisms: A Glossary of Words and Phrases Usually Regarded as Peculiar to the United States*. Boston: Little, Brown, 1859.

Bates, D. B. *Incidents on Land and Water*. 1857. Reprint, New York: Arno Press, 1974.

Beck, Ulrich. *World Risk Society*. Malden, Mass.: Polity Press, 1999.

Bederman, Gail. *Manliness and Civilization: A Cultural History of Gender and Race in the United States, 1880–1917*. Chicago: University of Chicago Press, 1995.

Beecher, Lyman. *A Plea for the West*. 1835. Reprint, New York: Arno Press, 1977.

Begbie, Matthew. *Journey into the Interior of British Columbia*. Vol. 3. London: Royal Geographic Society Journal, 1861.

Bell, R. "A Case of Intussusception, with Remarks." *California State Medical Journal* (1856): 203–10.

Benemann, William, ed. *A Year of Mud and Gold: San Francisco in Letters and Diaries, 1849–1850*. Lincoln: University of Nebraska Press, 1999.

Bennett, David. *The Party of Fear: From Nativist Movements to the New Right in American History*. Chapel Hill: University of North Carolina Press, 1988.

Berglund, Barbara. *Making San Francisco American: Cultural Frontiers in the Urban West, 1846–1906*. Lawrence: University Press of Kansas, 2007.

Berkhofer, Robert F. *The White Man's Indian: Images of the American Indian from Columbus to the Present*. New York: Knopf, 1978.

Billington, Ray Allen. *Land of Savagery / Land of Promise: The European Image of the American Frontier in the Nineteenth Century*. New York: Norton, 1981.

———. *The Protestant Crusade, 1800–1860: A Study of the Origins of American Nativism* (Chicago: Quadrangle Books, 1964.

Blight, David W. *Race and Reunion: The Civil War in American Memory*. Cambridge, Mass.: Harvard University Press, 2001.

Blodgett, Peter. "Worlds of Wonder and Ambition: Gold Rush California and the Culture of Mining Bonanzas in the North American West." In *A Companion to the Literature and Culture of the American West*, edited by Nicolas Witschi, 29–47. Malden, Mass.: Wiley-Blackwell, 2011.

Boag, Peter. *Re-dressing America's Frontier Past*. Berkeley: University of California Press, 2011.

Bolt, Christine. *Victorian Attitudes to Race*. Toronto: University of Toronto Press, 1971.

Borthwick, John David. *The Gold Hunters: A First Hand Picture of Life in California Mining Camps in the Early Fifties*. Edited by Horace Kephart. 1857. Reprint, New York: International Fiction Library, 1917.

Bottoms, D. Michael. *An Aristocracy of Color: Race and Reconstruction in California and the West, 1850–1890*. Norman: University of Oklahoma Press, 2013.

Bowen, William A. *The Willamette Valley: Migration and Settlement on the Oregon Frontier*. Seattle: University of Washington Press, 1978.

Bowles, Samuel. *Our New West: Records of Travel between the Mississippi River and the Pacific Ocean; over the Plains—over the Mountains—through the Great Interior Basin—over the Sierra Nevada—to and Up and Down the Pacific Coast; with Details of the Wonderful Natural Scenery, Agriculture, Mines, Business, Social Life, Progress, and Prospects . . . Including a Full Description of the Pacific Railroad; and of the Life of the Mormons, Indians, and Chinese; with Map, Portraits, and Twelve Full Page Illustrations*. Hartford, Conn.: Hartford Publishing, 1869.

Brands, H. W. *The Age of Gold: The California Gold Rush and the New American Dream*. New York: Doubleday, 2002.

Brechin, Gray A. *Imperial San Francisco: Urban Power, Earthly Ruin*. Berkeley: University of California Press, 1999.

Brown, Kathleen M. *Good Wives, Nasty Wenches, and Anxious Patriarchs: Gender, Race, and Power in Colonial Virginia*. Chapel Hill: Published for the Institute of Early American History and Culture by the University of North Carolina Press, 1996.

Brown, Richard Maxwell. *Strain of Violence: Historical Studies of American Violence and Vigilantism*. New York: Oxford University Press, 1975.

Browne, J. Ross. *Crusoe's Island: A Ramble in the Footsteps of Alexander Selkirk; with Sketches of Adventure in California and Washoe*. New York: Harper & Brothers, 1864.

———— *Report of the Debates in the Convention of California on the Formation of the State Constitution in September and October, 1849*. Washington, D.C.: Jon T. Towers, 1850.

Bruff, Joseph Goldsborough. *Gold Rush: The Journals, Drawings and Other Papers of J. Goldsborough Bruff, Captain, Washington City and California Mining Association, April 2, 1849–July 20, 1851*. Edited by Georgia Willis Read, Ruth Louise Gaines, and Frederick Webb Hodge. New York: Columbia University Press, 1949.

Buckbee, Edna Bryan. *The Saga of Old Tuolumne*. New York: Press of the Pioneers, 1935.

Buffum, E. Gould. *Six Months in the Gold Mines*. 1850. Reprint, Ann Arbor: University of Michigan Press, 1966.

Burchell, R. A. *The San Francisco Irish, 1848–1880*. Manchester, U.K.: Manchester University Press, 1979.

Burns, John, and Richard J. Orsi. *Taming the Elephant: Politics, Government, and Law in Pioneer California*. Berkeley: University of California Press, 2003.

Bushby, Arthur Thomas. "The Journal of Arthur Thomas Bushby, 1858–1859." *British Columbia Historical Quarterly* 21, no. 1 (January 1957): 101–57.

California State Legislature. *The Statutes of California, First Session of the Legislature, 1849–1850*. San Jose, Calif.: J. Winchester, State Printer, 1850.

Campbell, Malcolm. *Ireland's New Worlds: Immigrants, Politics, and Society in the United States and Australia, 1815–1922*. Madison: University of Wisconsin Press, 2007.

Canfield, Chauncey L. *The Diary of a Forty-Niner*. Boston: Houghton Mifflin, 1920.

Capron, Elisha Smith. *History of California, from Its Discovery to the Present Time: Comprising Also a Full Description of Its Climate, Surface, Soil, Rivers, Towns,*

Beasts, Birds, Fishes, State of its Society, Agriculture, Commerce, Mines, Mining, &c., with a Journal of the Voyage from New York, via Nicaragua, to San Francisco, and Back, via Panama. Cleveland, Ohio: Jewett, Proctor and Worthington, 1854.

Cariboo: The Newly Discovered Gold Fields of British Columbia. Fairfield, Wash.: Ye Galleon Press, 1975.

Carnes, Mark C. Secret Ritual and Manhood in Victorian America. New Haven, Conn.: Yale University Press, 1989.

Carnes, Mark C., and Clyde Griffen. Meanings for Manhood: Constructions of Masculinity in Victorian America. Chicago: University of Chicago Press, 1990.

Carr, John. Pioneer Days in California: Historical and Personal Sketches. Eureka, Calif.: Times Publishing, 1891.

Carson, James H. Early Recollections of the Mines, and a Description of the Great Tulare Valley. Stockton, Calif.: published to accompany the steamer edition of the "San Joaquin Republican," 1852.

Champness, W. To Cariboo and Back. London: Religious Tract Society, 1865.

Chaudhuri, Nupur, and Margaret Strobel, eds. Western Women and Imperialism: Complicity and Resistance. Bloomington: Indiana University Press, 1992.

Chen, Yong. Chinese San Francisco, 1850–1943: A Trans-Pacific Community. Asian America series. Stanford, Calif.: Stanford University Press, 2000.

Chilton, Lisa. Agents of Empire: British Female Migration to Canada and Australia, 1860s–1930. Toronto: University of Toronto Press, 2007.

Clappe, Louise Amelia Knapp. California in 1851: The Letters of Dame Shirley. Edited by Carl Wheat. San Francisco: Grabhorn Press, 1933.

———. The Shirley Letters from California Mines in 1851–52: Being a Series of Twenty-Three Letters from Dame Shirley (Mrs. Louise Amelia Knapp Smith Clappe) to Her Sister in Massachusetts, and Now Reprinted from the Pioneer Magazine of 1854–55; with Synopses of the Letters, a Foreword, and Many Typographical and Other Corrections and Emendations, by Thomas C. Russell. San Francisco: Thomas C. Russell, 1922.

Coblentz, Stanton. Villains and Vigilantes: The Story of James King, of William, and Pioneer Justice in California. New York: Wilson-Erickson, 1936.

Cohn, Bernard. Colonialism and Its Forms of Knowledge: The British in India. Princeton, N.J.: Princeton University Press, 1996.

Colton, Walter. Three Years in California [1846–49]. New York: A. S. Barnes, 1850.

Cooper, Frederick, and Ann Laura Stoler. Tensions of Empire: Colonial Cultures in a Bourgeois World. Berkeley: University of California Press, 1997.

Cornwallis, Kinahan. The New El Dorado; or, British Columbia. London: Thomas Cautley Newby, 1858.

Courtwright, David T. *Violent Land: Single Men and Social Disorder from the Frontier to the Inner City*. Cambridge, Mass.: Harvard University Press, 1996.

Cracroft, Sophia. *Lady Franklin Visits the Pacific Northwest: Being Extracts from the Letters of Miss Sophia Cracroft, Sir John Franklin's Niece, February to April 1861 and April to July 1870*. Victoria, B.C.: [Provincial Archives of British Columbia], 1974.

Crosby, Elisha Oscar. *Memoirs of Elisha Oscar Crosby: Reminiscences of California and Guatemala from 1849 to 1864*. Edited by Charles A. Barker. San Marino, Calif.: Huntington Library, 1945.

Cunliffe, Marcus. *Chattel Slavery and Wage Slavery: The Anglo-American Context, 1830–1860*. Athens: University of Georgia Press, 1979.

Curry, Richard Orr, and Thomas M. Brown. *Conspiracy: The Fear of Subversion in American History*. New York: Holt, Rinehart and Winston, 1972.

Dain, Bruce R. *A Hideous Monster of the Mind: American Race Theory in the Early Republic*. Cambridge, Mass.: Harvard University Press, 2002.

Dana, Richard Henry. *Two Years before the Mast and Other Voyages*. New York: Library of America, 2005.

Darwin, Charles. *The Origin of Species by Means of Natural Selection, or, The Preservation of Favored Races in the Struggle for Life*. New York: D. Appleton, 1896.

Davis, Stephen Chapin. *California Gold Rush Merchant: The Journal of Stephen Chapin Davis*. San Marino, Calif.: Huntington Library, 1956.

Decker, Peter. *The Diaries of Peter Decker: Overland to California in 1849 and Life in the Mines, 1850–1851*. Edited by Helen S. Giffen. Georgetown, Calif.: Talisman Press, 1966.

Defoe, Daniel. *The Life and Strange Surprising Adventures of Robinson Crusoe*. 1719. Reprint, New York: Grossett & Dunlap, 1946.

DeGuzmán, María. *Spain's Long Shadow: The Black Legend, Off-Whiteness, and Anglo-American Empire*. Minneapolis: University of Minnesota Press, 2005.

Delano, Alonzo. *A Live Woman in the Mines, or, Pike County Ahead!* 1857. Reprint, Cambridge: ProQuest Information and Learning Company, 2003.

———. *Pen Knife Sketches; or, Chips of the Old Block, a Series of Original Illustrated Letters, Written by One of California's Pioneer Miners*. Sacramento, Calif.: Published at the Union office, 1853.

———. *To California by Sea: A Maritime History of the California Gold Rush*. Columbia: University of South Carolina Press, 1990.

Delgado, James. *To California by Sea: A Maritime History of the California Gold Rush*. Columbia: University of South Carolina Press, 1990.

de Massey, Ernest. *A Frenchman in the Gold Rush: The Journal of Ernest de Massey, Argonaut of 1849*. Edited by Marguerite Eyer Wilber. San Francisco: California Historical Society, 1927.

de Russailh, Albert Benard. *Last Adventure: San Francisco in 1851; Translated from the Original Journal of Albert Benard de Russailh by Clarkson Crane*. Edited by Clarkson Crane. San Francisco: Westgate Press, 1931.

Dilsaver, Larry M. "After the Gold Rush." *Geographical Review* 75, no. 1 (January 1985): 1–18.

Domer, John. *New British Gold Fields: A Guide to British Columbia and Vancouver with Coloured Map Showing the Gold and Coal Fields, Constructed from Authentic Sources*. London: Hugh Barclay, 1858.

Doten, Alfred. *The Journals of Alfred Doten, 1849–1903*. Edited by Walter Van Tilburg Clark. Reno: University of Nevada Press, 1973.

Downie, William. *Hunting for Gold: Reminisences [sic] of Personal Experience and Research in the Early Days of the Pacific Coast from Alaska to Panama*. San Francisco: California Publishing, 1893.

Downs, Art. *Wagon Road North The Story of the Cariboo Gold Rush in Historical Photos*. Quesnel, B.C.: Northwest Digest, 1960.

Driesbach, Janice Tolhurst, Harvey Jones, and Katherine Church Holland. *Art of the Gold Rush*. Berkeley: University of California Press; Oakland: Oakland Museum; Sacramento: Crocker Art Museum, 1998.

Dubois, Ellen Carol, and Vicki Ruiz, eds. *Unequal Sisters: A Multi-Cultural Reader in U.S. Women's History*. New York: Routledge, 1990.

Dummitt, Chris. *The Manly Modern: Masculinity in Postwar Canada*. Sexuality Studies Series. Vancouver: University of British Columbia Press, 2007.

Dyer, Richard. *White*. New York: Routledge, 1997.

Ebrey, Patricia. *The Cambridge Illustrated History of China*. New York: Cambridge University Press, 2010.

Edelblute, Lucius A. *A True Story of the Adventures of Cariboo Ed in the Far West*. Bountiful, Utah: Family History Publishers, 1998.

Eldridge, C. C., ed. *British Imperialism in the Nineteenth Century*. London: Macmillan, 1984.

Ellison, William Henry. *A Self-Governing Dominion: California, 1849–1860*. Chronicles of California. Berkeley: University of California Press, 1950.

Erie, Steven P. *Rainbow's End: Irish-Americans and the Dilemmas of Urban Machine Politics, 1840–1985*. Berkeley: University of California Press, 1988.

Ethington, Philip J. *The Public City: The Political Construction of Urban Life in San Francisco, 1850–1900*. New York: Cambridge University Press, 1994.

Eyal, Yonatan. *The Young America Movement and the Transformation of the Democratic Party, 1828–61*. New York: Cambridge University Press, 2007.

Fabian, Ann. *Card Sharps and Bucket Shops: Gambling in Nineteenth-Century America*. New York: Routledge, 1999.

Faragher, John Mack. *Women and Men on the Overland Trail*. Yale Historical Publications: Miscellany 121. New Haven, Conn.: Yale University Press, 1979.

Farnham, Eliza W. *California, In-doors and Out; or, How We Farm, Mine, and Live Generally in the Golden State*. New York: Dix, Edwards, 1856.

Faust, Drew Gilpin. *James Henry Hammond and the Old South: A Design for Mastery*. Baton Rouge: Louisiana State University Press, 1982.

———. *This Republic of Suffering: Death and the American Civil War*. New York: Alfred A. Knopf, 2008.

Fawcett, Edgar. *Some Reminiscences of Old Victoria*. Toronto: W. Briggs, 1912.

Fetherling, George. *The Gold Crusades: A Social History of Gold Rushes, 1849–1929*. Toronto: University of Toronto Press, 1997.

Findlay, John M. *People of Chance: Gambling in American Society, from Jamestown to Las Vegas*. New York: Oxford University Press, 1986.

Fischer, Gayle V. *Pantaloons and Power: Nineteenth-Century Dress Reform in the United States*. Kent, Ohio: Kent State University Press, 2001.

Fisher, Robin. *Contact and Conflict: Indian-European Relations in British Columbia, 1774–1890*. Vancouver: University of British Columbia Press, 1992.

Foner, Eric. *Free Soil, Free Labor, Free Men: The Ideology of the Republican Party before the Civil War*. New York: Oxford University Press, 1995.

———. *Reconstruction: America's Unfinished Revolution, 1863–1877*. New York: Harper & Row, 1988.

Forsythe, Mark, and Greg Dickson. *The Trail of 1858: British Columbia's Gold Rush Past*. Madeira Park, B.C.: Harbour Publishing, 2007.

Frémont, John Charles, John Torrey, and James Hall. *Report of the Exploring Expedition to the Rocky Mountains in the Year 1842, and to Oregon and North California in the Years 1843–44*. Washington, D.C.: Gales and Seaton, printers, 1845.

Friend, Craig Thompson, and Lorri Glover. *Southern Manhood: Perspectives on Masculinity in the Old South*. Athens: University of Georgia Press, 2004.

Furniss, Elizabeth. *Dakelh Keyoh: The Southern Carrier in Earlier Times*. Quesnel, B.C.: Quesnel School District no. 28, 1993.

Furniss, Norman F. *The Mormon Conflict, 1850–1859*. New Haven, Conn.: Yale University Press, 1960.

Gallay, Allan. *The Indian Slave Trade: The Rise of the English Empire in the American South, 1670–1717*. New Haven, Conn.: Yale University Press, 2002.

Galois, Robert M. "Gold Mining and Its Effects on Landscapes of the Cariboo." Master's thesis, University of Calgary, 1972.

Gardiner, Howard C. *In Pursuit of the Golden Dream: Reminiscences of San Francisco and the Northern and Southern Mines, 1849–1857*. Edited by Dale Lowell Morgan. Stoughton, Mass.: Western Hemisphere, 1970.

Gerstäcker, Friedrich. *Scenes of Life in California*. Translated by George Cosgrave and Gustave Revilliod. 1856. Reprint, San Francisco: J. Howell, 1942.

Gibbs, Mifflin W. *Shadow and Light: An Autobiography*. New York: Arno Press and New York Times, 1968.

Gilmore, Glenda. *Gender and Jim Crow: Women and the Politics of White Supremacy in North Carolina, 1896–1920*. Chapel Hill: University of North Carolina Press, 1996.

Glaab, Charles Nelson, and A. Theodore Brown. *A History of Urban America*. New York: Macmillan, 1967.

Glare, P. G. W. *Oxford Latin Dictionary*. Oxford: Oxford University Press, 2007.

Gonzales-Day, Ken. *Lynching in the West, 1850–1935*. Durham, N.C.: Duke University Press, 2006.

Goodman, David. *Gold Seeking: Victoria and California in the 1850s*. Stanford, Calif.: Stanford University Press, 1994.

Gordon, Linda. *The Great Arizona Orphan Abduction*. Cambridge, Mass.: Harvard University Press, 1999.

Gossett, Thomas F. *Race: The History of an Idea in America*. Dallas, Tex.: Southern Methodist University Press, 1963.

Gould, Stephen Jay. *The Mismeasure of Man*. New York: W. W. Norton, 1981.

Grant, Robert. *Representations of British Emigration, Colonisation, and Settlement: Imagining Empire, 1800–1860*. Houndmills, Basingstoke, Hampshire: Palgrave Macmillan, 2005.

Great Britain, Emigration Commission. "Colonization Circular," no. 26. G. E. Eyre and W. Spottiswoode for H. M. Stationary Office, 1866.

Green, Rayna. "The Pocahontas Perplex: The Image of Indian Women in American Culture." *Massachusetts Review* 16, no. 4 (Autumn 1975): 698–714.

Greenberg, Amy S. *Manifest Manhood and the Antebellum American Empire*. New York: Cambridge University Press, 2005.

Greenberg, Kenneth S. *Honor and Slavery: Lies, Duels, Noses, Masks, Dressing as a Woman, Gifts, Strangers, Humanitarianism, Death, Slave Rebellions, the Pro-slavery Argument, Baseball, Hunting, and Gambling in the Old South*. Princeton, N.J.: Princeton University Press, 1996.

Gutiérrez, Ramón A., and Richard J. Orsi. *Contested Eden: California before the Gold Rush*. Berkeley: University of California Press, 1998.

Hale, Richard Lunt. *The Log of a Forty-Niner: Journal of a Voyage from Newburyport to San Francisco in the Brig. Genl. Worth, Commanded by Captain Samuel Walton*. Edited by Carolyn Ernestine Hale Russ. Boston: B. J. Brimmer, 1923.

Haley, Bruce. *The Healthy Body and Victorian Culture*. Cambridge, Mass.: Harvard University Press, 1978.

Hall, Catherine. *Civilising Subjects: Colony and Metropole in the English Imagination, 1830–1867.* Chicago: University of Chicago Press, 2002.

———, ed. *Cultures of Empire: Colonizers in Britain and the Empire in the Nineteenth and Twentieth Centuries: A Reader.* New York: Routledge, 2000.

Hall, Catherine, and Sonya O. Rose, eds. *At Home with the Empire: Metropolitan Culture and the Imperial World.* New York: Cambridge University Press, 2006.

Hall, William Henry Harrison. *The Private Letters and Diaries of Captain Hall: An Epic of an Argonaut in the California Gold Rush, Oregon Territories, Civil War, and Oil City.* Edited by Eric Schneirsohn. Glendale, Calif.: London Book Company, 1974.

Halttunen, Karen. *Confidence Men and Painted Women: A Study of Middle-Class Culture in America, 1830–1870.* Yale Historical Publications 129. New Haven, Conn.: Yale University Press, 1982.

Harlow, Neal. *California Conquered: War and Peace on the Pacific, 1846–1850.* Berkeley: University of California Press, 1982.

Harris, Cole. *Making Native Space: Colonialism, Resistance, and Reserves in British Columbia.* Vancouver: University of British Columbia Press, 2002.

Harvey, Charles H. *California Gold Rush: Diary of Charles H. Harvey, February 12–November 12, 1852.* Indianapolis: Indiana Historical Society, 1983.

Hauka, Donald. *McGowan's War.* Vancouver, B.C.: New Star Books, 2003.

Helper, Hinton Rowan. *The Land of Gold, Reality versus Fiction.* Baltimore: H. Taylor, 1855.

Higgins, David. *The Mystic Spring, and Other Tales of Western Life.* Toronto: W. Briggs, 1904.

Hiltebeitel, Alf, and Barbara D. Miller, eds. *Hair: Its Power and Meanings in Asian Cultures.* Albany: State University of New York Press, 1998.

Himmelfarb, Gertrude. *Victorian Minds.* New York: Knopf, 1968.

Holland, R. F., S. E. Stockwell, and A. N. Porter, eds. *Ambiguities of Empire: Essays in Honour of Andrew Porter.* London: Routledge, 2008.

Holliday, J. S. *Rush for Riches: Gold Fever and the Making of California.* Oakland: Oakland Museum of California, 1999.

Horsman, Reginald. *Race and Manifest Destiny: The Origins of American Racial Anglo-Saxonism.* Cambridge, Mass.: Harvard University Press, 1981.

Howay, Frederic. *Early History of the Fraser River Mines.* Victoria, B.C.: C. F. Banfield, 1926.

Howe, Daniel Walker, ed. *Victorian America.* [Philadelphia]: University of Pennsylvania Press, 1976.

Hurtado, Albert L. *Indian Survival on the California Frontier.* Yale Western Americana 35. New Haven, Conn.: Yale University Press, 1988.

Jackson, Alfred T. *The Diary of a Forty-Niner.* Boston: Houghton Mifflin, 1930.

Jacobson, Matthew Frye. *Whiteness of a Different Color: European Immigrants and the Alchemy of Race*. Cambridge, Mass: Harvard University Press, 1998.

Jaksic, Ivan. *The Hispanic World and American Intellectual Life, 1820–1880*. Studies of the Americas. New York: Palgrave Macmillan, 2007.

Johannsen, Robert Walter. *To the Halls of the Montezumas: The Mexican War in the American Imagination*. New York: Oxford University Press, 1985.

Johnson, David Alan. *Founding the Far West: California, Oregon, and Nevada, 1840–1890*. Berkeley: University of California Press, 1992.

Johnson, R. Byron. *Very Far West Indeed: A Few Rough Experiences on the North-West Pacific Coast*. 3rd ed. London: S. Low, Martson, Low & Searle, 1872.

Johnson, Samuel. *A Dictionary of the English Language: In Which the Words Are Deduced from Their Originals, Explained in Their Different Meanings, and Authorized by the Names of the Writers in Whose Works They Are Found*. London: Printed for F. C. and J. Rivington, 1815.

———. *A Dictionary of the English Language: In Which Words Are Deduced from Their Originals; and Illustrated in Their Different Significations, by Examples from the Best Writers; Together with a History of the Language, and an English Grammar*. Vol. 2. London: printed for Longman, Rees, Orme, Brown, and Green et al., 1827.

Johnson, Susan Lee. *Roaring Camp: The Social World of the California Gold Rush*. New York: W. W. Norton, 2000.

Johnson, Theodore T. *Sights in the Gold Region, and Scenes by the Way*. New York: Baker and Scribner, 1849.

Jordan, Winthrop. *White over Black: American Attitudes toward the Negro, 1550–1812*. Chapel Hill: University of North Carolina Press, 1968.

Jung, Moon-Ho. *Coolies and Cane: Race, Labor, and Sugar in the Age of Emancipation*. Baltimore: Johns Hopkins University Press, 2006.

Kasson, John F. *Rudeness and Civility: Manners in Nineteenth-Century Urban America*. New York: Hill and Wang, 1990.

Kelley, Robert. "The Mining Debris Controversy in the Sacramento Valley." *Pacific Historical Review* 25, no. 4 (November 1956): 331–46.

Khan, Ava Fran. *Jewish Voices of the California Gold Rush: A Documentary History, 1849–1880*. Detroit: Wayne State University Press, 2002.

Kilian, Crawford. *Go Do Some Great Thing: The Black Pioneers of British Columbia*. Vancouver, B.C.: Douglas & McIntyre, 1978.

Kingsley, Nelson. *Diary of Nelson Kingsley, a California Argonaut of 1849*. Edited by Frederick Teggart. Berkeley: University of California, 1914.

Kramer, Paul. *The Blood of Government: Race, Empire, the United States, and the Philippines*. Chapel Hill: University of North Carolina Press, 2006.

Krebbs, Paula. *Gender, Race, and the Writing of Empire: Public Discourse and the Boer War*. New York: Cambridge University Press, 1999.

Lai, Chuen-yan David. *Chinatowns: Towns within Cities in Canada*. Vancouver: University of British Columbia Press, 1988.

Lakoff, George. *Women, Fire, and Dangerous Things: What Categories Reveal about the Mind*. Chicago: University of Chicago Press, 1987.

Lamson, Joseph. *Round Cape Horn: Voyage of the Passenger-Ship James W. Paige, from Maine to California in the Year 1852*. Bangor, Maine: Press of O. F. & W. H. Knowles, 1878.

Lane, Christopher. *Hatred and Civility: The Antisocial Life in Victorian England*. New York: Columbia University Press, 2006.

Langworthy, Franklin. *Scenery of the Plains, Mountains and Mines*. Princeton, N.J.: Princeton University Press, 1932.

Lears, T. J. Jackson. *Something for Nothing: Luck in America*. New York: Penguin, 2004.

Leduc, Joanne. *Overland from Canada to British Columbia*. Vancouver: University of British Columbia Press, 1981.

Lemire, Elise Virginia. *"Miscegenation": Making Race in America*. Philadelphia: University of Pennsylvania Press, 2002.

Letts, John M. *A Pictorial View of California: Including a Description of the Panama and Nicaragua Routes, with Information and Advice Interesting to All, Particularly Those Who Intend to Visit the Golden Region, by a Returned Californian*. New York: H. Bill, 1853.

Levine, Philippa, ed. *Gender and Empire*. Oxford History of the British Empire Companion Series. New York: Oxford University Press, 2004.

———. *Prostitution, Race, and Politics: Policing Venereal Disease in the British Empire*. New York: Routledge, 2003.

Lewis, Oscar. *Sea Routes to the Gold Fields: The Migration by Water to California in 1849–1852*. New York: A. A. Knopf, 1949.

Lidell, Henry George, Robert Scott, Henry Stuart Jones, Roderick McKenzie, and Eric Arthur Barber. *A Greek-English Lexicon*. Oxford: Oxford University Press, 1968.

Limerick, Patricia. *The Legacy of Conquest: The Unbroken Past of the American West*. New York: Norton, 1987.

Lindsay, Brendan C. *Murder State: California's Native American Genocide, 1846–1873*. Lincoln: University of Nebraska Press, 2012.

London, Jack. *Smoke Bellew*. New York: Century Company, 1912.

Loo, Tina. *Making Law, Order, and Authority in British Columbia, 1821–1871*. Social History of Canada, no. 50. Toronto: University of Toronto Press, 1994.

López, Ian Haney. *White by Law: The Legal Construction of Race*. New York: New York University Press, 2006.

Lott, Eric. *Love and Theft: Blackface Minstrelsy and the American Working Class*. New York: Oxford University Press, 1993.

Lutz, John. "We Do Not Know His Name." N.d. Canadian Mysteries.ca.

Macfie, Matthew. *Vancouver Island and British Columbia: Their History, Resources, and Prospects*. 1865. Reprint, New York: Arno Press, 1973.

Mackie, Richard. "The Colonization of Vancouver Island, 1849–1858." *BC Studies* 96 (Winter 1992–93): 3–40.

———. *Trading beyond the Mountains: The British Fur Trade on the Pacific, 1793–1843*. Vancouver: University of British Columbia Press, 1997.

Madley, Benjamin. *An American Genocide: The United States and the California Indian Catastrophe, 1846–1873*. Lamar Series in Western History. New Haven, Conn.: Yale University Press, 2016.

Madsen, Brigham D. *Gold Rush Sojourners in Great Salt Lake City, 1849 and 1850*. Salt Lake City: University of Utah Press, 1983.

Malamud, Margaret. *Ancient Rome and Modern America*. Malden, Mass.: Wiley-Blackwell, 2009.

Mangan, J. A., and James Walvin, eds. *Manliness and Morality: Middle-Class Masculinity in Britain and America, 1800–1940*. New York: St. Martin's Press, 1987.

Mann, Ralph. *After the Gold Rush: Society in Grass Valley and Nevada City, California, 1849–1870*. Stanford, Calif.: Stanford University Press, 1982.

Marcus, Steven. *The Other Victorians: A Study of Sexuality and Pornography in Mid-Nineteenth-Century England*. New York: Basic Books, 1966.

Mark, William. *Cariboo: A True and Correct Narrative*. Stockton, U.K.: W. M. Wright, 1863.

Marryat, Frank. *Mountains and Molehills; or, Recollections of a Burnt Journal*. 1855. Reprint, Philadelphia: Lippincott, 1962.

Marshall, Dan. "Claiming the Land: Indians, Goldseekers and the Rush to British Columbia." PhD diss., University of British Columbia, 2000.

Martin, Robert Bernard. *Enter Rumour: Four Early Victorian Scandals*. London: Faber and Faber, 1962.

Mattingly, Carol. *Appropriate[ing] Dress: Women's Rhetorical Style in Nineteenth-Century America*. Carbondale: Southern Illinois University Press, 2002.

Mayne, Richard. *Four Years in British Columbia and Vancouver Island: An Account of Their Forests, Rivers, Coasts, Gold Fields and Resources for Colonisation*. London: John Murray, 1862.

McCall, A. J. *The Great California Trail in 1849, Wayside Notes of an Argonaut . . . Reprinted from the Steuben Courier*. Bath, N.Y.: Steuben Courier Print, 1882.

McClintock, Anne. *Imperial Leather: Race, Gender, and Sexuality in the Colonial Contest*. New York: Routledge, 1995.

M'Collum, William S. *California as I Saw It: Correspondence, Manuscript, Prospectuses; Sherwood Anderson, a Bibliography: Manuscript, 1 letter; Western Reaches: Misc. Items; Early Day Letters from Aurora: Correspondence, Manuscript*. Buffalo, N.Y.: George H. Derby, 1850.

McDiarmid, Finely. *Letters to My Wife*. Fairfield, Wash.: Ye Galleon Press, 1997.

McGuinness, Aims. *Path of Empire: Panama and the California Gold Rush*. The United States in the World. Ithaca, N.Y.: Cornell University Press, 2008.

McKelvey, Blake. *American Urbanization: A Comparative History*. Glenview, Ill.: Scott, Foresman, 1973.

McKinstry, Byron. *The California Gold Rush Overland Diary of Byron McKinstry, 1850–1852*. Glendale, Calif.: A. H. Clark, 1975.

McLaren, John, Hamar Foster, and Chet Orloff, eds. *Law for the Elephant, Law for the Beaver: Essays in the Legal History of the North American West*. Regina, Sask.: Canadian Plains Research Center, 1992.

Megquier, Mary Jane. *Apron Full of Gold: The Letters of Mary Jane Megquier from San Francisco, 1849–1856*. Edited by Robert Glass Cleland. San Marino, Calif.: Huntington Library, 1949.

Meinig, D. W. *The Shaping of America: A Geographical Perspective on 500 Years of History*. Vol. 2. New Haven, Conn.: Yale University Press, 1993.

Melendy, H. Brett, and Benjamin Gilbert, *The Governors of California: Peter H. Burnett to Edmund G. Brown*. Georgetown, Calif.: Talisman Press, 1965.

Miers, David. *Regulating Commercial Gambling: Past, Present, and Future*. New York: Oxford University Press, 2004.

Miller, Edward F. *Ned McGowan's War*. [Don Mills, Ont.]: Burns and MacEachern, 1968.

Miller, Stuart Creighton. *The Unwelcome Immigrant: The American Image of the Chinese, 1785–1882*. Berkeley: University of California Press, 1969.

Monaghan, Jay. *Australians and the Gold Rush: California and Down Under, 1849–1854*. Berkeley: University of California Press, 1966.

Montgomery, David. *The Fall of the House of Labor: The Workplace, the State, and American Labor Activism, 1865–1925*. New York: Cambridge University Press, 1987.

Moody, Richard. "Letter to Arthur Blackwood, 1 February, 1859." *British Columbia Historical Quarterly* 25, nos. 1–2 (January–April 1951): 91–103.

Moore, James. "The Discovery of Hill's Bar in 1858." *British Columbia Historical Quarterly* 3, no. 3 (July 1939): 217–19.

Morgan, Edmund S. "Slavery and Freedom: The American Paradox." *Journal of American History* 59, no. 1 (June 1972): 5–29.

Morgan, Martha. *A Trip across the Plains in the Year 1849; with Notes of a Voyage to California, by Way of Panama; also, Some Spiritual Songs, &c.* San Francisco: Pioneer Press, 1864.

Morison, James. *By Sea to San Francisco, 1849–1850: The Journal of Dr. James Morison.* Memphis, Tenn.: Memphis State University Press, 1977.

Morse, Samuel. *Foreign Conspiracy against the Liberties of the United States: The Numbers of Brutus.* 1835. Reprint, New York: Arno Press, 1977.

Mulford, Prentice. *Prentice Mulford's Story.* Edited by Frederic Remington. 1889. Reprint, Oakland, Calif.: Biobooks, 1953.

Mullen, Kevin. *Dangerous Strangers: Minority Newcomers and Criminal Violence in the Urban West, 1850–2000.* New York: Palgrave, 2005.

Munting, Roger. *An Economic and Social History of Gambling in Britain and the USA.* Manchester, U.K.: Manchester University Press, 1996.

Nash, Linda Lorraine. *Inescapable Ecologies: A History of Environment, Disease, and Knowledge.* Berkeley: University of California Press, 2006.

Navarro, Ramón Gil. *The Gold Rush Diary of Ramón Gil Navarro.* Edited by Maria del Carmen Ferreyra and David Sven Reher. Lincoln: University of Nebraska Press, 2000.

Nelson, Dana D. *National Manhood: Capitalist Citizenship and the Imagined Fraternity of White Men.* New Americanists. Durham, N.C.: Duke University Press, 1998.

Newell, Diane. *Tangled Webs of History: Indians and the Law in Canada's Pacific Coast Fisheries.* Toronto: University of Toronto Press, 1999.

Newsome, David. *The Victorian World Picture: Perceptions and Introspections in an Age of Change.* New Brunswick, N.J.: Rutgers University Press, 1997.

Ngai, Mae M. "The Architecture of Race in American Immigration Law: A Reexamination of the Immigration Act of 1924." *Journal of American History* 86, no. 1 (June 1999): 67–92.

Oldstone-Moore, Christopher. "The Beard Movement in Victorian Britain." *Victorian Studies* 48, no. 1 (Autumn 2005): 7–34.

Ormsby, Margaret. *British Columbia, a History.* Toronto: Macmillan, 1958.

Paddison, Joshua. *American Heathens: Religion, Race, and Reconstruction in California.* Berkeley: University of California Press, 2012.

———. *A World Transformed: Firsthand Accounts of California before the Gold Rush.* Berkeley, Calif.: Heyday Books, 1998.

Palmer, John Williamson. *The New and the Old; or, California and India in Romantic Aspects.* New York: Rudd & Carleton, 1859.

Pancoast, Charles Edward. *A Quaker Forty-Niner: The Adventures of Charles Edward Pancoast on the American Frontier.* Edited by Anna Paschall Hannum. Philadelphia: University of Pennsylvania Press, 1930.

Parke, Charles Ross. *Dreams to Dust: A Diary of the California Gold Rush, 1849–1850*. Edited by James Davis. Lincoln: University of Nebraska Press, 1989.

Parry, John T., ed. *Evil, Law and the State: Perspectives on State Power and Violence*. Amsterdam: Rodopi, 2006.

Parsons, Timothy. *The British Imperial Century, 1815–1914: A World History Perspective*. Lanham, Md.: Rowman & Littlefield, 1999.

Paul, Rodman W. *California Gold: The Beginning of Mining in the Far West*. Cambridge, Mass.: Harvard University Press, 1947.

———. *Mining Frontiers of the Far West, 1848–1880*. New York: Holt, Rinehart and Winston, 1963.

Payson, George. *Golden Dreams and Leaden Realities*. New York: G. P. Putnam, 1853.

Peck, Gunther. *Reinventing Free Labor: Padrones and Immigrant Workers in the North American West, 1880–1930*. New York: Cambridge University Press, 2000.

Peck, Washington. *On the Western Trails: The Overland Diaries of Washington Peck*. Edited by Susan M. Erb. Norman, Okla.: Arthur H. Clark, 2009.

Perry, Adele. *On the Edge of Empire: Gender, Race, and the Making of British Columbia, 1849–1871*. Toronto: University of Toronto Press, 2001.

Pfeifer, Michael J. *Rough Justice: Lynching and American Society, 1874–1947*. Urbana: University of Illinois Press, 2004.

Picard, Liza. *Victorian London: The Life of a City, 1840–1870*. New York: St. Martin's Press, 2006.

Pierce, Jason. *Making the White Man's West: Whiteness and the Creation of the American West*. Boulder: University of Colorado Press, 2016.

Pike, Fredrick B. *The United States and Latin America: Myths and Stereotypes of Civilization and Nature*. Austin: University of Texas Press, 1992.

Pilton, James. "Negro Settlement in British Columbia, 1858–1871." Master's thesis, University of British Columbia, 1951.

Polk, James. "Message to Congress, 5 December, 1848." *Journal of the Senate of the United States of America, 1789–1873*, 13th Cong., 2nd sess., 5 December 1848.

Pomeroy, Earl S. *The Pacific Slope: A History of California, Oregon, Washington, Idaho, Utah, and Nevada*. New York: Knopf, 1965.

Pomfret, John E., Charles Henry Ellis, and John N. Stone. *California Gold Rush Voyages, 1848–1849: Three Original Narratives*. San Marino, Calif.: Huntington Library, 1954.

Poole, Francis. *Queen Charlotte Islands: A Narrative of Discovery and Adventure in the North Pacific*. London: Hurst and Blackett, 1872.

Porsild, Charlene. *Gamblers and Dreamers: Women, Men, and Community in the Klondike*. Vancouver: University of British Columbia Press, 1988.

Prucha, Francis Paul. *The Great Father: The United States Government and the American Indians*. Vols. 1 and 2. Unabridged. Lincoln: University of Nebraska Press, 1984.

Pullman, John. *History of Education in America*. Columbus, Ohio: Merrill, 1982.

Raibmon, Paige. *Authentic Indians: Episodes of Encounter from the Late-Nineteenth-Century Northwest Coast*. Durham, N.C.: Duke University Press, 2005.

Rawls, James J. *Indians of California: The Changing Image*. Norman: University of Oklahoma Press, 1984.

Rawls, James J., Richard J. Orsi, and Marlene Smith-Baranzini, eds. *A Golden State: Mining and Economic Development in Gold Rush California*. Berkeley: University of California Press, 1999.

Reid, Bernard J. *Overland to California with the Pioneer Line: The Gold Rush Diary of Bernard J. Reid*. Edited by Mary McDougall Gordon. Stanford, Calif.: Stanford University Press, 1983.

Reinhart, Herman. *The Golden Frontier: The Recollections of Herman Francis Reinhart, 1851–1869*. Austin: University of Texas Press, 1962.

Reinhold, Meyer. *Classica Americana: The Greek and Roman Heritage in the United States*. Detroit: Wayne State University Press, 1984.

Rickard, T. A. "Indian Participation in the Gold Discoveries." *British Columbia Historical Quarterly* 2, no. 1 (January 1938): 3–18.

Riley, Glenda. *Confronting Race: Women and Indians on the Frontier, 1815–1915*. Albuquerque: University of New Mexico Press, 2004.

Roach-Higgins, Mary Ellen, Joanne Bubolz Eicher, and Kim K. P. Johnson, eds. *Dress and Identity*. New York: Fairchild, 1995.

Roberts, Brian. *American Alchemy: The California Gold Rush and Middle-Class Culture*. Chapel Hill: University of North Carolina Press, 2000.

Roediger, David R. *The Wages of Whiteness: Race and the Making of the American Working Class*. London: Verso, 1999.

———. *Working toward Whiteness: How America's Immigrants Became White; The Strange Journey from Ellis Island to the Suburbs*. New York: Basic Books, 2005.

Rohrbough, Malcolm J. *Days of Gold: The California Gold Rush and the American Nation*. Berkeley: University of California Press, 1997.

Roosevelt, Theodore. *Ranch Life and the Hunting-Trail*. 1888. Reprint, Ann Arbor, MI: University Microfilms, 1966.

Roske, Ralph J. "The World Impact of the California Gold Rush, 1849–1857." *Arizona and the West* 5, no. 3 (Autumn 1963): 187–232.

Rotundo, E. Anthony. *American Manhood: Transformations in Masculinity from the Revolution to the Modern Era*. New York: Basic Books, 1993.

Royce, Josiah. *California, from the Conquest in 1846 to the Second Vigilance Committee in San Francisco: A Study of American Character*. Edited by Robert Glass Cleland. New York: A. A. Knopf, 1948.

Royce, Sarah Bayliss. *A Frontier Lady: Recollections of the Gold Rush and Early California*. Edited by Ralph Henry Gabriel. New Haven, Conn.: Yale University Press, 1932.

Rozwadowski, Helen M. *Fathoming the Ocean: The Discovery and Exploration of the Deep Sea*. Cambridge, Mass: Belknap Press of Harvard University Press, 2005.

Ryan, William Redmond. *Personal Adventures in Upper and Lower California, in 1848–9*. 2 vols. New York: Arno Press, 1973.

Sandage, Scott. *Born Losers: A History of Failure in America*. Cambridge, Mass.: Harvard University Press, 2005.

Saum, Lewis O. *The Popular Mood of Pre–Civil War America*. Westport, Conn: Greenwood Press, 1980.

Sawyer, Lorenzo. *Way Sketches: Containing Incidents of Travel across the Plains from St. Joseph to California in 1850, with Letters Describing Life and Conditions in the Gold Region*. Edited by Edward Eberstadt. New York: E. Eberstadt, 1926.

Saxton, Alexander. *The Rise and Fall of the White Republic: Class Politics and Mass Culture in Nineteenth-Century America*. London: Verso, 1990.

Scholefield, E. O. S. *British Columbia from the Earliest Times to the Present*. Vol. 1. Vancouver: S. J. Clarke, 1914.

Seacole, Mary. *Wonderful Adventures of Mrs. Seacole in Many Lands*. 1857. Reprint, New York: Oxford University Press, 1988.

Sears, Clare. "All That Glitters: Trans-ing California's Gold Rush Migrations." *GLQ: A Journal of Lesbian and Gay Studies* 14, nos. 2–3 (2008): 383–402.

Seltz, Jennifer. "Embodying Nature: Health, Place, and Identity in Nineteenth-Century America." PhD diss., University of Washington, 2005.

Senkewicz, Robert M. *Vigilantes in Gold Rush San Francisco*. Stanford, Calif.: Stanford University Press, 1985.

Shah, Nayan. *Contagious Divides: Epidemics and Race in San Francisco's Chinatown*. Berkeley: University of California Press, 2001.

Shaw, Pringle. *Ramblings in California: Containing a Description of the Country, Life at the Mines, State of Society, &c.; Interspersed with Characteristic Anecdotes, and Sketches from Life*. Toronto: J. Bain, [1856?].

Shaw, William. *Golden Dreams and Waking Realities: Being the Adventures of a Gold-Seeker in California and the Pacific Islands*. London: Smith, Elder, 1851.

Shelton, W. George. *British Columbia and Confederation*. Victoria, B.C.: published for the University of Victoria by the Morriss Print Co., 1967.

Shinn, Charles Howard. *Mining Camps: A Study in American Frontier Government.* New York: Charles Scribner's Sons, 1885. Reprint, New York: Harper & Row, 1965.

Smith, Andrea. *Conquest: Sexual Violence and American Indian Genocide.* Cambridge, Mass.: South End Press, 2005.

Smith, Azariah. *The Gold Discovery Journal of Azariah Smith.* Edited by John Bigler. Logan: Utah State University Press, 1996.

Smith, Catherine, and Cynthia Greig. *Women in Pants: Manly Maidens, Cowgirls, and Other Renegades.* New York: H. N. Abrams, 2003.

Smith, Stacey. *Freedom's Frontier: California and the Struggle over Unfree Labor, Emancipation, and Reconstruction.* Chapel Hill: University of North Carolina Press, 2013.

Soulé, Frank. *The Annals of San Francisco: Containing a Summary of the History of . . .* California, and a Complete History of . . . Its Great City. New York: Appleton, 1855.

Spence, Jonathan. *The Search for Modern China.* New York: Norton, 1990.

Spickard, Paul R. *Almost All Aliens: Immigration, Race, and Colonialism in American History and Identity.* New York: Routledge, 2007.

Stannard, M. *Memoirs of a Professional Lady Nurse.* London: Simpkin, Marshall, 1873.

Stanton, William Ragan. *The Leopard's Spots: Scientific Attitudes toward Race in America, 1815–59.* [Chicago]: University of Chicago Press, 1960.

Starr, Kevin, and Richard J. Orsi, eds. *Rooted in Barbarous Soil: People, Culture, and Community in Gold Rush California.* Berkeley: University of California Press, 2000.

Stepan, Nancy. *The Idea of Race in Science: Great Britain, 1800–1960.* Hamden, Conn.: Archon Books, 1982.

Stephens, John Lloyd. *Incidents of Travel in Central America, Chiapas and Yucatan.* 1841. Reprint, New York: Dover, 1969.

Stevens, Errol Wayne. *Incidents of a Voyage to California, 1849: A Diary Aboard the Bark Hersilia, and in Sacramento, 1850.* Los Angeles: Western History Association, 1987.

Stillson, Richard T. *Spreading the Word: A History of Information in the California Gold Rush.* Lincoln: University of Nebraska Press, 2006.

Stokes, Melvyn, and Stephen Conway. *The Market Revolution in America: Social, Political, and Religious Expressions, 1800–1880.* Charlottesville: University Press of Virginia, 1996.

Stoler, Ann Laura. *Carnal Knowledge and Imperial Power: Race and the Intimate in Colonial Rule.* Berkeley: University of California Press, 2002.

Taleb, Nassim. *The Black Swan: The Impact of the Highly Improbable*. New York: Random House, 2007.

Taniguchi, Nancy. *Dirty Deeds: Land, Violence, and the 1856 San Francisco Vigilance Committee*. Norman: University of Oklahoma Press, 2016.

Tate, Michael L. *Indians and Emigrants: Encounters on the Overland Trails*. Norman: University of Oklahoma Press, 2006.

Taylor, Bayard. *Eldorado; or, Adventures in the Path of Empire, Comprising a Voyage to California, via Panama; Life in San Francisco and Monterey; Pictures of the Gold Region, and Experiences of Mexican Travel*. New York: G. P. Putnam's Sons, 1879.

Taylor, Quintard. *In Search of the Racial Frontier: African Americans in the American West, 1528–1990*. New York: W. W. Norton, 1998.

Taylor, William. *California Life Illustrated*. New York: Carlton & Porter, 1860.

Terry, David. *Trial of David S. Terry by the Committee of Vigilance, San Francisco*. San Francisco: R. C. Moore, 1856.

Thomson, Guy P. C., ed. *The European Revolutions of 1848 and the Americas*. London: Institute of Latin American Studies, 2002.

Tosh, John. *A Man's Place: Masculinity and the Middle-Class Home in Victorian England*. New Haven, Conn.: Yale University Press, 1999.

Trafzer, Clifford, and Joel Hyer, eds. *Exterminate Them: Written Accounts of the Murder, Rape, and Slavery of Native Americans during the California Gold Rush, 1848–1868*. East Lansing: Michigan State University Press, 1999.

Treaty of Guadalupe Hidalgo [exchange copy], February 2, 1848 [Electronic Records], Perfected Treaties, 1778–1945, Record Group 11, General Records of the United States Government, 1778–1992, National Archives.

Trowbridge, J. T., Lucy Larcom, and Gail Hamilton, eds. *Our Young Folks*. Vols. 1–9. Boston: Ticknor and Fields [James R. Osgood and Company], 1865–73.

Unruh, John David. *The Plains Across: The Overland Emigrants and the Trans-Mississippi West, 1840–1860*. Urbana: University of Illinois Press, 1979.

Vancouver Island. "An Act to Provide for the Naturalization of Aliens, 1861." In *A Collection of the Public General Statues of the Colony of Vancouver Island, Passed in the Year 1859, 1860, 1861, 1862, and 1863*. Victoria: British Colonist Office, 1866.

Van Kirk, Sylvia. "Tracing the Fortunes of Five Founding Families of Victoria." *BC Studies*, 115-16 (Autumn–Winter 1997–98): 149–79.

Van Vugt, William E. *Britain to America: Mid-Nineteenth-Century Immigrants to the United States*. Urbana: University of Illinois Press, 1999.

Veracini, Lorenzo. *Settler Colonialism: A Theoretical Overview*. New York: Palgrave Macmillan, 2010.

Verney, Edmund Hope. *Vancouver Island Letters of Edmund Hope Verney, 1862–65*. Edited by Allan Pritchard. Vancouver: University of British Columbia Press, 1996.

Wakefield, Edward. *The Collected Works of Edward Gibbon Wakefield*. Edited by Muriel F. Lloyd Prichard. Glasgow: Colins, 1968.

———. *A View of the Art of Colonization, with Present Reference to the British Empire: In Letters between a Statesman and a Colonist*. Kitchener, Ont.: Batoche Books, 2001.

Waldrep, Christopher. *The Many Faces of Judge Lynch: Extralegal Violence and Punishment in America*. New York: Palgrave Macmillan, 2002.

Ward, W. Peter. *White Canada Forever: Popular Attitudes and Public Policy toward Orientals in British Columbia*. Montreal: McGill-Queen's University Press, 1978.

Waters, Hazel. *Racism on the Victorian Stage: Representation of Slavery and the Black Character*. Cambridge: Cambridge University Press, 2007.

Webster, Noah. *An American Dictionary of the English Language: Containing the Whole Vocabulary of the First Edition in Two Volumes Quarto; the Entire Corrections and Improvements of the Second Edition in Two Volumes Royal Octavo; to Which Is Prefixed an Introductory Dissertation on the Origin, History, and Connection, of the Languages of Western Asia and Europe, with an Explanation of the Principles on Which Languages Are Formed*. Springfield, Mass.: George and Charles Merriam, 1855.

———. *An American Dictionary of the English Language Exhibiting the Origin, Orthography, Pronunciation, and Definitions of Words . . .* Springfield, Mass.: Merriam, 1853.

Webster, Noah, and Noah Parker. *An American Dictionary of the English Language: Containing the Whole Vocabulary of the First Edition . . . the Entire Corrections and Improvements of the Second Edition . . . to Which Is Prefixed an Introductory Dissertation on the Origin, History, and Connection, of the Languages of Western Asia and Europe, with an Explanation of the Principles on Which Languages Are Formed*. Springfield, Mass.: George and Charles Merriam, 1856.

West, Elliott. *Growing Up with the Country: Childhood on the Far-Western Frontier*. Histories of the American Frontier. Albuquerque: University of New Mexico Press, 1989.

Weston, Silas. *Life in the Mountains; or, Four Months in the Mines of California*. Providence, R.I.: B. T. Albro, 1854.

Wheat, Carl I. "Ned, the Ubiquitous." *California Historical Society Quarterly* 6, no. 1 (March 1927): 3–36.

White, Richard. *"It's Your Misfortune and None of My Own": A History of the American West*. Norman: University of Oklahoma Press, 1991.

Wierzbicki, Felix Paul. *California as It Is and as It May Be; or, A Guide to the Gold Region*. 1849. Reprint, New York: Grabhorn Press, 1970.

Wilentz, Sean. *Chants Democratic: New York City and the Rise of the American Working Class, 1788–1850.* New York: Oxford University Press, 1986.

Wingate, Benjamin. *Uncertain Country: The Wingate Letters, San Francisco, California—Meriden, New Hampshire, 1851–1854.* Edited by Stephen Vincent. Berkeley, Calif.: Friends of the Bancroft Library, 2000.

Winks, Robin. *The Blacks in Canada: A History.* Buffalo, N.Y.: McGill-Queen's University Press, 1997.

Wolfe, Patrick. *Settler Colonialism and the Transformation of Anthropology: The Politics and Poetics of an Ethnographic Event.* New York: Cassell, 1999.

Wood, Gordon S. *The Creation of the American Republic, 1776–1787.* Chapel Hill: Published for the Institute of Early American History and Culture at Williamsburg, Va., by the University of North Carolina Press, 1969.

Woods, Robert. *The Demography of Victorian England and Wales.* Cambridge: Cambridge University Press, 2000.

Young, G. M. *Victorian England: Portrait of an Age.* 2nd ed. New York: Oxford University Press, 1953.

Zakim, Michael. *Ready-Made Democracy: A History of Men's Dress in the American Republic, 1760–1860.* Chicago: University of Chicago Press, 2003.

INDEX

A

aboriginals. *See* indigenous peoples

Act for the Government and Protection of the Indians (1850), 60

African Americans. *See* African descent, people of

African Canadians. *See* African descent, people of

African descent, people of: and Americans, 83; Aurora-Davis dispute, 105–7; black bodies, 7; colonialism, 61, 78, 82, 93, 96–97; colorblindness, 79, 104; cross-dressing, 146; dandy, 140*fig.*, 141; economic threat of, 50, 55; effeminate, 26; gambling, 120–21; indigenous peoples and, 149–51; jokes about, 30–31, 44; juries, 100; lucky, 113; Panamanians, 35–37; resistance to colonialism, 93–94, 96, 98–99, 106–8, 166; segregation in British Columbia, 93–96; slavery, 20, 32–33, 49; stereotypes, 8, 22, 50; threat to republicanism, 44–52, 61; terminology, 205n25; voting, 49–50, 97–100, 107–8, 168

Alta California: on beards, 138–39; on bloomers, 149; on Chinese people, 149, 153, 155; on the Hounds, 65–67; on immigrants, 66–67; on the Vigilance Committee (1856), 70–74, 159–60; on white women, 152

appearance. *See* bodies; dress

Argonauts: characteristics, 19–23; Chinese people and, 40–41; colonialism, 17–19; definition, 14, 17; expertise, 26; Latin American built environment, 34–35, 36; Latin American environment, 32; Latin Americans and, 32–33, 35–36; leisure, 27–29; organization, 23–25; practical jokes, 30–31; San Francisco, 37–40; Victoria, 43. *See also* Incidente de la Tajada de Sandia; Overlanders

Aurora Company, 105–6

Australians: immigrants, 58, 74, 141; as off-white, 66; supposed criminality, 54, 65–67, 68–70; terminology, 198nn121,123; Vigilance Committee (1851) and, 68–70

B

Barkerville, 129, 146

Begbie, Matthew Baillie, 82–83, 90–92, 104–7, 132

Birch, Arthur, 39, 103

black settlers: *See* African descent, people of

Blanshard, Richard, 80, 204n13

bodies: and character, 16, 135, 136–37, 161–62; Chinese, 150–53; hardened, 112, 119, 141–43; masculinity, 165–67; physical hardships, 128–29; racial characteristics and, 145, 150–53; sickness, 112, 153–58. *See also* death and dying; dress

Bowen, Ben, 56

Brace, Philander, 159–61

Brannan, Samuel, 64, 67–70

Brew, Chartres, 90, 92, 101, 103

British people: and African descent, people of, 78–79, 82, 83, 93, 95, 97, 100, 106–8; as

British people (*continued*)
Argonauts, 24–25; attitudes toward
Americans, 36–37, 39–40, 44–45, 81–
82, 83, 89, 91–92; beards, 138; British
Empire, 42; Chinese people and, 40–
41; gambling, 131–33; in Great Britain, 5;
the Hounds and, 63; indigenous peoples
and, 44–45; values, 5–8, 9, 78–82, 166;
Welsh, 5, 141; white women, 42. *See also*
Irish people
Buckley, Cecil, 24–25, 36–37

C
California Constitutional Convention,
Monterey, 49–52
Californio. *See* Hispanic peoples
Cariboo: Anderson, James, 125; beards, 145;
executions in, 160; gambling in, 132; gold
discovery, 126; isolation of, 100, 126–29;
mining region, 41, 105, 107, 129, 131
Casey, James, 71
Catholicism, 21–22, 47, 73
Champness, W., 40, 128, 143, 159
chance: and character, 111–15, 122–23; definition, 110; and failure, 112–14, 122–23;
gambling, 15, 119; mining, 15, 109–13, 115,
129. *See also* gambling; risk; work-reward
relationship
Chilean Gulch, 56
Chileans. *See* Hispanic peoples
Chilean War, 56–57
Chinese people: appearance, 152–53; changing
views of, 58; Chinatown, 41, 44, 153–55; as
colonized subjects, 49, 52, 55, 59, 79, 100,
149, 156, 166; death and dying, 159; disease,
153–56; as economic threat, 55, 56, 58, 116,
130; Fraser River War, 86, 88; gambling,
133; immigration (1852), 58–59; mining
licenses, 58; resistance to colonialism, 11,
41, 56, 166; as risk-averse, 116, 130; white
commentary on, 40–41, 56, 58
Civil War, American, 39, 43, 108, 158, 165
Clarke, William, 94–95

colonialism: and African descent, people of,
50; Chinese people and, 58, 116; class and,
5–8; competing visions of, 49–58, 93–97;
and control over mining, 52–61; Foreign
Miner's Tax and, 54, 58; and gender, 4–9,
11–12; gold rush as watershed moment
for, 9, 11; gold rush society and, 3–4, 46–
47; Hispanic peoples and, 32–33, 36; indigenous peoples and, 33, 36, 44, 50–51, 59–
60, 85, 101, 150, 151; individual emphasized
in, 27; off-whites and, 62, 65; and race,
4–9, 46–47, 49, 50, 60–61, 74, 93, 150, 151;
resistance to, 54–55, 58; San Francisco,
62; settler colonialism, 9, 11, 46, 152, 163;
transnational, 8–9, 10–11; Wakefield,
Edward, 80–81; westward migration as
training for, 14, 17–18, 27, 30; white manliness and, 4, 15, 20, 24, 60–61, 77, 135, 164,
165, 166; white women and, 135, 148–49.
See also colorblindness; indigenous peoples; republicanism; sex; Vigilance Committee (1851); Vigilance Committee (1856);
vigilantism
Colonial Theatre, 96
colorblindness: Americans and, 83, 93, 166;
Chinese people and, 79; contested, 95–96;
decline of, 80, 104–6; definition, 15, 79;
indigenous peoples and, 79, 85; and white
supremacy, 98–99, 106–8, 131
Colton, Walter, 46, 48
Consolidation Act, 1856, 61
Cora, Charles, 71, 73, 201n174
Cox, George, 101, 103–5
Cridge, Edward, 93–95
cross-dressing, 146–49
Crusoe, Robinson. *See* Juan Fernandez
Island
culture transmission, 4, 8, 11

D
Dame Fortune, 109–10, 113–14, 129
Dana, Richard Henry, 13, 22
Davis Company, 105–7

death and dying, 154, 158–61

Decker, Peter, 17, 25

de Cosmos, Amor, 97–98, 102

de la Guerra, Pablo Noriego, 51

democracy, idea of: Argonauts and, 23–24; British Columbia, 164; dress and, 148; over-democratic, 37, 81–82, 91; religion and, 21; white manhood, 24

Democratic Party: California, 63, 166; the Hounds, 63; Ned McGowan's War, 89–90; Vigilance Committee (1851), 67; Vigilance Committee (1856), 71, 74–76, 89

discovery of gold, California, 3–4, 12–13

Douglas, James: and African descent, peoples of, 78, 83, 96, 98; Americans and, 81–82; Amor de Cosmos, 97–98; Family-Company-Compact, 43, 80, 97, 99–100; Fraser River, access to, 43, 126–27; gambling, 132; governorship, 204n13; indigenous-settler conflict, 84–85, 88–89; Ned McGowan's War, 89–90; Tsilhqot'in and, 102–3

dress: beards, 137–39, 145–46; bloomers, 147–49; Chinese people, 149; dandy, 139–41; gamblers, 139; Greenhorn, 141–42; and identity, 15, 21, 63, 143–45; miner's costume, 137–39, 143; weapons, 137–38;

E

eastern audiences: gambling and, 110, 111, 114–15, 117–18, 122–24; importance to gold rushers, 164–65, 167; mining and, 128–29; skepticism of, 12–13; vigilantism and, 74, 76. See also bodies; cross-dressing

Emmerson, John, 37, 41

Evans, John, 129

F

failure: and the body, 143; fear of, 10; gold rush as test of, 13, 15, 38, 114; temporary setback, 111–12; weakness of character, 7, 112–13, 139. See also work-reward relationship

families, 8, 12, 15. See also white women

Family-Company-Compact, 80–81, 97

Foreign Miner's Tax (1850), 53–55, 58

Fortuna. See Dame Fortune

Fraser River: conflict on, 83–92; Fraser Canyon, 85–89, 128; gold discovery (1858), 19, 42, 126; hazards, 128; humbug, 92; indigenous peoples, 85–88, 134; restricted access to, 43; travel, 127–28

Fraser River War, 85–89

French people: British Columbia, 86; expelled from mines, 55; French Revolution (1850), 54–55; Frenchwomen, 147; Frenchwomen, fictional, 122

G

gambling: anti-gambling, British Columbia, 132–33; anti-gambling, California, 120, 124; British Columbia, 131, 132; California, 117–18, 122–23; halls, 120–21; pervasiveness, 122, 133; private games, 121–22; risk, 117–23; social implications, 118–20, 122–23, 130–33. See also chance

Germans, 61, 74, 149

Gibbs, Mifflin, 93–94, 98–99

Gilbert, Edward, 51–52, 77

goldfield system, 8–11, 18–19, 167

Great Fire (San Francisco, 1851), 68

Guadalupe Hidalgo, Treaty of, 51, 55

H

Hale, Richard, 28, 38

Harvey-Dixon Company, 105

Hawaiian people, 54–55

Hetherington, Joseph, 159–60

Hicks, Richard, 90

Hill's Bar, 84–85, 89–92, 206n34

Hispanic peoples: Catholicism, 21, 22, 47, 54; Chileans, 54–58, 63, 65, 149; as colonized subjects, 36, 48, 52–56, 61, 149, 163, 166; decayed society of, 18, 32, 35; and gambling, 119–21; mine ownership, 55–57; perceived weakness of, 32, 34–36; resistance to colonialism, 11, 54, 56–57, 166;

Hispanic peoples (*continued*)
  stereotypes, 21–22, 32, 38, 45; targets of
  mob violence, 53, 54–55, 56–57, 63–64;
  threat to republicanism, 49, 51–52; wage
  labor, 53–54, 55–56. *See also* Latin America
Hope, Fort, 86, 88, 127
Hopkins, Sterling, 75–76
Hounds, the, 62–65, 67, 196n101, 197n107
Hudson's Bay Company: history of, 80, 164;
  indigenous peoples and, 44, 84–85, 133;
  monopoly, 43. *See also* Douglas, James;
  Family-Company-Compact

I
Incidente de la Tajada de Sandia, 35–36
independence (trait): British Columbia, 24;
  non-whites, 8, 49, 54; republicanism, 14,
  24, 48, 53, 62, 67, 70, 72; threats, 8, 55, 59;
  western archetypes, 20, 116; white manhood, 7–8, 25, 110–11
indigenous peoples: American policy toward,
  33, 36, 42, 46, 50–53, 59–61, 102, 138, 150, 163–
  64; appearance, 149–50, 153–58; bodies,
  149–52; British policy toward, 36, 44, 84–
  88, 100–104, 153, 155–56, 163–64; as colonized subjects, 50–51, 59–61, 79, 84–88,
  100–104, 133–34, 154–58, 160–61; death
  practices, 159; demographics, 18, 61, 134;
  Diggers, 33, 149–52; exclusion from mines,
  52–53; genocide, 36, 84–87, 164; Hill's
  Bar, 84; natural environment and, 33;
  Nlaka'pamux, 84, 86–88, 206n34; Overlanders and, 18, 21, 26–27, 30, 31–36; physical threat, 21, 26–27, 33–34, 116, 138, 150;
  sex, 133–34; squaw, 63, 103, 134, 151–52;
  stereotypes, 7, 21, 33–34, 44–45, 79, 83–
  84, 101–3, 141; Sto:lo, 84, 206n34; villages,
  44–45, 86, 153, 155–56. *See also* Fraser
  River War; Kar-le; Klatsassin; Nikel
  Palsk; Tsilqhot'in;
Irish people: and Australians, 66; class, 74;
  colonialism, 61; racial categorization, 7,
  11–12, 149; social threat, 74, 121

J
Jenkins, John, 68–70
J. M. E., 55–56
Johnson, Byron, 24–25, 37, 39
Johnson, John Neely, 73–75
Juan Fernandez Island, 20, 28, 29*fig.*

K
Kar-le, 157
Kennedy, Arthur, 96, 102, 108, 204n13
Klatsassin, 100–101, 103–4, 211n104

L
Lady Luck. *See* Dame Fortune
Latin America: built environment, 34–36, 38–
  39; decay, 18, 22, 32–33, 35, 38–39; knowledge of, 21–22; natural environment, 22,
  32. *See also* Incidente de la Tajada de Sandia; Mexican-American War
Latin Americans. *See* Hispanic peoples
Law-and-Order Faction, 68, 73, 75–76, 89–90
Leavenworth, Thaddeus, 64, 67
leisure: class and, 111; dancing, 27, 146; deviation from East, 27–28, 111; play, 27–29;
  practical jokes, 30–31; respectability, 110;
  violation of Sabbath, 40; weapons and,
  28–30; white manhood and, 20, 110–11,
  117, 146. *See also* gambling; sex
Letts, John, 37, 120
luck. *See* chance

M
Macfie, Matthew, 39, 94–95, 154
McGowan, Edward (Ned), 89–90, 92
Mexican-American War, 12, 21–22, 34, 51, 82
Mexicans. *See* Hispanic peoples
Mexico, 3, 22, 51
migration, 14. *See also* Overlanders;
  Argonauts
miner's meetings: British Columbia, 85, 88,
  91–92; California, 52–53, 55–56
mining: as gamble, 15, 112–15; justification of
  risk, 112–14, 115–16, 117; physical hardship,

114–15, 126–27, 128–29; racial exclusion, 116, 124; skill, 129–30. *See also* wage labor

mining licenses: British Columbia, 88; California, 58–59

Moody, Richard, 89–92

Moses, W. D. (Wellington Delaney), 78

N

Native Americans. *See* indigenous peoples

Ned McGowan's War, 89–92

New Westminster, 146, 155

Nlaka'pamux, 84, 86–88, 206n34

not quite white. *See* off-white

O

off-whites: behavior, 65–66, 77, 112, 117, 158–60; bodies of, 156–57, 161; definition, 7, 173n18; intersectionality and, 12; luck and, 113; republicanism and, 52, 62, 76, 77; as threat, 61–62, 65, 133; uncertain status of, 47, 61

Overlanders: California, arrival in, 41–42; characteristics, 19–21; colonialism, 20–21; definition, 14, 17; expertise, 21, 26–27; indigenous peoples and, 18, 21, 22–23, 33–34, 36, 60; leisure, 28–30; Oregonians, 20, 60; organization, 23–24; practical jokes, 30; white women, absence of, 23, 25. *See also* Argonauts

P

Palmer, John, 117

Palsk, Nikel, 160–61

Panama. *See* Latin America

Payson, George, 20, 147

Perrier, George, 85, 89, 91

play. *See* leisure

Polk, James K., 13

Poole, Francis, 40

Q

Quesnellemouth, 101

R

rape: non- or off-whites accused of, 65, 157–58; non-white victims deemed illegitimate, 156–57; white male dominance and, 113–14, 157–58

Rathbun, Alonzo, 30, 34, 138

republicanism: colonial hierarchy, and, 46–47, 49–53, 57, 58–59, 62, 74, 165; definition, 48; "good citizens" and "bad men" and, 48, 62–65, 72–75; local governance, 52, 62; national expansion and, 22; non-whites' place in, 51, 76, 166; non-whites unsuitable for, 49, 53, 58, 65, 166; republican virtues, 14, 50, 55, 59, 166; threats to California republicanism, 50–51, 53, 55, 59, 61, 63, 66, 72; as threat to British governance, 15, 78, 81–82, 98, 104; vigilantism, and, 62, 68, 70–75, 168; white men and, 14, 48, 49, 52–53, 57, 59, 166

risk: British Columbia, 126–27, 129; Chinese people as risk-averse, 116, 130; colonialism, 116, 130–31; definition, 110; physical dangers of mining and, 112, 114, 127–29; respectability, 110–11; shift to skill, 119, 129–30; and wage labor, 115–16, 125–28. *See also* chance; gambling; work-reward relationship

Royce, Sarah, 33–34,

Ryan, William, 58, 149

S

San Francisco: built environment, 37–38, 39–40, 120; character of inhabitants, 38, 40; Chinatown, 41, 44, 153–55; crime, 62, 65–67, 70, 71–72, 124; municipal government, 52, 61–62, 64, 67–68, 71, 76; regional hub, 14, 18, 61. *See also* Vigilance Committee (1851); Vigilance Committee (1856); Hounds

sex: cross-dressing and homoeroticism, 146; hypersexualized non-whites, 22, 118, 134, 151–52, 156–57; interracial, 118, 133–34; rejection of eastern norms, 118; repressive attitudes toward, 5

Seymour, Frederick, 103, 204n13

Shattuck, David, 68

slavery: and African descent, people of, 20; indigenous peoples, and, 50–51, 60–61, 150–51; national debate, 12; prohibited in California, 49; rhetoric, 55–56, 72; threat to free labor, 50, 55–56

slumming, 123–24, 134, 218n43

Snyder, Harry, 87–88

Stuart and Wildred Affair, 67–68

Sutter's Mill, 12

Sydney Ducks. *See* Australians

T

Terry, David, 75–76

Thompson, Charles, 53, 122, 141

Tsilhqot'in, 100–104, 211n103

U

urbanization, 4–5, 10, 115. *See also* San Francisco

V

Victoria: and African descent, people of, 83, 93; American accounts of, 43–44; Chinatown, 44; 1858 rush, 19; entry to Fraser River, 126–27; Hudson's Bay Company and, 80; indigenous village (Songhee), 44, 155–56; police, 83; spatial organization, 44–45, 155; Tsilhqot'in resistance and, 102; Vancouver Island Volunteer Rifle Corps, 96, 108; volunteer fire company, 95–96

Victorianism, 3

Vigilance Committee (1851), 64, 67–71

Vigilance Committee (1856): actions of, 70–71, 75–76; crime, 71–72; defense of, 72–75; executions, 71, 159–60; Law-and-Order Faction, 73, 75–76; McGowan, Edward (Ned), 89; membership, 72–74; off-whites and, 74; republicanism, 70, 71–73, 74, 76, 168; Terry, David, 75–76; women, 73

vigilantism: Argonauts and, 23–24; "bad men" and "good citizens" and, 48, 52, 62, 70; lynch law, 67–68, 70, 75; mob rule, 67–68, 70, 75, 96. *See also* republicanism; Vigilance Committee (1851); Vigilance Committee (1856)

W

Waddington, Alfred, 100, 102

wage labor: and British Columbia gold rush, 126–28, 131; as constraining, 13; as emerging eastern norm, 5, 8, 10, 19, 115; end of gold rush and, 10, 163, 167; mining-as-gamble rhetoric and, 115–16; non-white labor, 52–56, 58–60, 116, 130; shift to wage labor in California, 18–19, 115; as threat to white male independence, 7–8, 19, 59

Wakefield, Edward, 80–81

Welsh, 129, 141

western archetypes: colonialism, 30, 168; cowboy, 167–68; dandy, 114, 123, 139–41, 143–44, 161, 168; gambler, 118–19, 121–23, 139, 141; greenhorn, 26, 141–43, 161; martial manhood and, 6, 20, 29, 167–68; pioneer, 6, 20–21, 29–30, 129, 137, 144, 168; prospector, 115–16, 130–31; squaw man, 63, 103, 134. *See also* indigenous peoples: stereotypes

Whannell, Peter, 89–91

white manhood: and colonialism, 4–6, 124; and performance, 11–12; behavior, impact of, 7, 11–12; forces shaping, 4–6, 10, 13–14; ideology, 5, 7–8; martial manhood, 6, 20–21, 27–28, 31, 38, 138, 145; play, 27–31; resistance to, 6, 11; restrained manhood, 5–6, 20, 27–28, 31, 38, 145. *See also* white men; whiteness; white womanhood; white women

white men: characteristics, 110–11, 135; class and, 62, 74; colonial hierarchy and, 11, 24, 25, 45, 77, 109, 131; concerns about respectability, 3, 7, 86, 110, 118–20, 124–25; empire as platform for, 42–43; mining as performance, 59, 112, 137–39, 145–46; national identity and, 83, 97, 104; non-white labor and, 54–55; performed identity, 11–12, 26, 27, 73, 87, 111; republicanism, 48, 63, 67, 70; status imperiled in East, 7; unlucky, 112–13; white supremacy, 34, 53, 72, 94. *See also* bodies; chance; dress; gambling; risk; slumming; whiteness; white womanhood; white women

whiteness: British and American bond of, 63, 89, 92, 100; changing boundaries of, 11–12, 74, 149; and gender, 12; independence and, 7–8; and republicanism, 14. *See also* white manhood; white men; white womanhood; white women

white womanhood, 16. *See also* white manhood; white men; whiteness; white women

white women: absence of, 8, 23, 25–26, 118, 146, 152, 167; as civilizing force, 134, 135, 152, 167; ideal, 144, 151, 152, 157; immigration encouraged, 42; justification for violence, 35; and non-white women, 118, 134, 152; and womanhood, 6, 34, 124, 148–49. *See also* white manhood; white men; whiteness; white womanhood

William, James King of, 71

work-reward relationship: attempts to reestablish, 113–14, 130; challenges to, 110, 111, 113; character, 13, 15, 109, 112–13, 119; and colonialism, 13–14; dandy, 114, 139–40; failure, 111–13; pre-rush assumptions about, 13–14, 110–11

Y

Yale, Fort, 86–87, 89–90, 92, 127

EMIL AND KATHLEEN SICK SERIES IN WESTERN HISTORY AND BIOGRAPHY

The Great Columbia Plain: A Historical Geography, 1805–1910, by Donald W. Meinig

Mills and Markets: A History of the Pacific Coast Lumber Industry to 1900, by Thomas R. Cox

Radical Heritage: Labor, Socialism, and Reform in Washington and British Columbia, 1885–1917, by Carlos A. Schwantes

The Battle for Butte: Mining and Politics on the Northern Frontier, 1864–1906, by Michael P. Malone

The Forging of a Black Community: Seattle's Central District from 1870 through the Civil Rights Era, by Quintard Taylor

Warren G. Magnuson and the Shaping of Twentieth-Century America, by Shelby Scates

The Atomic West, edited by Bruce Hevly and John M. Findlay

Power and Place in the North American West, edited by Richard White and John M. Findlay

Henry M. Jackson: A Life in Politics, by Robert G. Kaufman

Parallel Destinies: Canadian-American Relations West of the Rockies, edited by John M. Findlay and Ken S. Coates

Nikkei in the Pacific Northwest: Japanese Americans and Japanese Canadians in the Twentieth Century, edited by Louis Fiset and Gail M. Nomura

Bringing Indians to the Book, by Albert Furtwangler

Death of Celilo Falls, by Katrine Barber

The Power of Promises: Perspectives on Indian Treaties of the Pacific Northwest, edited by Alexandra Harmon

Warship under Sail: The USS Decatur *in the Pacific West*, by Lorraine McConaghy

Shadow Tribe: The Making of Columbia River Indian Identity, by Andrew H. Fisher

A Home for Every Child: Relinquishment, Adoption, and the Washington Children's Home Society, 1896–1915, by Patricia Susan Hart

Atomic Frontier Days: Hanford and the American West, by John M. Findlay and Bruce Hevly

The Nature of Borders: Salmon, Boundaries, and Bandits on the Salish Sea, by Lissa K. Wadewitz

Encounters in Avalanche Country: A History of Survival in the Mountain West, 1820–1920, by Diana L. Di Stefano

The Rising Tide of Color: Race, State Violence, and Radical Movements across the Pacific, edited by Moon-Ho Jung

Trout Culture: How Fly Fishing Forever Changed the Rocky Mountain West, by Jen Corrinne Brown

Japanese Prostitutes in the North American West, 1887–1920, by Kazuhiro Oharazeki

In Defense of Wyam: Native-White Alliances and the Struggle for Celilo Village, by Katrine Barber

Gold Rush Manliness: Race and Gender on the Pacific Slope, by Christopher Herbert

CPSIA information can be obtained
at www.ICGtesting.com
Printed in the USA
FSHW012004070121
77499FS